All Star

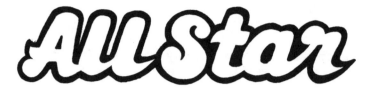

This book would never have come together without the help and support of Avani Agarwal, Colleen AF Venable, Dan Mazur, Jen Vaughn, Mo Oh, Ryan Mita, the Boston Comics Roundtable, my friends, and my family.

All Star

by Jesse Lonergan

NBM ComicsLit

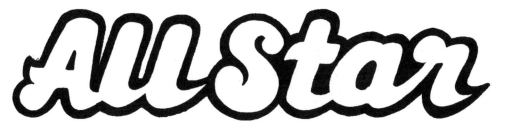

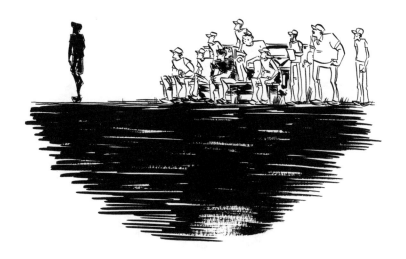

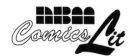

ISBN 978-1-56163-835-2
© 2014 Jesse Lonergan
Library of Congress Control Number 2013957612
Third printing

This is also available wherever e-books are sold

Comicslit is an imprint
and trademark of

NANTIER • BEALL • MINOUSTCHINE
Publishing inc.
new york

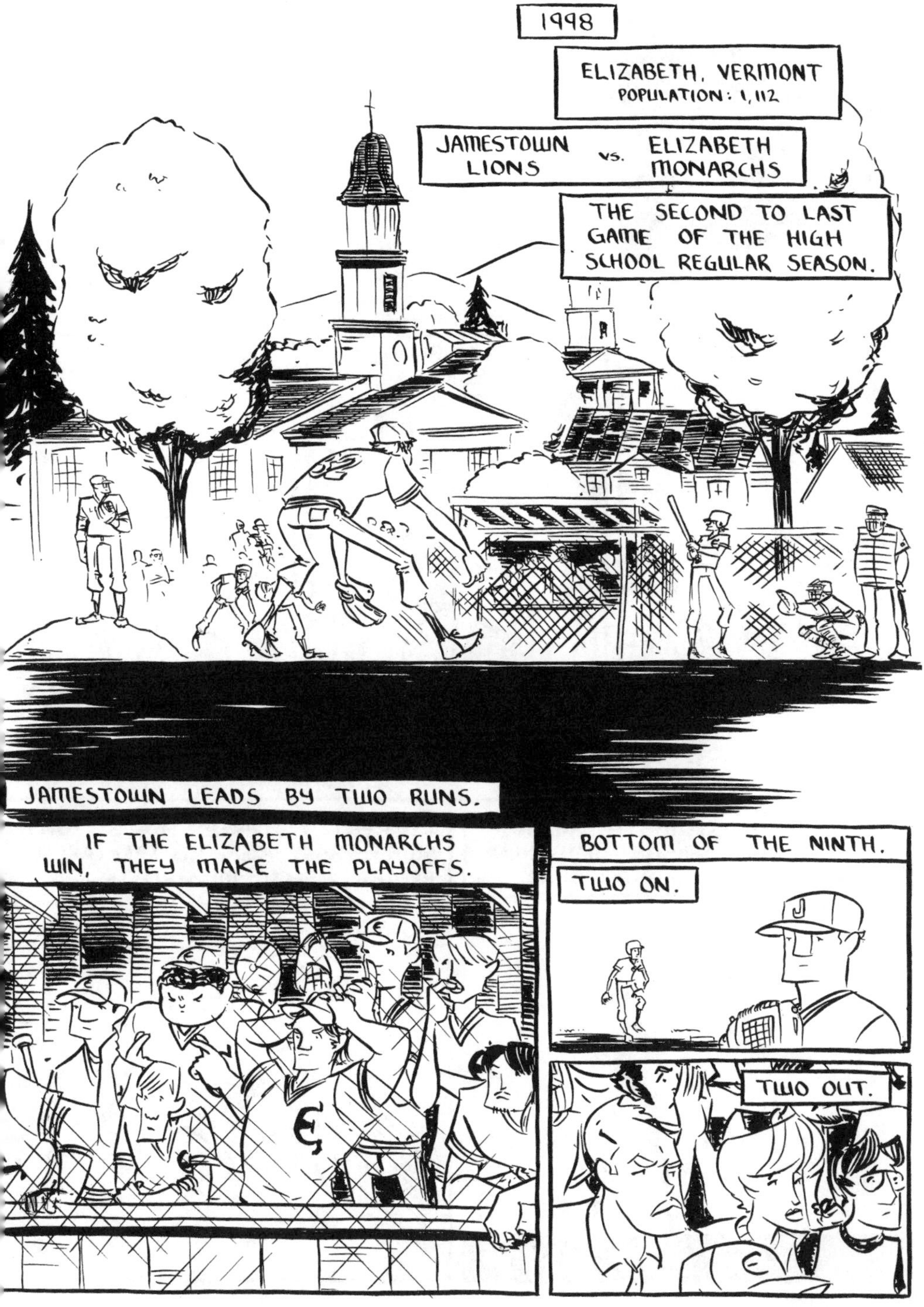
1998
ELIZABETH, VERMONT
POPULATION: 1,112
JAMESTOWN LIONS vs. ELIZABETH MONARCHS
THE SECOND TO LAST GAME OF THE HIGH SCHOOL REGULAR SEASON.
JAMESTOWN LEADS BY TWO RUNS.
IF THE ELIZABETH MONARCHS WIN, THEY MAKE THE PLAYOFFS.
BOTTOM OF THE NINTH.
TWO ON.
TWO OUT.

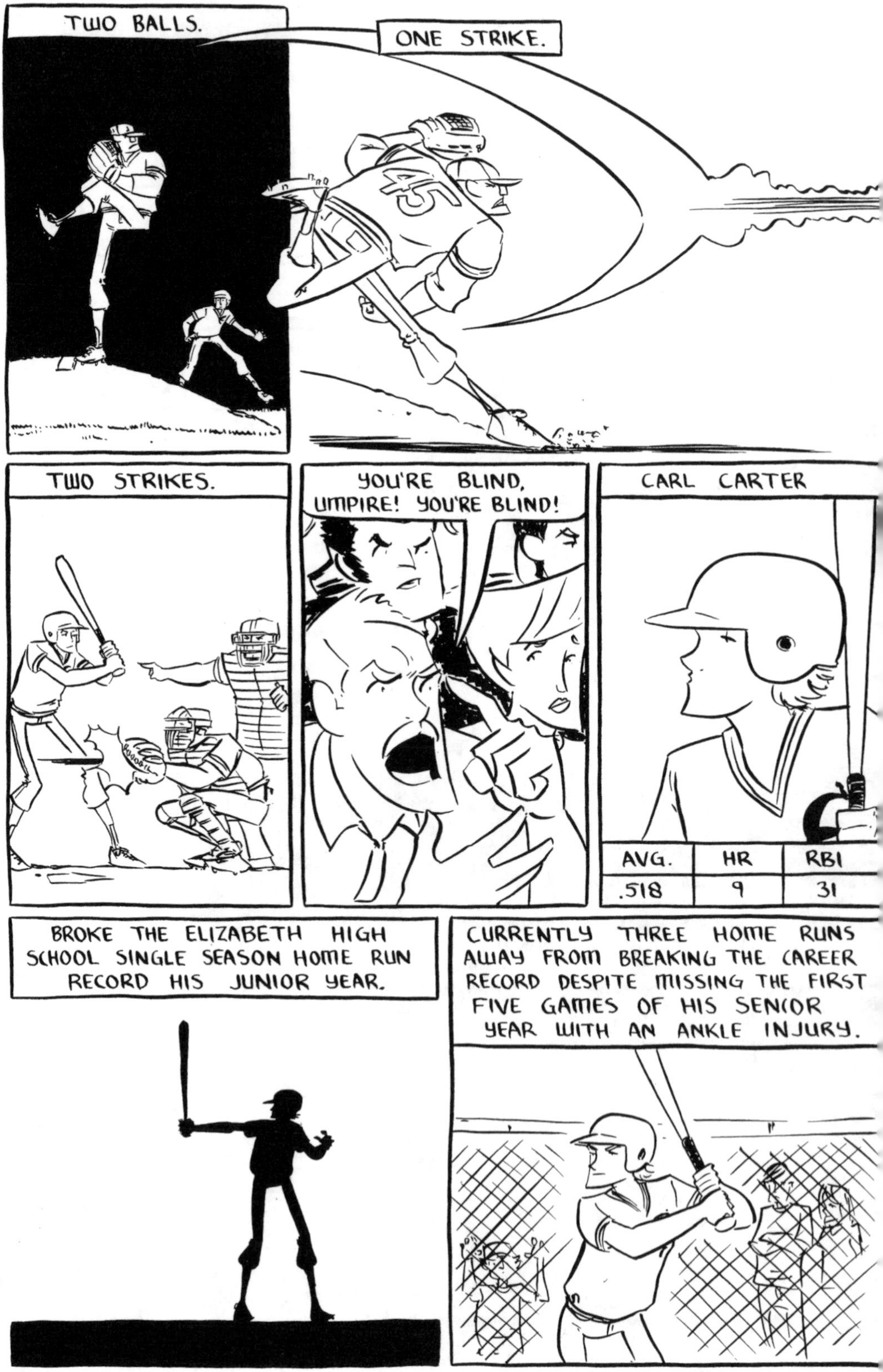
TWO BALLS.
ONE STRIKE.
TWO STRIKES.
YOU'RE BLIND, UMPIRE! YOU'RE BLIND!
CARL CARTER
AVG. .518
HR 9
RBI 31
BROKE THE ELIZABETH HIGH SCHOOL SINGLE SEASON HOME RUN RECORD HIS JUNIOR YEAR.
CURRENTLY THREE HOME RUNS AWAY FROM BREAKING THE CAREER RECORD DESPITE MISSING THE FIRST FIVE GAMES OF HIS SENIOR YEAR WITH AN ANKLE INJURY.

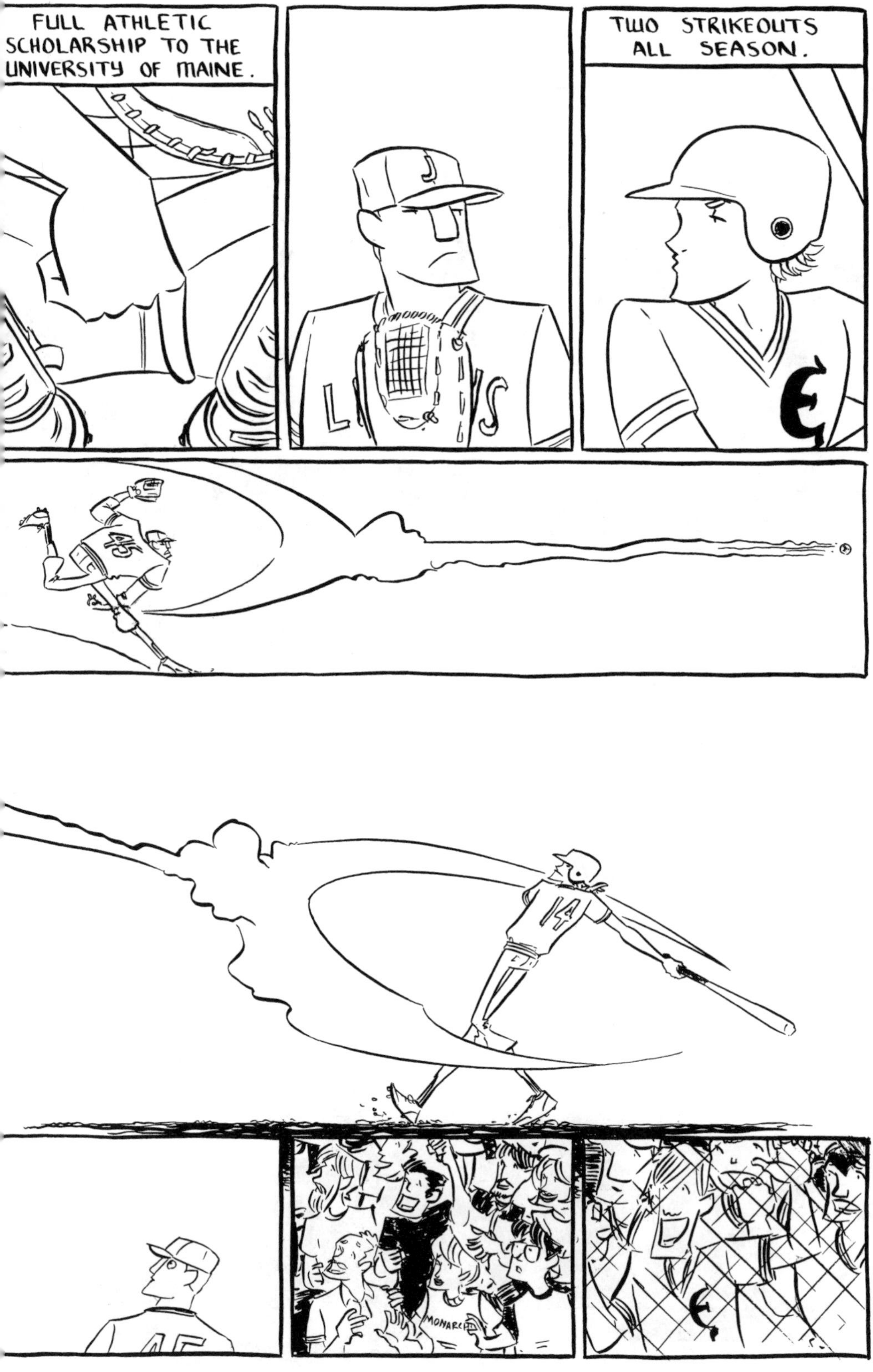
FULL ATHLETIC SCHOLARSHIP TO THE UNIVERSITY OF MAINE.
TWO STRIKEOUTS ALL SEASON.
MONARCH

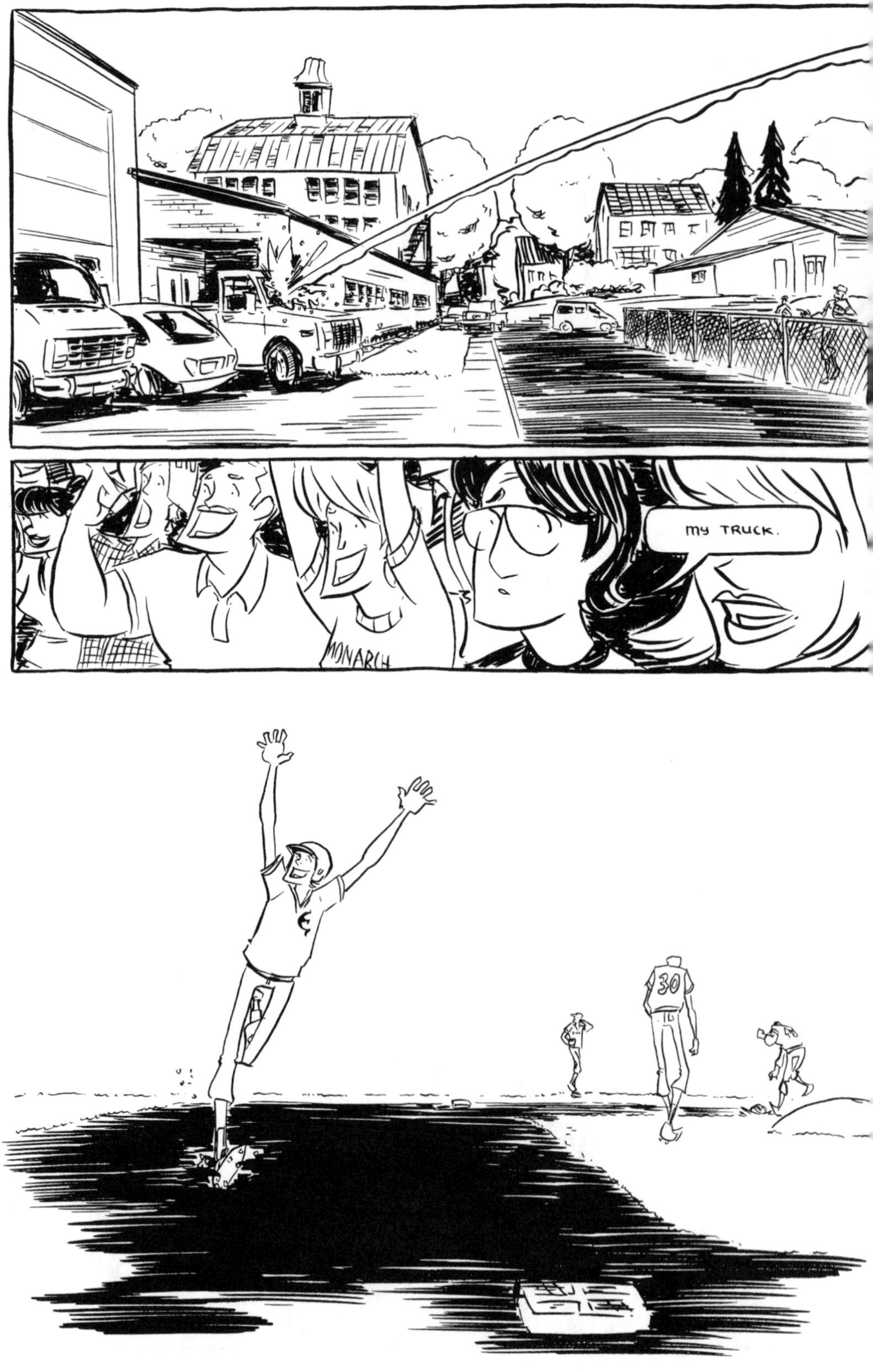
MY TRUCK.
MONARCH

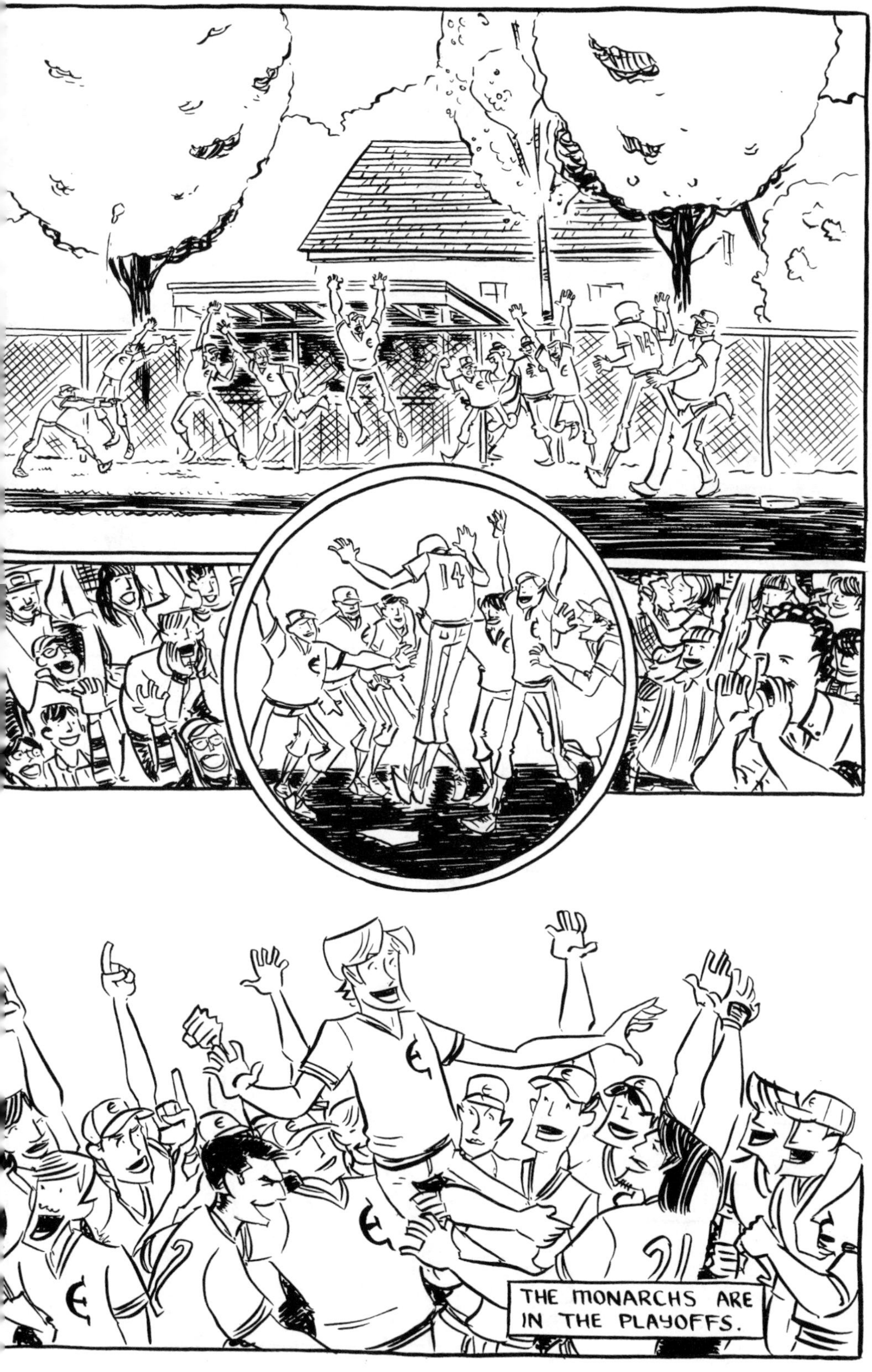
THE MONARCHS ARE IN THE PLAYOFFS.

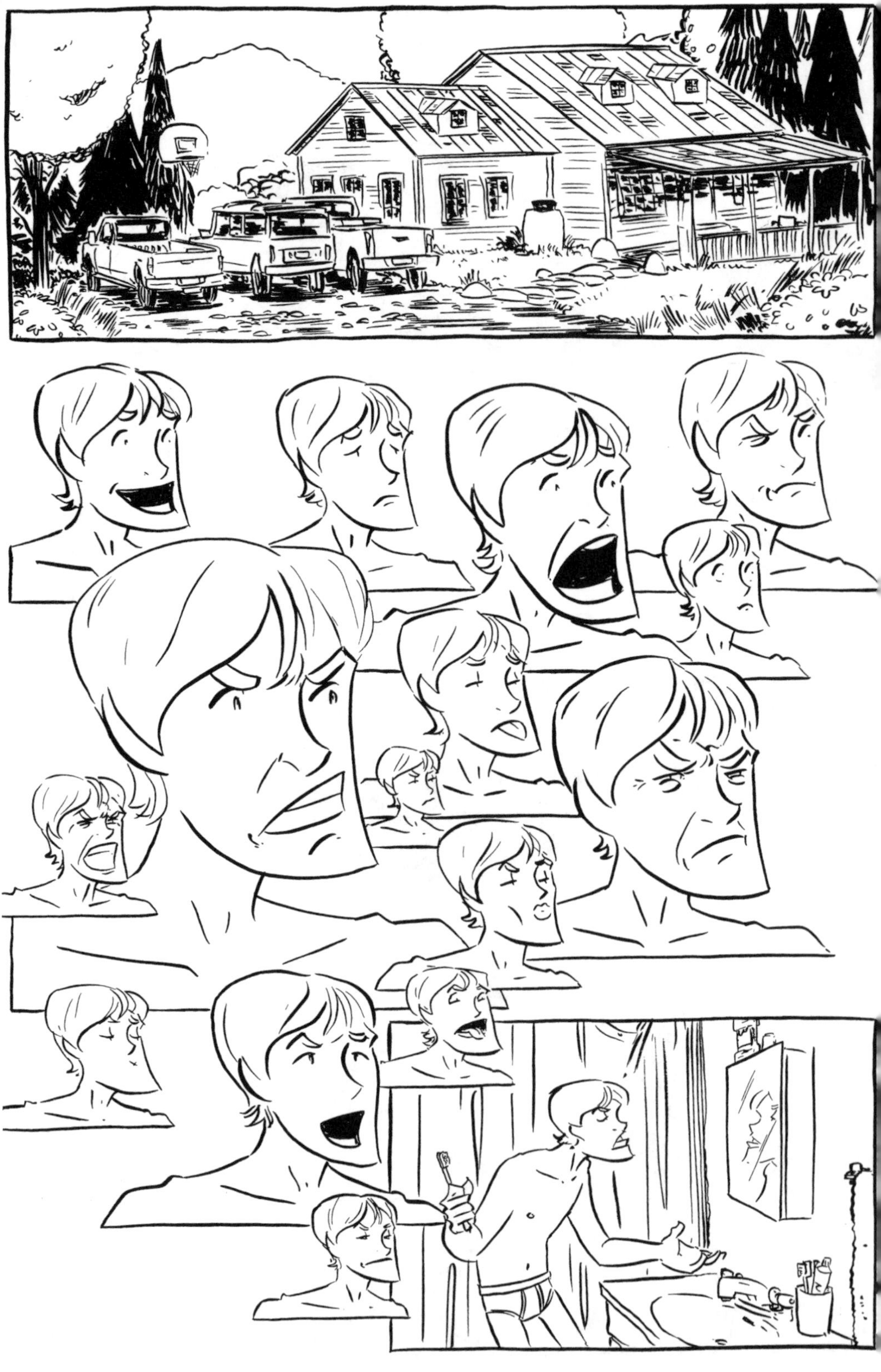

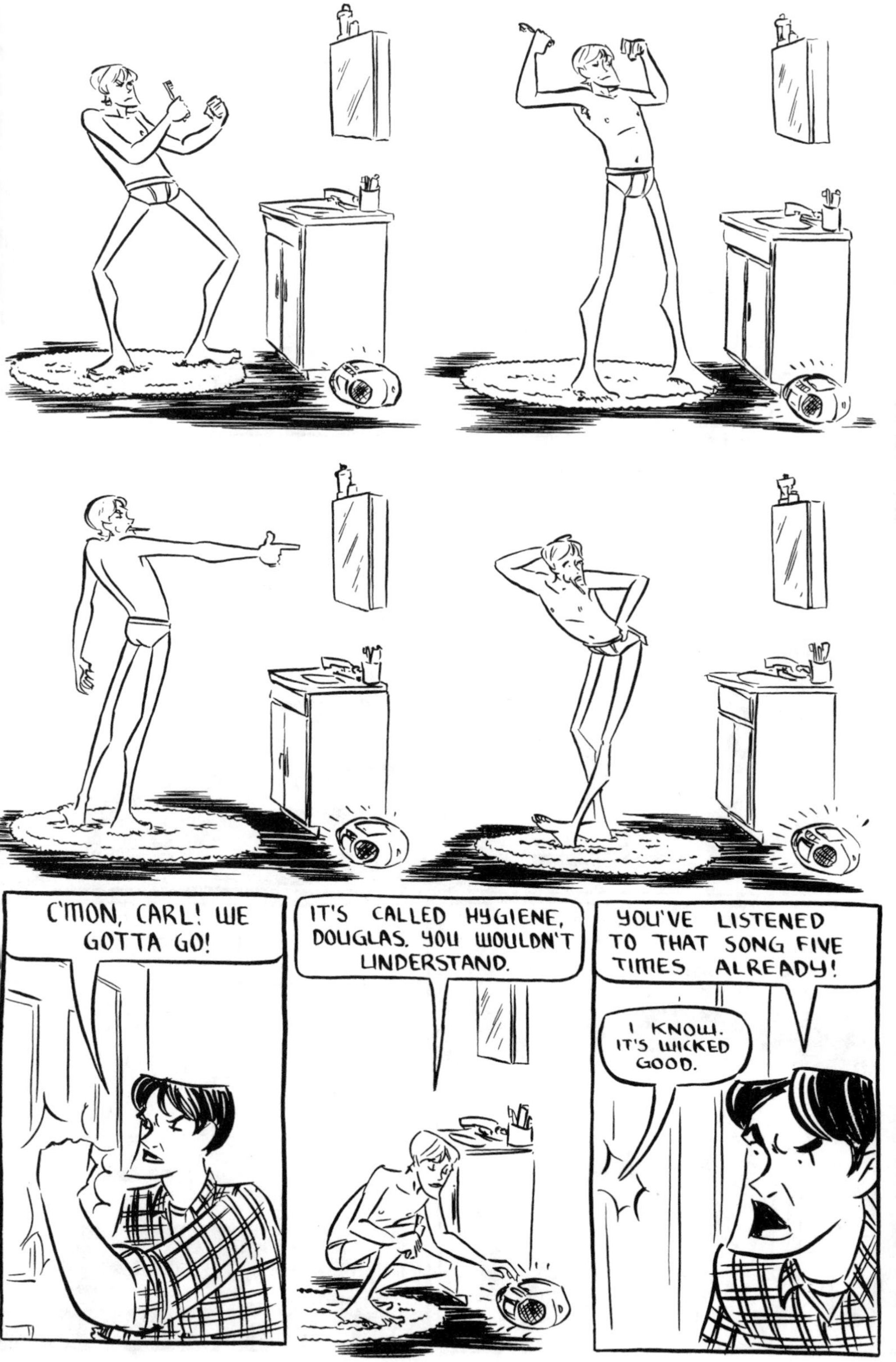
C'MON, CARL! WE GOTTA GO!
IT'S CALLED HYGIENE, DOUGLAS. YOU WOULDN'T UNDERSTAND.
YOU'VE LISTENED TO THAT SONG FIVE TIMES ALREADY!
I KNOW. IT'S WICKED GOOD.

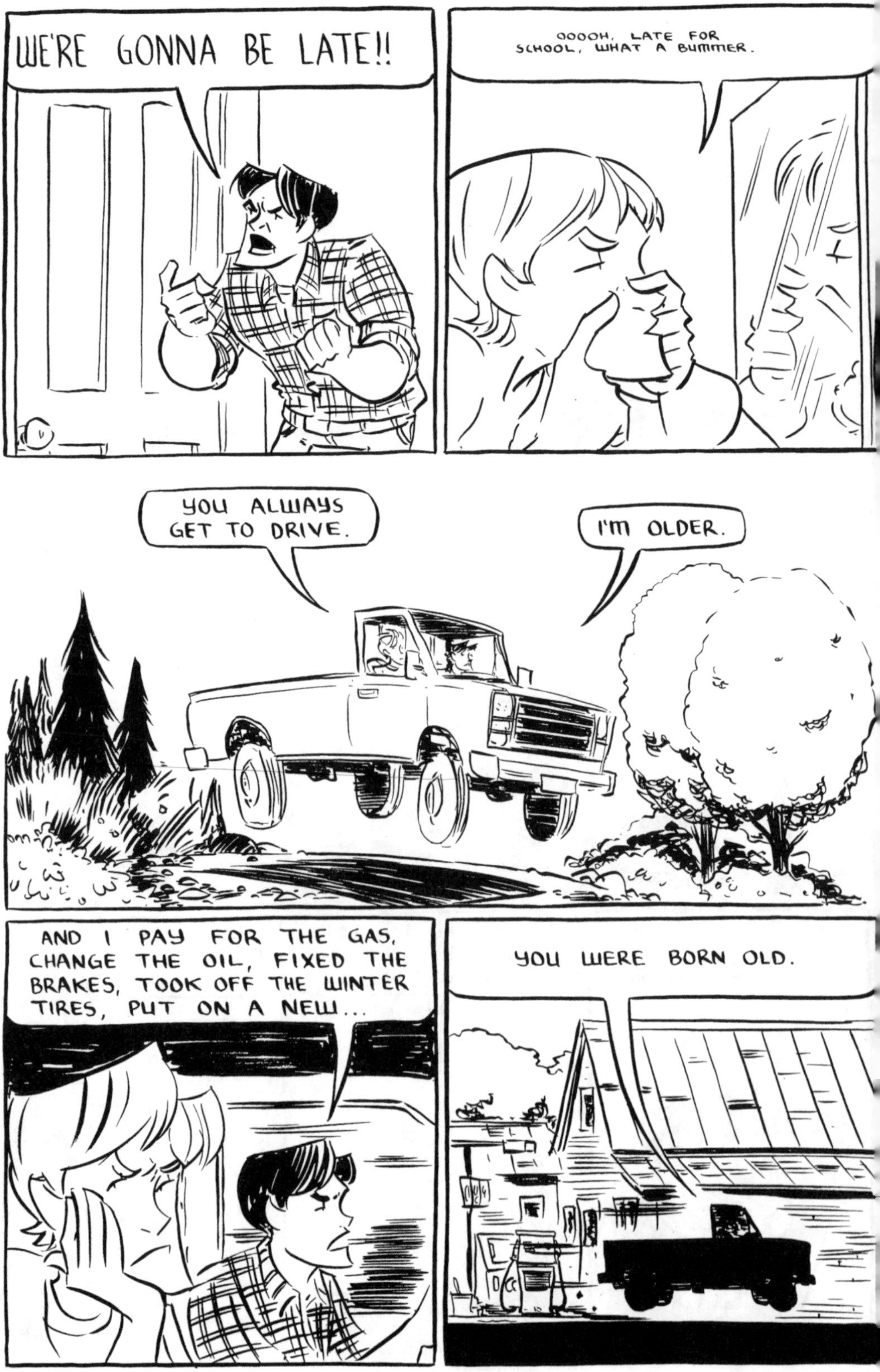
WE'RE GONNA BE LATE!!
OOOOH, LATE FOR SCHOOL, WHAT A BUMMER.
YOU ALWAYS GET TO DRIVE.
I'M OLDER.
AND I PAY FOR THE GAS, CHANGE THE OIL, FIXED THE BRAKES, TOOK OFF THE WINTER TIRES, PUT ON A NEW...
YOU WERE BORN OLD.

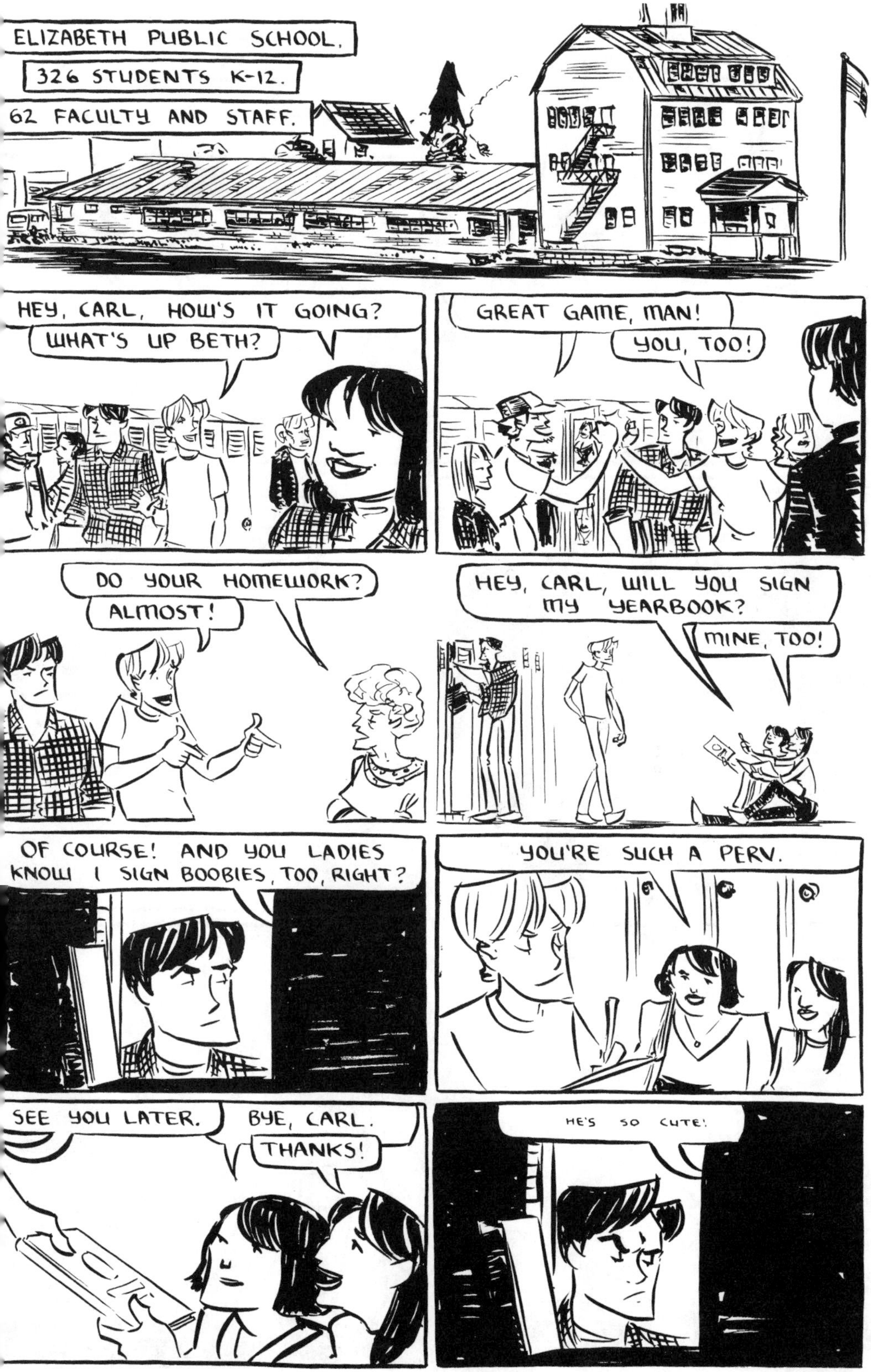
ELIZABETH PUBLIC SCHOOL.
326 STUDENTS K-12.
62 FACULTY AND STAFF.
HEY, CARL, HOW'S IT GOING?
WHAT'S UP BETH?
GREAT GAME, MAN!
YOU, TOO!
DO YOUR HOMEWORK?
ALMOST!
HEY, CARL, WILL YOU SIGN MY YEARBOOK?
MINE, TOO!
OF COURSE! AND YOU LADIES KNOW I SIGN BOOBIES, TOO, RIGHT?
YOU'RE SUCH A PERV.
SEE YOU LATER.
BYE, CARL.
THANKS!
HE'S SO CUTE!

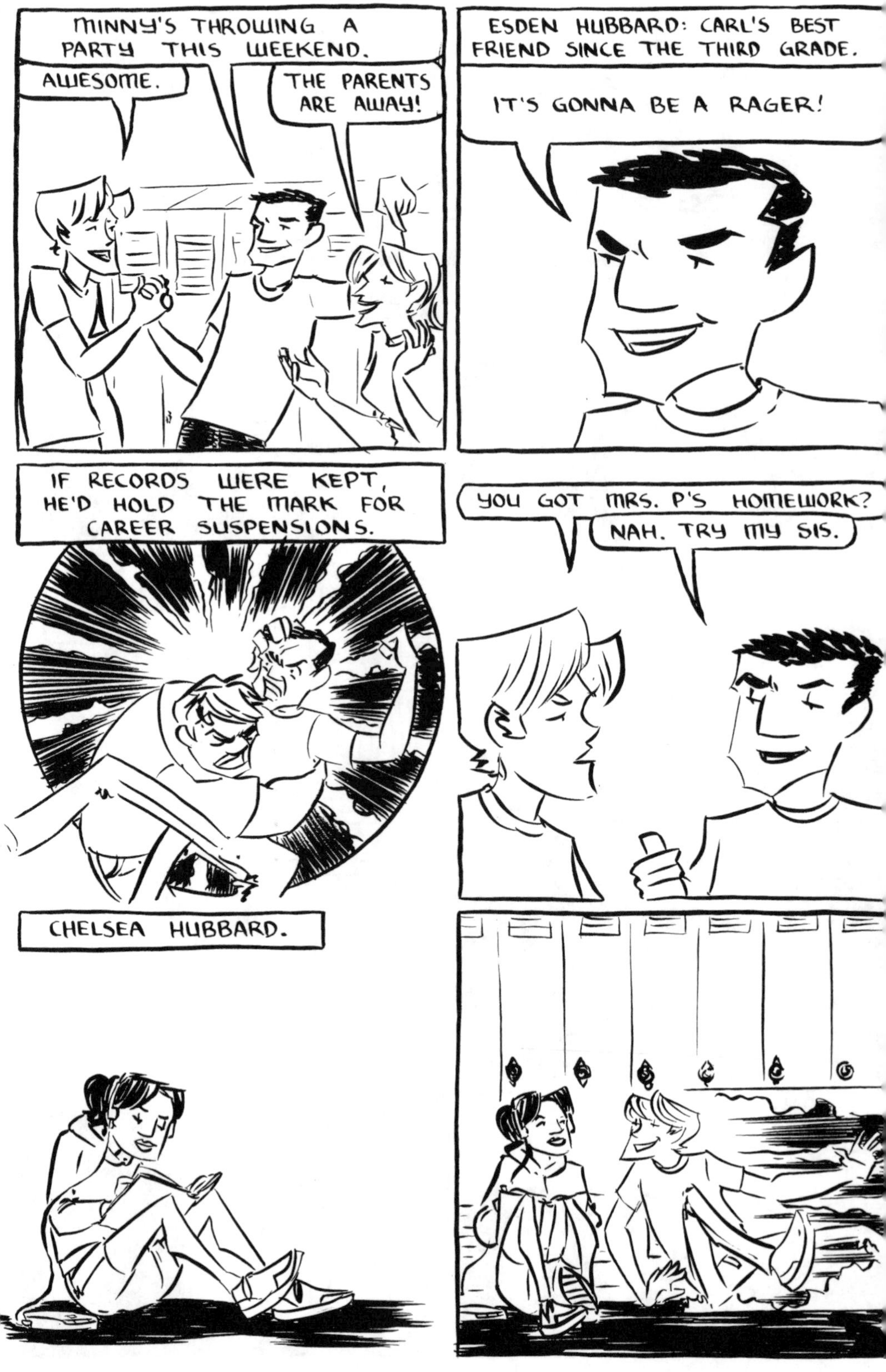

MINNY'S THROWING A PARTY THIS WEEKEND.
AWESOME.
THE PARENTS ARE AWAY!
ESDEN HUBBARD: CARL'S BEST FRIEND SINCE THE THIRD GRADE.
IT'S GONNA BE A RAGER!
IF RECORDS WERE KEPT, HE'D HOLD THE MARK FOR CAREER SUSPENSIONS.
YOU GOT MRS. P'S HOMEWORK?
NAH. TRY MY SIS.
CHELSEA HUBBARD.

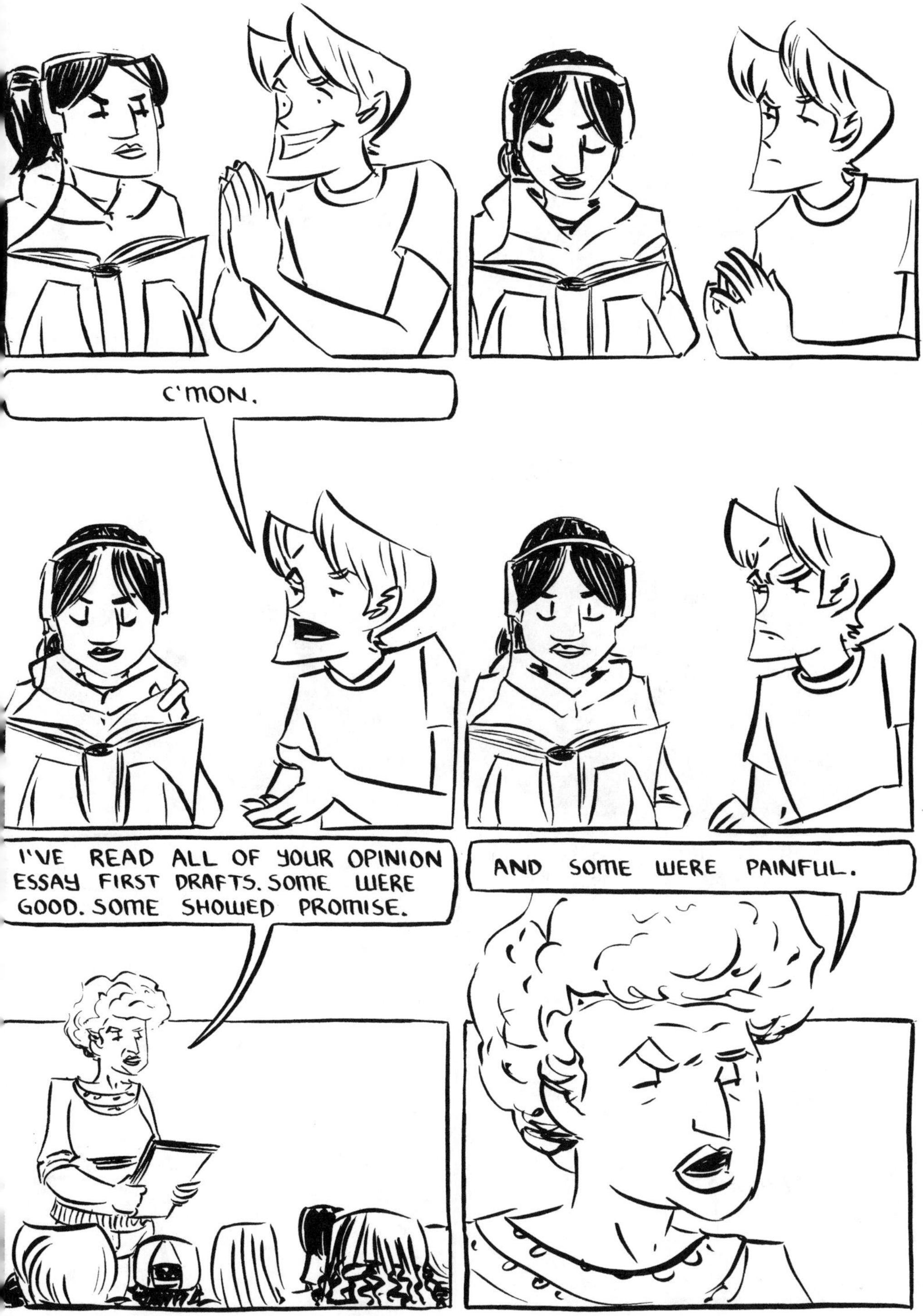
C'MON.
I'VE READ ALL OF YOUR OPINION ESSAY FIRST DRAFTS. SOME WERE GOOD. SOME SHOWED PROMISE.
AND SOME WERE PAINFUL.

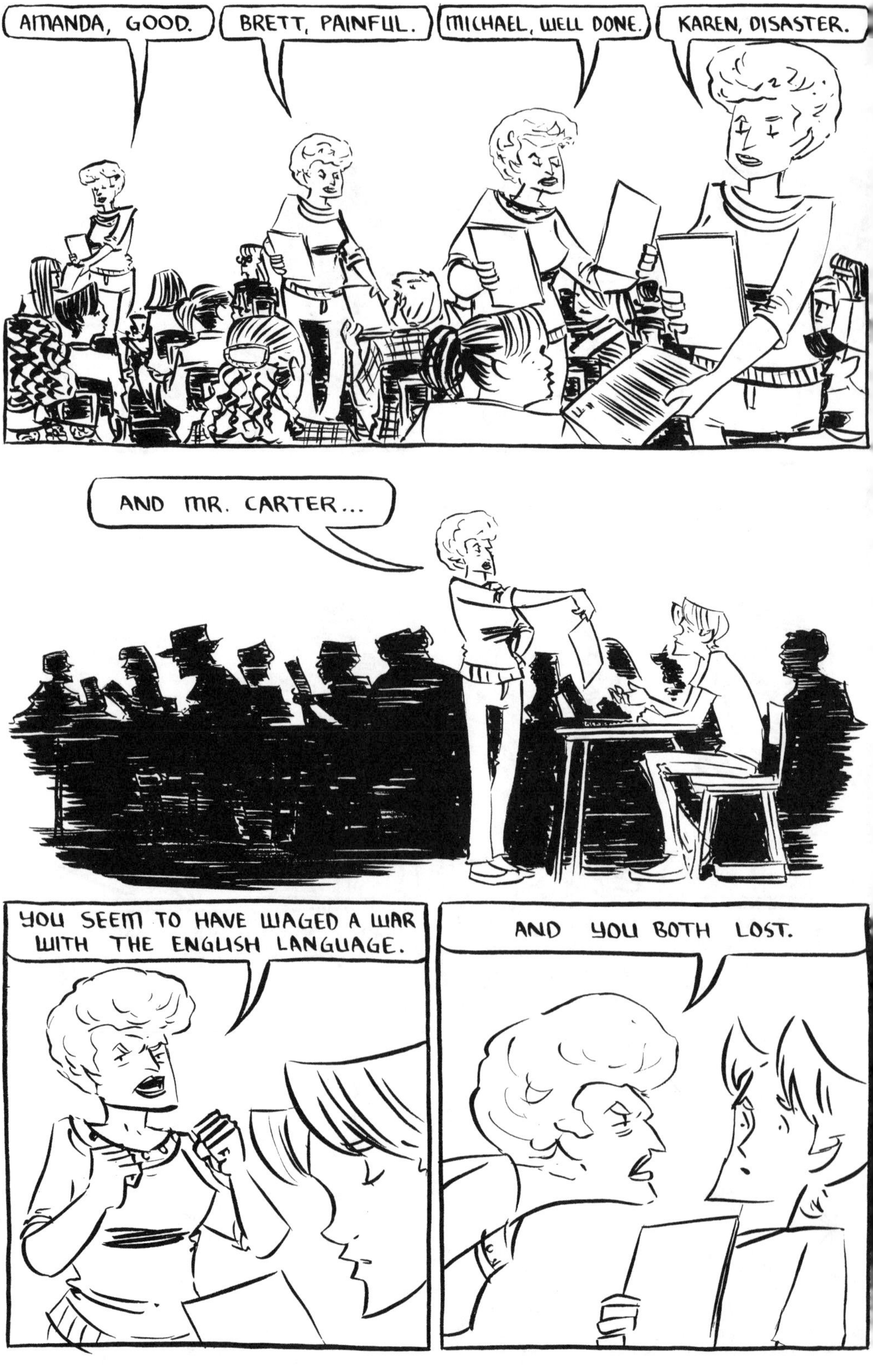
AMANDA, GOOD.
BRETT, PAINFUL.
MICHAEL, WELL DONE.
KAREN, DISASTER.
AND MR. CARTER...
YOU SEEM TO HAVE WAGED A WAR WITH THE ENGLISH LANGUAGE.
AND YOU BOTH LOST.

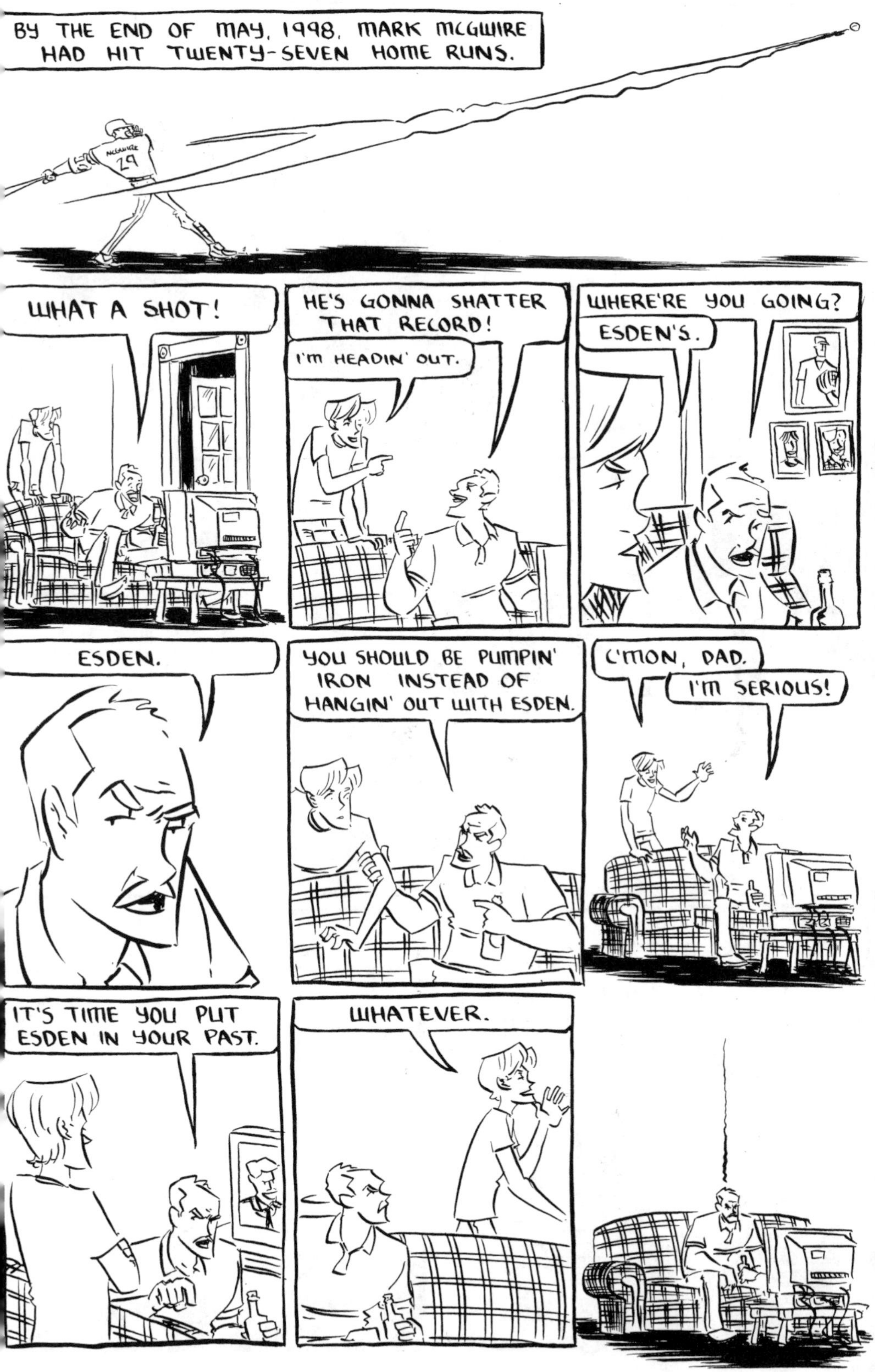
BY THE END OF MAY, 1998, MARK MCGWIRE HAD HIT TWENTY-SEVEN HOME RUNS.
MCGWIRE 29
WHAT A SHOT!
HE'S GONNA SHATTER THAT RECORD!
I'M HEADIN' OUT.
WHERE'RE YOU GOING?
ESDEN'S.
ESDEN.
YOU SHOULD BE PUMPIN' IRON INSTEAD OF HANGIN' OUT WITH ESDEN.
C'MON, DAD.
I'M SERIOUS!
IT'S TIME YOU PUT ESDEN IN YOUR PAST.
WHATEVER.

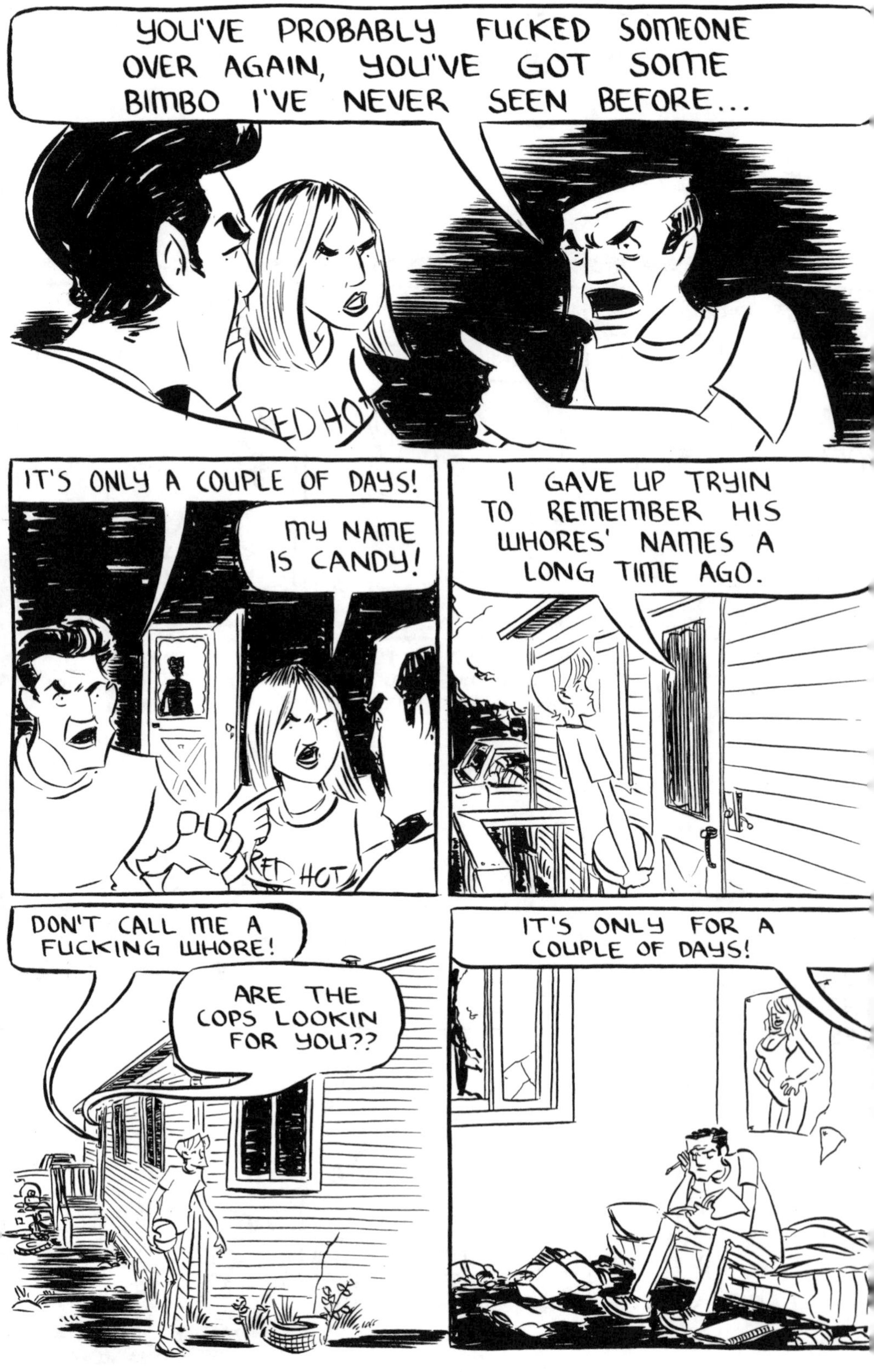
YOU'VE PROBABLY FUCKED SOMEONE OVER AGAIN, YOU'VE GOT SOME BIMBO I'VE NEVER SEEN BEFORE...
RED HOT
IT'S ONLY A COUPLE OF DAYS!
MY NAME IS CANDY!
RED HOT
I GAVE UP TRYIN TO REMEMBER HIS WHORES' NAMES A LONG TIME AGO.
DON'T CALL ME A FUCKING WHORE!
ARE THE COPS LOOKIN FOR YOU??
IT'S ONLY FOR A COUPLE OF DAYS!

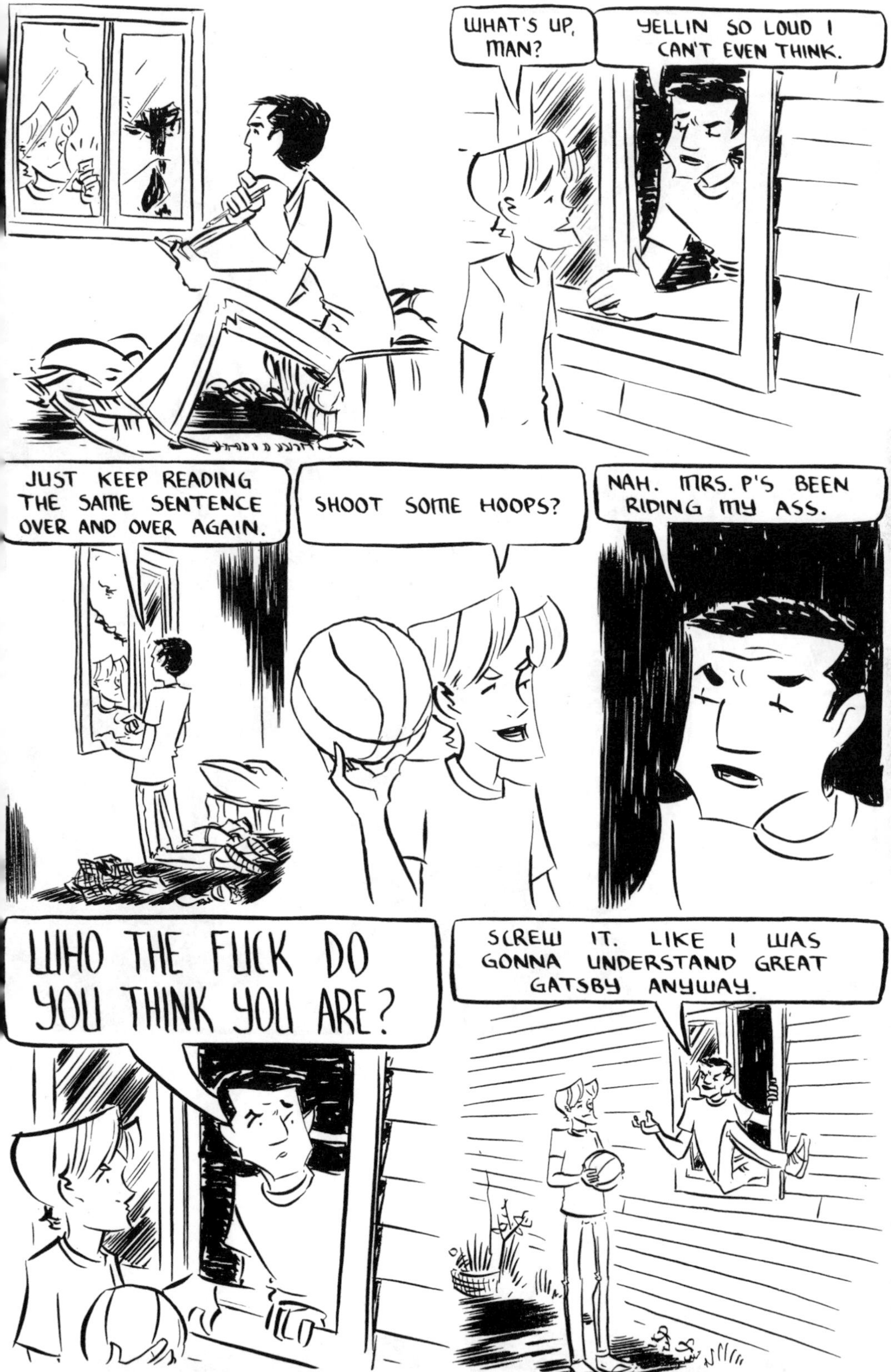
WHAT'S UP, MAN?
YELLIN SO LOUD I CAN'T EVEN THINK.
JUST KEEP READING THE SAME SENTENCE OVER AND OVER AGAIN.
SHOOT SOME HOOPS?
NAH. MRS. P'S BEEN RIDING MY ASS.
WHO THE FUCK DO YOU THINK YOU ARE?
SCREW IT. LIKE I WAS GONNA UNDERSTAND GREAT GATSBY ANYWAY.

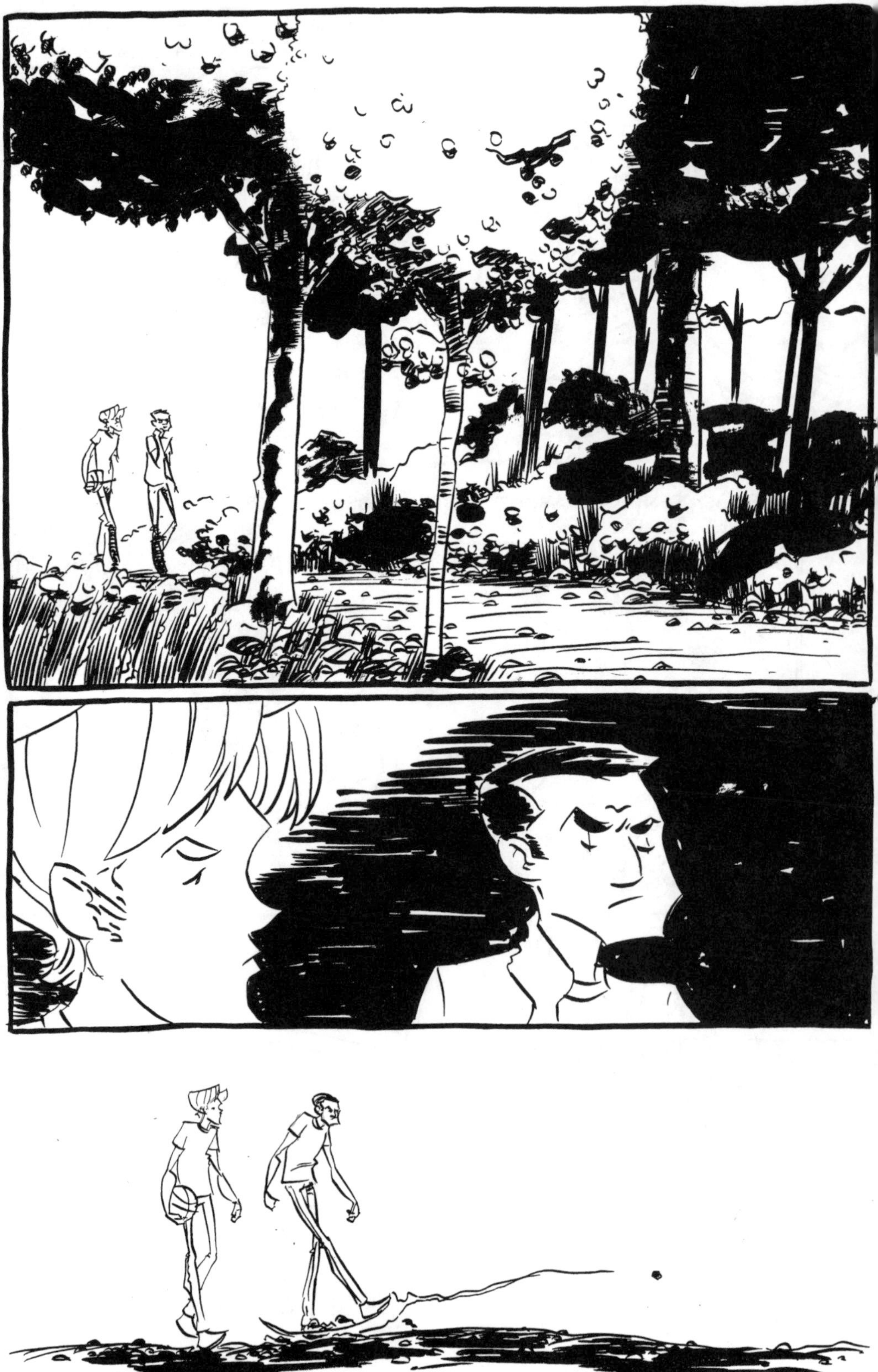

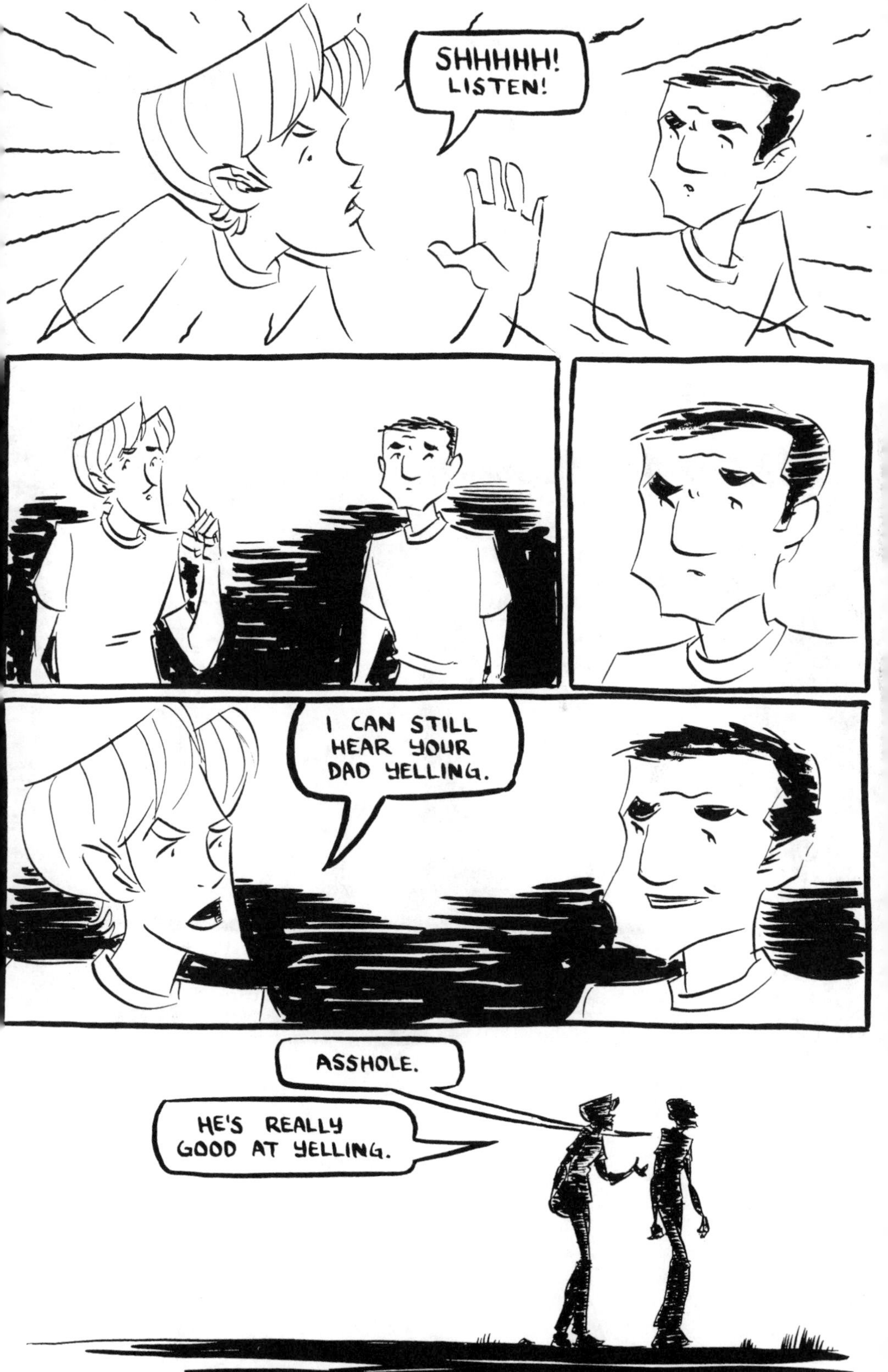
SHHHHH! LISTEN!
I CAN STILL HEAR YOUR DAD YELLING.
ASSHOLE.
HE'S REALLY GOOD AT YELLING.

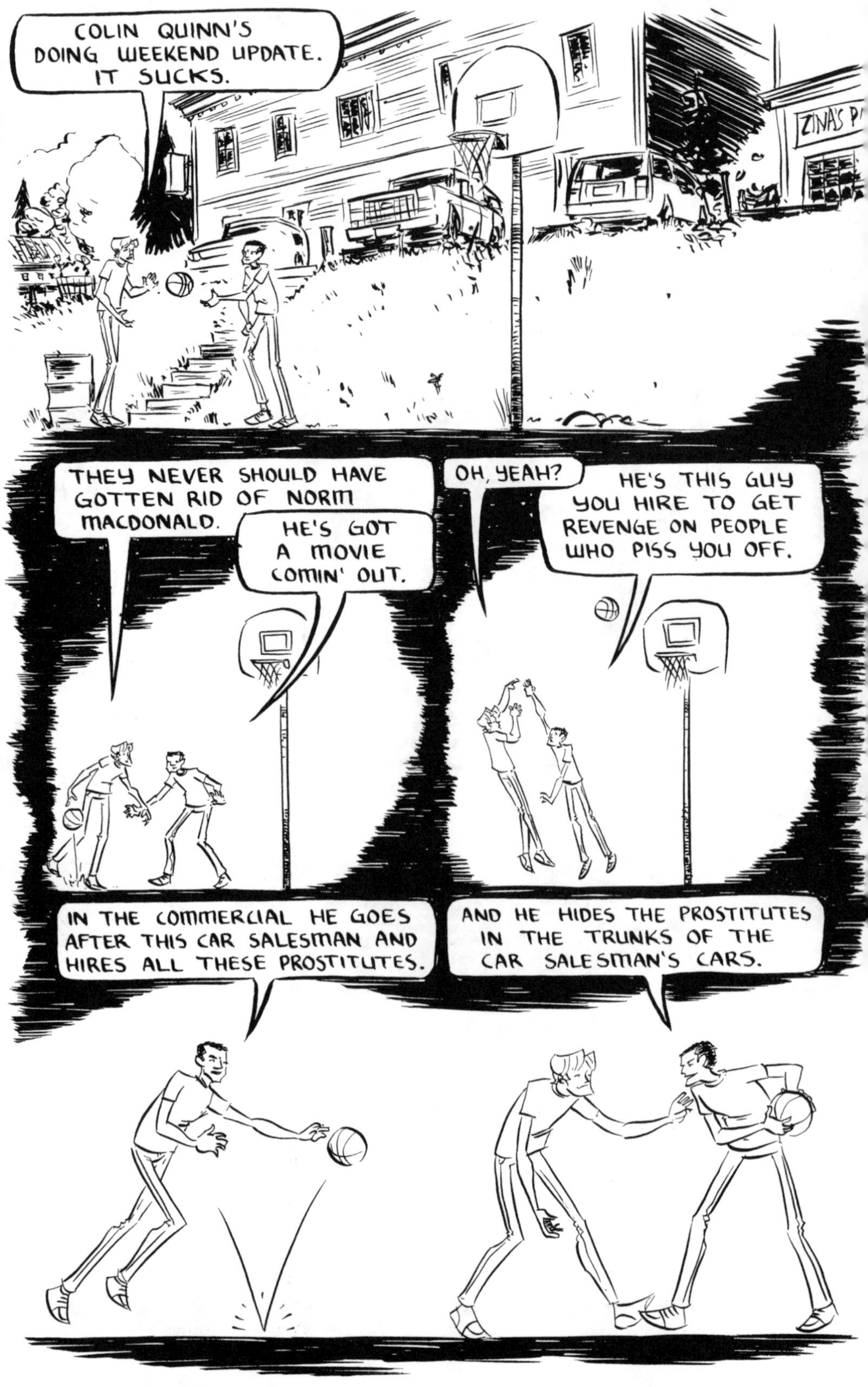
COLIN QUINN'S DOING WEEKEND UPDATE. IT SUCKS.
ZINA'S P
THEY NEVER SHOULD HAVE GOTTEN RID OF NORM MACDONALD.
HE'S GOT A MOVIE COMIN' OUT.
OH, YEAH?
HE'S THIS GUY YOU HIRE TO GET REVENGE ON PEOPLE WHO PISS YOU OFF.
IN THE COMMERCIAL HE GOES AFTER THIS CAR SALESMAN AND HIRES ALL THESE PROSTITUTES.
AND HE HIDES THE PROSTITUTES IN THE TRUNKS OF THE CAR SALESMAN'S CARS.

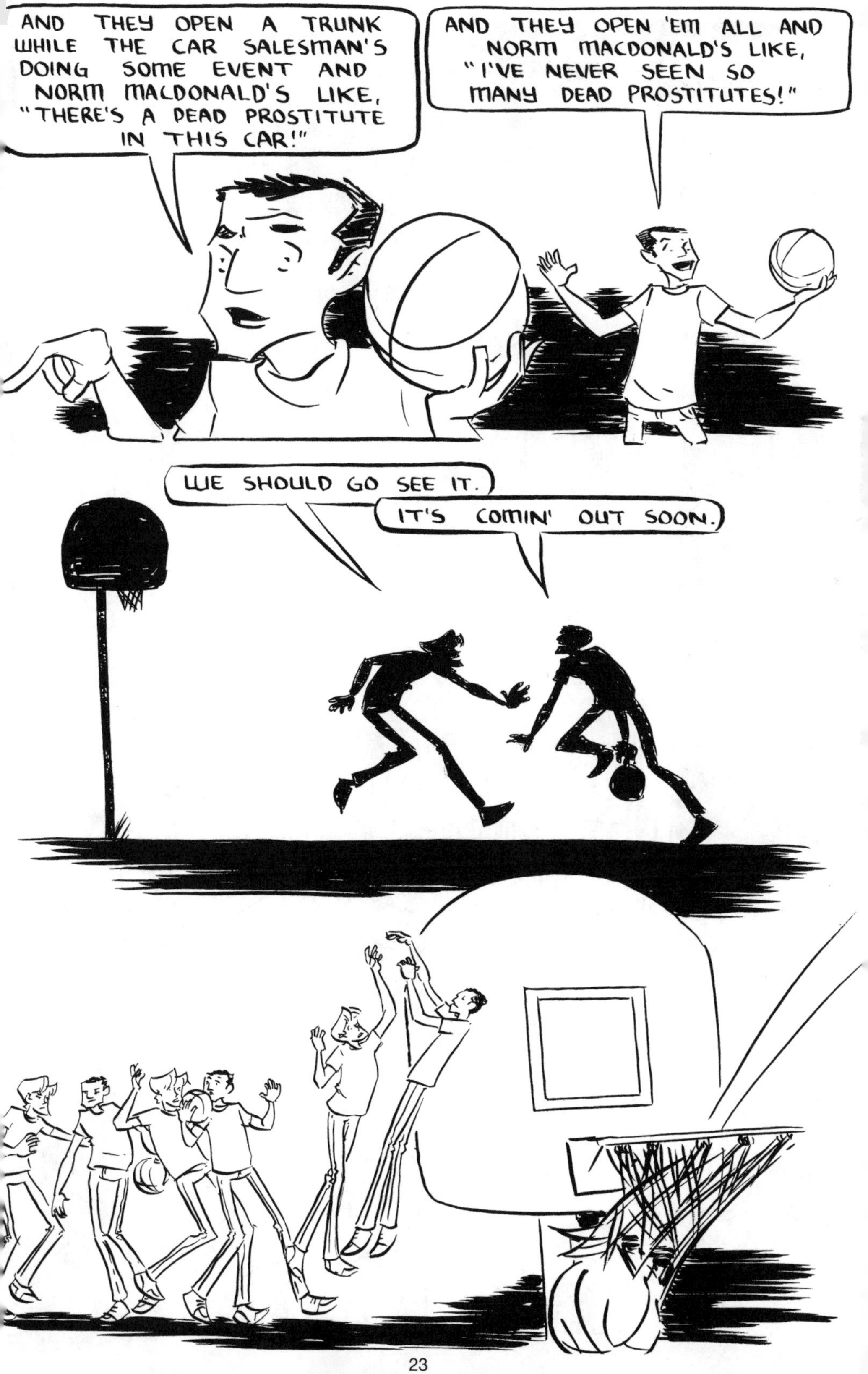
AND THEY OPEN A TRUNK WHILE THE CAR SALESMAN'S DOING SOME EVENT AND NORM MACDONALD'S LIKE, "THERE'S A DEAD PROSTITUTE IN THIS CAR!"
AND THEY OPEN 'EM ALL AND NORM MACDONALD'S LIKE, "I'VE NEVER SEEN SO MANY DEAD PROSTITUTES!"
WE SHOULD GO SEE IT.
IT'S COMIN' OUT SOON.

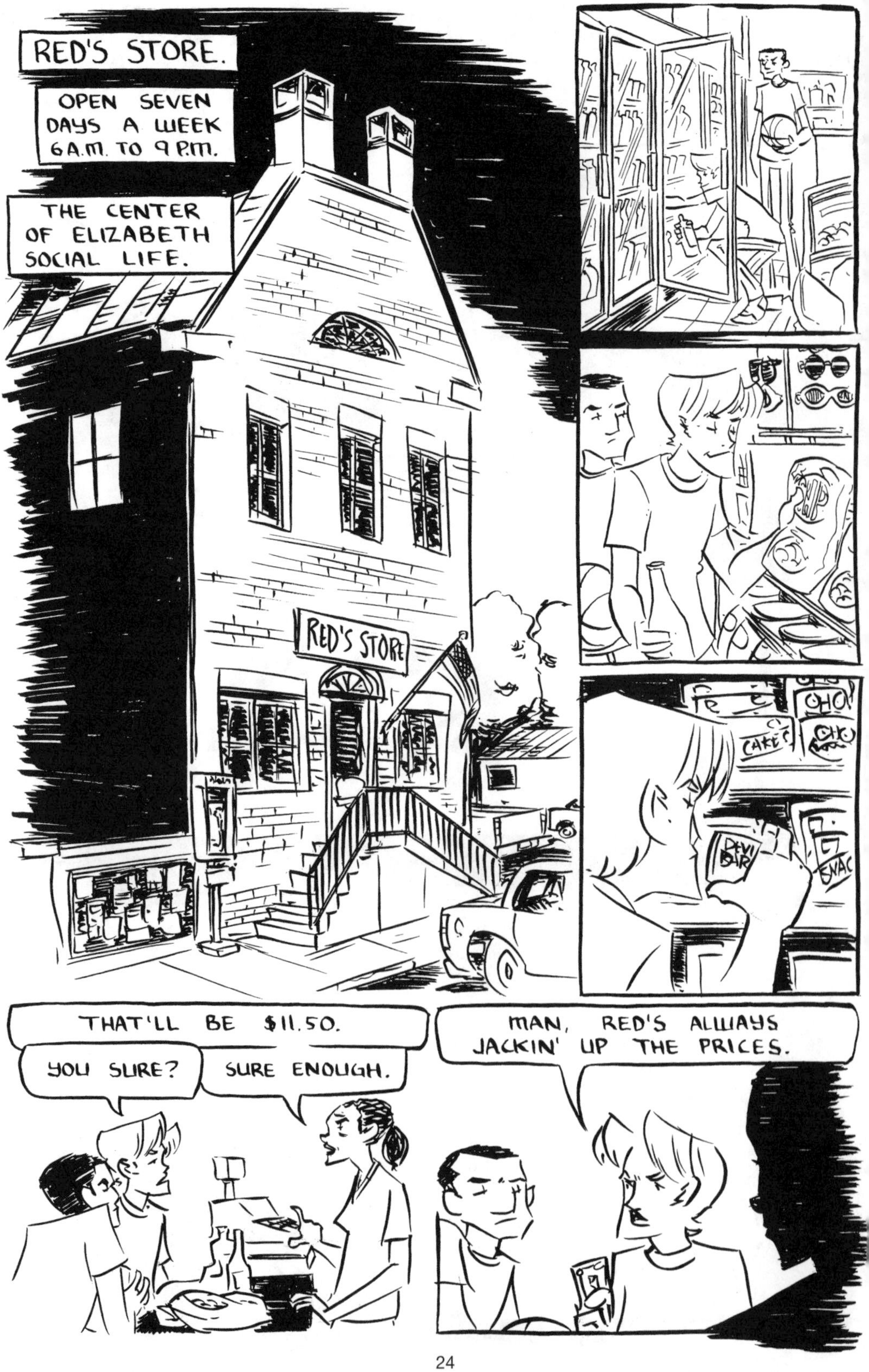
RED'S STORE.
OPEN SEVEN DAYS A WEEK 6 A.M. TO 9 P.M.
THE CENTER OF ELIZABETH SOCIAL LIFE.
RED'S STORE
CAKES
THAT'LL BE $11.50.
YOU SURE?
SURE ENOUGH.
MAN, RED'S ALWAYS JACKIN' UP THE PRICES.

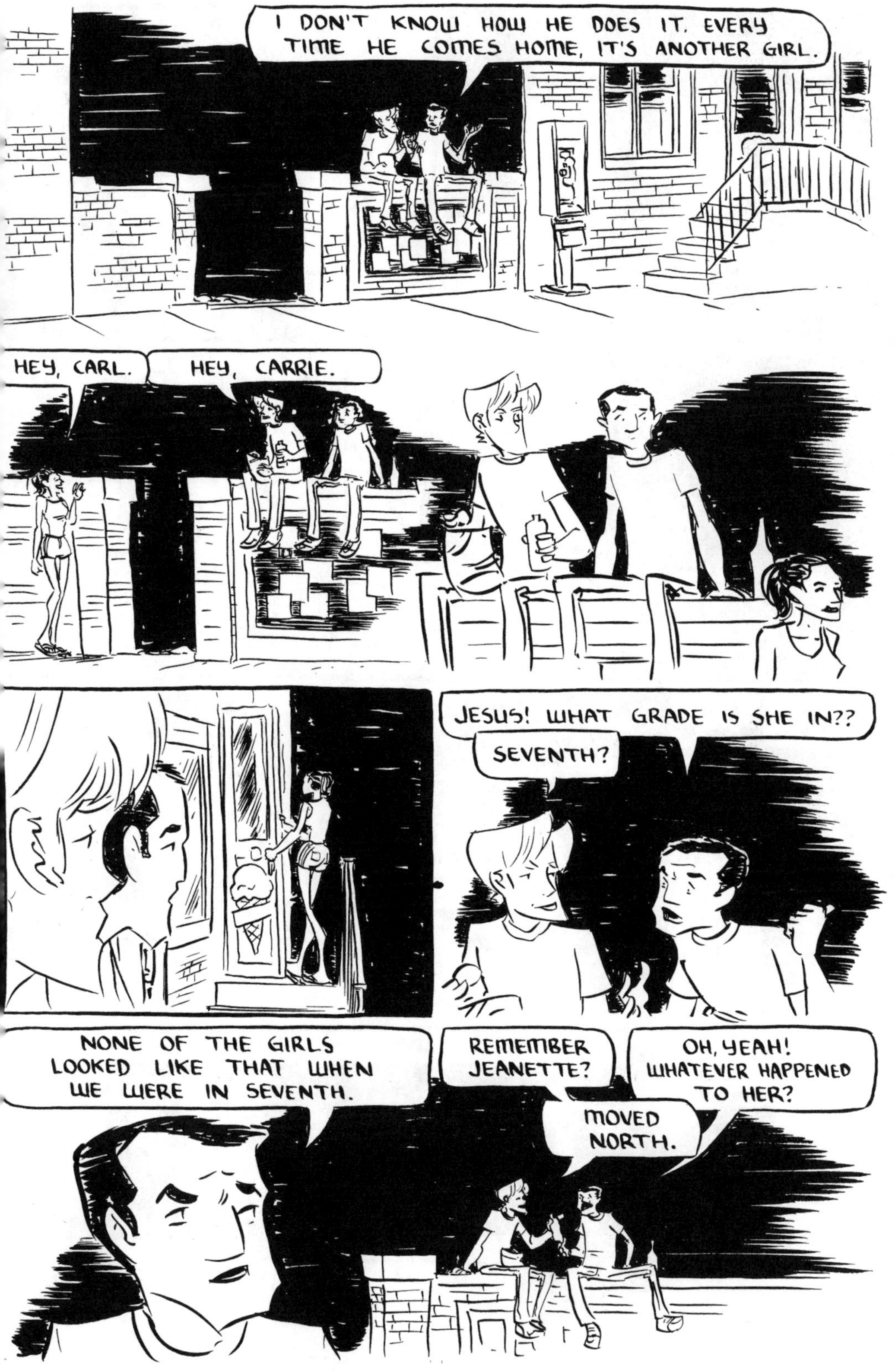
I DON'T KNOW HOW HE DOES IT. EVERY TIME HE COMES HOME, IT'S ANOTHER GIRL.
HEY, CARL.
HEY, CARRIE.
JESUS! WHAT GRADE IS SHE IN??
SEVENTH?
NONE OF THE GIRLS LOOKED LIKE THAT WHEN WE WERE IN SEVENTH.
REMEMBER JEANETTE?
OH, YEAH! WHATEVER HAPPENED TO HER?
MOVED NORTH.

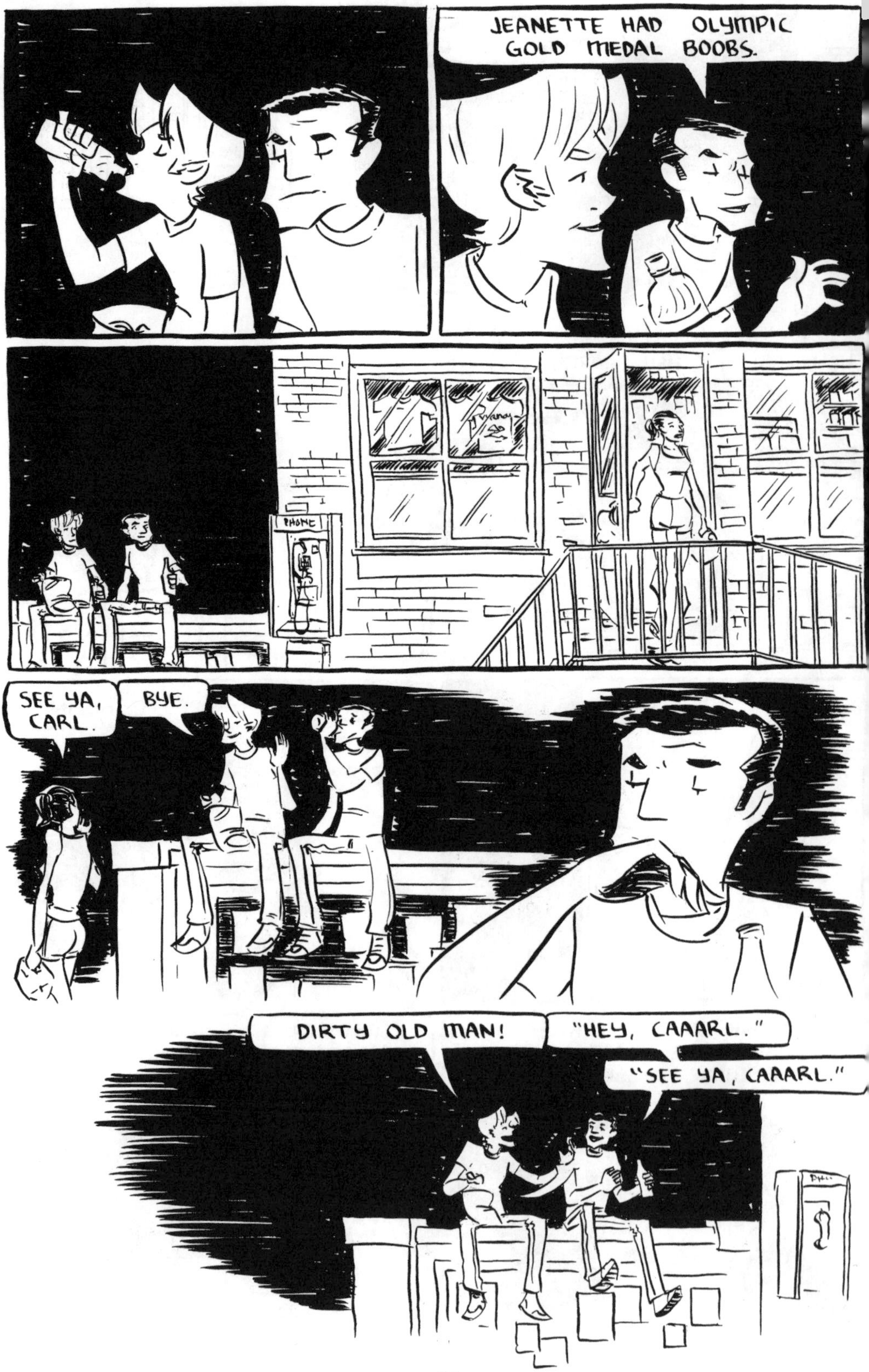
JEANETTE HAD OLYMPIC GOLD MEDAL BOOBS.
PHONE
SEE YA, CARL.
BYE.
DIRTY OLD MAN!
"HEY, CAAARL."
"SEE YA, CAAARL."

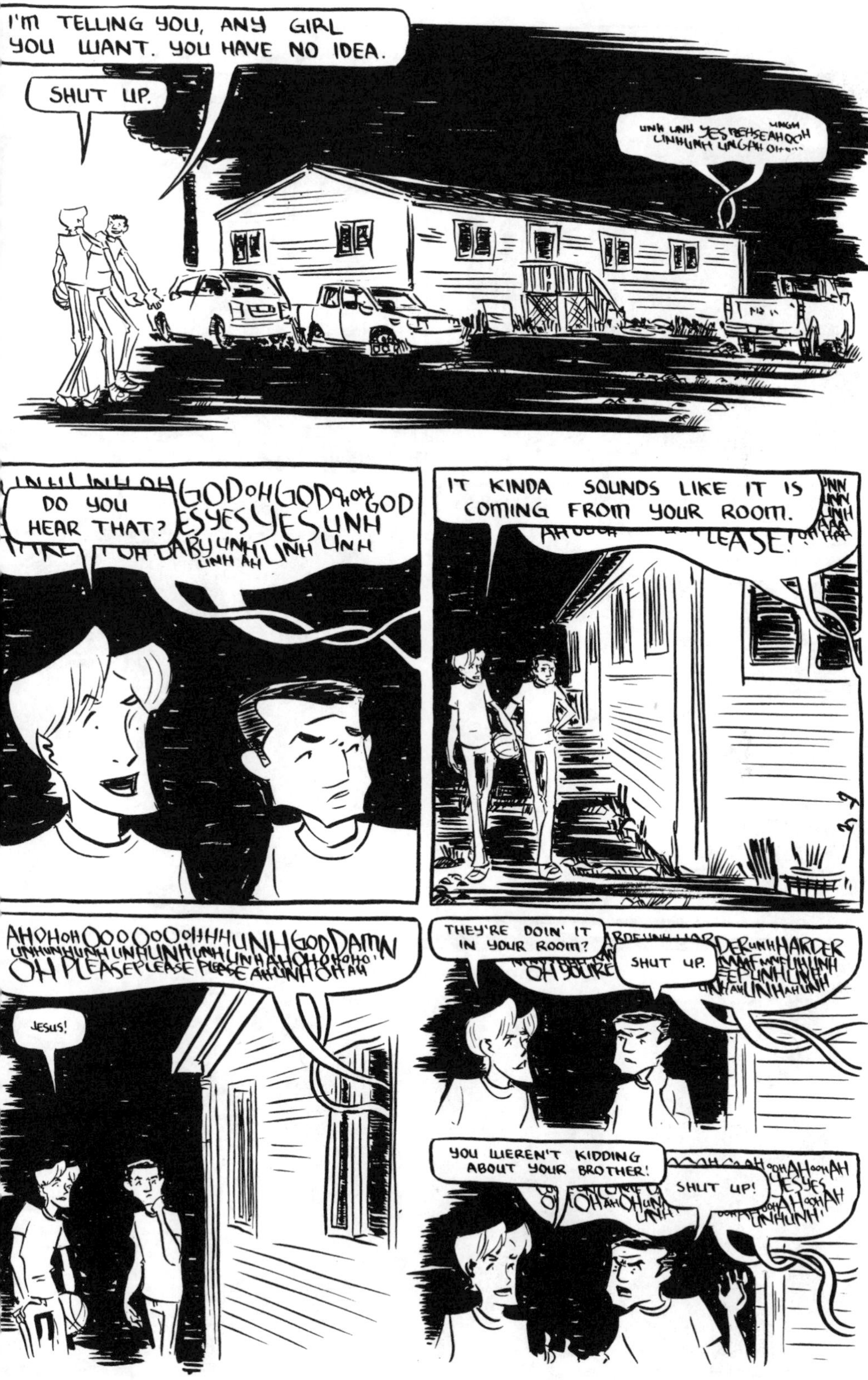
I'M TELLING YOU, ANY GIRL YOU WANT. YOU HAVE NO IDEA.
SHUT UP.
DO YOU HEAR THAT?
IT KINDA SOUNDS LIKE IT IS COMING FROM YOUR ROOM.
AHOHOHOOOOOOOHHHUNHGODDAMN
OH PLEASEPLEASE PLEASE AHUNH OHAH
JESUS!
THEY'RE DOIN' IT IN YOUR ROOM?
SHUT UP.
YOU WEREN'T KIDDING ABOUT YOUR BROTHER!
SHUT UP!

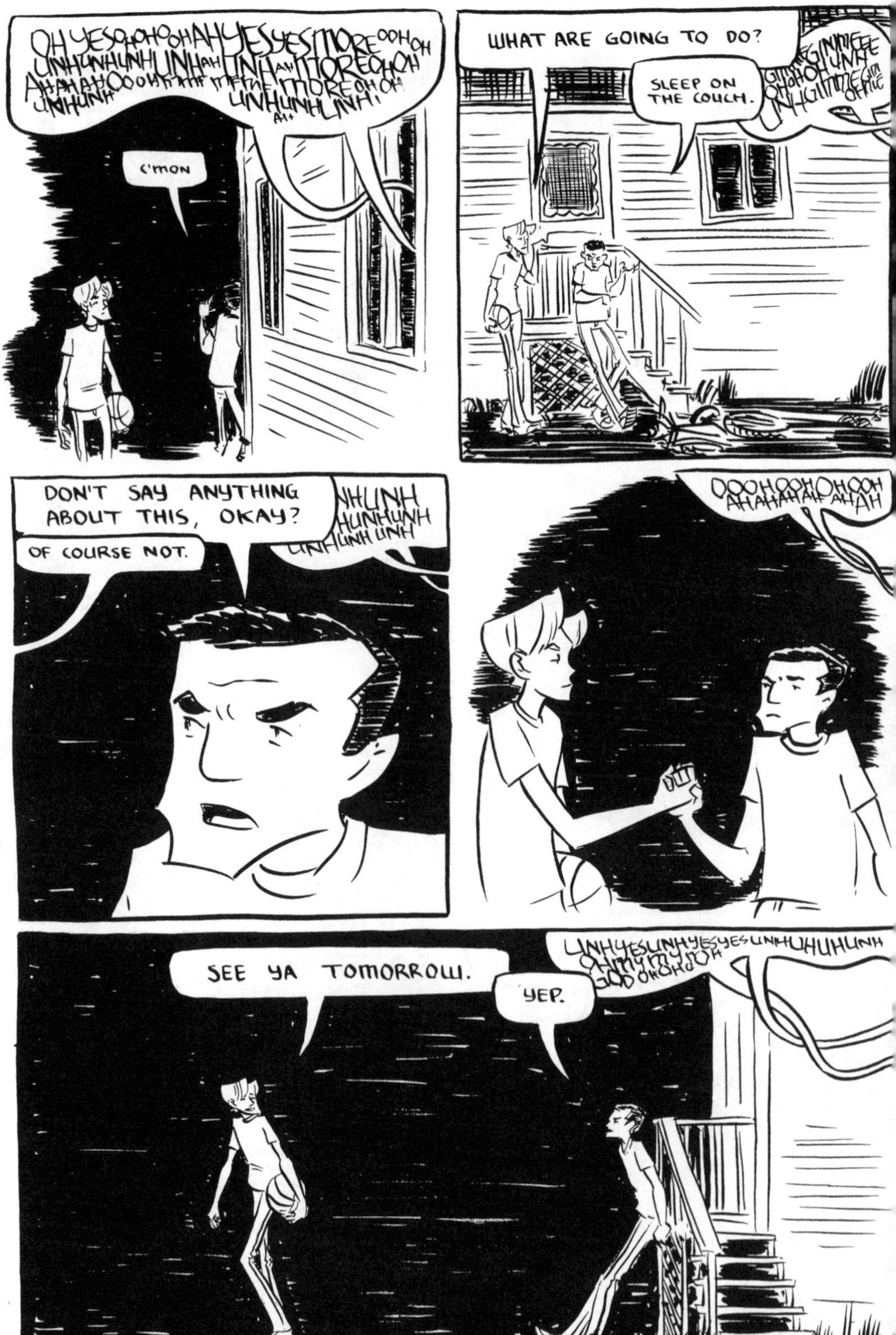
OH YES OHOHOOH AH YES YES MORE OOH OH
UNH UNH UNH UNH AH UNH AH MORE OH OH
UNH UNH UNH UNH
C'MON
WHAT ARE GOING TO DO?
SLEEP ON THE COUCH.
DON'T SAY ANYTHING ABOUT THIS, OKAY?
OF COURSE NOT.
UNH UNH
UNH UNH UNH
UNH UNH UNH
OOOH OOH OH OOH
AH AH AH AH AH AH
SEE YA TOMORROW.
YEP.
UNH YES UNH YES YES UNH UH UH UNH

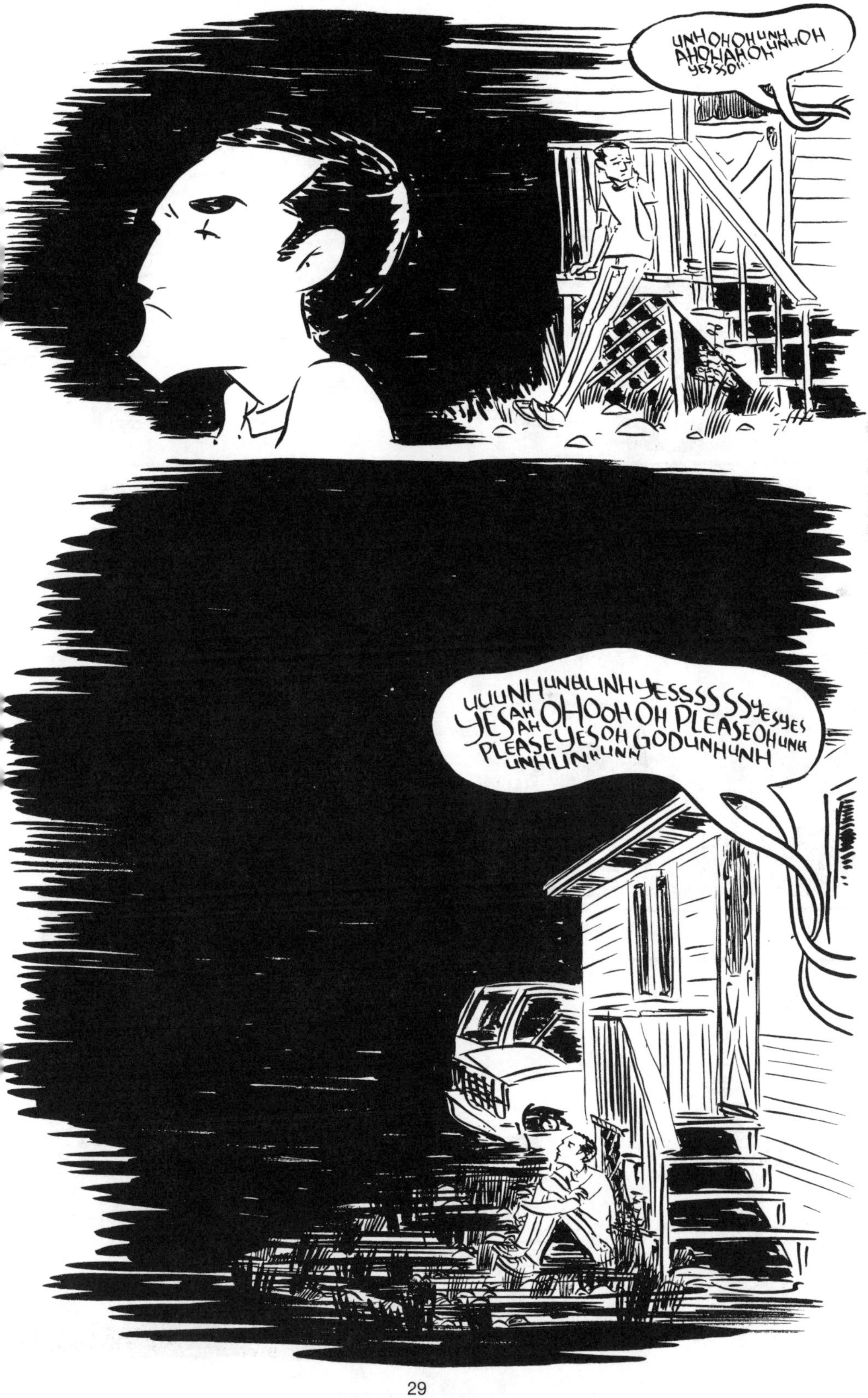
UNHOHOHUNHUNHOH AHOHAHOH YESSSOH
UUUNHUNHUNHYESSSSSSYESYES YESAHAHOHOOHOH PLEASEOHUNH PLEASEYESOH GODUNHUNH UNHUNHUNH

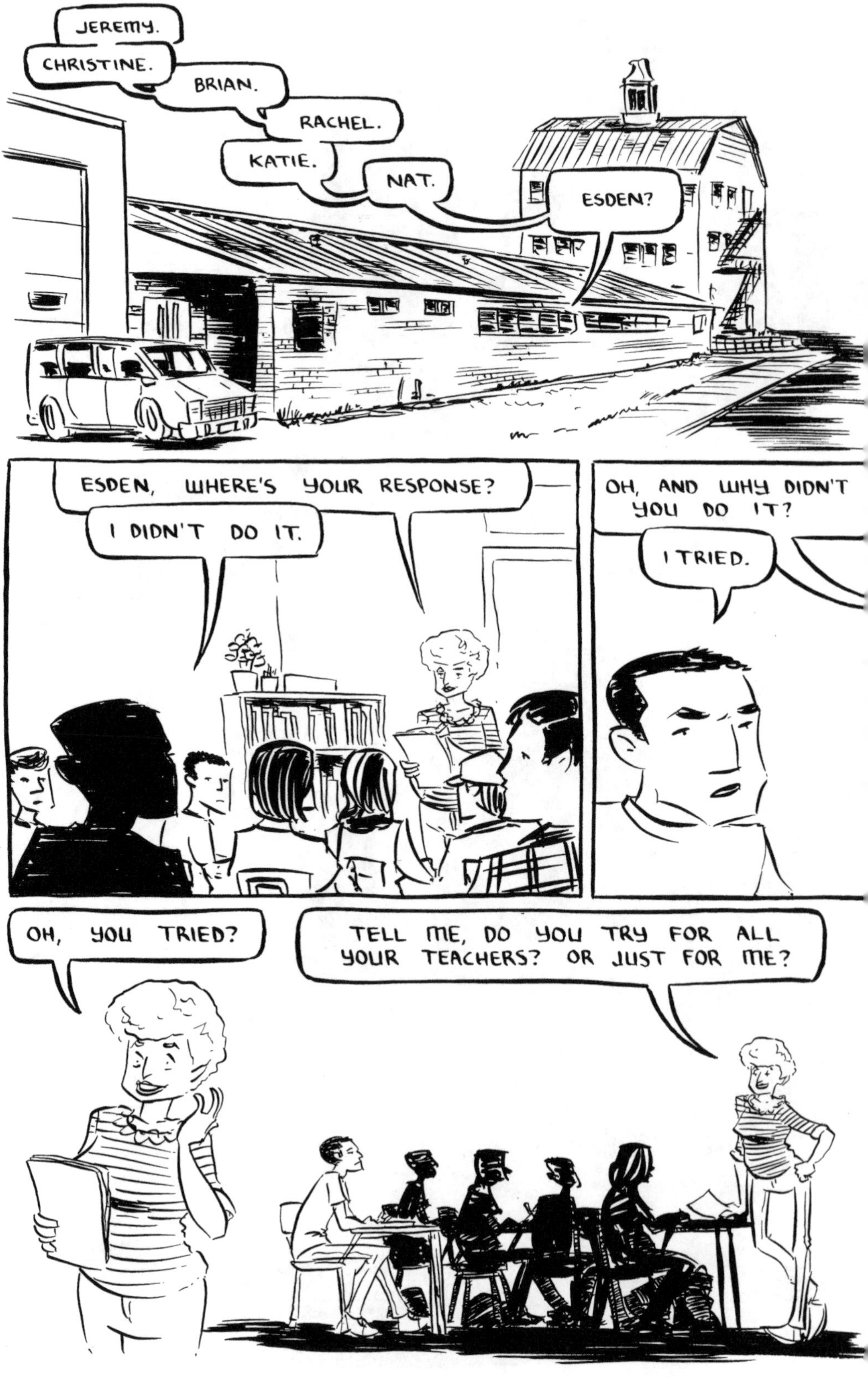
JEREMY.
CHRISTINE.
BRIAN.
RACHEL.
KATIE.
NAT.
ESDEN?
ESDEN, WHERE'S YOUR RESPONSE?
I DIDN'T DO IT.
OH, AND WHY DIDN'T YOU DO IT?
I TRIED.
OH, YOU TRIED?
TELL ME, DO YOU TRY FOR ALL YOUR TEACHERS? OR JUST FOR ME?

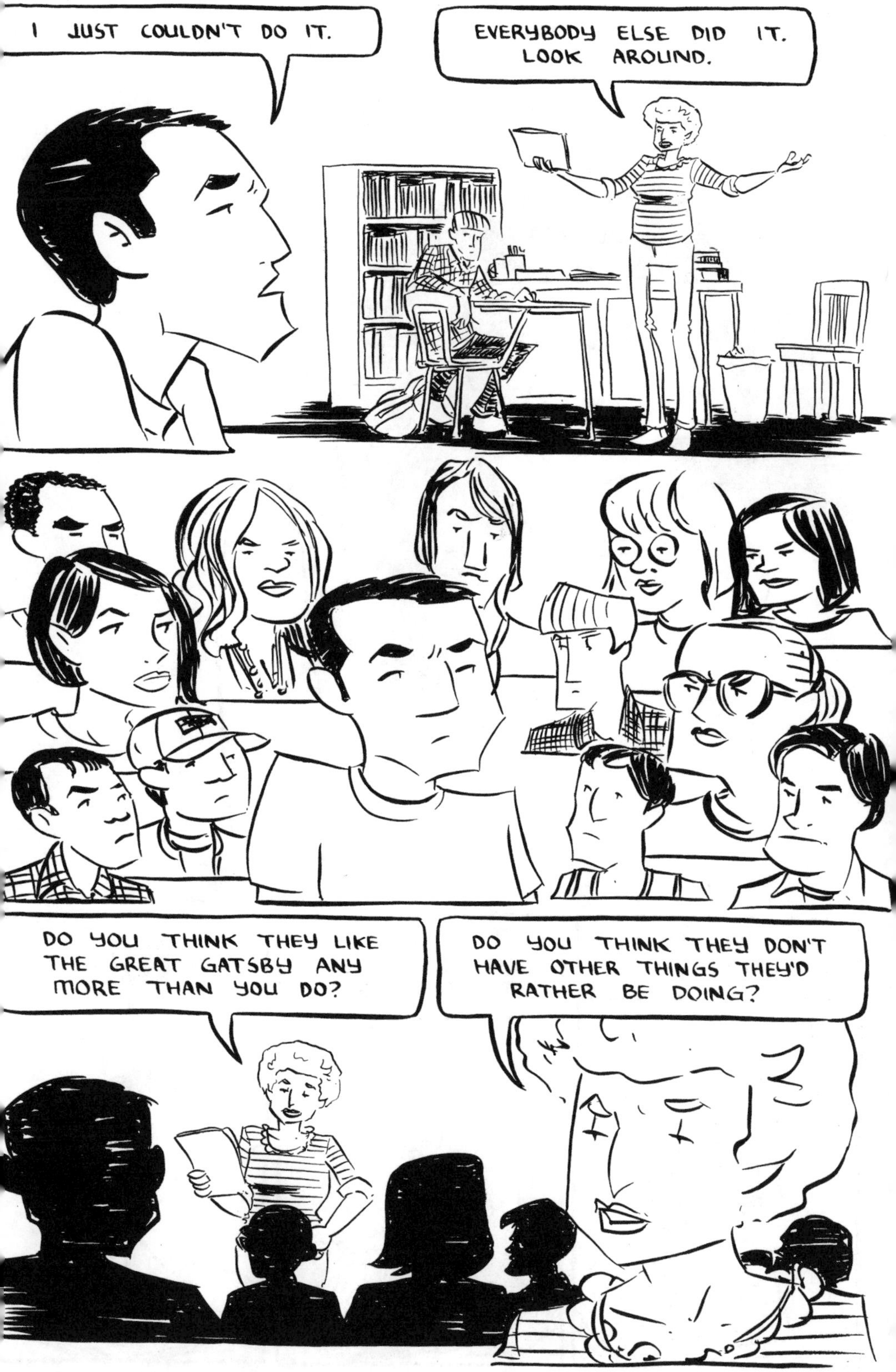
I JUST COULDN'T DO IT.
EVERYBODY ELSE DID IT. LOOK AROUND.
DO YOU THINK THEY LIKE THE GREAT GATSBY ANY MORE THAN YOU DO?
DO YOU THINK THEY DON'T HAVE OTHER THINGS THEY'D RATHER BE DOING?

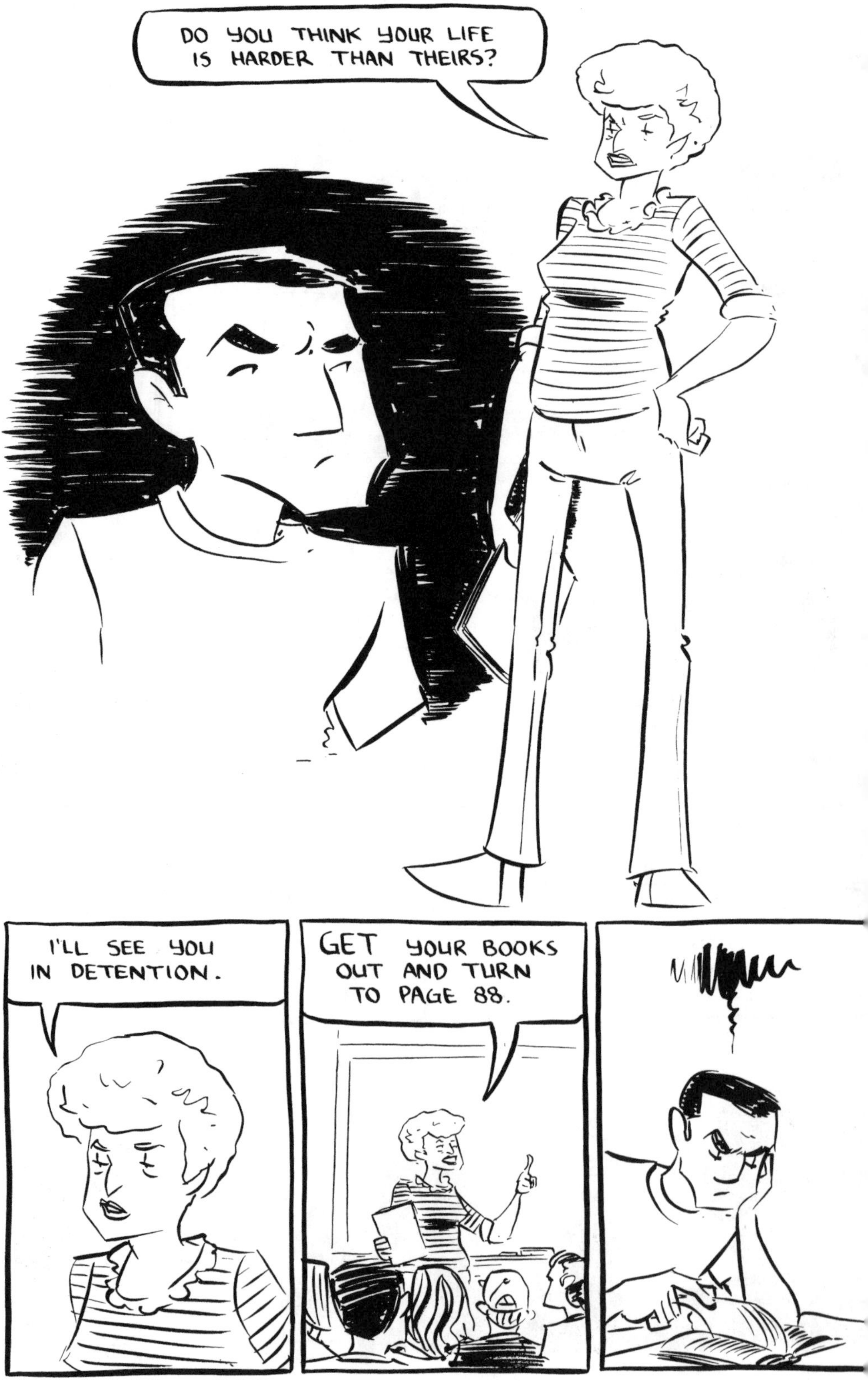
DO YOU THINK YOUR LIFE IS HARDER THAN THEIRS?
I'LL SEE YOU IN DETENTION.
GET YOUR BOOKS OUT AND TURN TO PAGE 88.

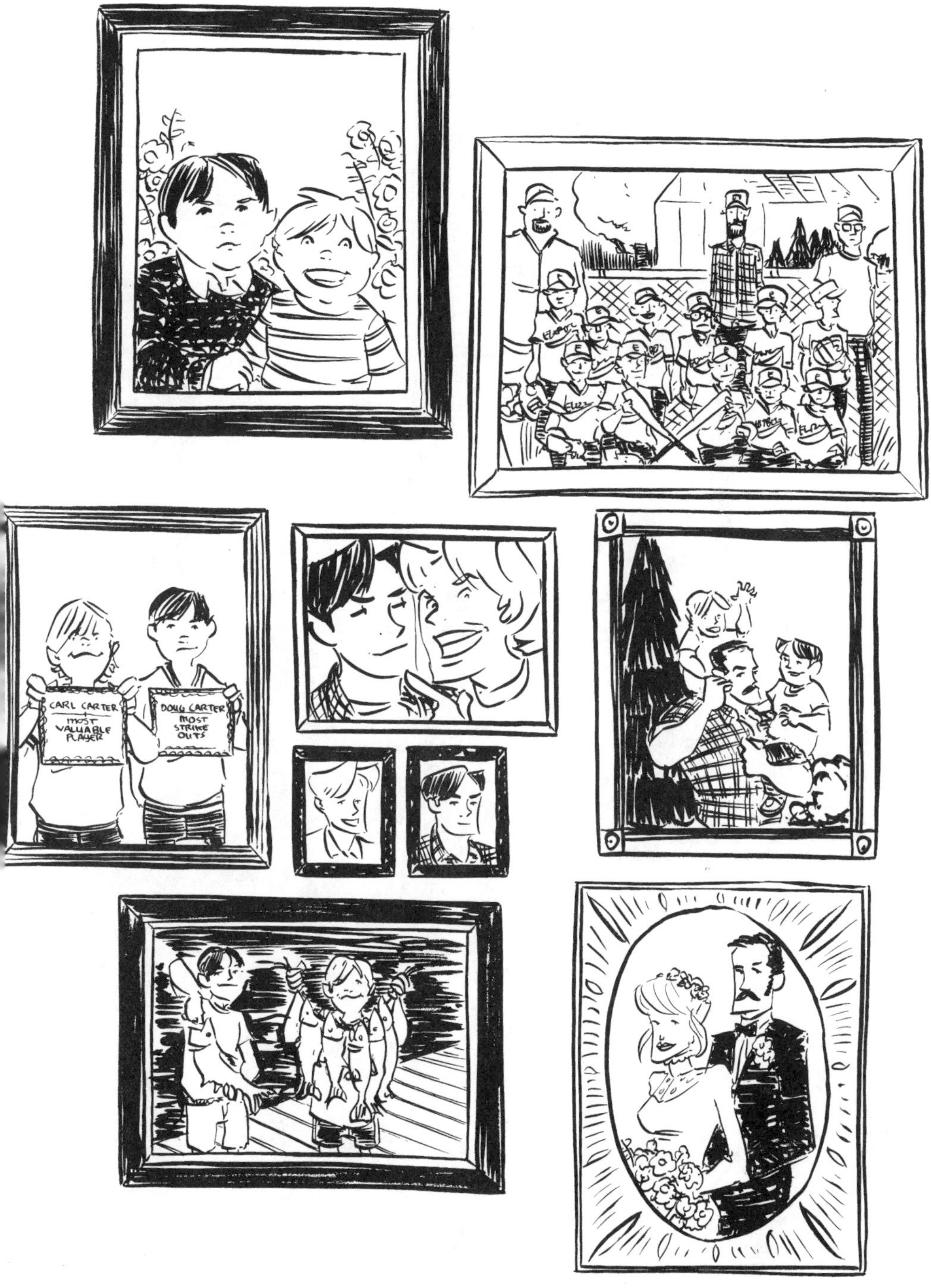
CARL CARTER
MOST VALUABLE PLAYER
DOUG CARTER
MOST STRIKE OUTS

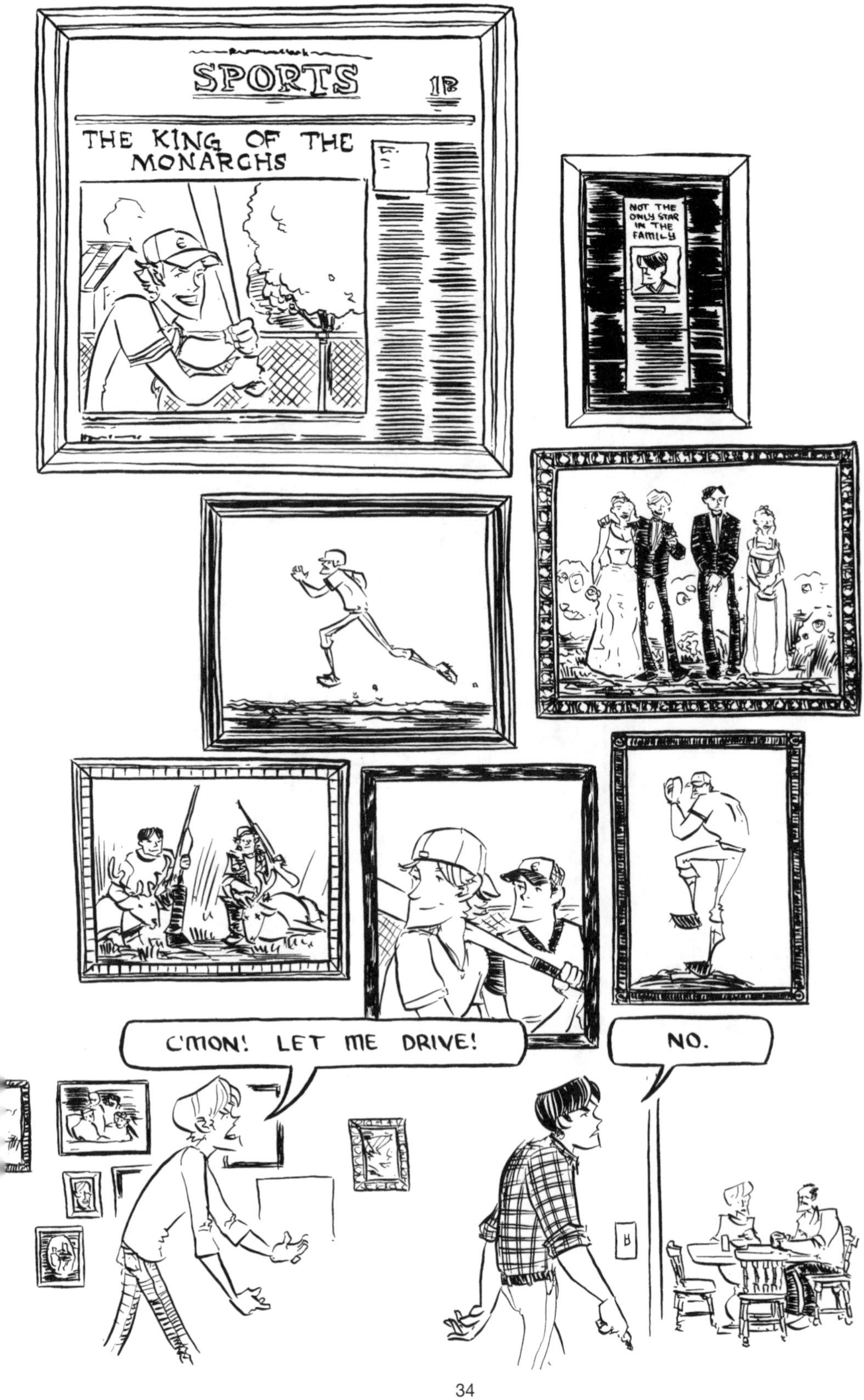
SPORTS
1B
THE KING OF THE MONARCHS
NOT THE ONLY STAR IN THE FAMILY
C'MON! LET ME DRIVE!
NO.

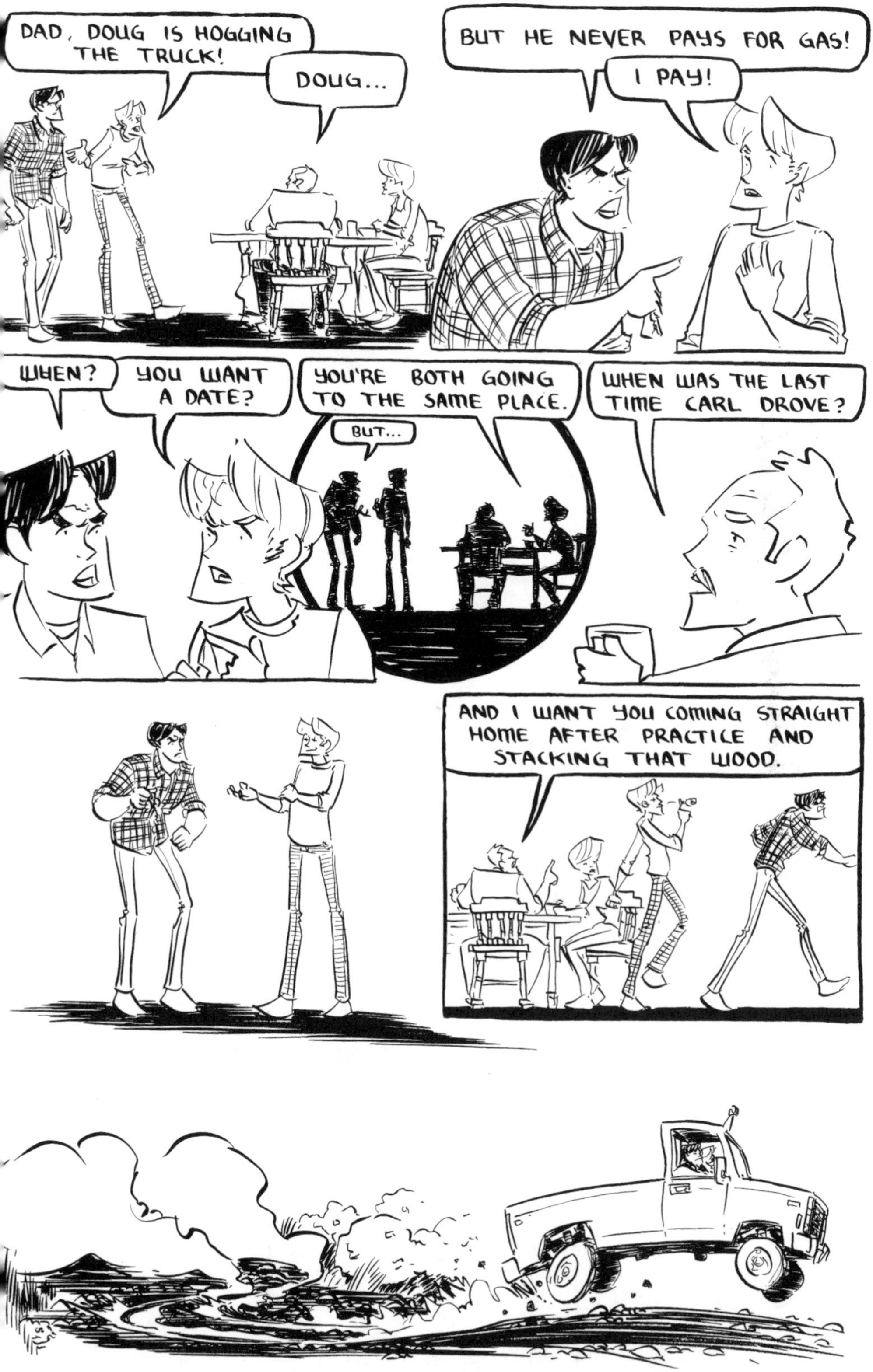
DAD, DOUG IS HOGGING THE TRUCK!
DOUG...
BUT HE NEVER PAYS FOR GAS!
I PAY!
WHEN?
YOU WANT A DATE?
YOU'RE BOTH GOING TO THE SAME PLACE.
BUT...
WHEN WAS THE LAST TIME CARL DROVE?
AND I WANT YOU COMING STRAIGHT HOME AFTER PRACTICE AND STACKING THAT WOOD.

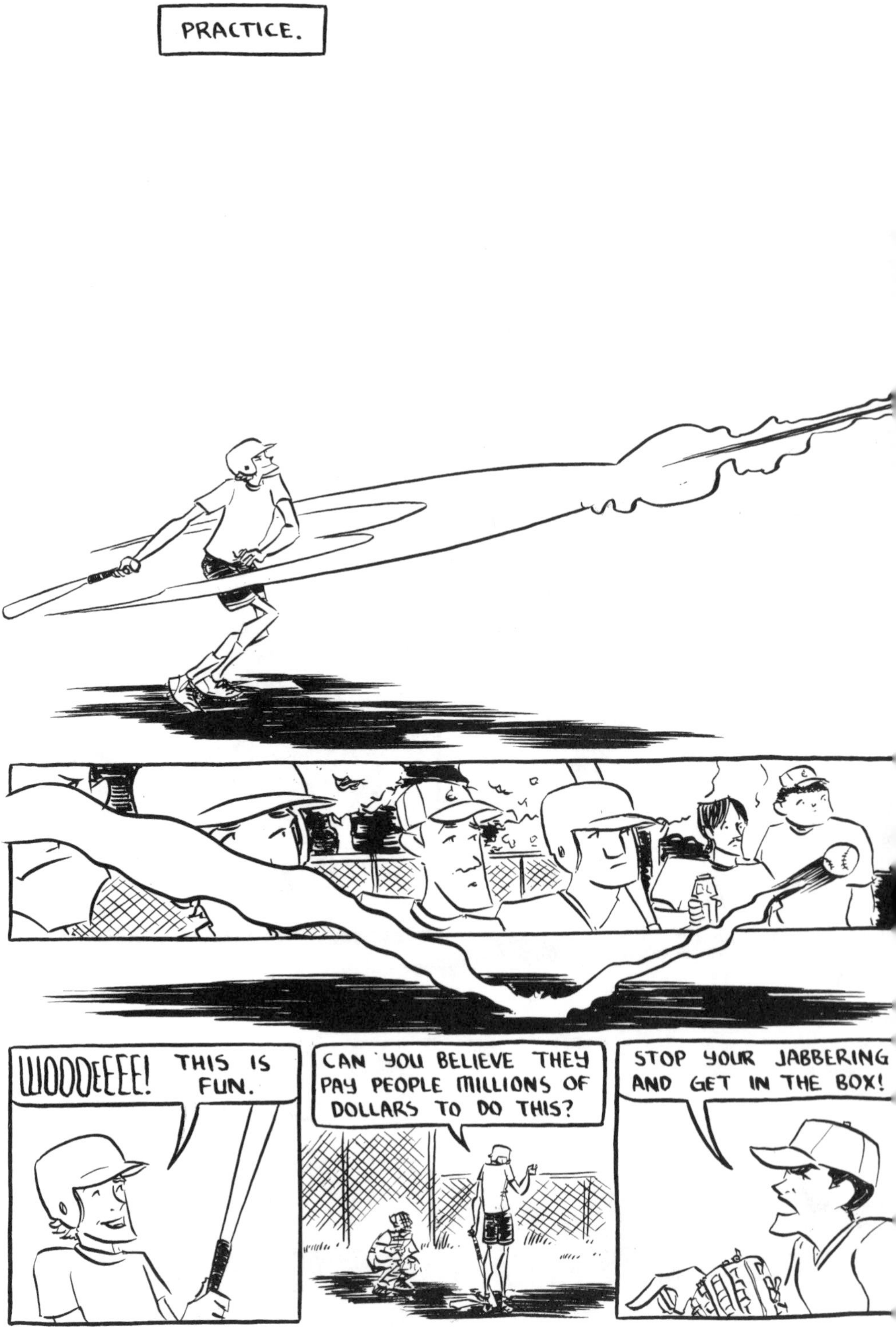
PRACTICE.
WOOOEEEE! THIS IS FUN.
CAN YOU BELIEVE THEY PAY PEOPLE MILLIONS OF DOLLARS TO DO THIS?
STOP YOUR JABBERING AND GET IN THE BOX!

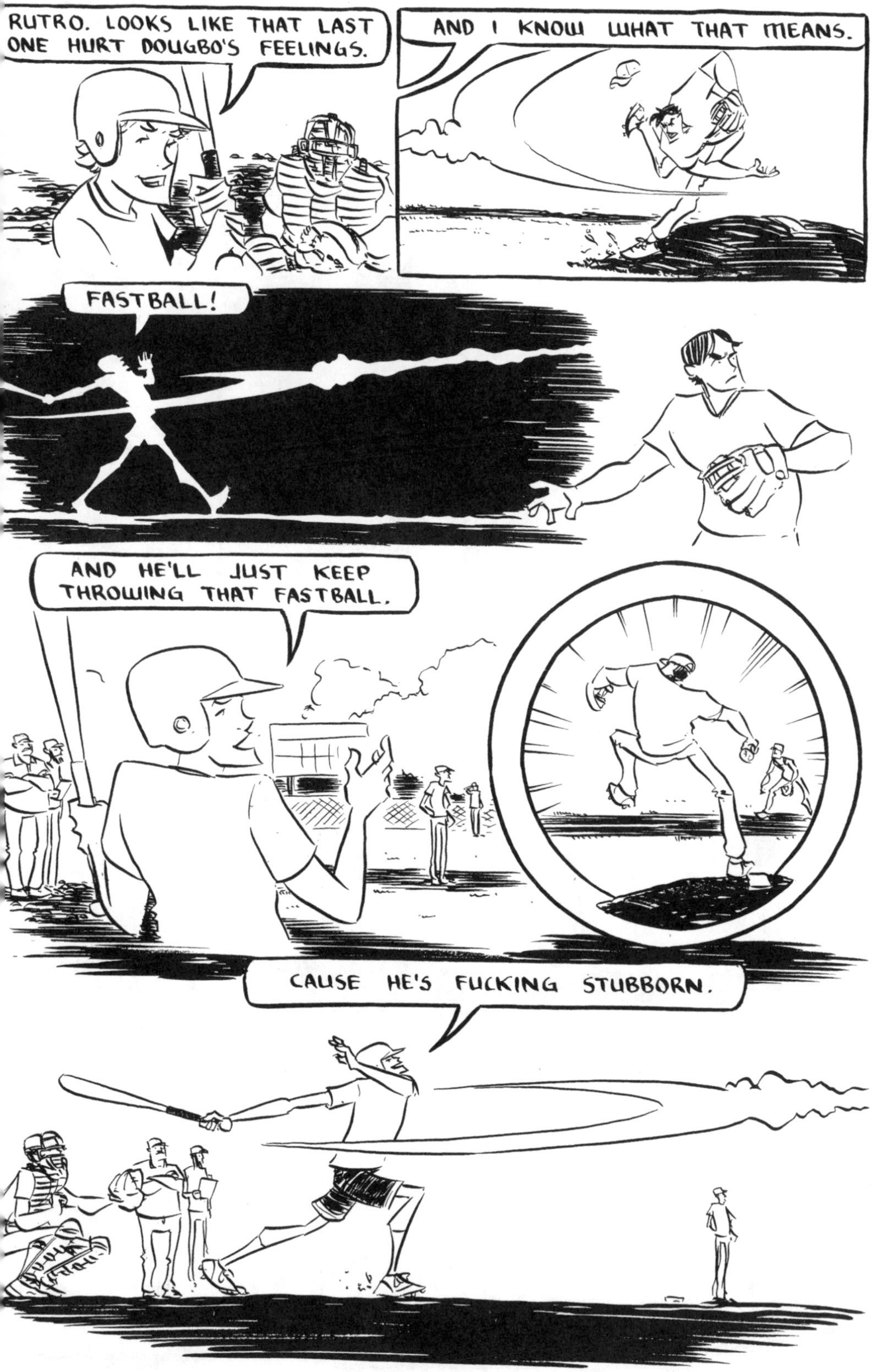
RUTRO. LOOKS LIKE THAT LAST ONE HURT DOUGBO'S FEELINGS.
AND I KNOW WHAT THAT MEANS.
FASTBALL!
AND HE'LL JUST KEEP THROWING THAT FASTBALL.
CAUSE HE'S FUCKING STUBBORN.

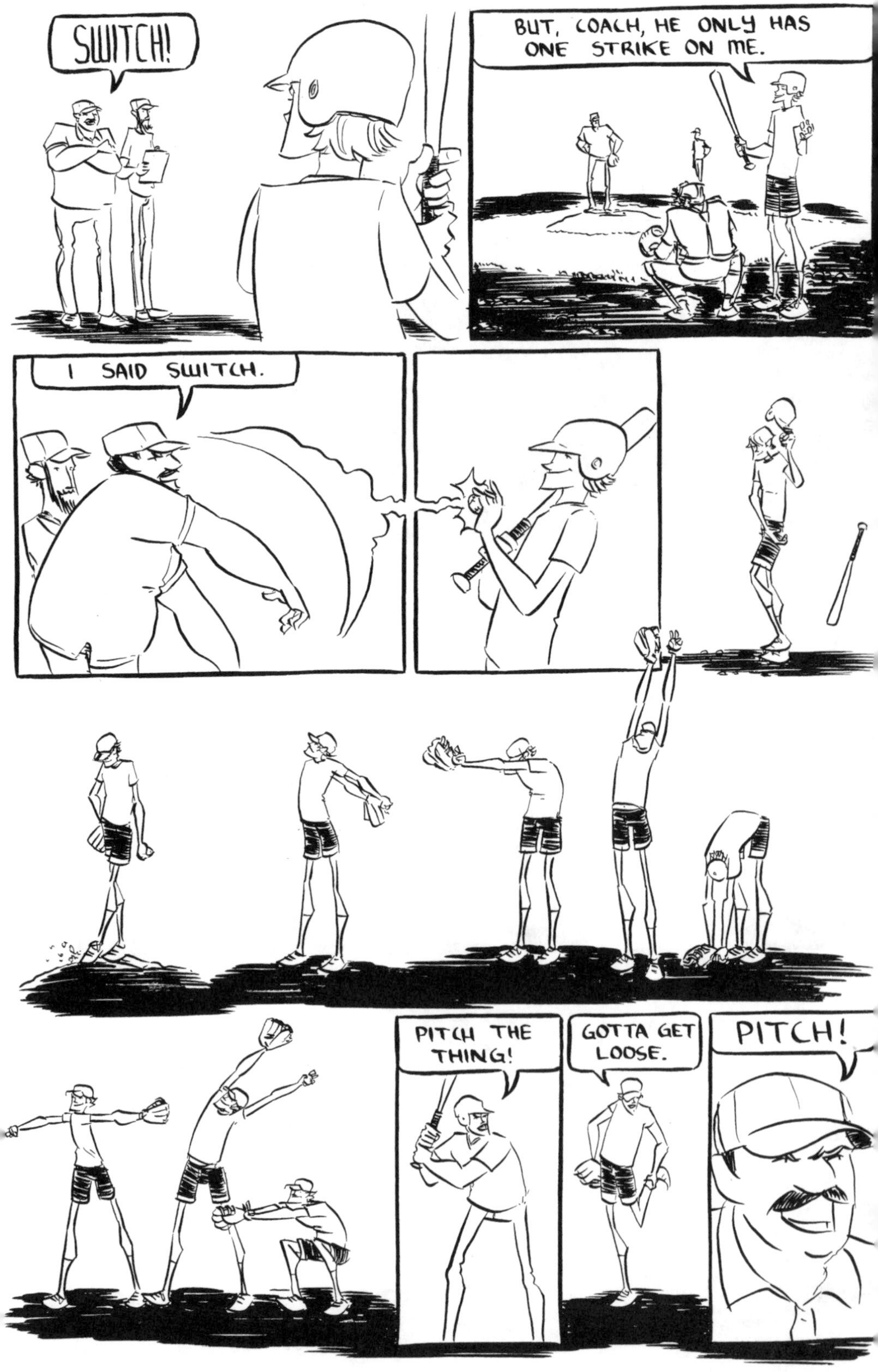
SWITCH!
BUT, COACH, HE ONLY HAS ONE STRIKE ON ME.
I SAID SWITCH.
PITCH THE THING!
GOTTA GET LOOSE.
PITCH!

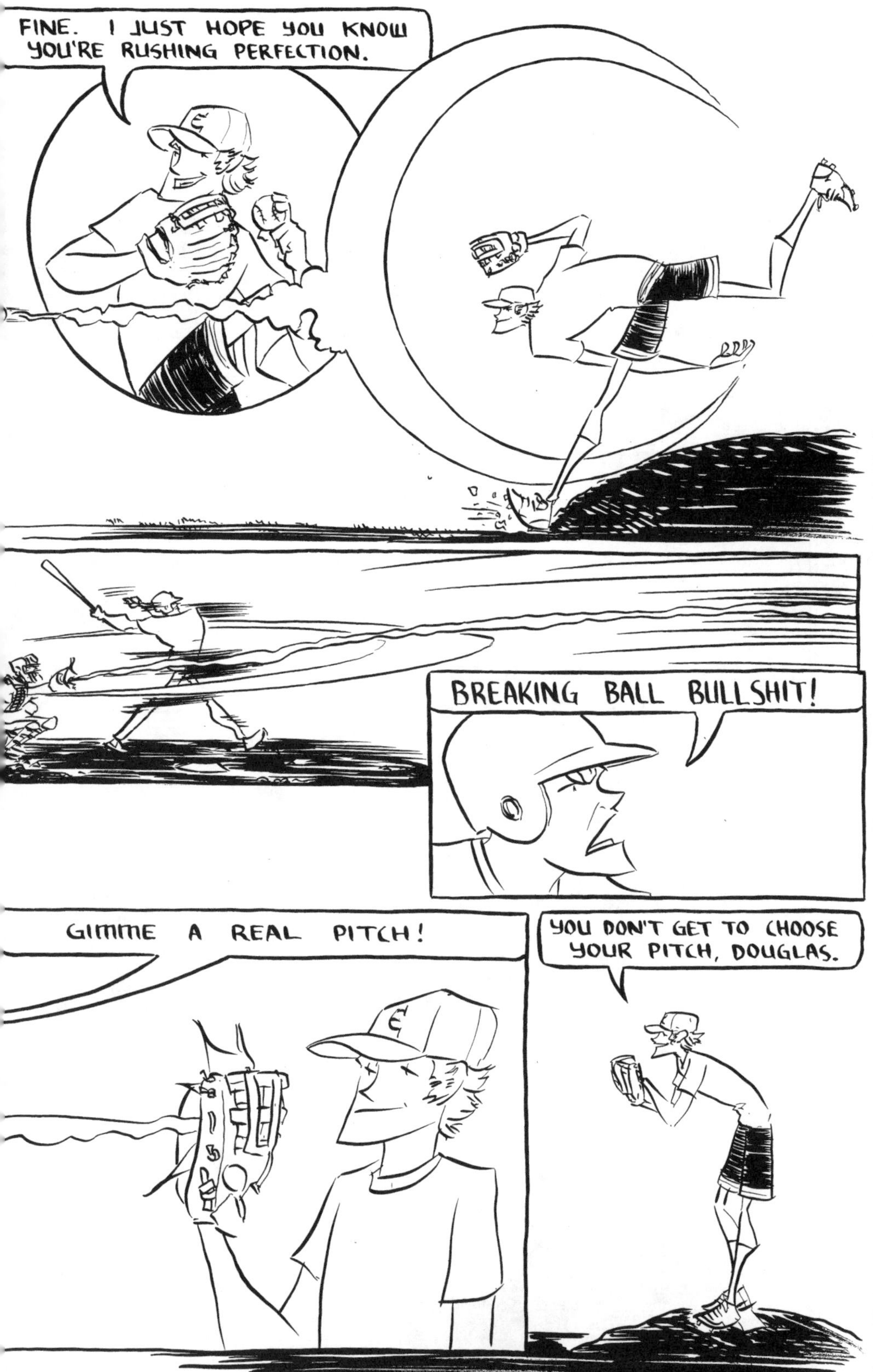
FINE. I JUST HOPE YOU KNOW YOU'RE RUSHING PERFECTION.
BREAKING BALL BULLSHIT!
GIMME A REAL PITCH!
YOU DON'T GET TO CHOOSE YOUR PITCH, DOUGLAS.

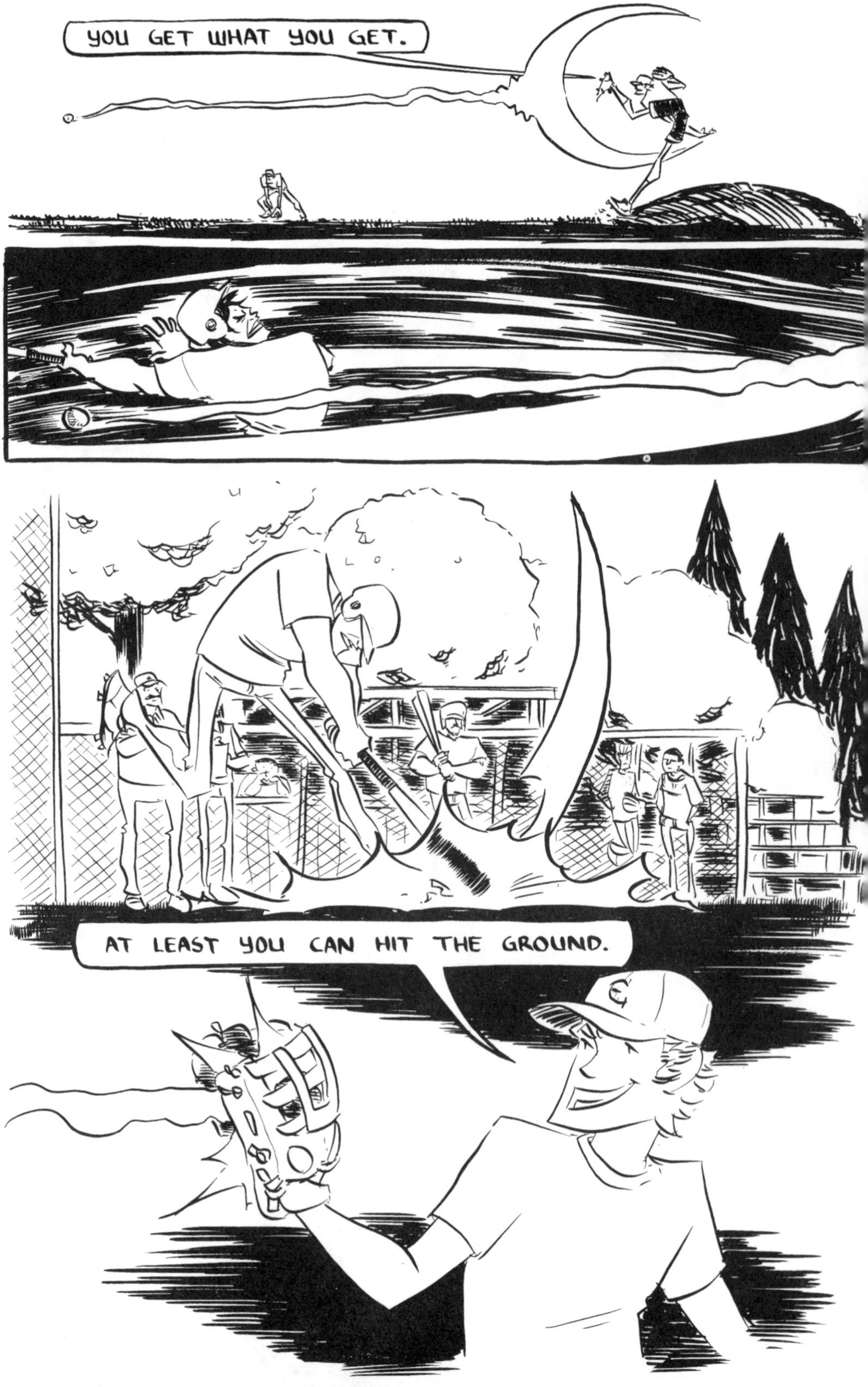
YOU GET WHAT YOU GET.
AT LEAST YOU CAN HIT THE GROUND.

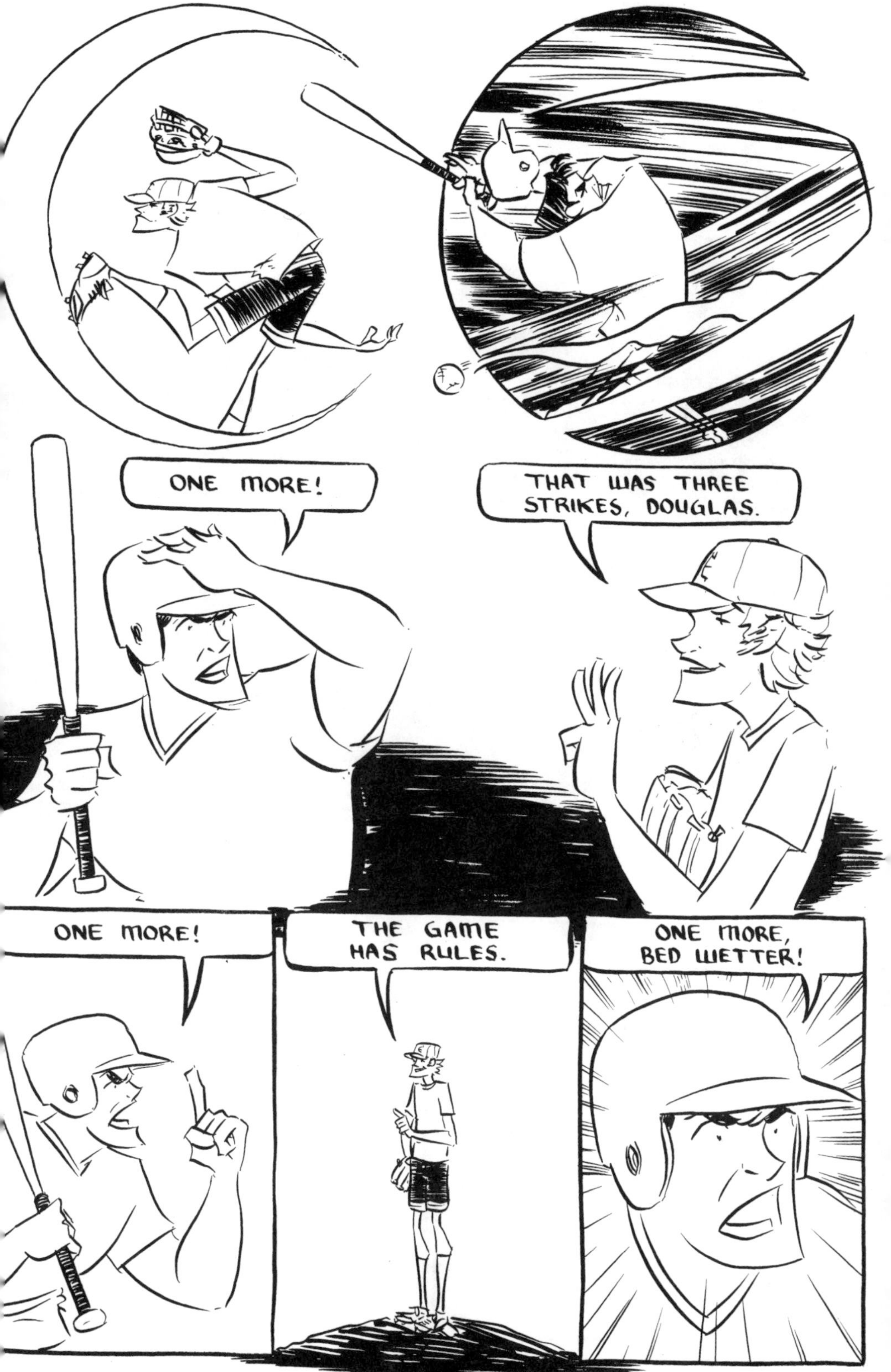
ONE MORE!
THAT WAS THREE STRIKES, DOUGLAS.
ONE MORE!
THE GAME HAS RULES.
ONE MORE, BED WETTER!

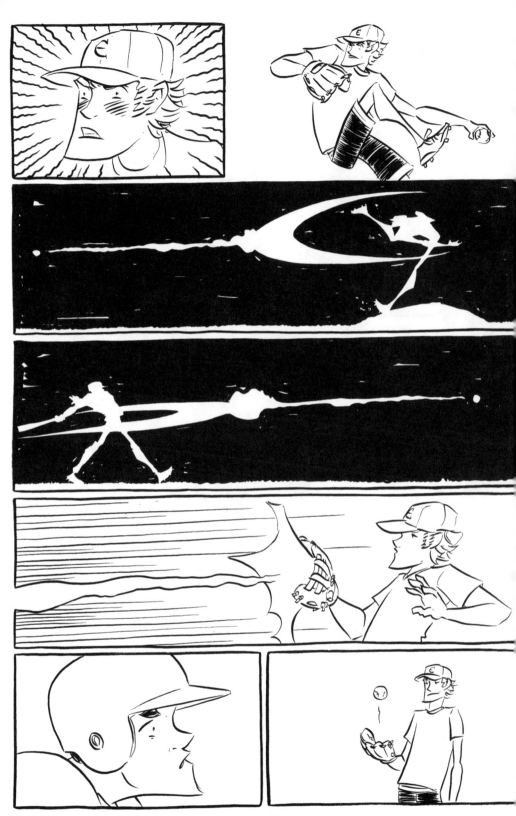

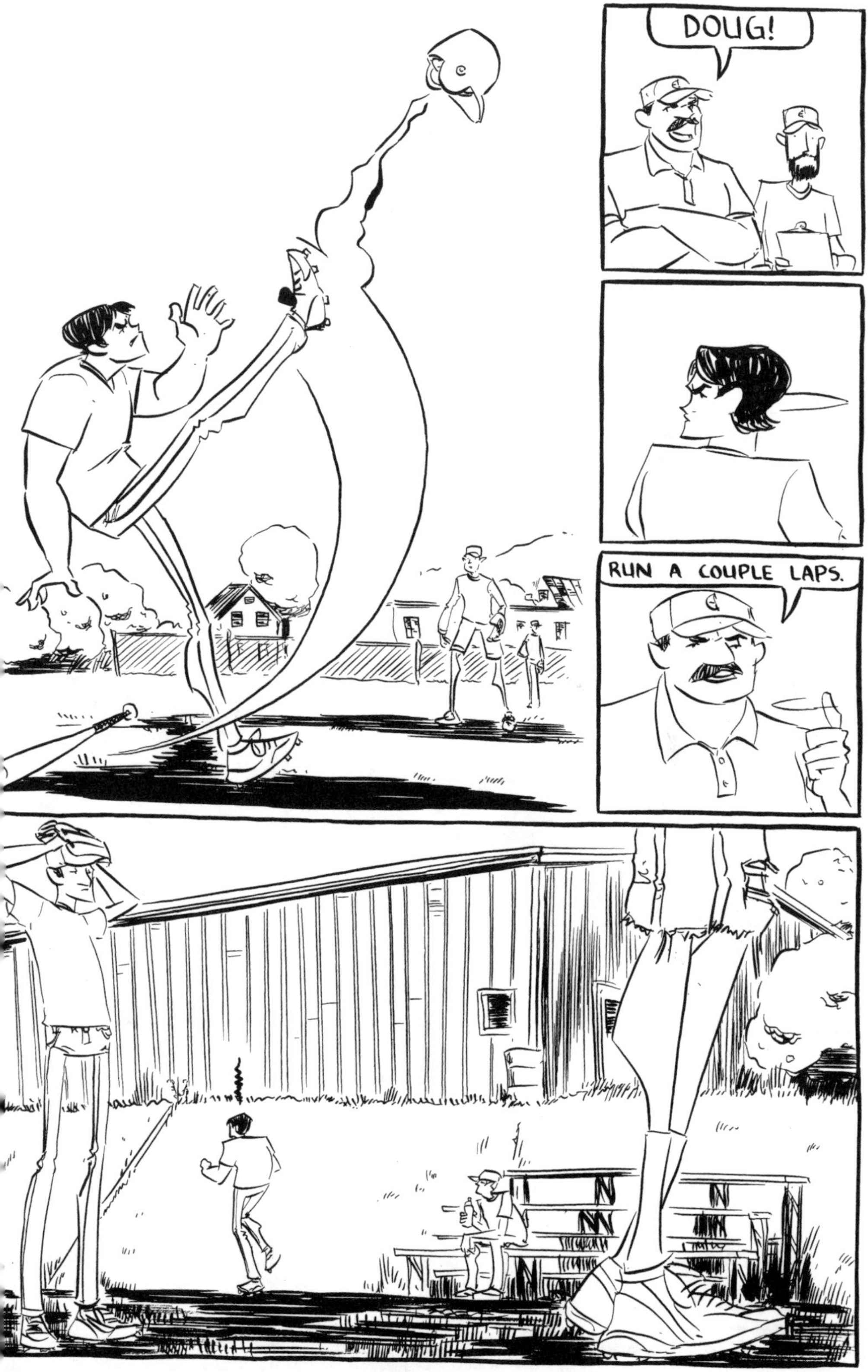
DOUG!
RUN A COUPLE LAPS.

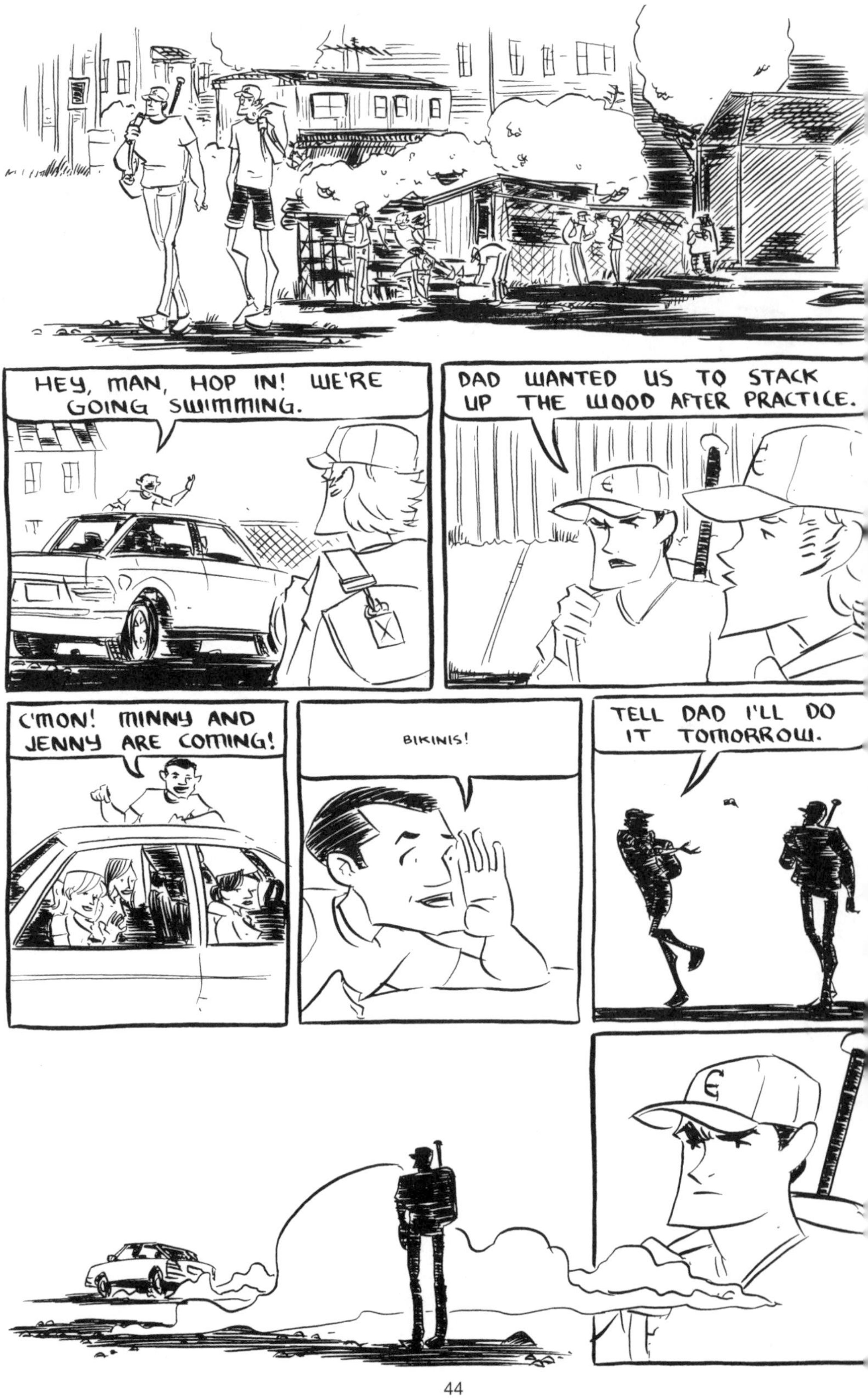
HEY, MAN, HOP IN! WE'RE GOING SWIMMING.
DAD WANTED US TO STACK UP THE WOOD AFTER PRACTICE.
C'MON! MINNY AND JENNY ARE COMING!
BIKINIS!
TELL DAD I'LL DO IT TOMORROW.

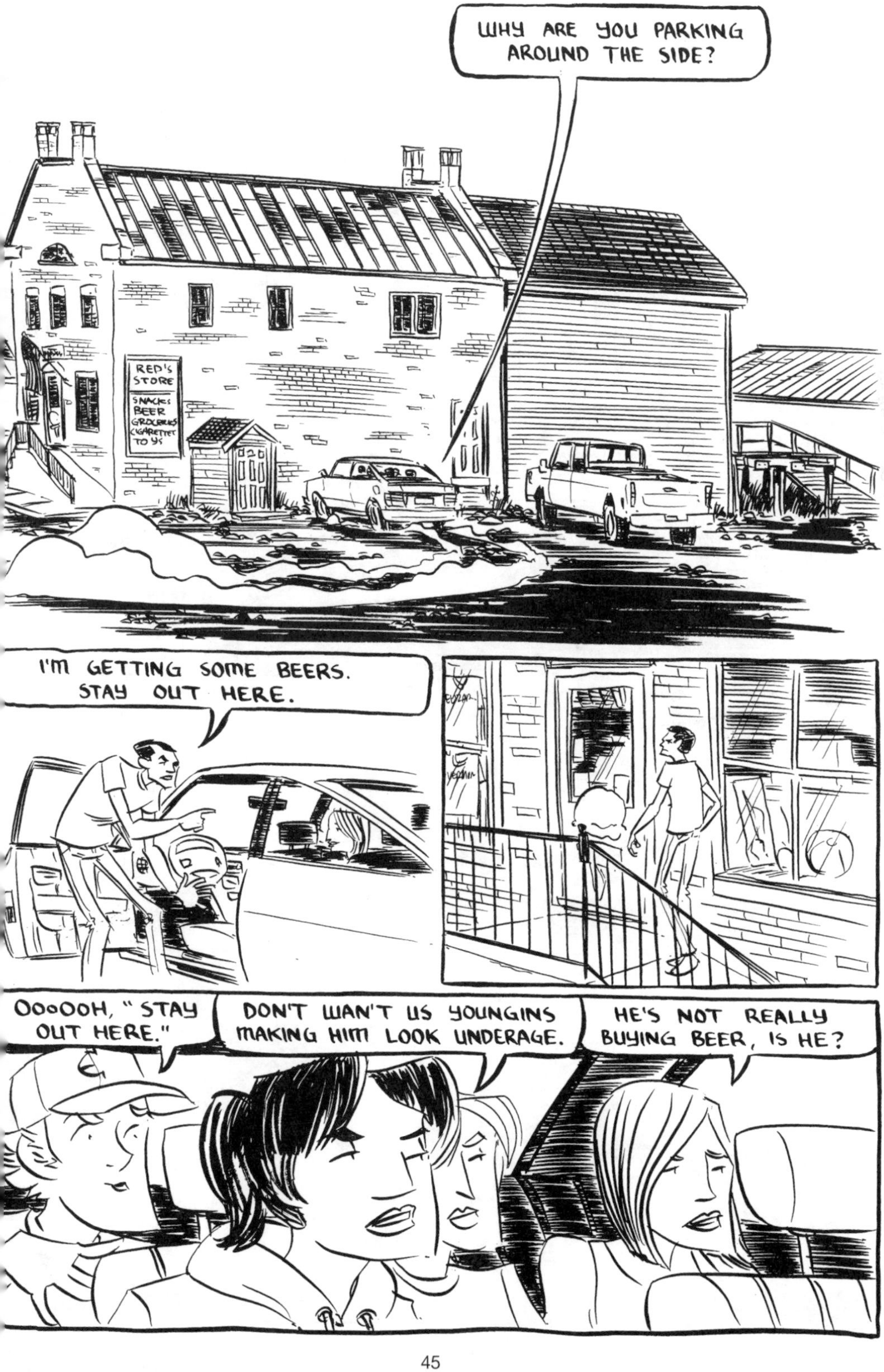
WHY ARE YOU PARKING AROUND THE SIDE?
RED'S STORE
SNACKS
BEER
I'M GETTING SOME BEERS. STAY OUT HERE.
OOoOOH, "STAY OUT HERE."
DON'T WAN'T US YOUNGINS MAKING HIM LOOK UNDERAGE.
HE'S NOT REALLY BUYING BEER, IS HE?

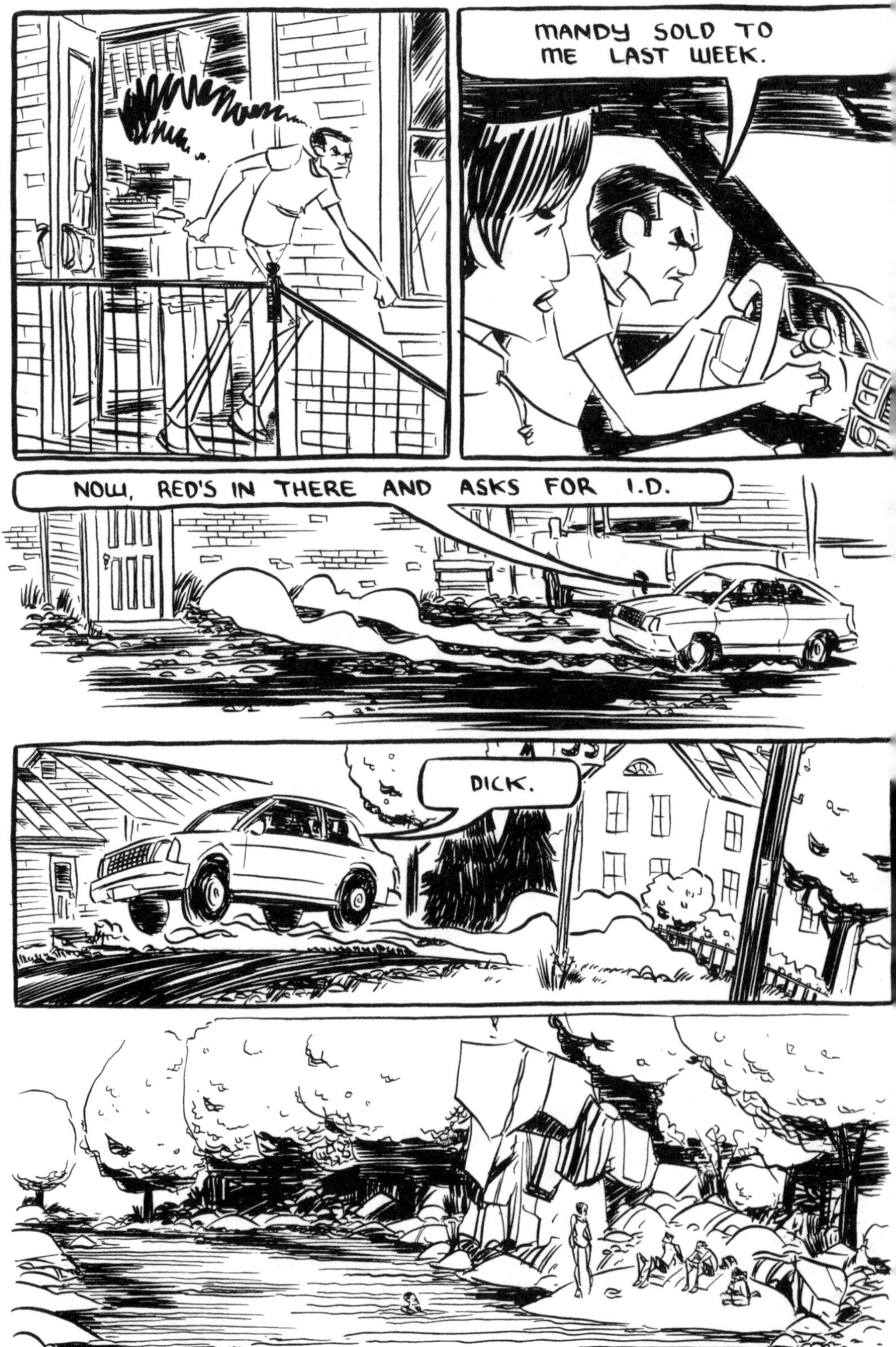
MANDY SOLD TO ME LAST WEEK.
NOW, RED'S IN THERE AND ASKS FOR I.D.
DICK.

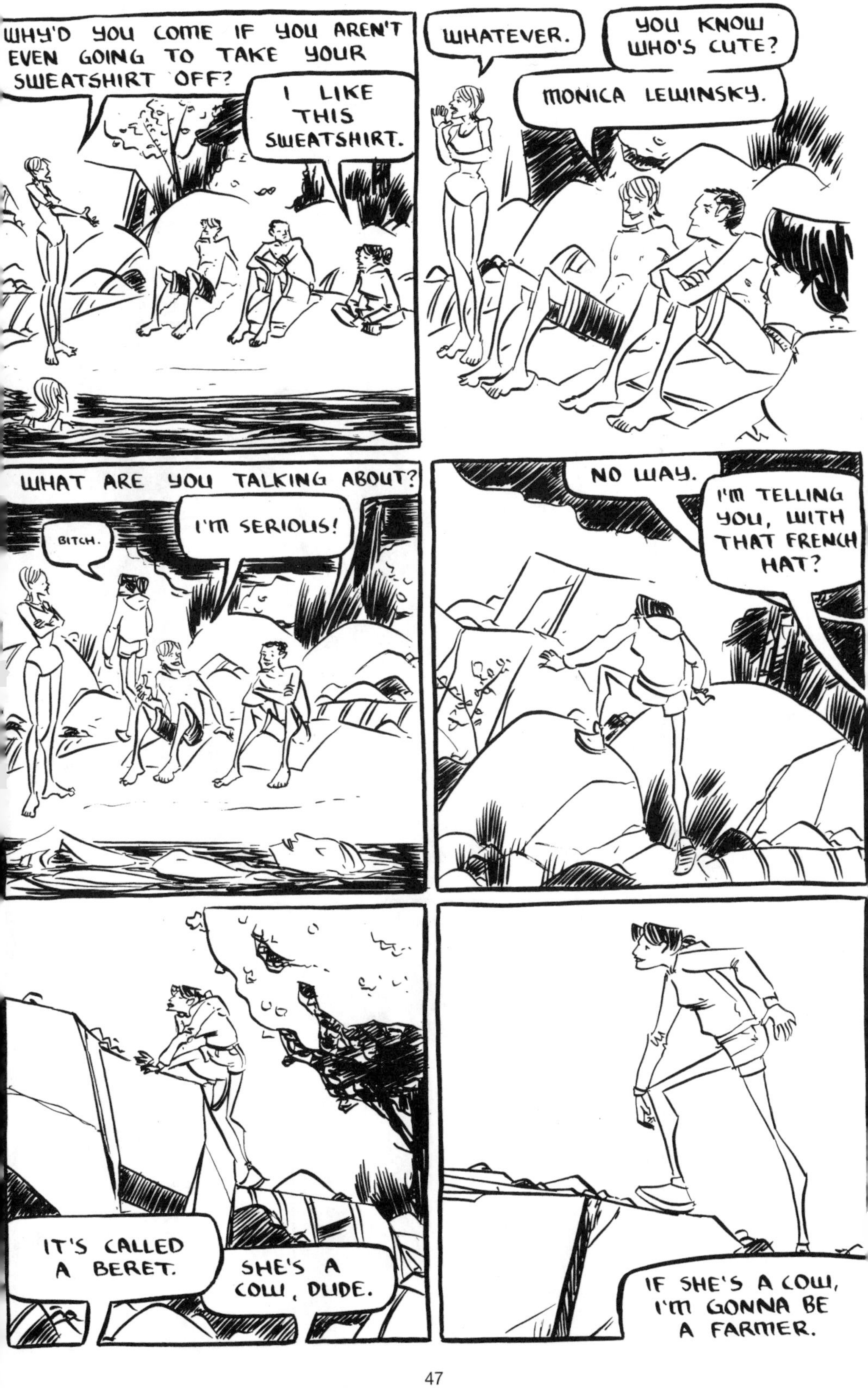
WHY'D YOU COME IF YOU AREN'T EVEN GOING TO TAKE YOUR SWEATSHIRT OFF?
I LIKE THIS SWEATSHIRT.
WHATEVER.
YOU KNOW WHO'S CUTE?
MONICA LEWINSKY.
WHAT ARE YOU TALKING ABOUT?
BITCH.
I'M SERIOUS!
NO WAY.
I'M TELLING YOU, WITH THAT FRENCH HAT?
IT'S CALLED A BERET.
SHE'S A COW, DUDE.
IF SHE'S A COW, I'M GONNA BE A FARMER.

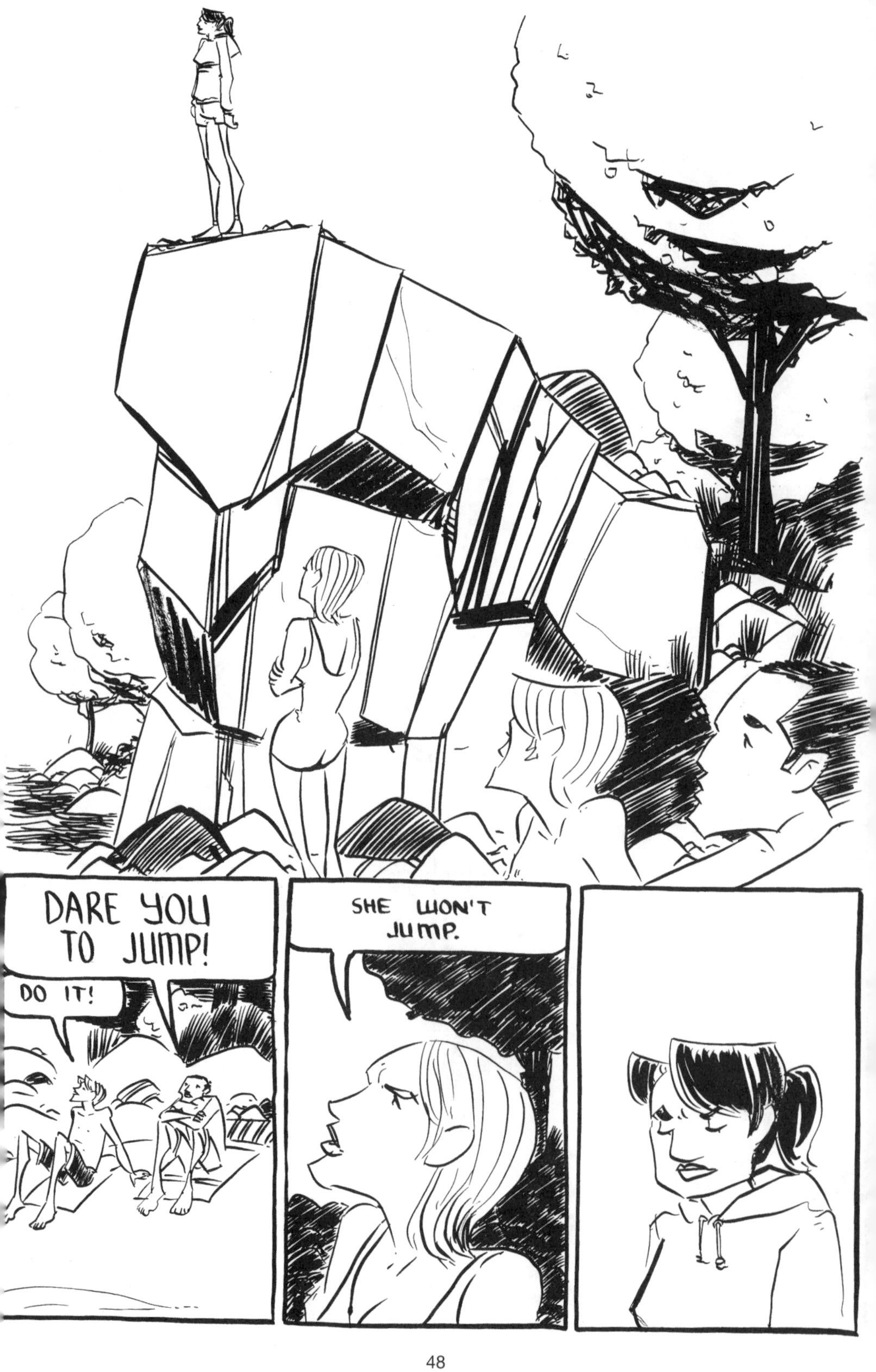
DARE YOU TO JUMP!
DO IT!
SHE WON'T JUMP.

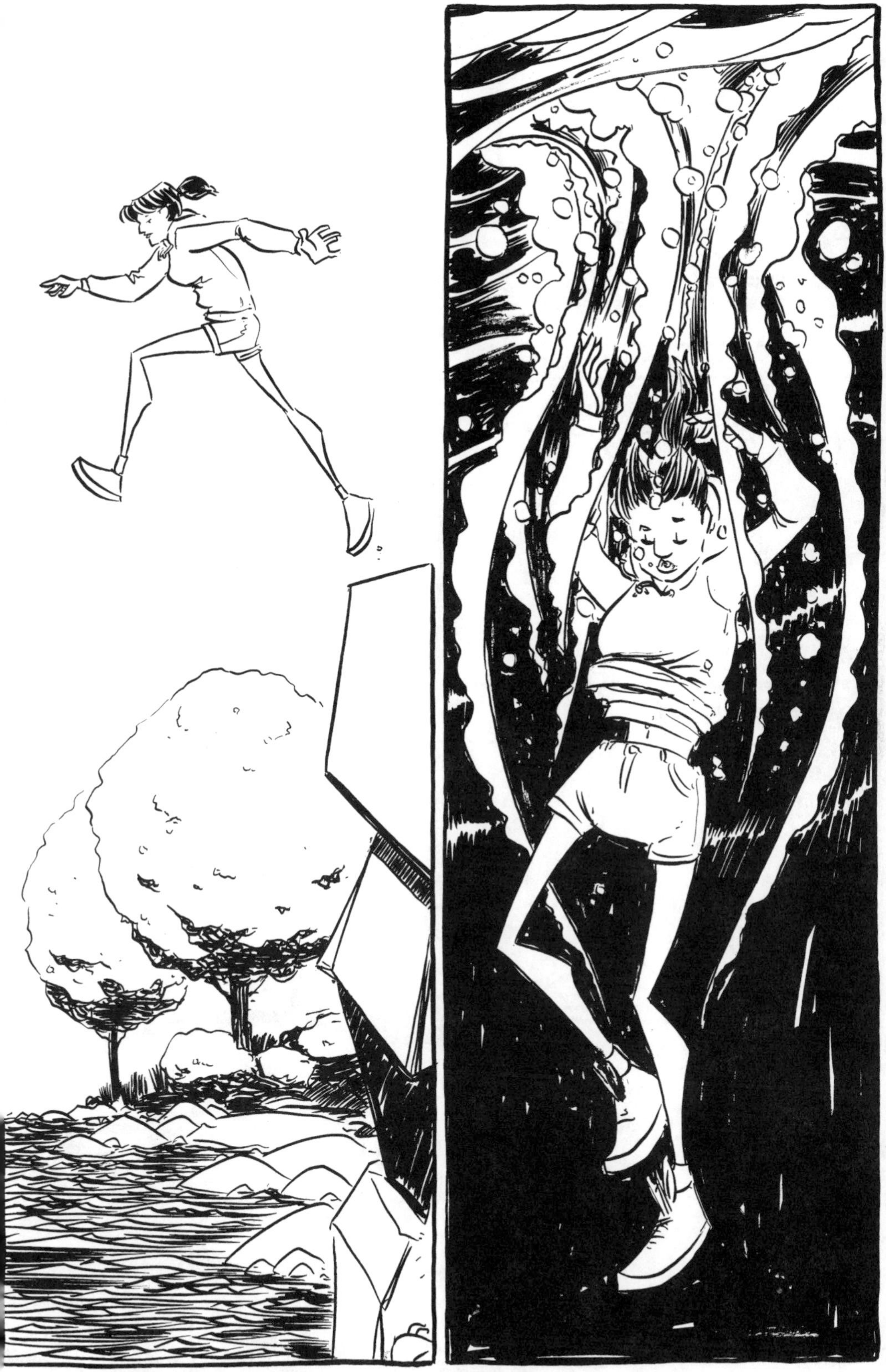

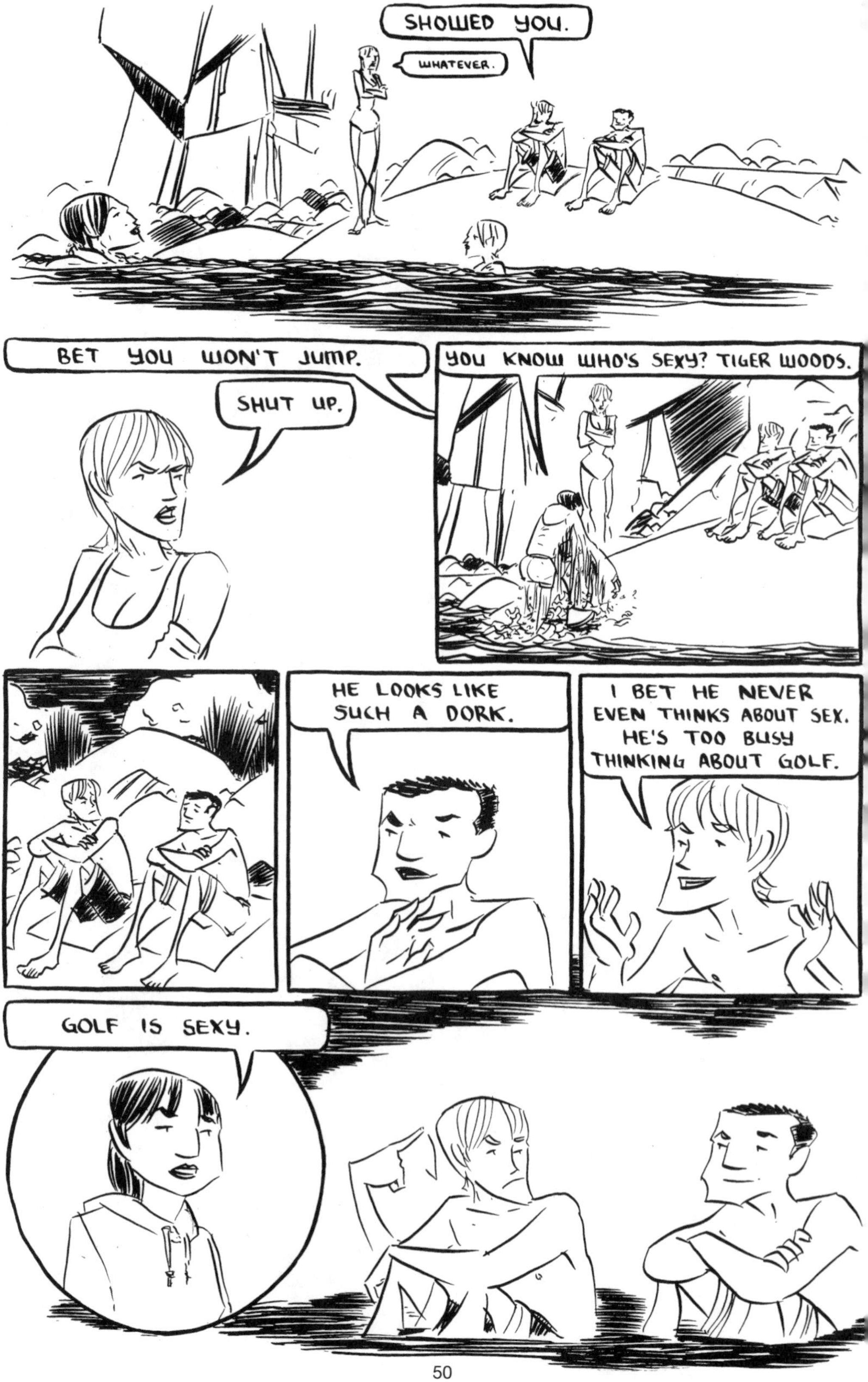
SHOWED YOU.
WHATEVER.
BET YOU WON'T JUMP.
SHUT UP.
YOU KNOW WHO'S SEXY? TIGER WOODS.
HE LOOKS LIKE SUCH A DORK.
I BET HE NEVER EVEN THINKS ABOUT SEX. HE'S TOO BUSY THINKING ABOUT GOLF.
GOLF IS SEXY.

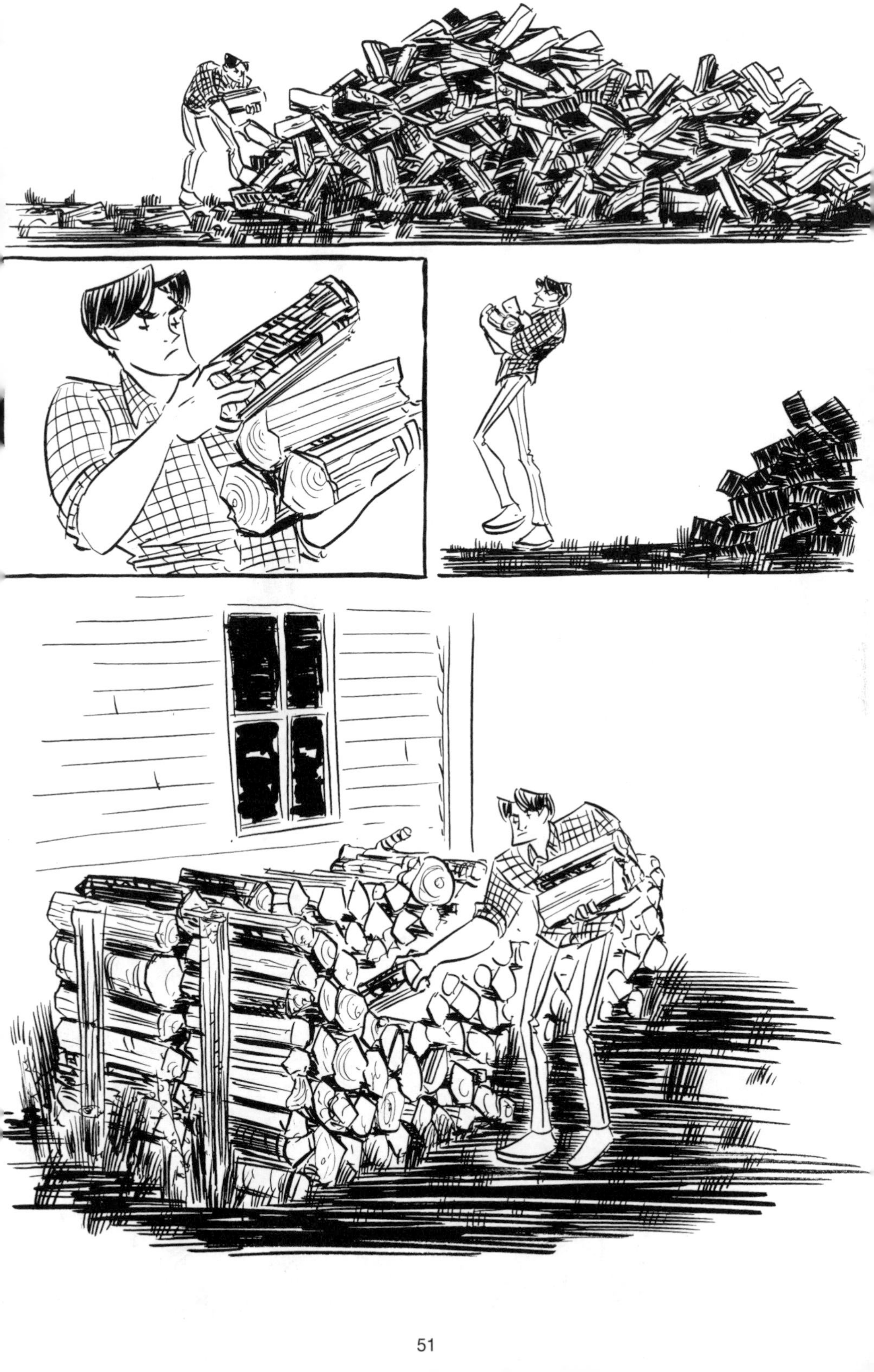

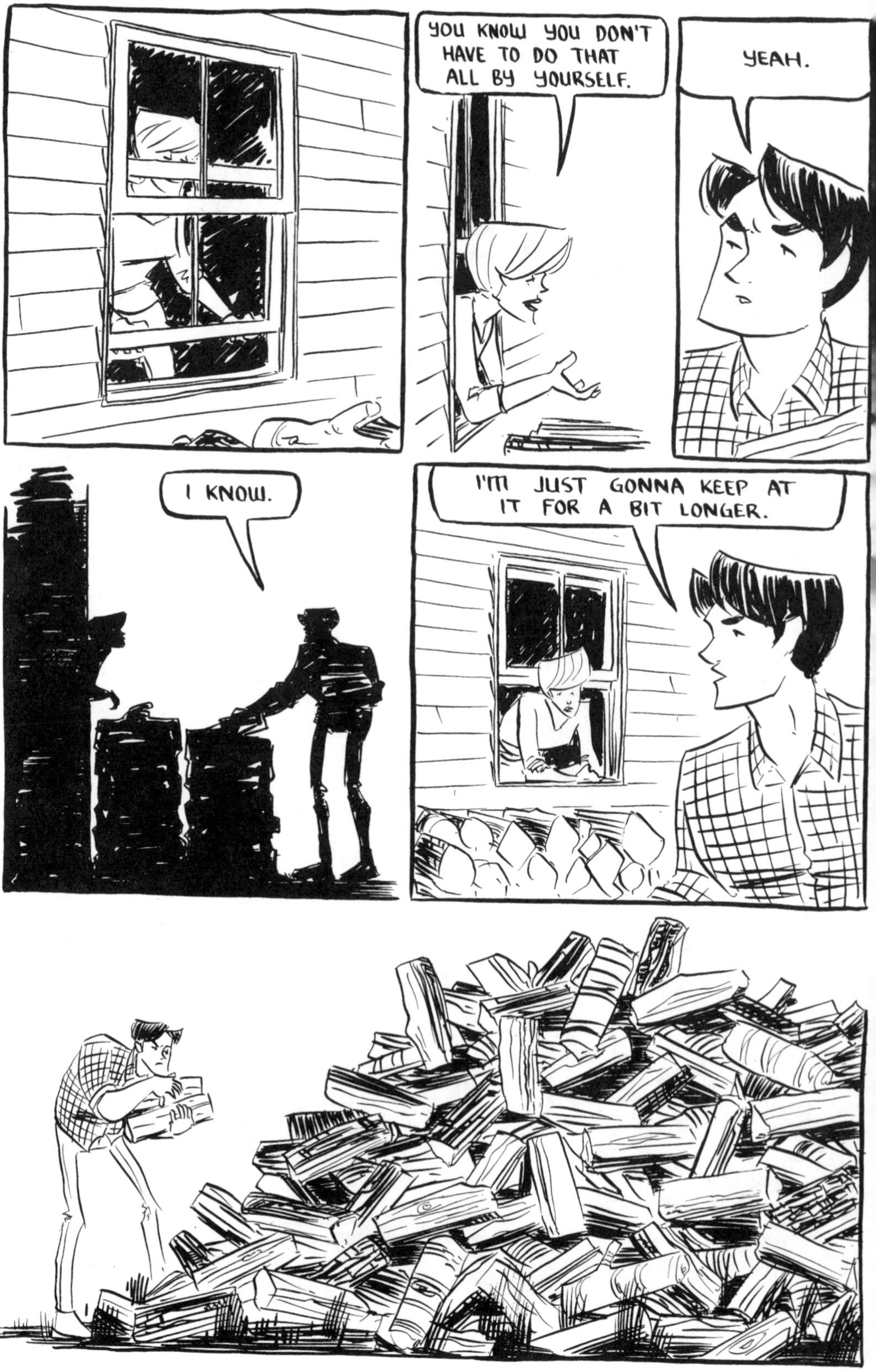
YOU KNOW YOU DON'T HAVE TO DO THAT ALL BY YOURSELF.
YEAH.
I KNOW.
I'M JUST GONNA KEEP AT IT FOR A BIT LONGER.

MINNY'S PARTY
FORD

DENISE RICHARDS.

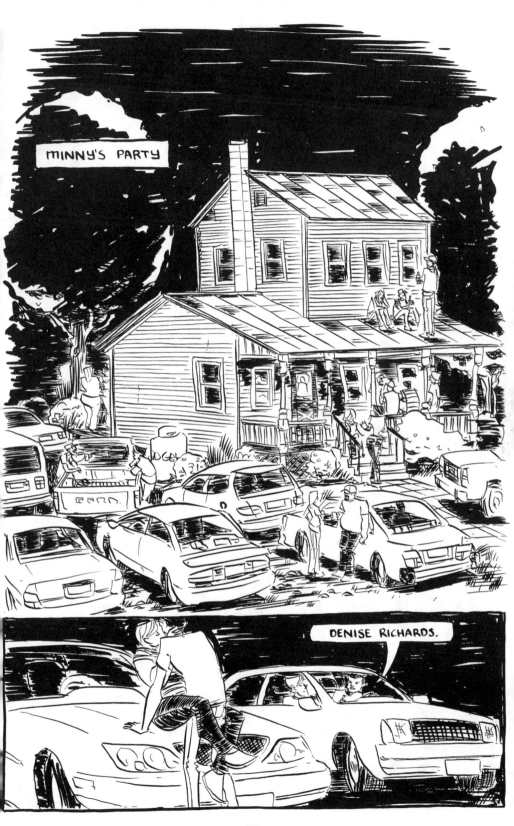

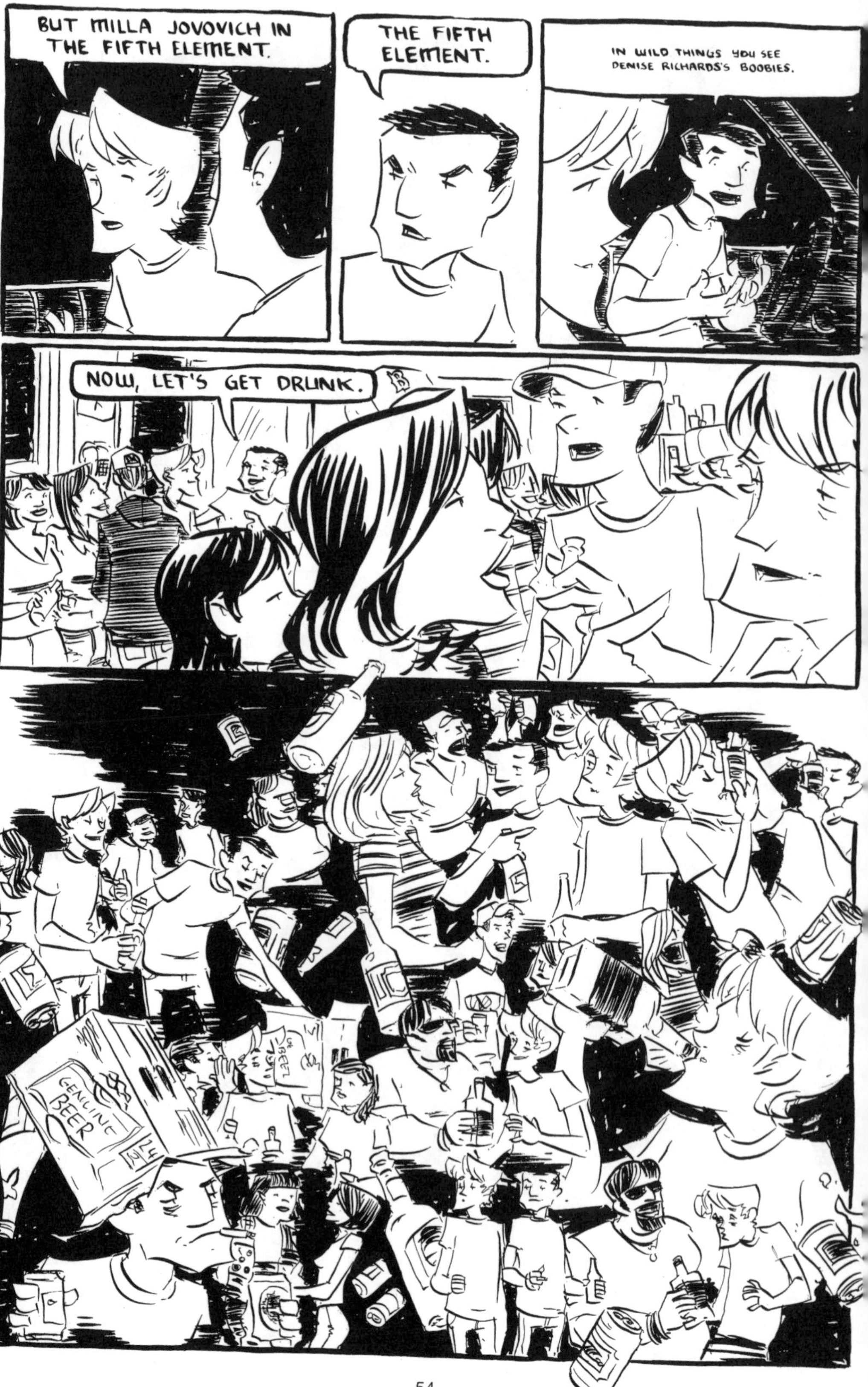

BUT MILLA JOVOVICH IN THE FIFTH ELEMENT.
THE FIFTH ELEMENT.
IN WILD THINGS YOU SEE DENISE RICHARDS'S BOOBIES.
NOW, LET'S GET DRUNK.
GENUINE BEER

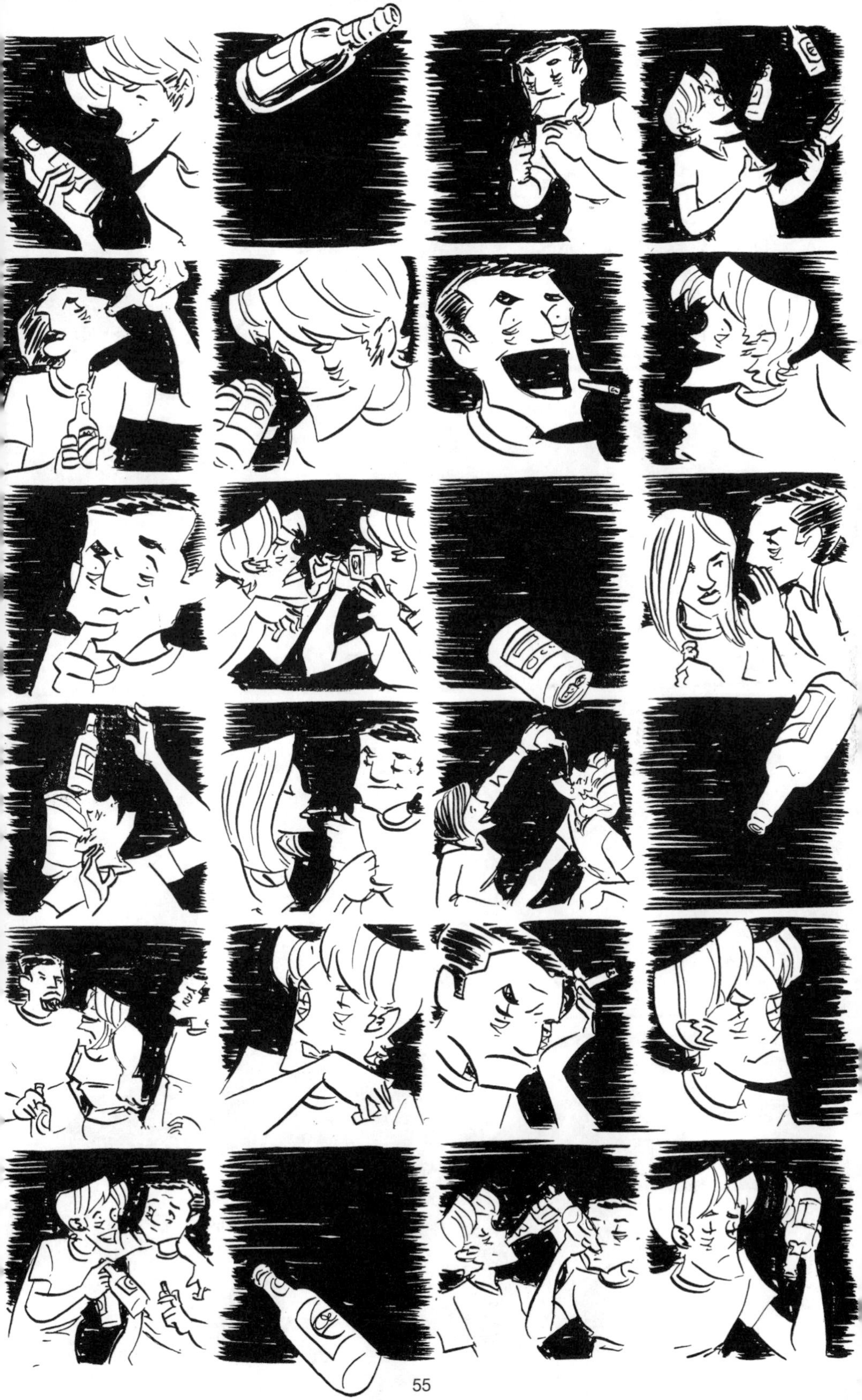

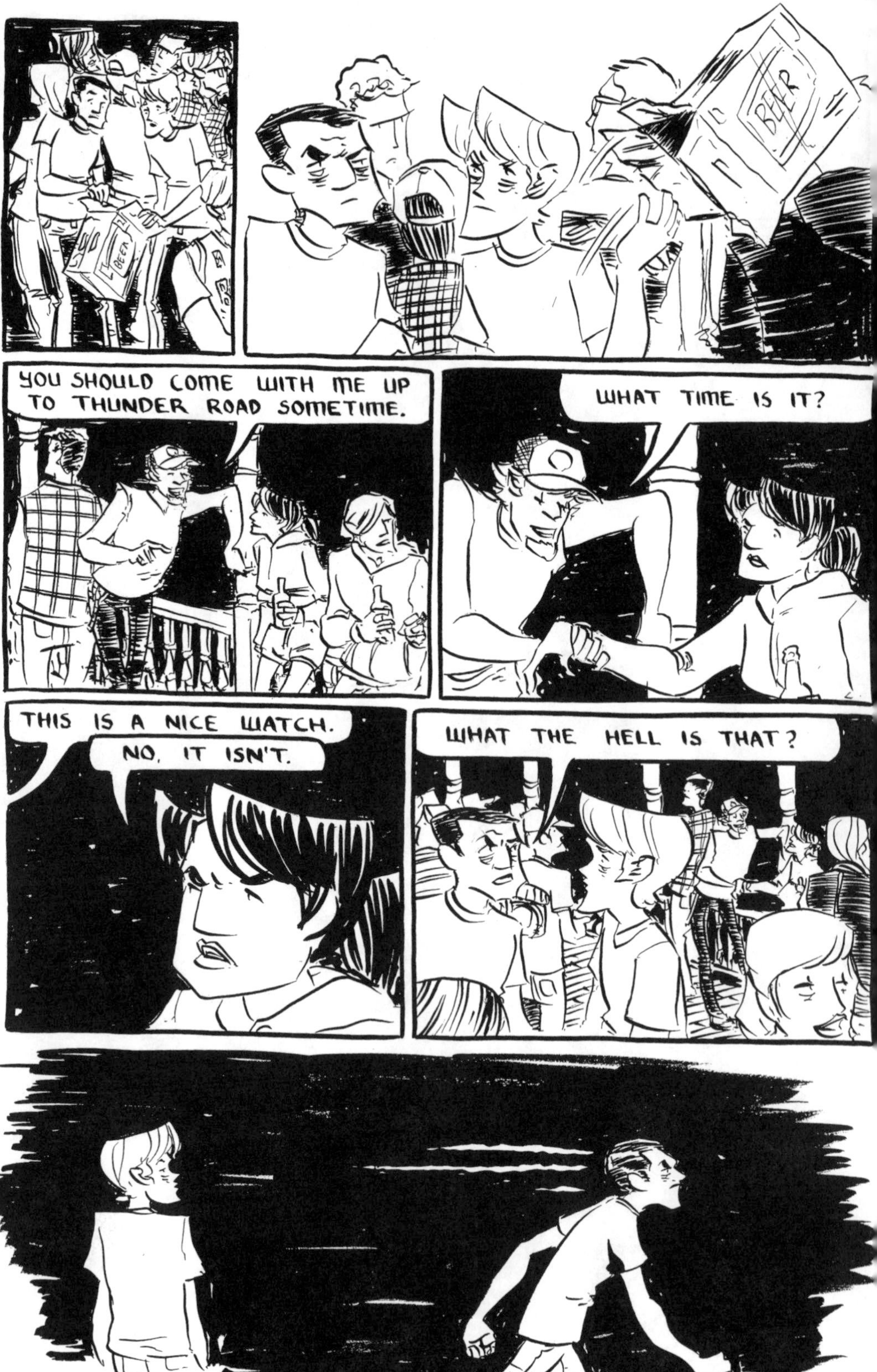
YOU SHOULD COME WITH ME UP TO THUNDER ROAD SOMETIME.
WHAT TIME IS IT?
THIS IS A NICE WATCH.
NO, IT ISN'T.
WHAT THE HELL IS THAT?

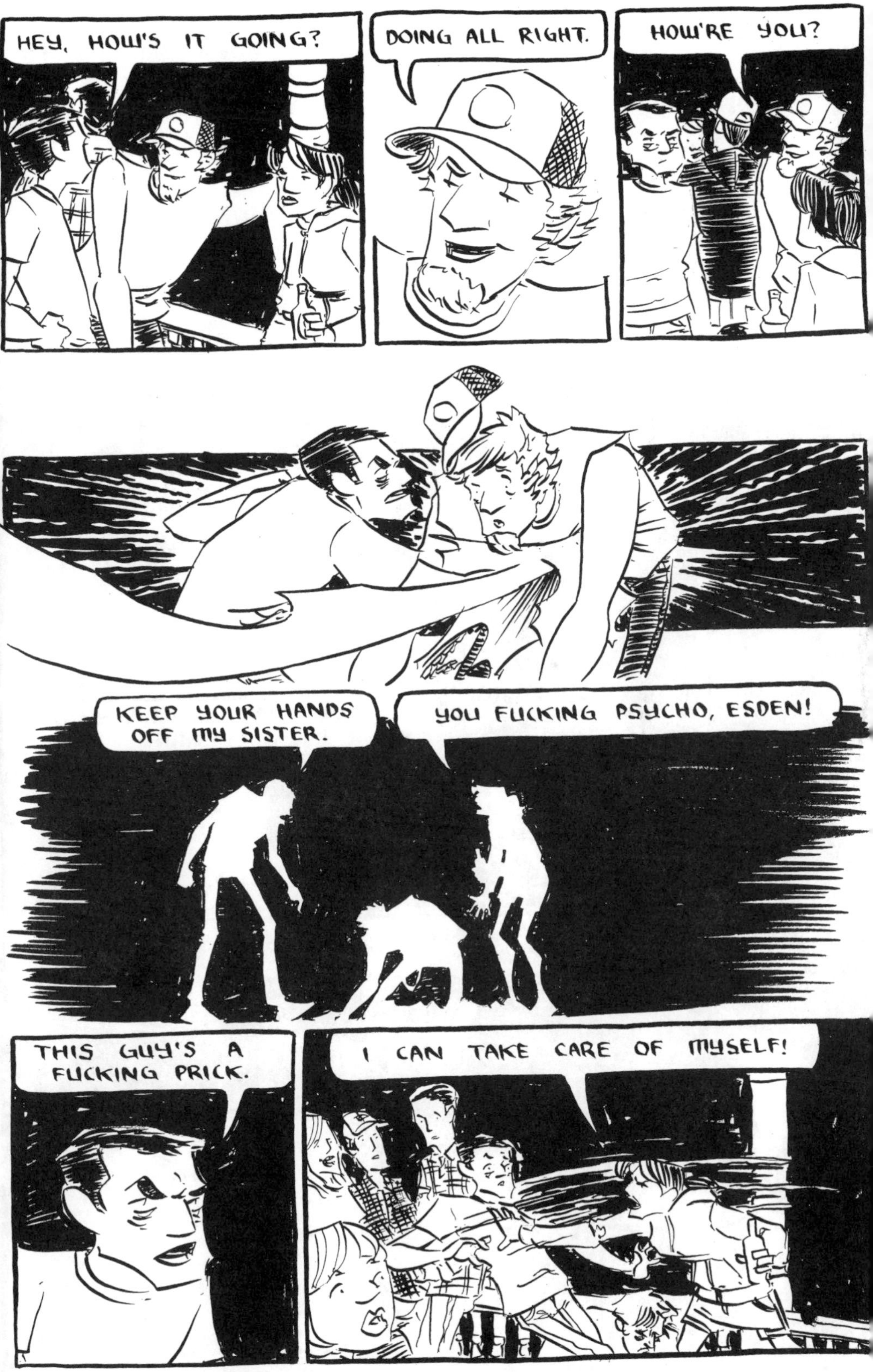
HEY, HOW'S IT GOING?
DOING ALL RIGHT.
HOW'RE YOU?
KEEP YOUR HANDS OFF MY SISTER.
YOU FUCKING PSYCHO, ESDEN!
THIS GUY'S A FUCKING PRICK.
I CAN TAKE CARE OF MYSELF!

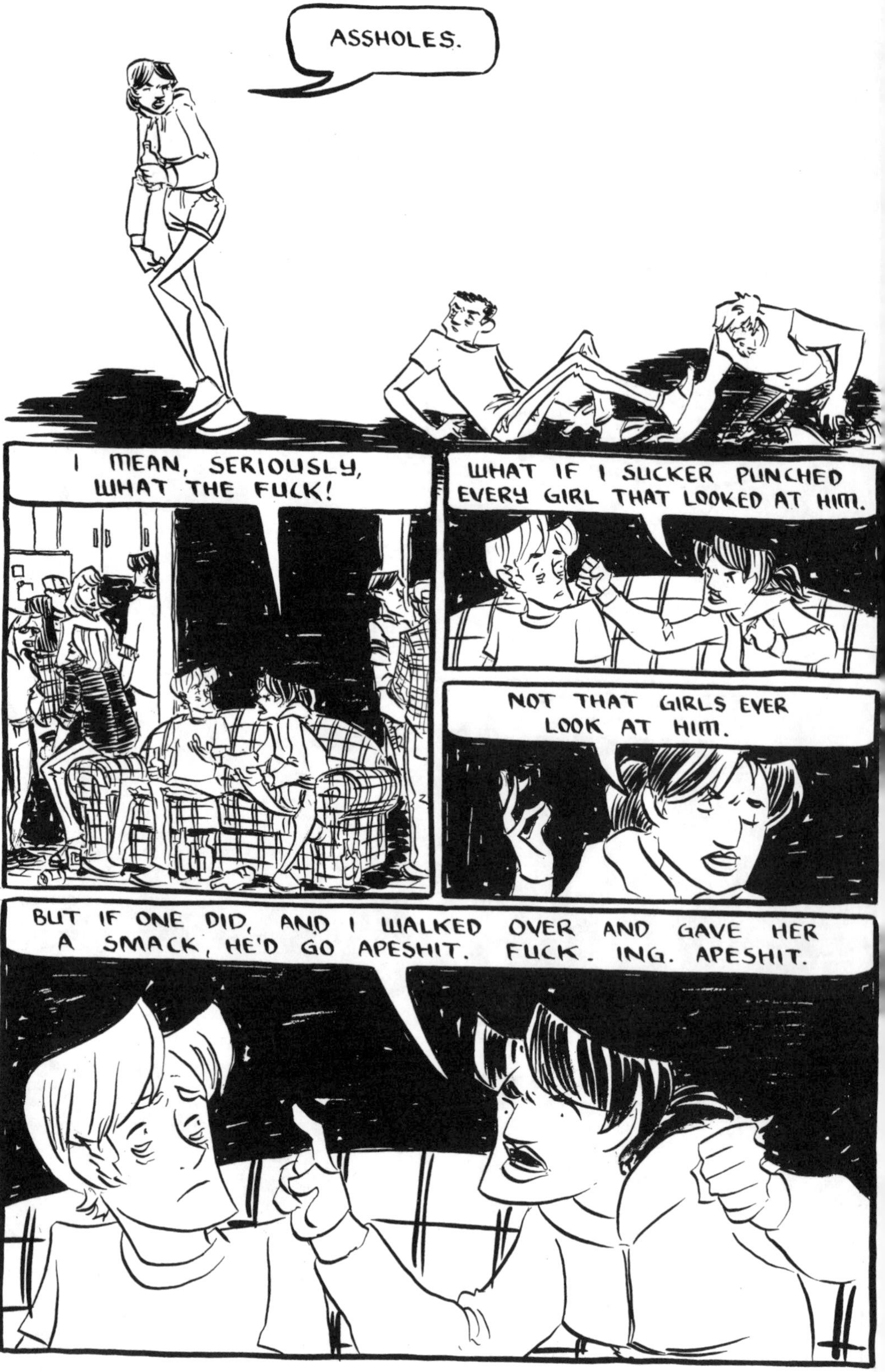
ASSHOLES.
I MEAN, SERIOUSLY, WHAT THE FUCK!
WHAT IF I SUCKER PUNCHED EVERY GIRL THAT LOOKED AT HIM.
NOT THAT GIRLS EVER LOOK AT HIM.
BUT IF ONE DID, AND I WALKED OVER AND GAVE HER A SMACK, HE'D GO APESHIT. FUCK. ING. APESHIT.

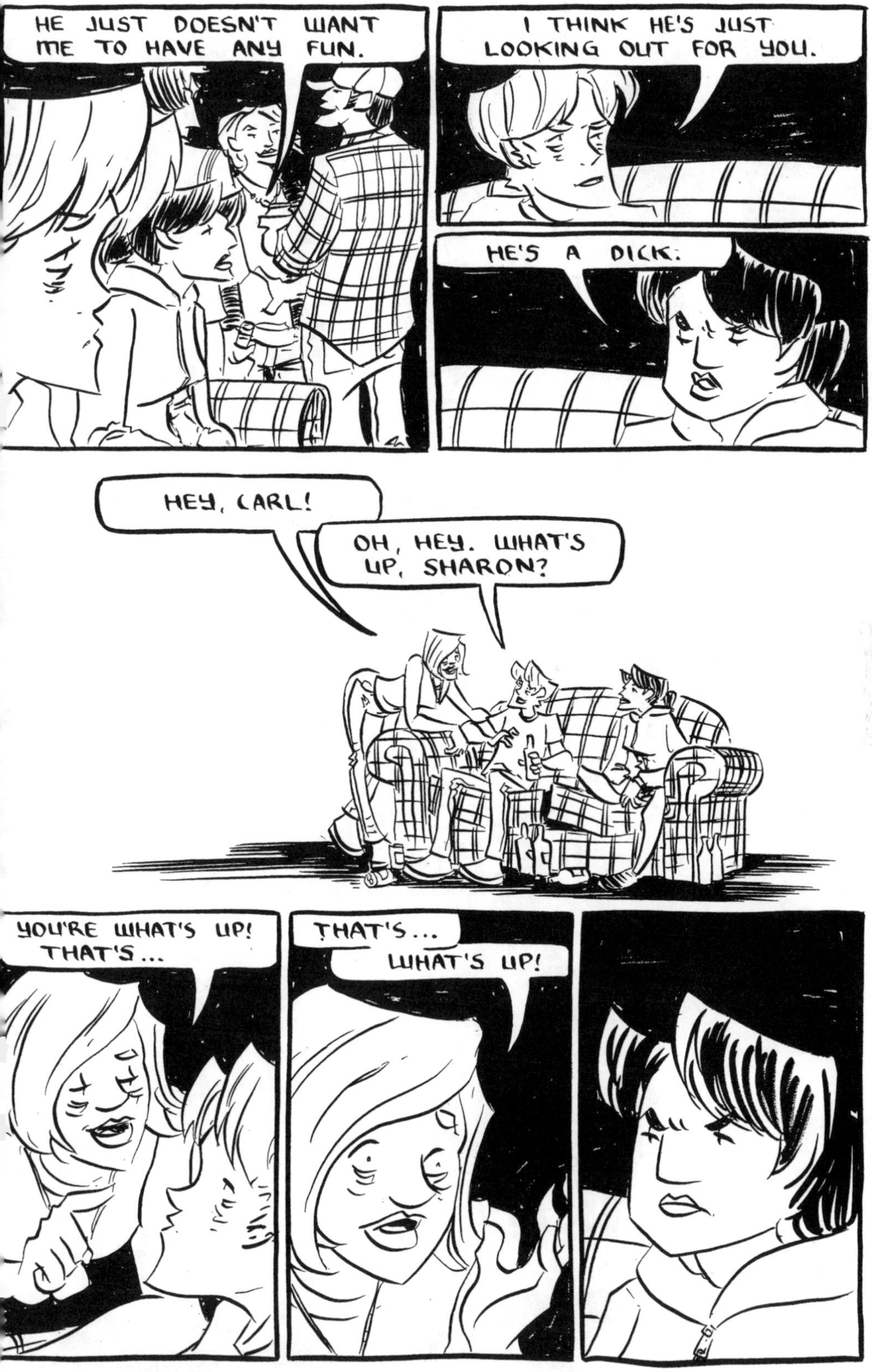
HE JUST DOESN'T WANT ME TO HAVE ANY FUN.
I THINK HE'S JUST LOOKING OUT FOR YOU.
HE'S A DICK.
HEY, CARL!
OH, HEY. WHAT'S UP, SHARON?
YOU'RE WHAT'S UP! THAT'S...
THAT'S...
WHAT'S UP!

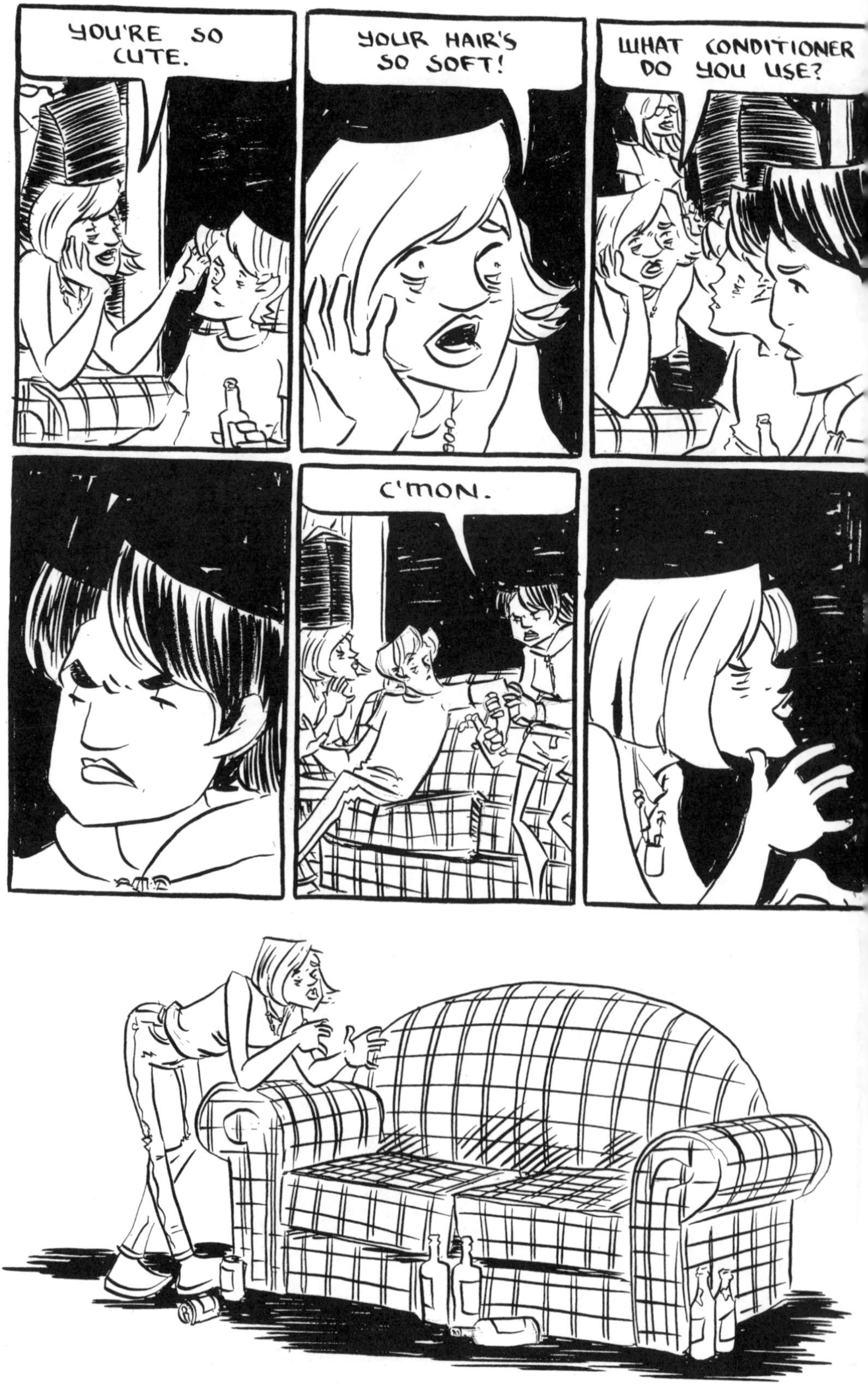
YOU'RE SO CUTE.
YOUR HAIR'S SO SOFT!
WHAT CONDITIONER DO YOU USE?
C'MON.

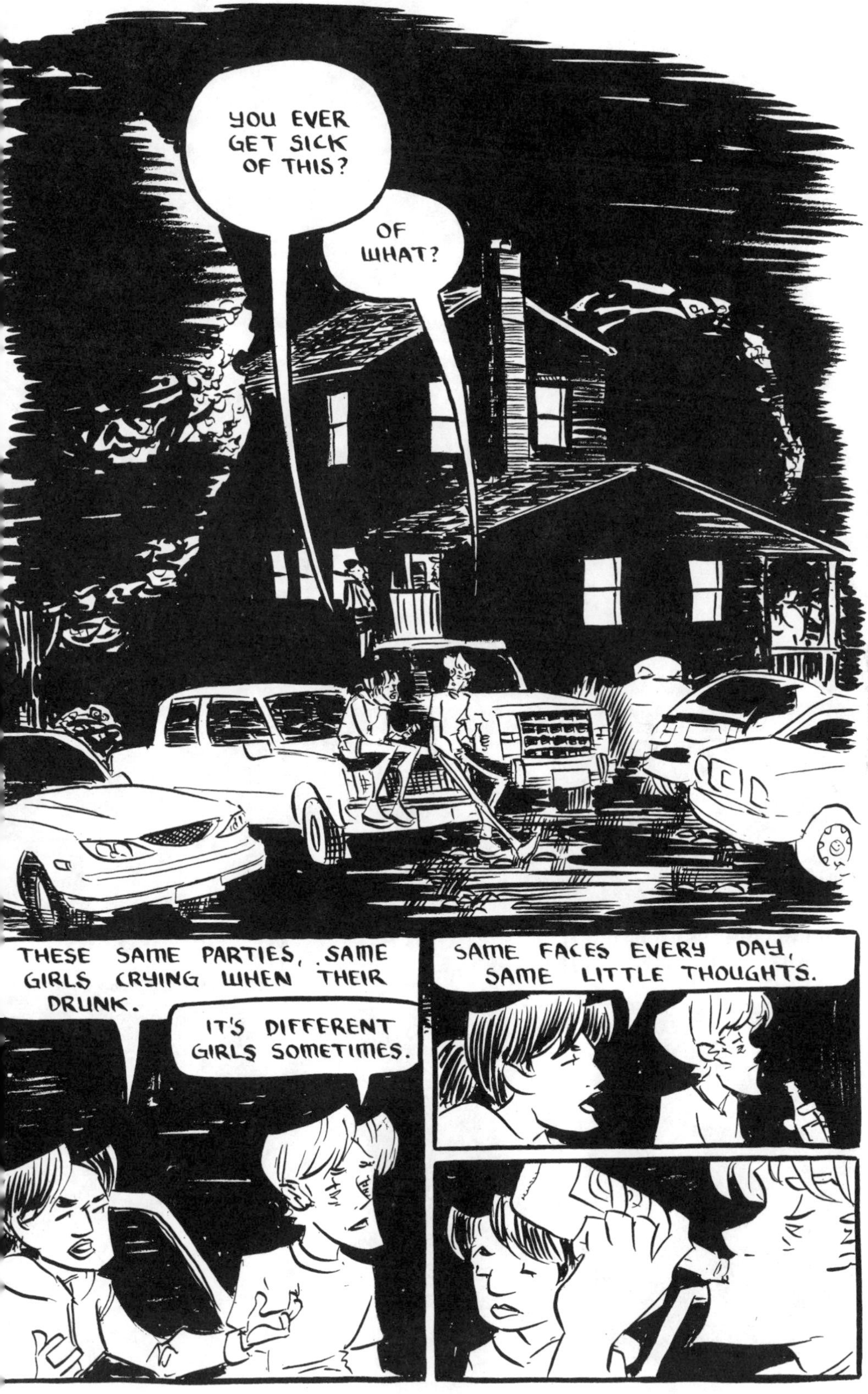
YOU EVER GET SICK OF THIS?
OF WHAT?
THESE SAME PARTIES, SAME GIRLS CRYING WHEN THEIR DRUNK.
IT'S DIFFERENT GIRLS SOMETIMES.
SAME FACES EVERY DAY, SAME LITTLE THOUGHTS.

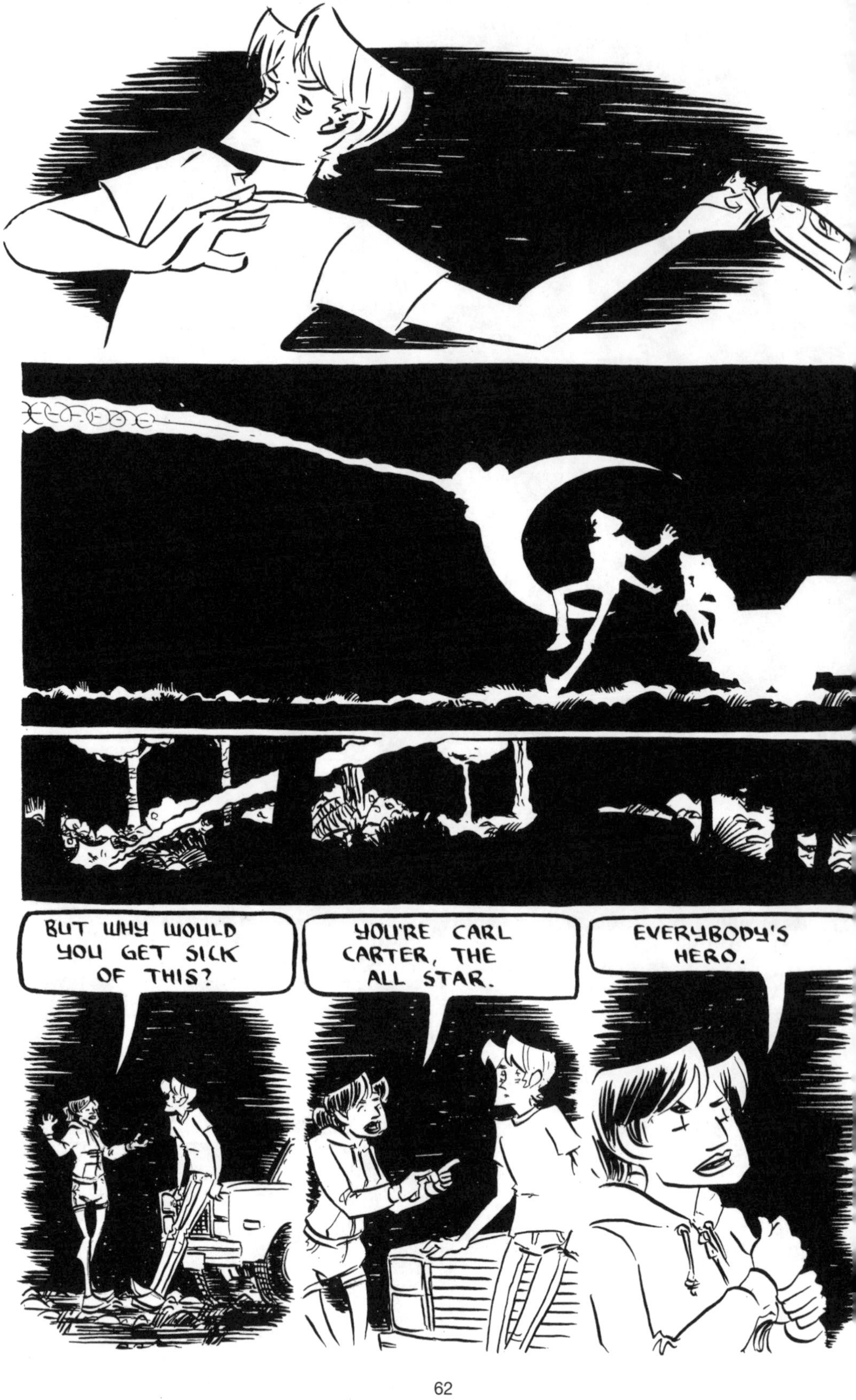
BUT WHY WOULD YOU GET SICK OF THIS?
YOU'RE CARL CARTER, THE ALL STAR.
EVERYBODY'S HERO.

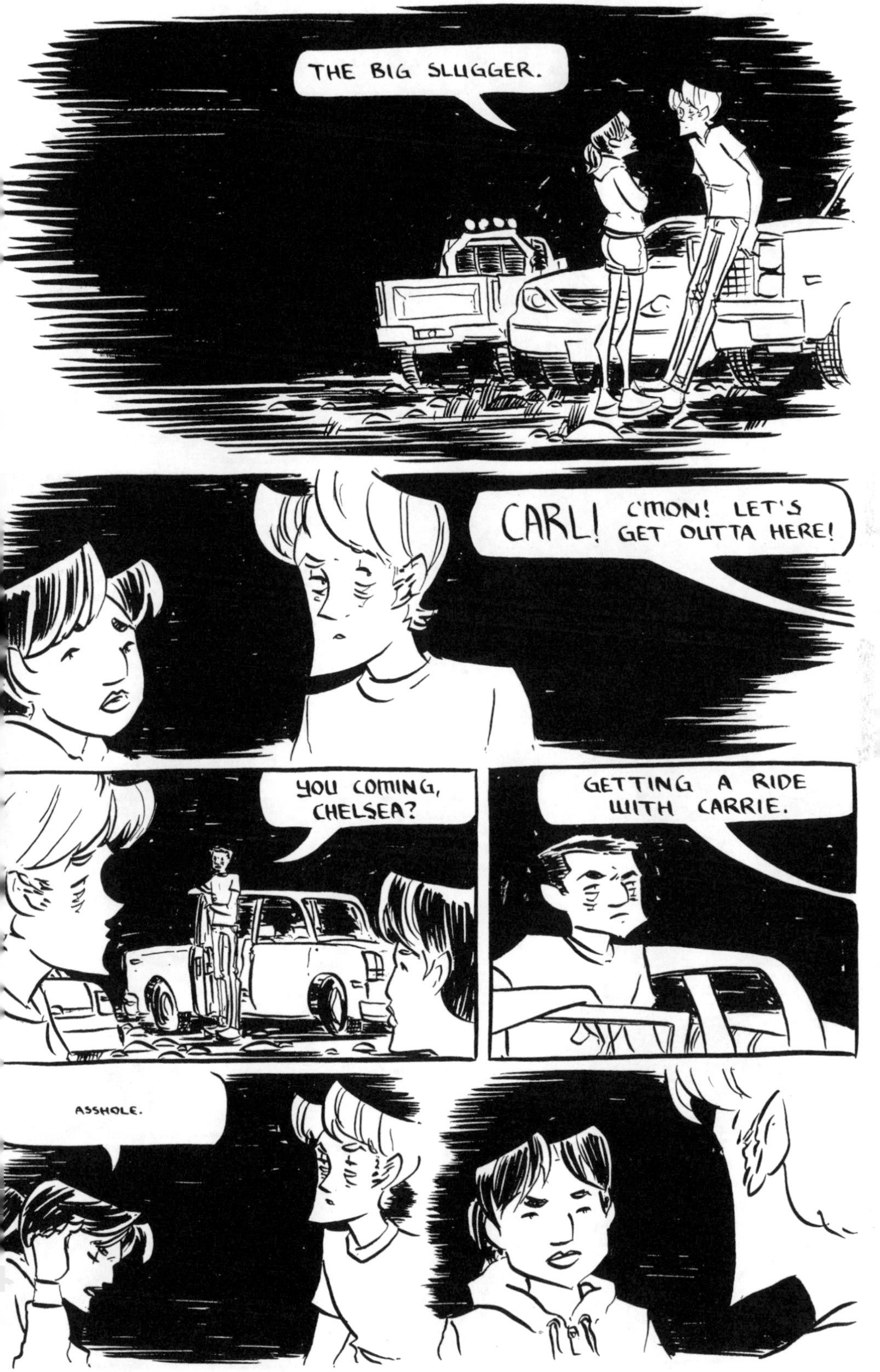
THE BIG SLUGGER.
CARL! C'MON! LET'S GET OUTTA HERE!
YOU COMING, CHELSEA?
GETTING A RIDE WITH CARRIE.
ASSHOLE.

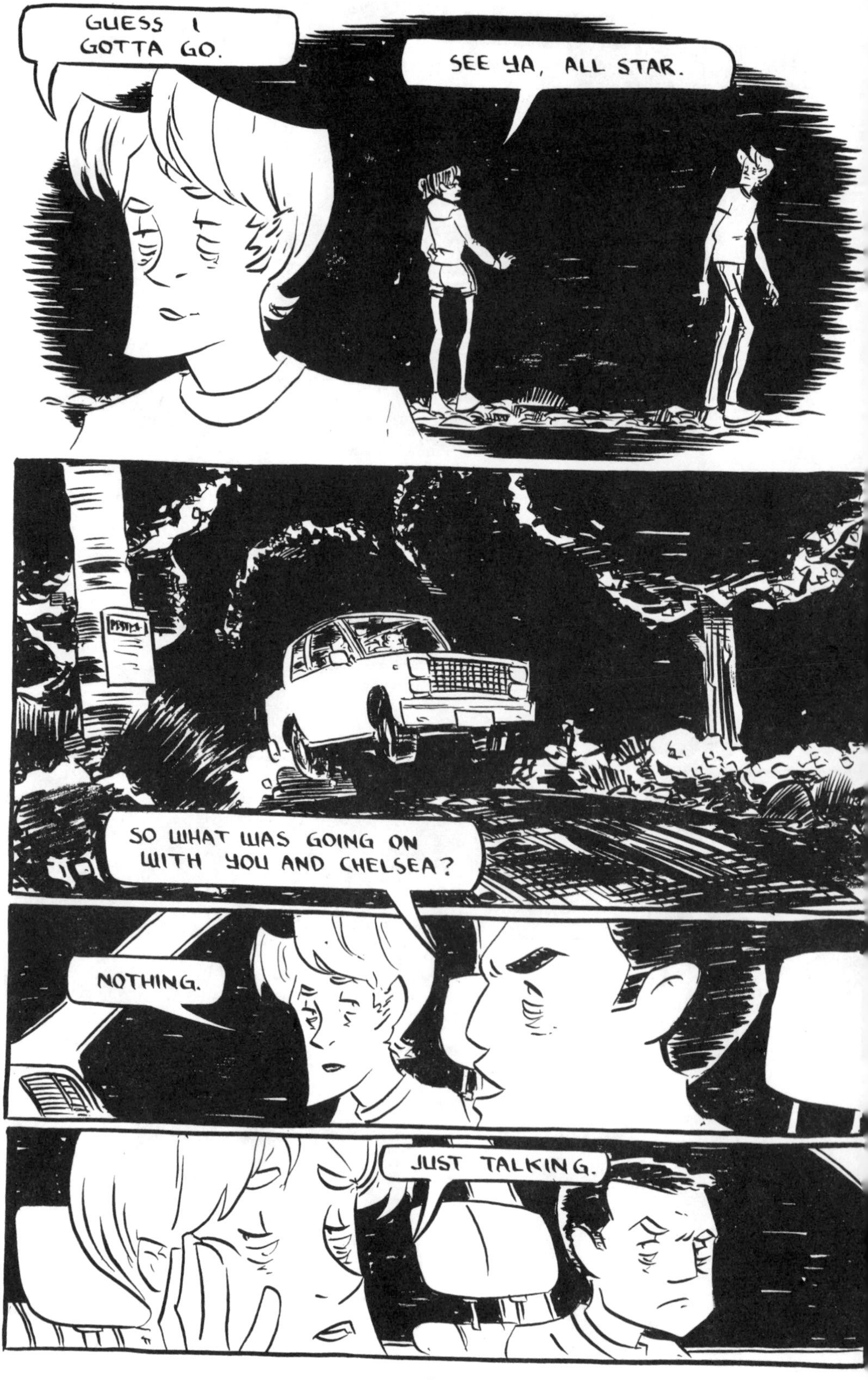
GUESS I GOTTA GO.
SEE YA, ALL STAR.
SO WHAT WAS GOING ON WITH YOU AND CHELSEA?
NOTHING.
JUST TALKING.

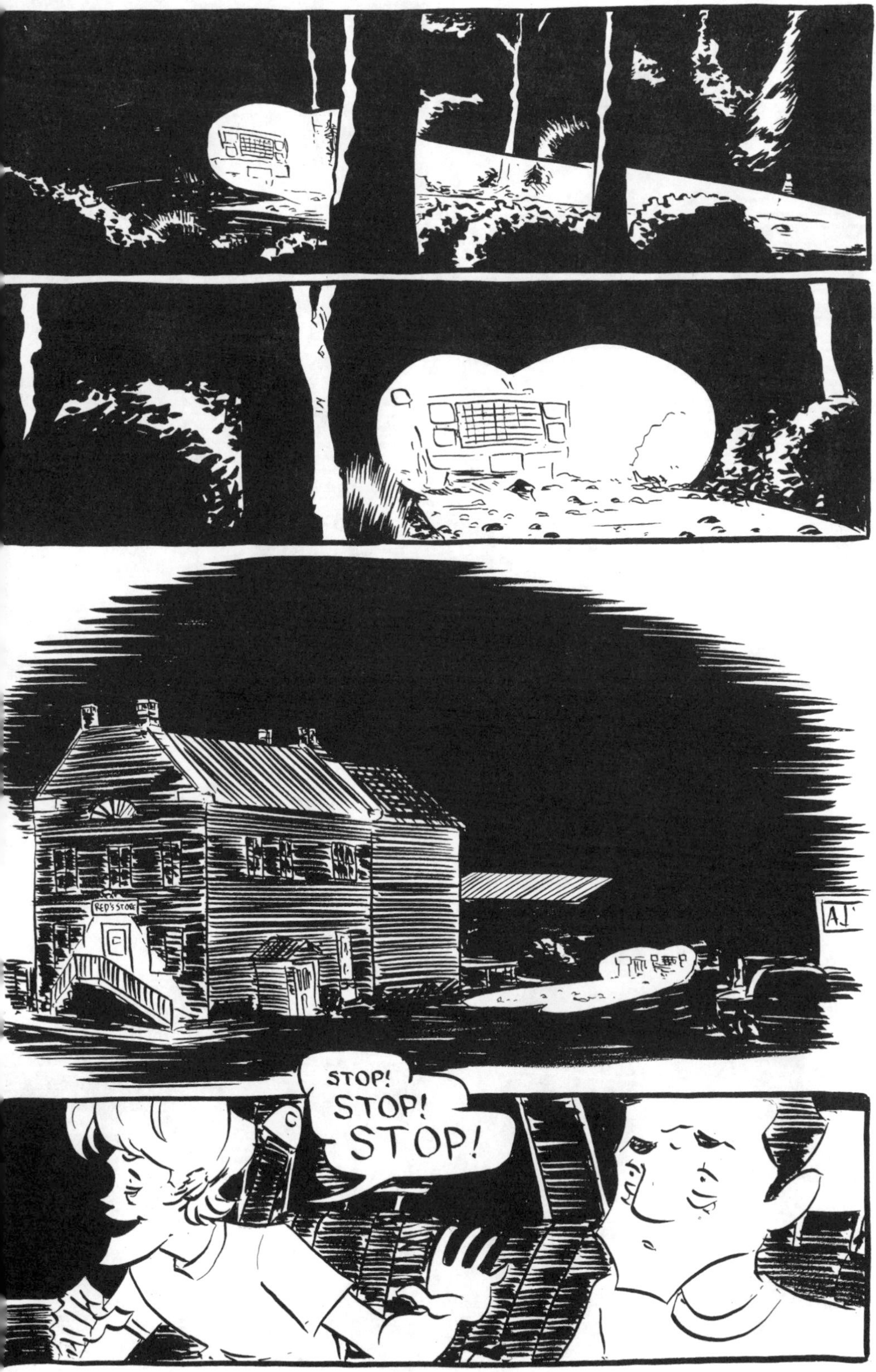
RED'S STORE
AJ
STOP!
STOP!
STOP!

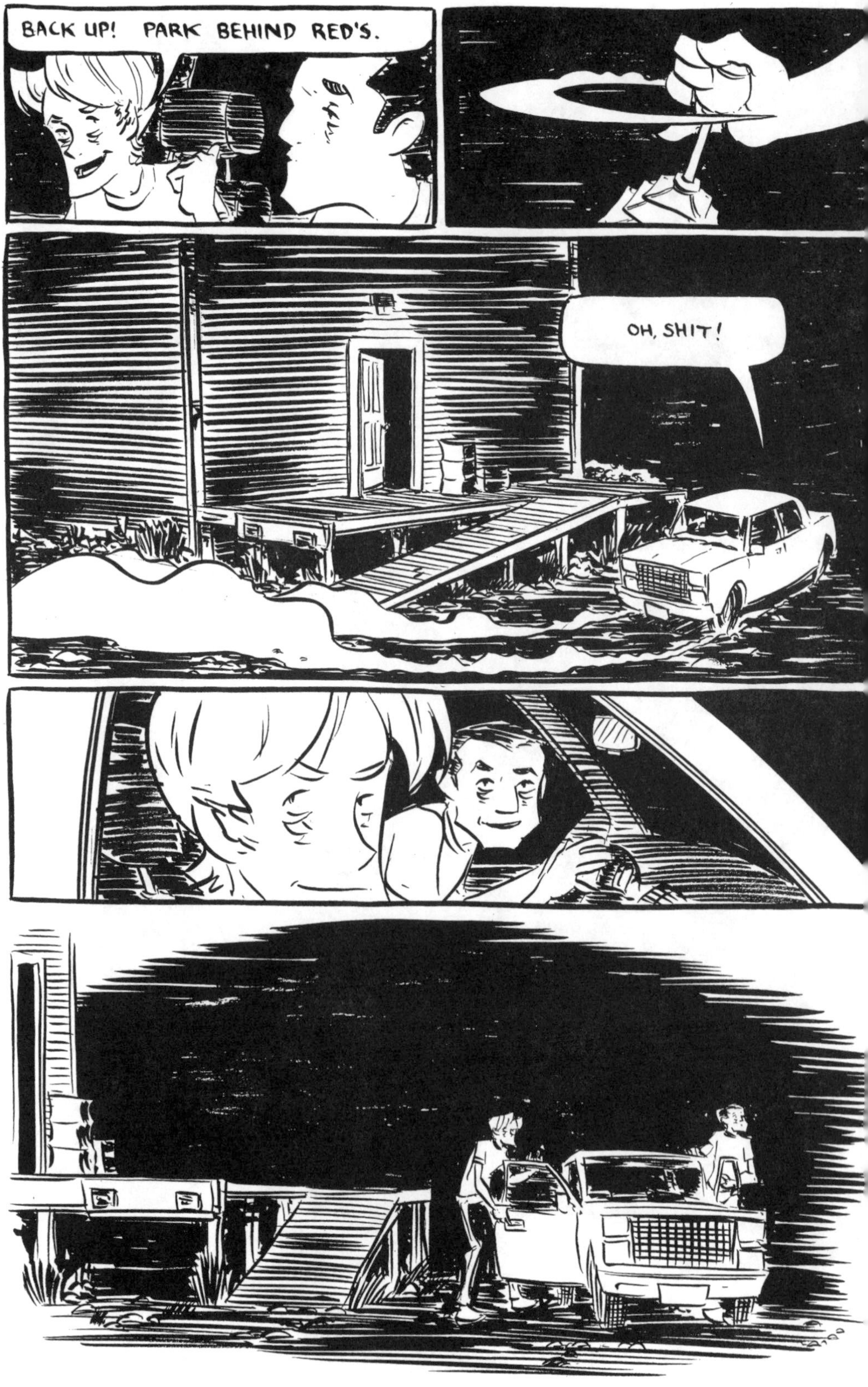
BACK UP! PARK BEHIND RED'S.
OH, SHIT!

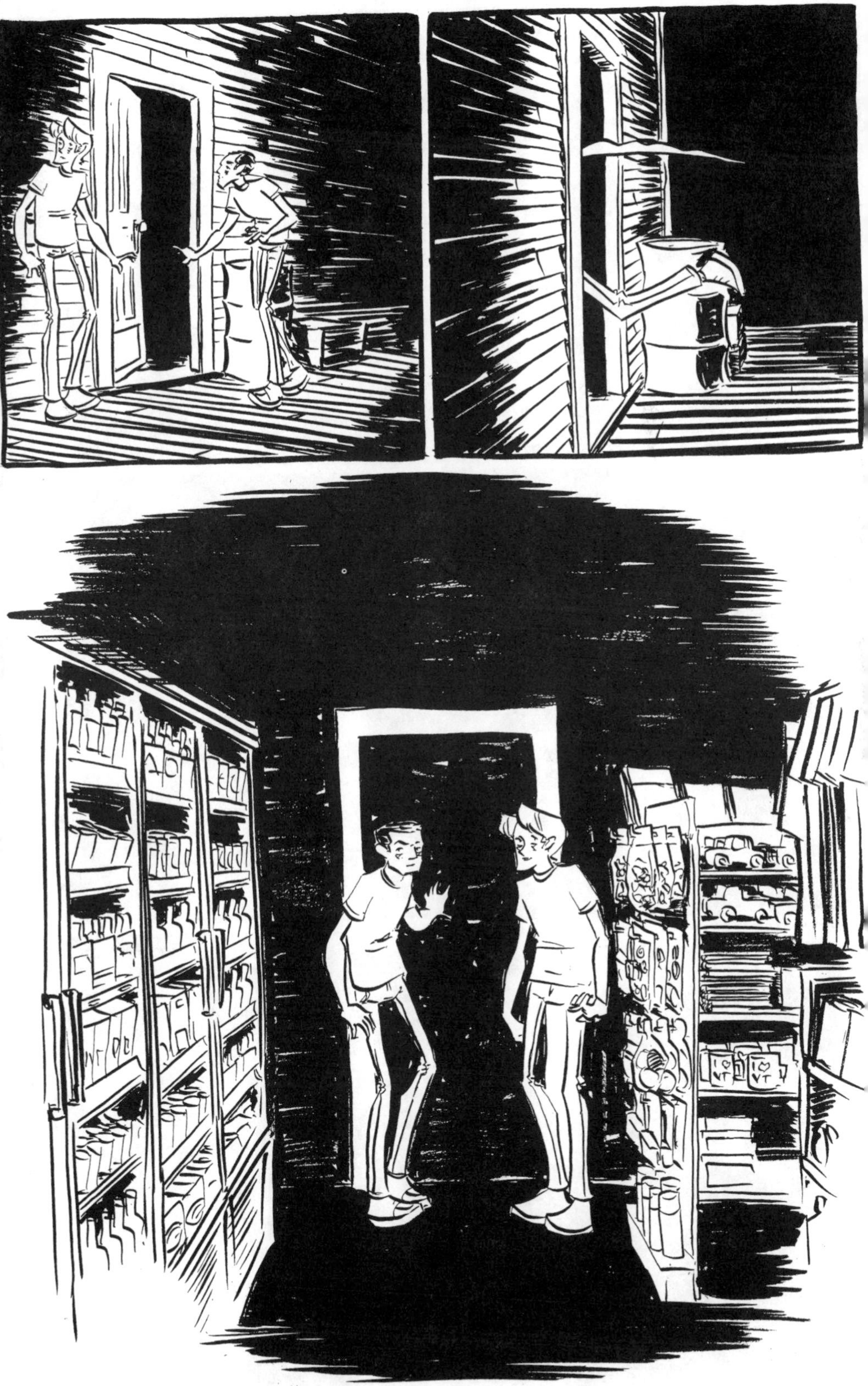

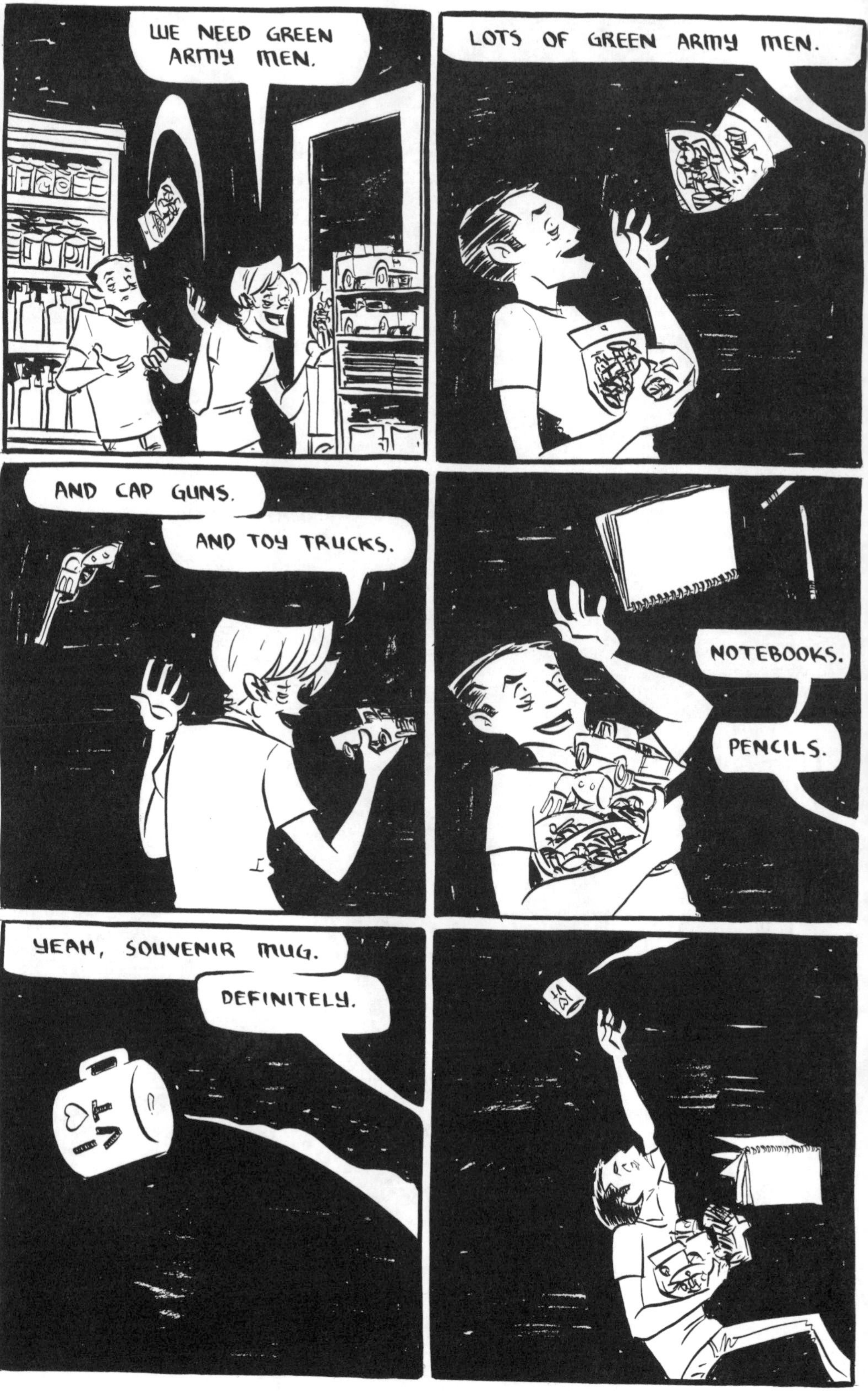
WE NEED GREEN ARMY MEN.
LOTS OF GREEN ARMY MEN.
AND CAP GUNS.
AND TOY TRUCKS.
NOTEBOOKS.
PENCILS.
YEAH, SOUVENIR MUG.
DEFINITELY.

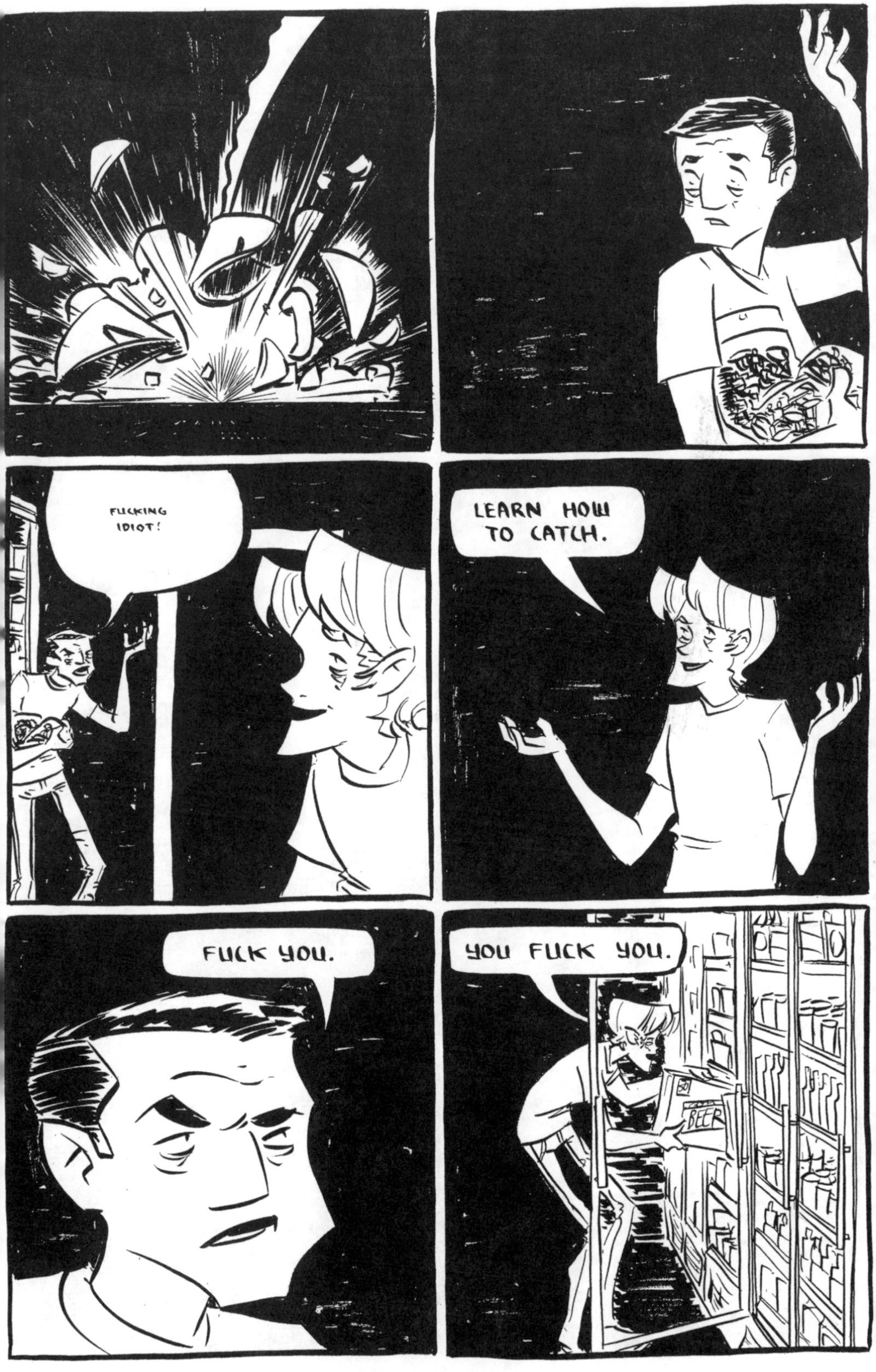
FUCKING IDIOT!
LEARN HOW TO CATCH.
FUCK YOU.
YOU FUCK YOU.
BEER

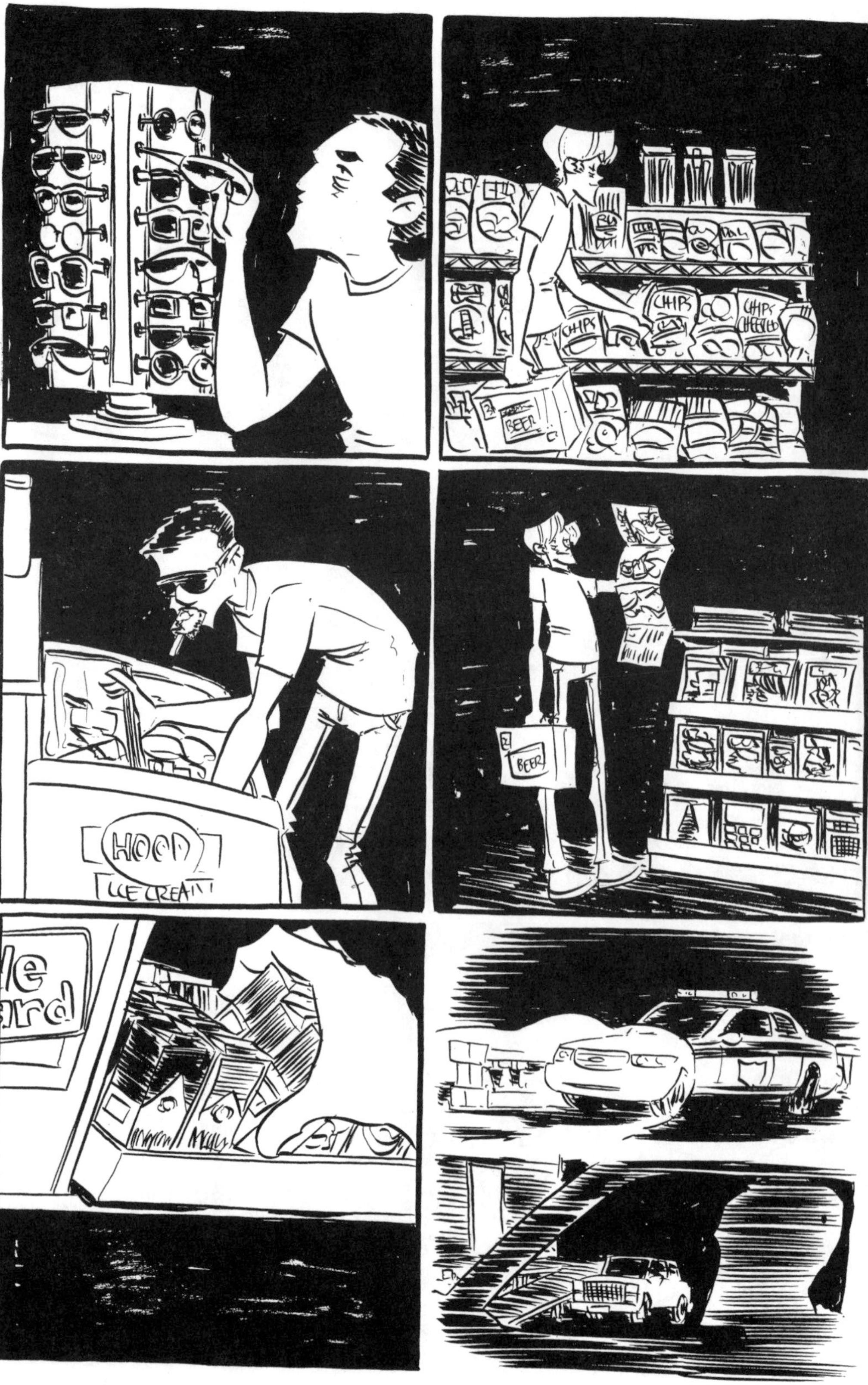
CHIPS
BEER
HOOD
BEER

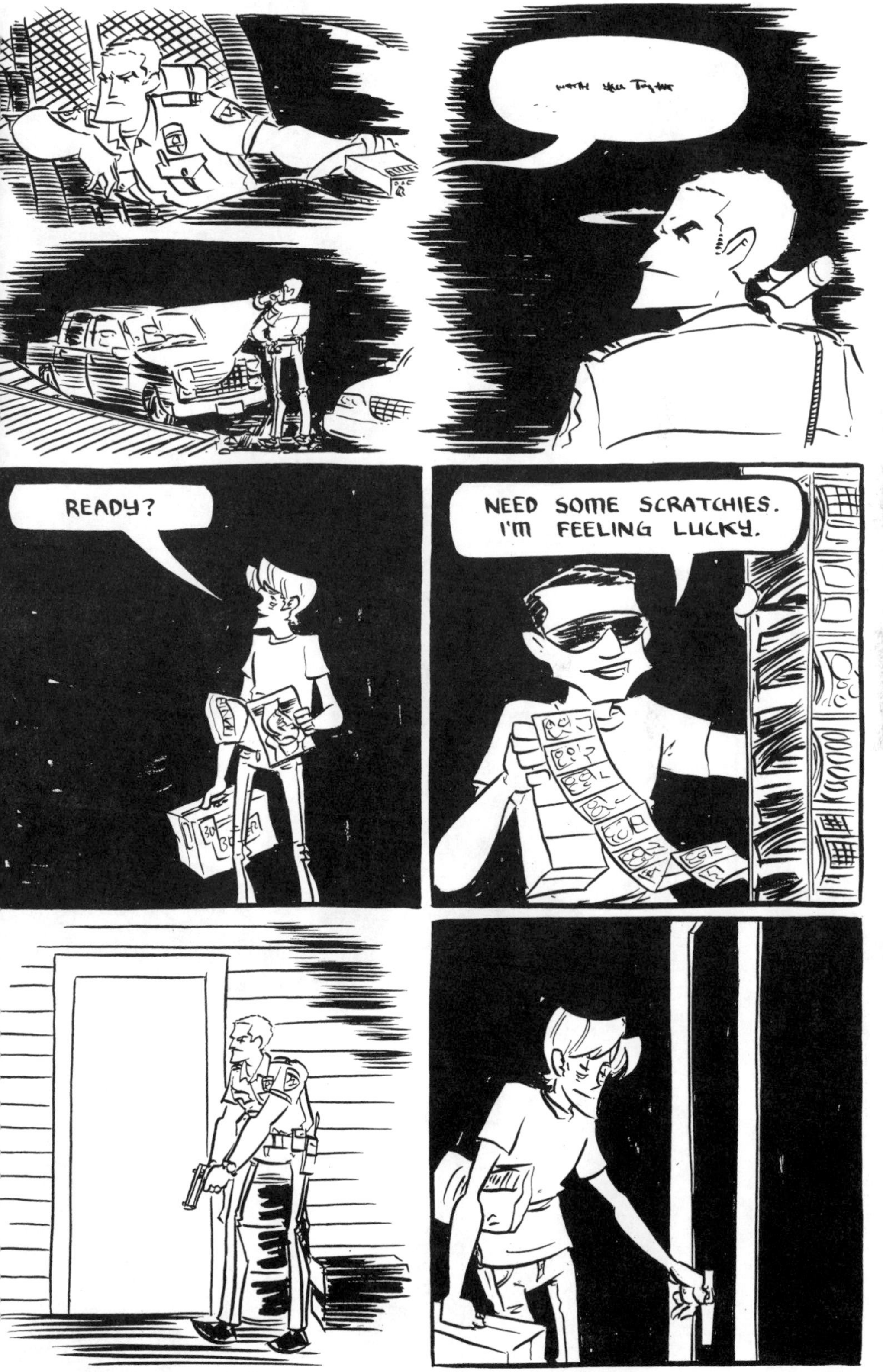
READY?
NEED SOME SCRATCHIES. I'M FEELING LUCKY.

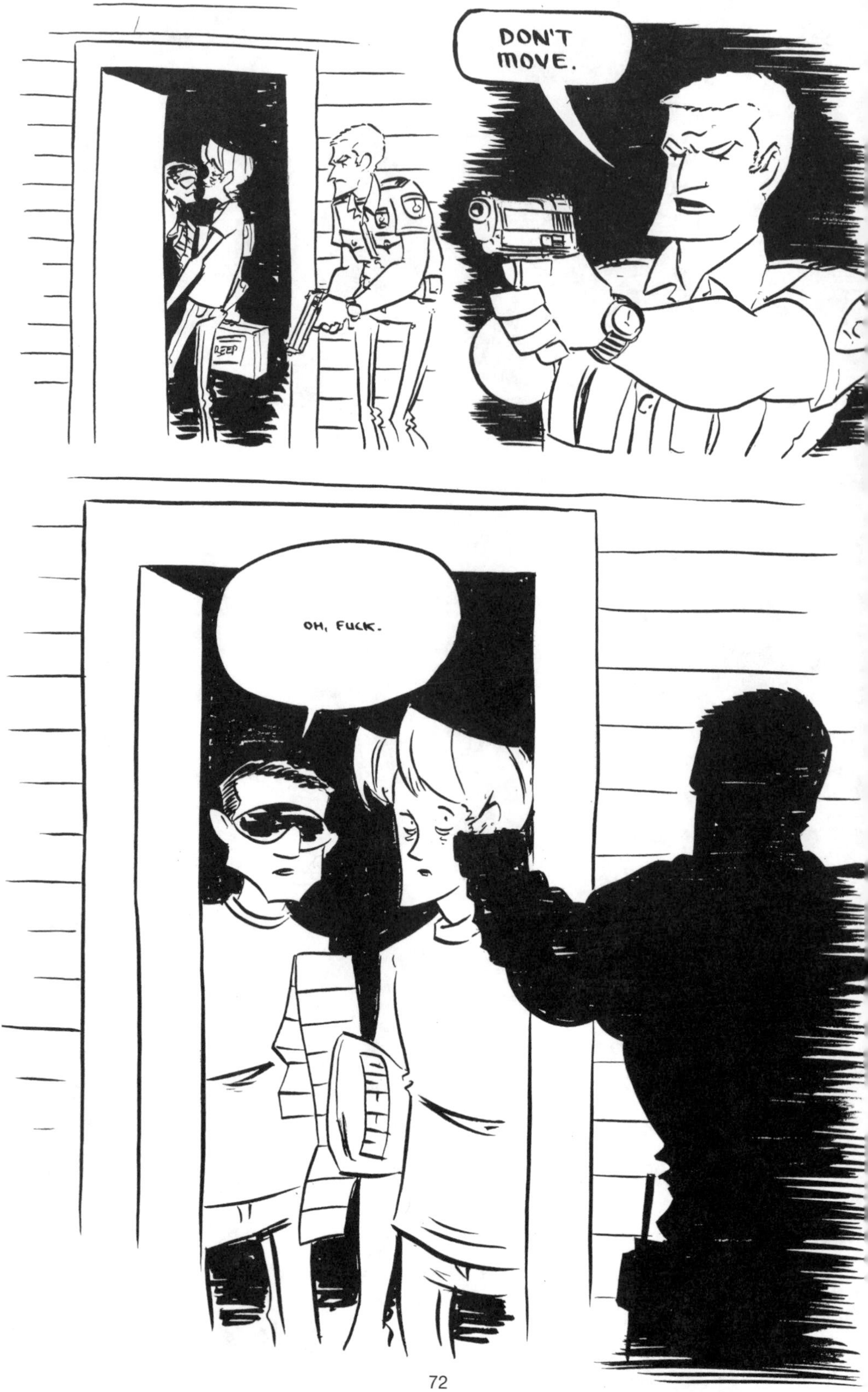
DON'T MOVE.
OH, FUCK.

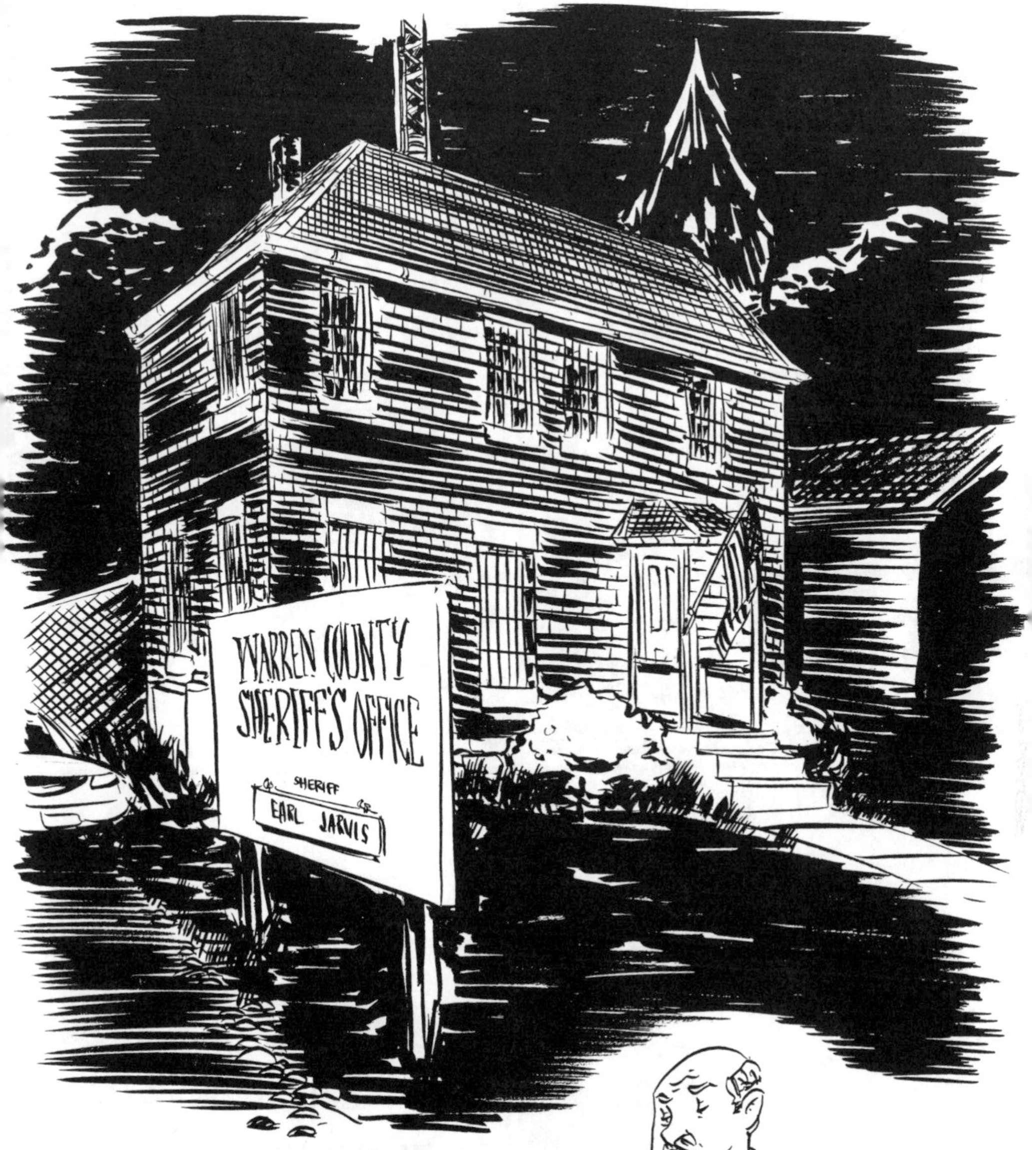
WARREN COUNTY
SHERIFF'S OFFICE
SHERIFF
EARL JARVIS

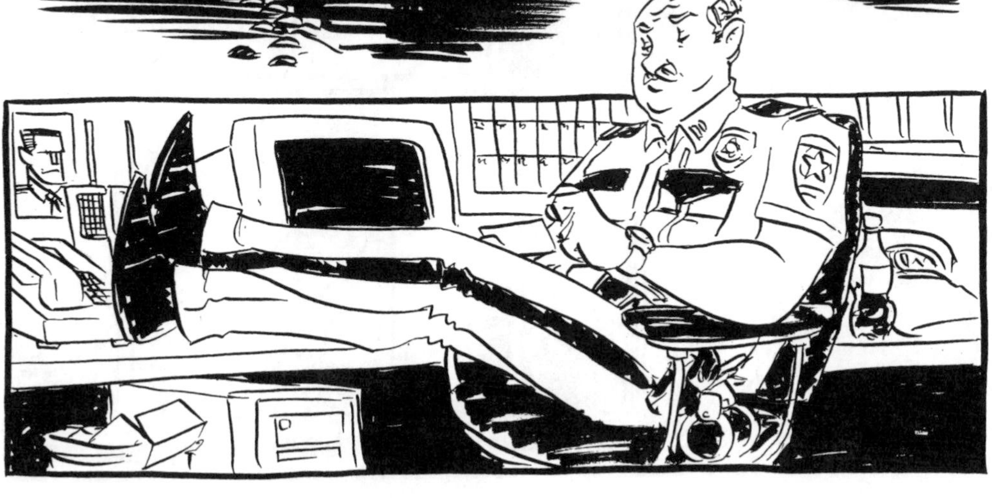

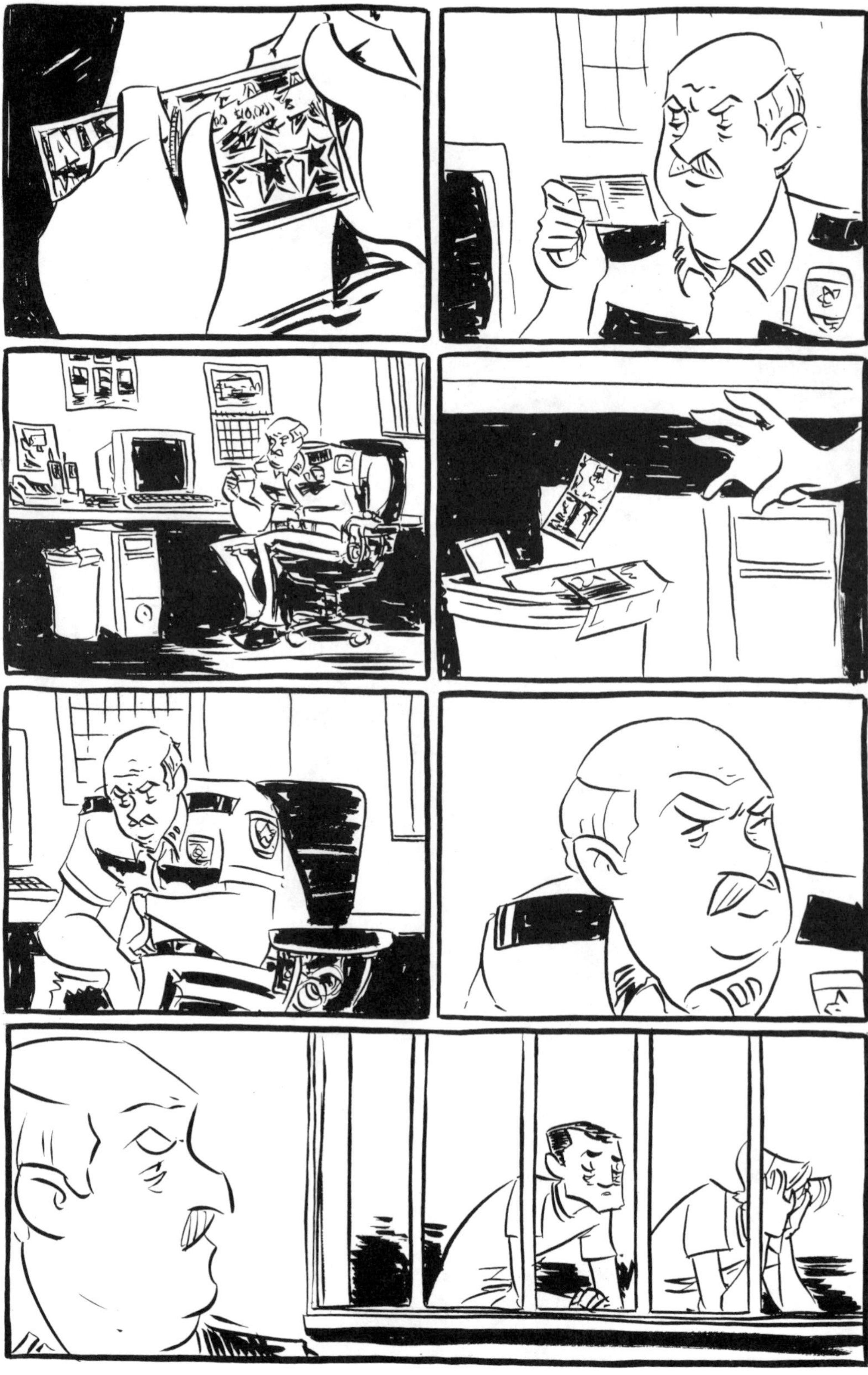

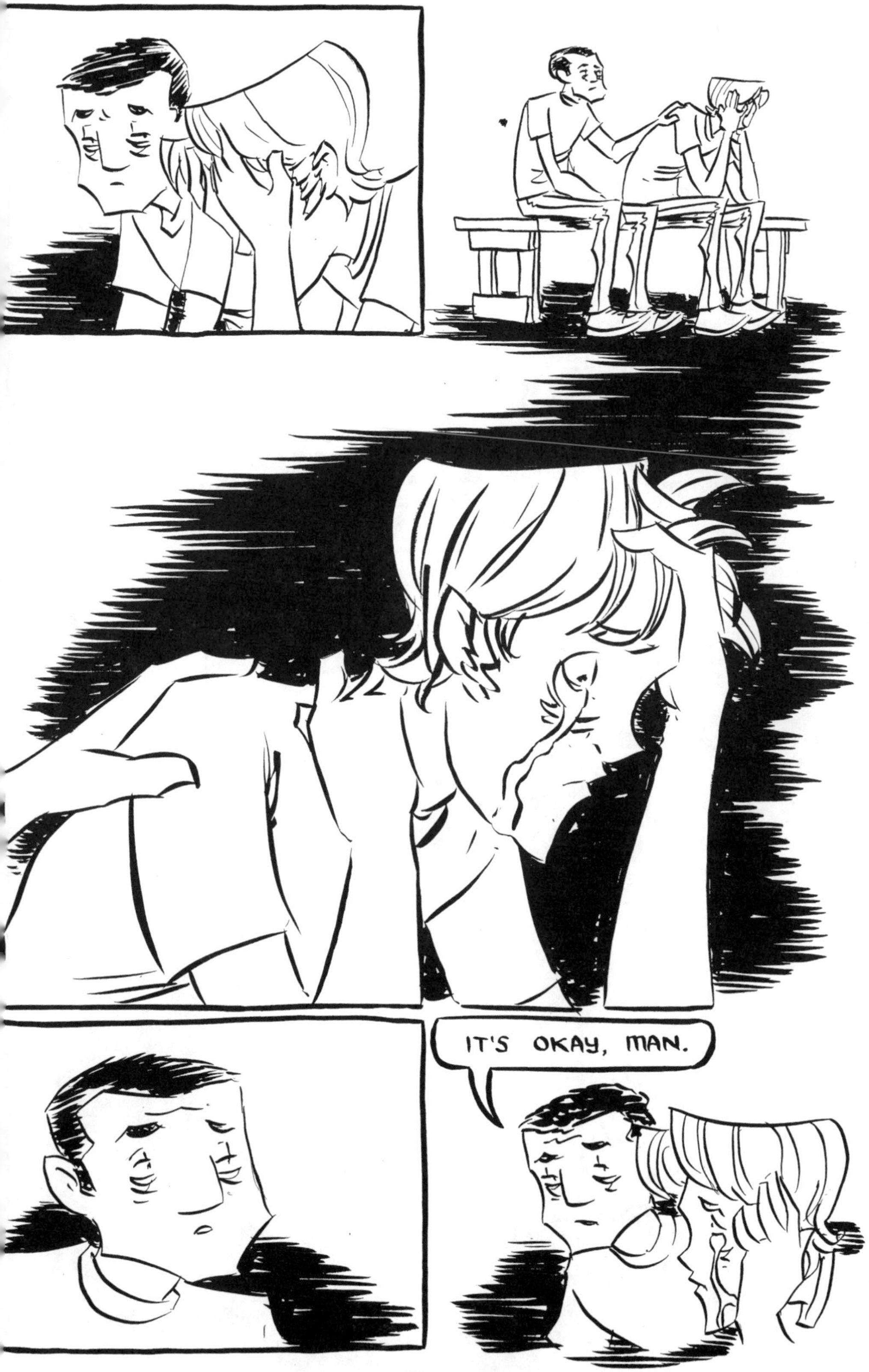
IT'S OKAY, MAN.

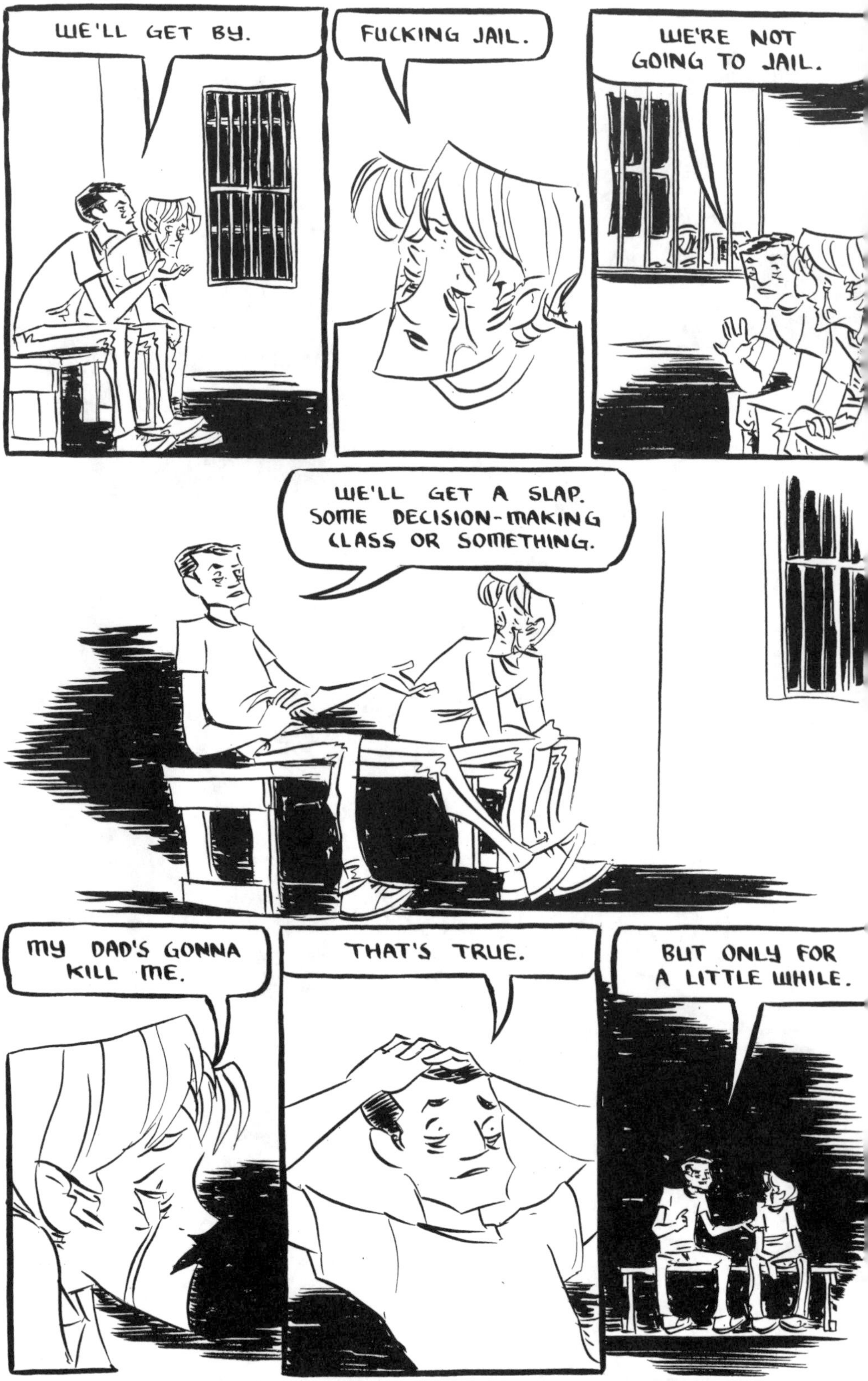
WE'LL GET BY.
FUCKING JAIL.
WE'RE NOT GOING TO JAIL.
WE'LL GET A SLAP. SOME DECISION-MAKING CLASS OR SOMETHING.
MY DAD'S GONNA KILL ME.
THAT'S TRUE.
BUT ONLY FOR A LITTLE WHILE.

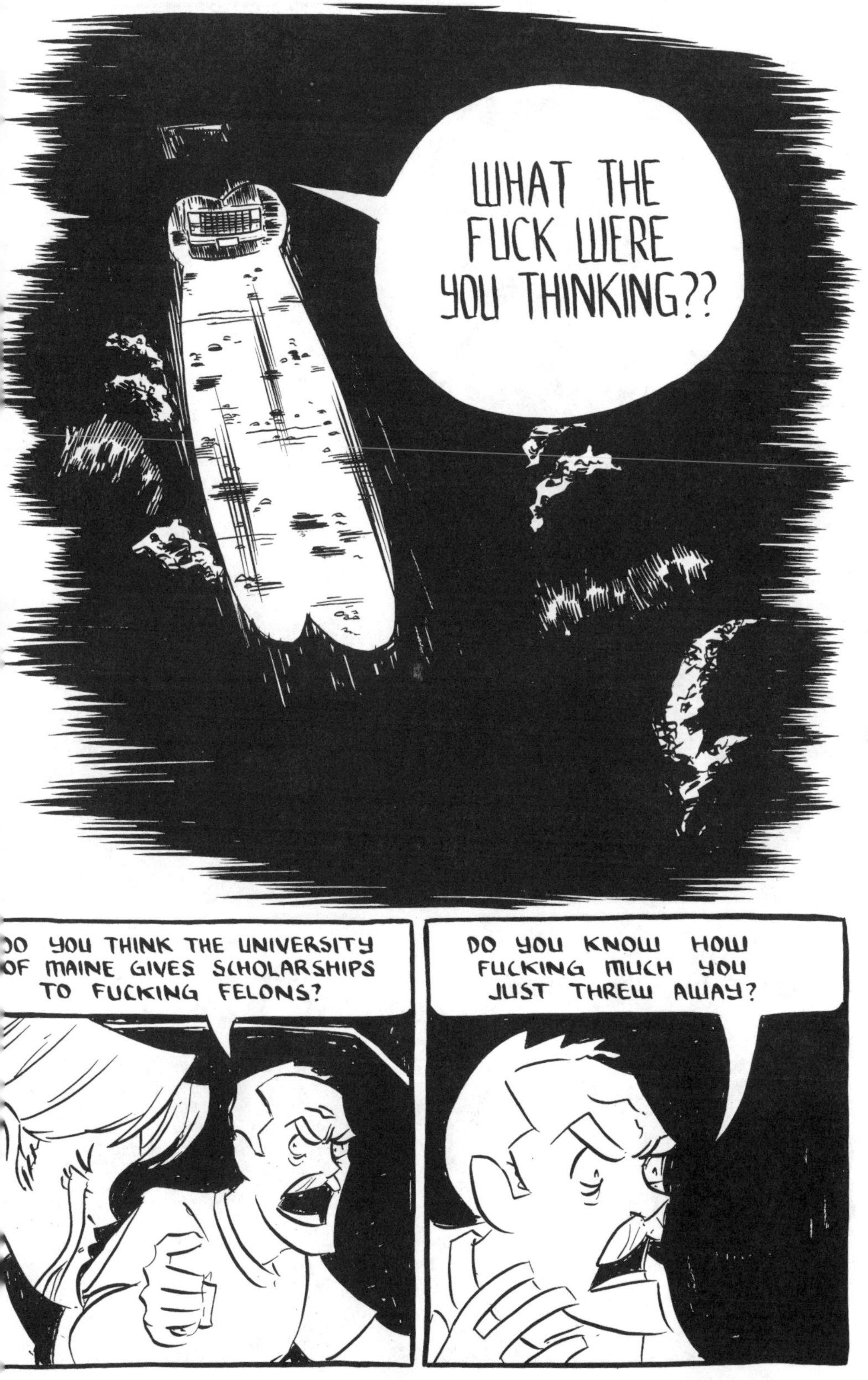
WHAT THE FUCK WERE YOU THINKING??
DO YOU THINK THE UNIVERSITY OF MAINE GIVES SCHOLARSHIPS TO FUCKING FELONS?
DO YOU KNOW HOW FUCKING MUCH YOU JUST THREW AWAY?

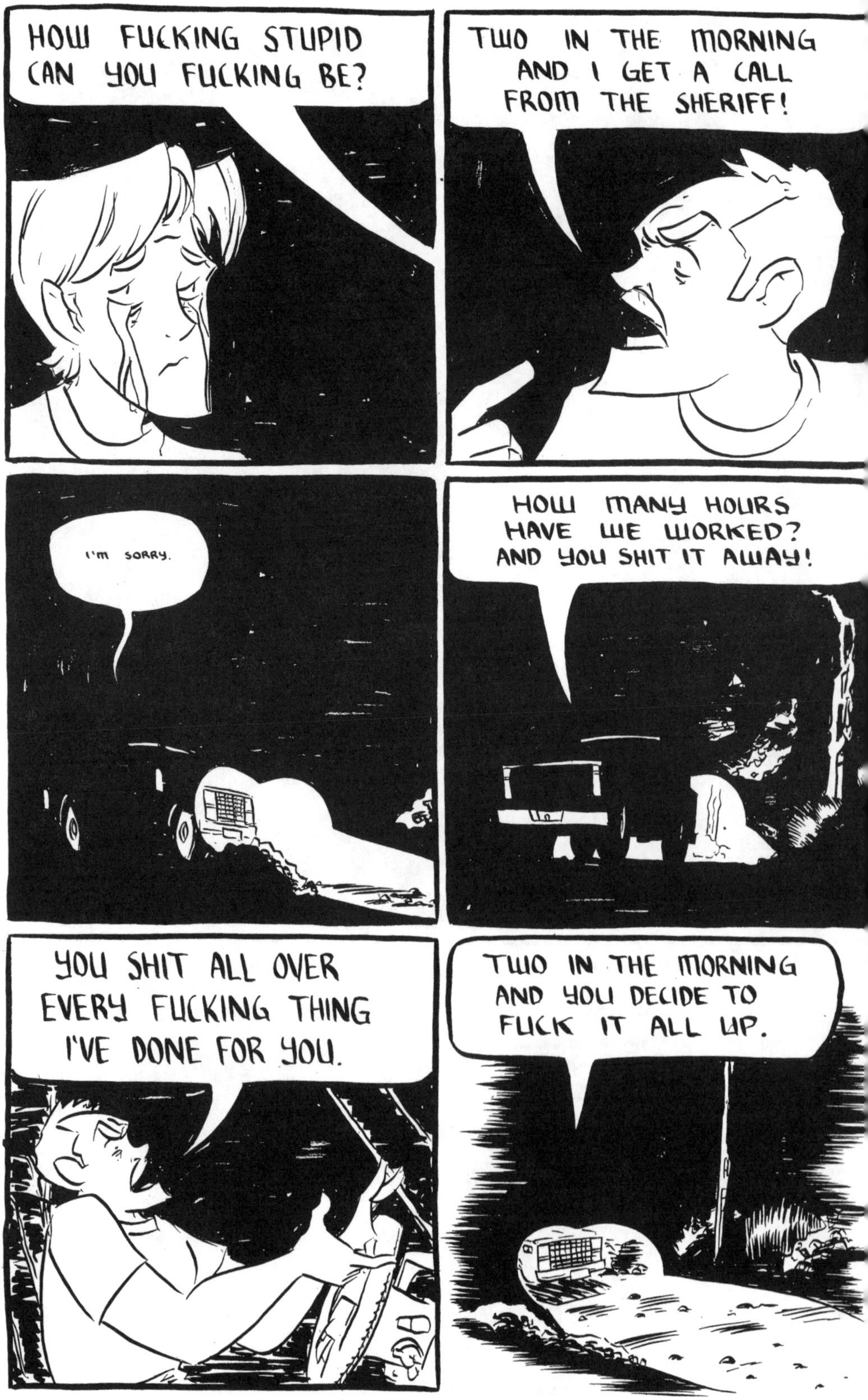

HOW FUCKING STUPID CAN YOU FUCKING BE?
TWO IN THE MORNING AND I GET A CALL FROM THE SHERIFF!
I'M SORRY.
HOW MANY HOURS HAVE WE WORKED? AND YOU SHIT IT AWAY!
YOU SHIT ALL OVER EVERY FUCKING THING I'VE DONE FOR YOU.
TWO IN THE MORNING AND YOU DECIDE TO FUCK IT ALL UP.

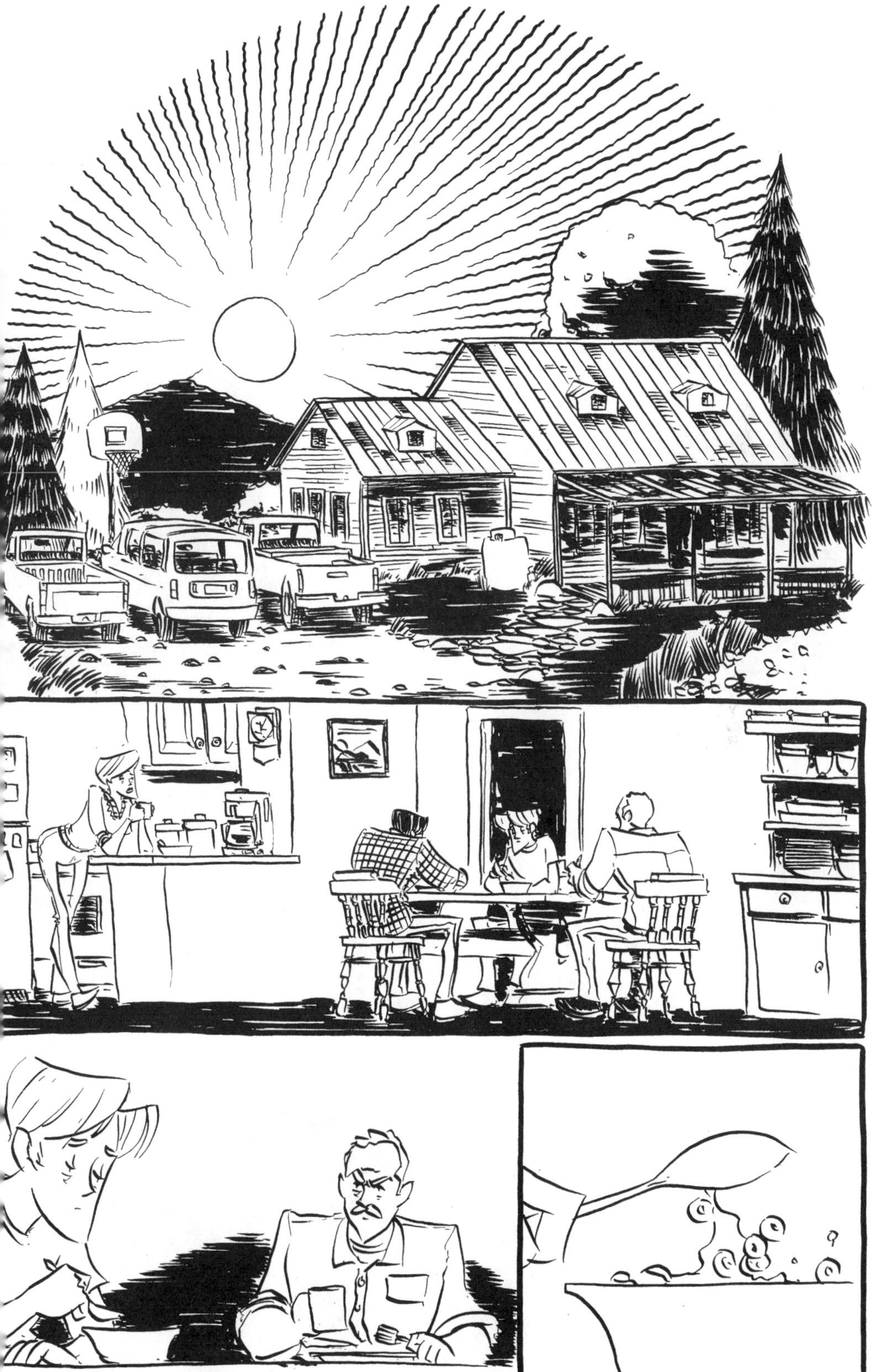

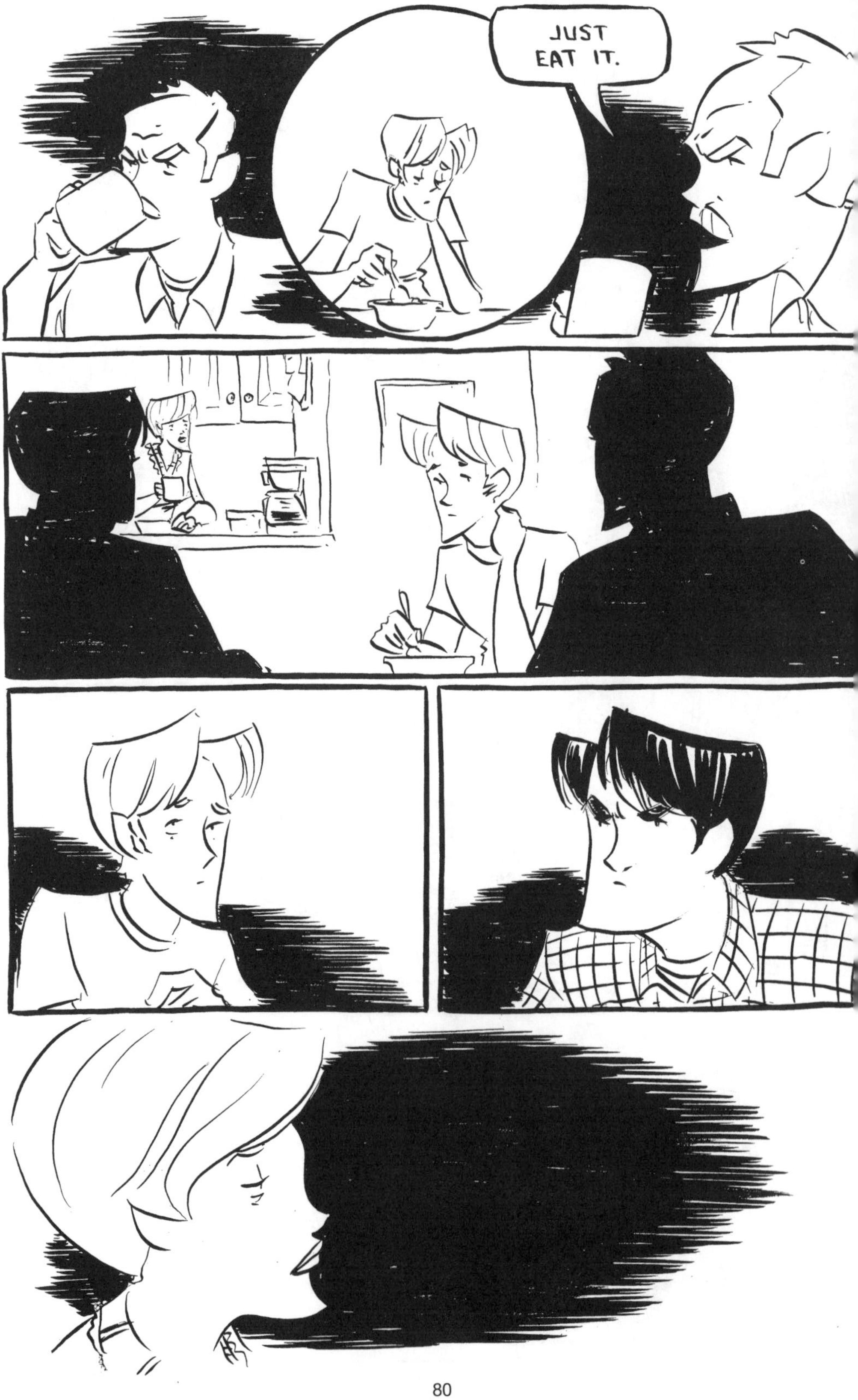
JUST EAT IT.

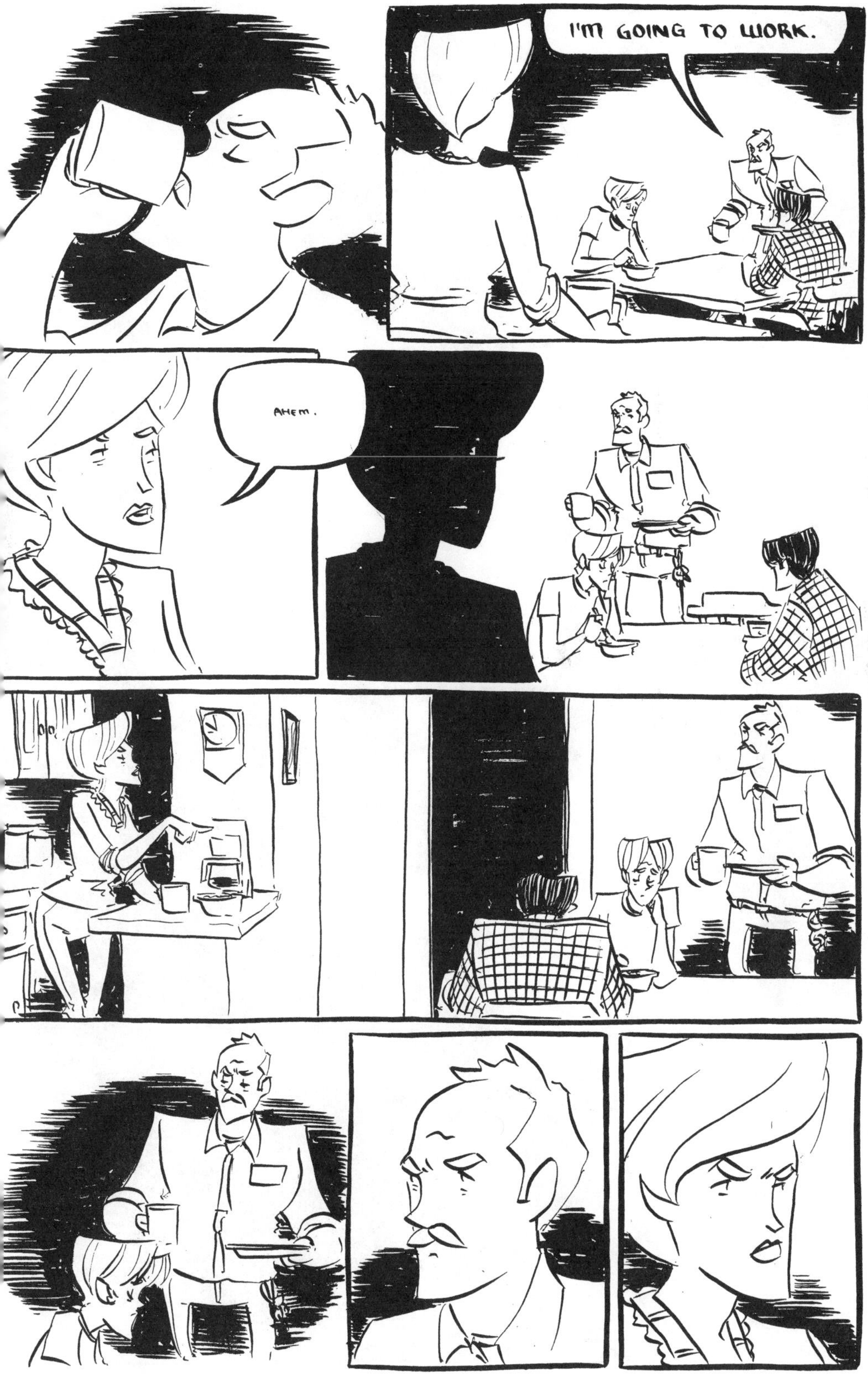
I'M GOING TO WORK.
AHEM.

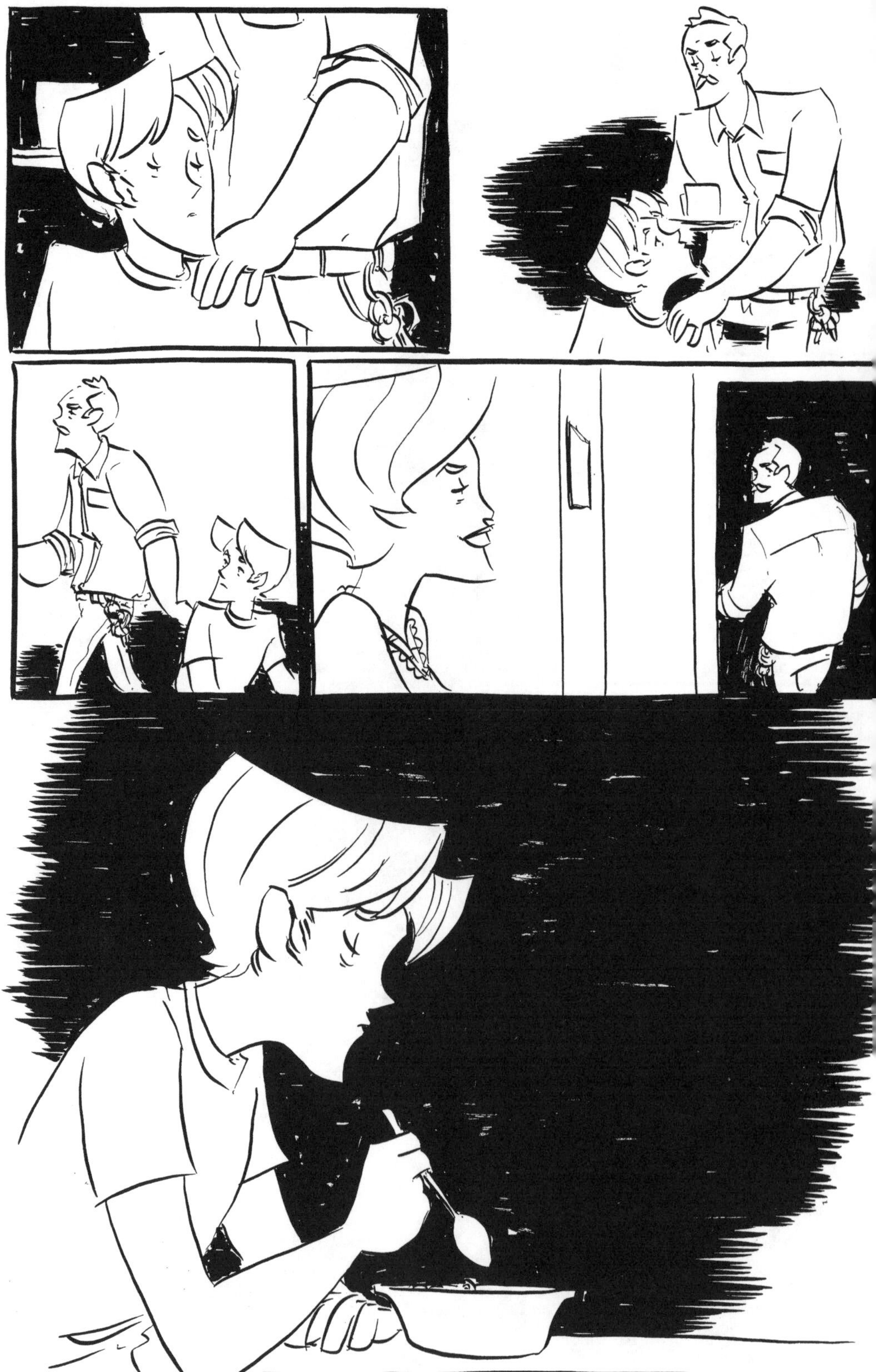

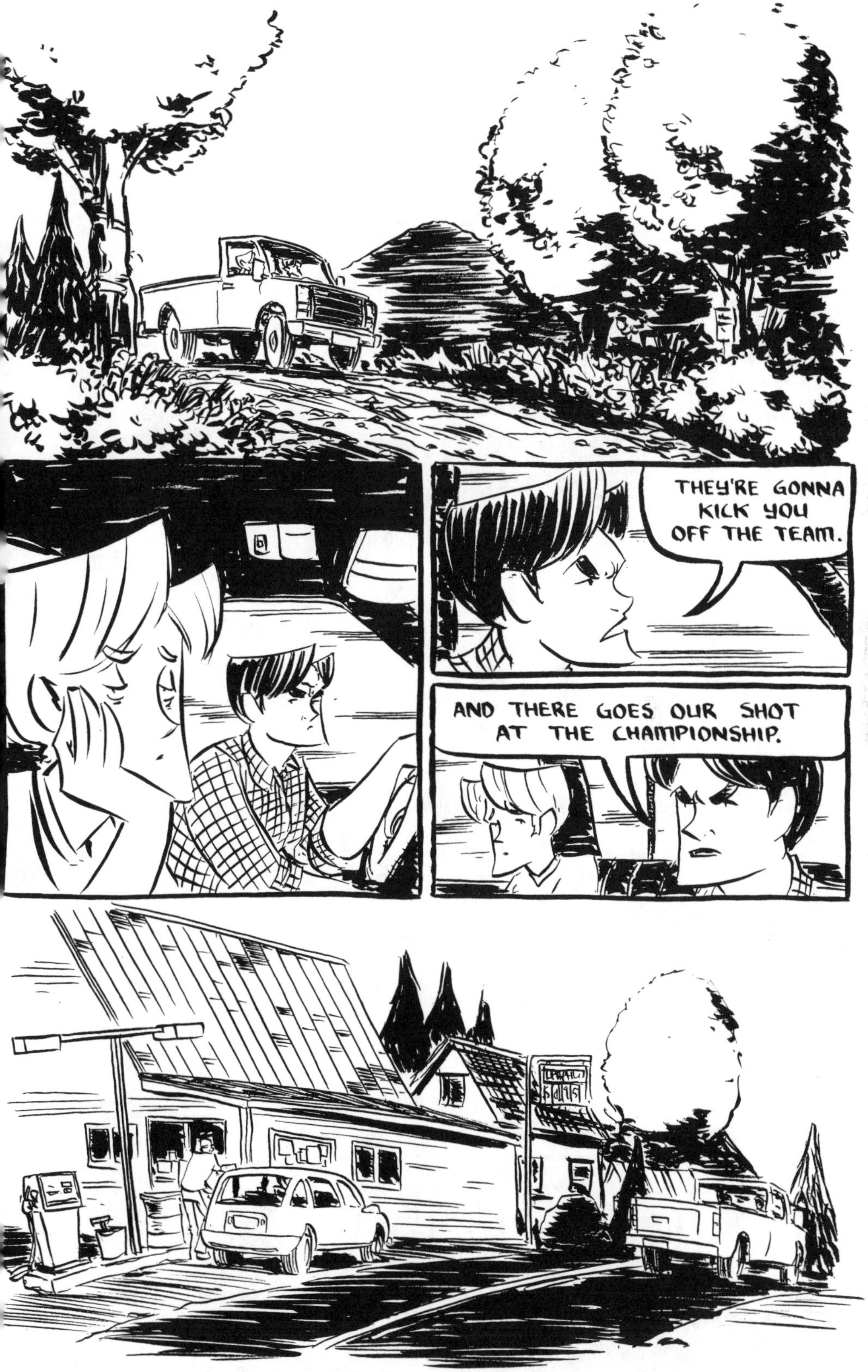
THEY'RE GONNA KICK YOU OFF THE TEAM.
AND THERE GOES OUR SHOT AT THE CHAMPIONSHIP.

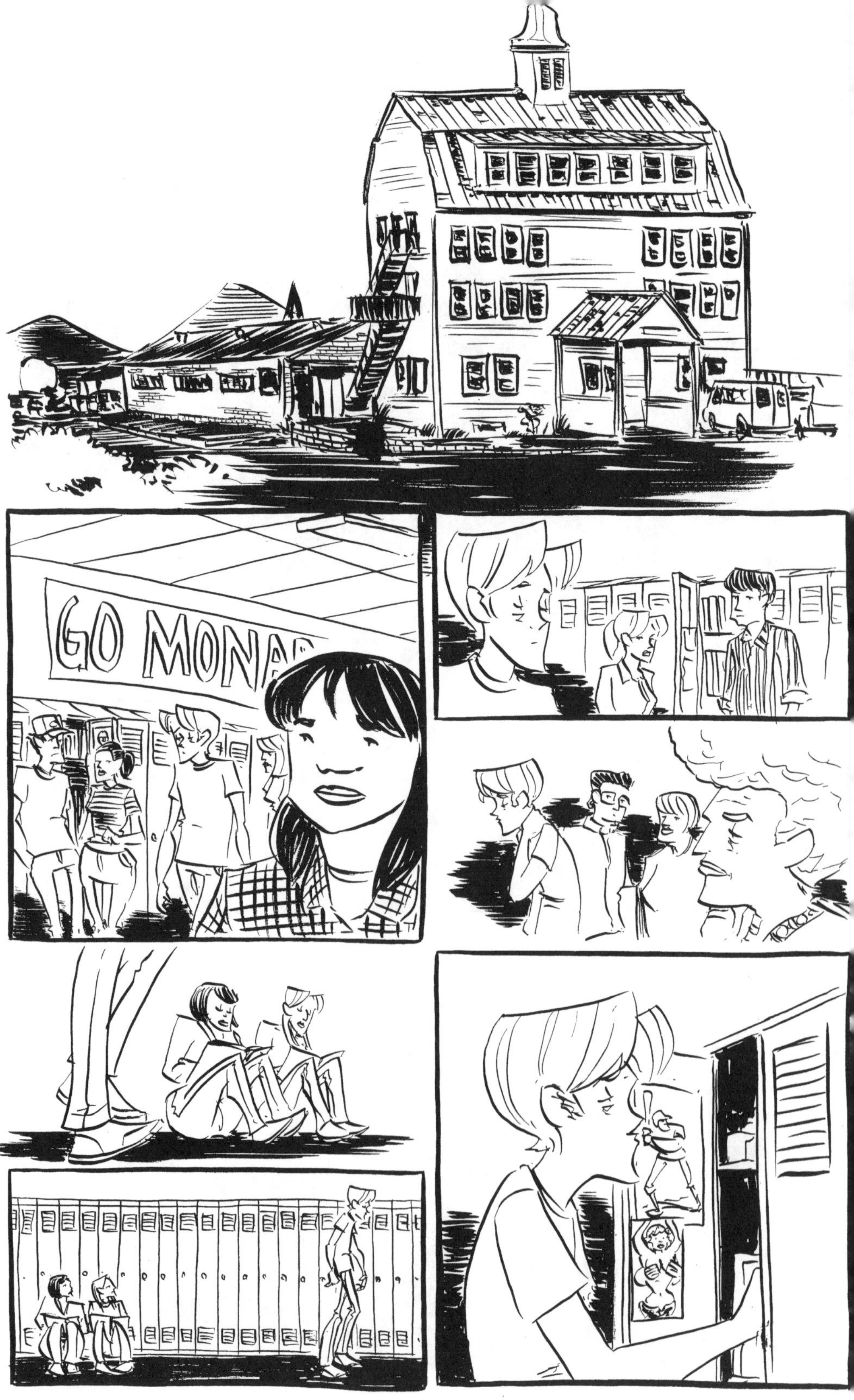
GO MONA

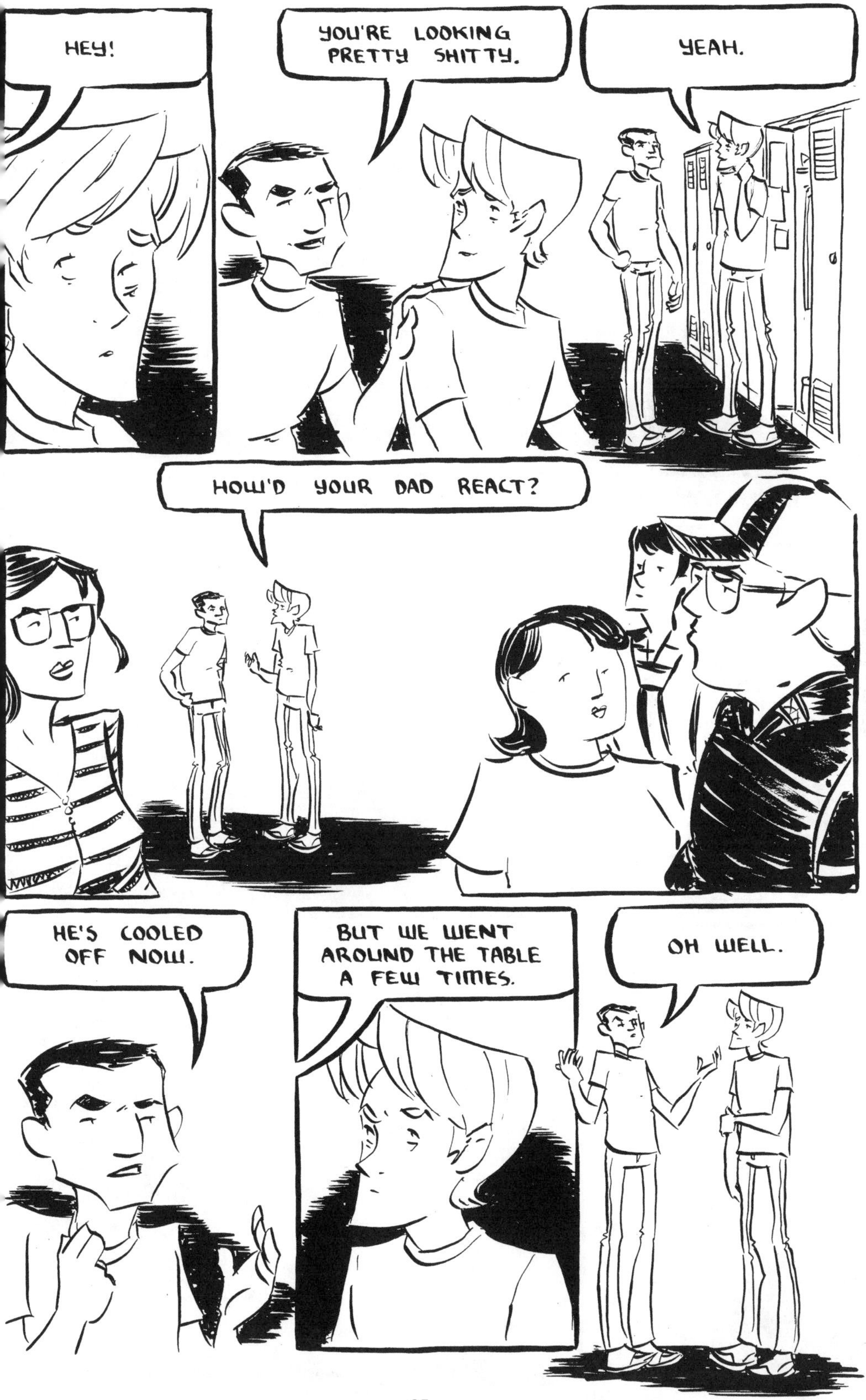
HEY!
YOU'RE LOOKING PRETTY SHITTY.
YEAH.
HOW'D YOUR DAD REACT?
HE'S COOLED OFF NOW.
BUT WE WENT AROUND THE TABLE A FEW TIMES.
OH WELL.

"... LOOK ON MY WORKS, YE MIGHTY, AND DESPAIR!"

NOTHING BESIDES REMAINS.

ROUND THE DECAY OF THAT COLO... CO...

COLOSSAL.

... COLOSSAL WRECK, BOUNDLESS AND BARE.

... THE LONE AND LEVEL SANDS STRETCH FAR AWAY.

THANK YOU FOR THAT MOVING READING, MATT. NOW, WHAT DOES...

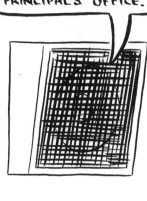

ESDEN HUBBARD, PLEASE COME TO THE PRINCIPAL'S OFFICE.

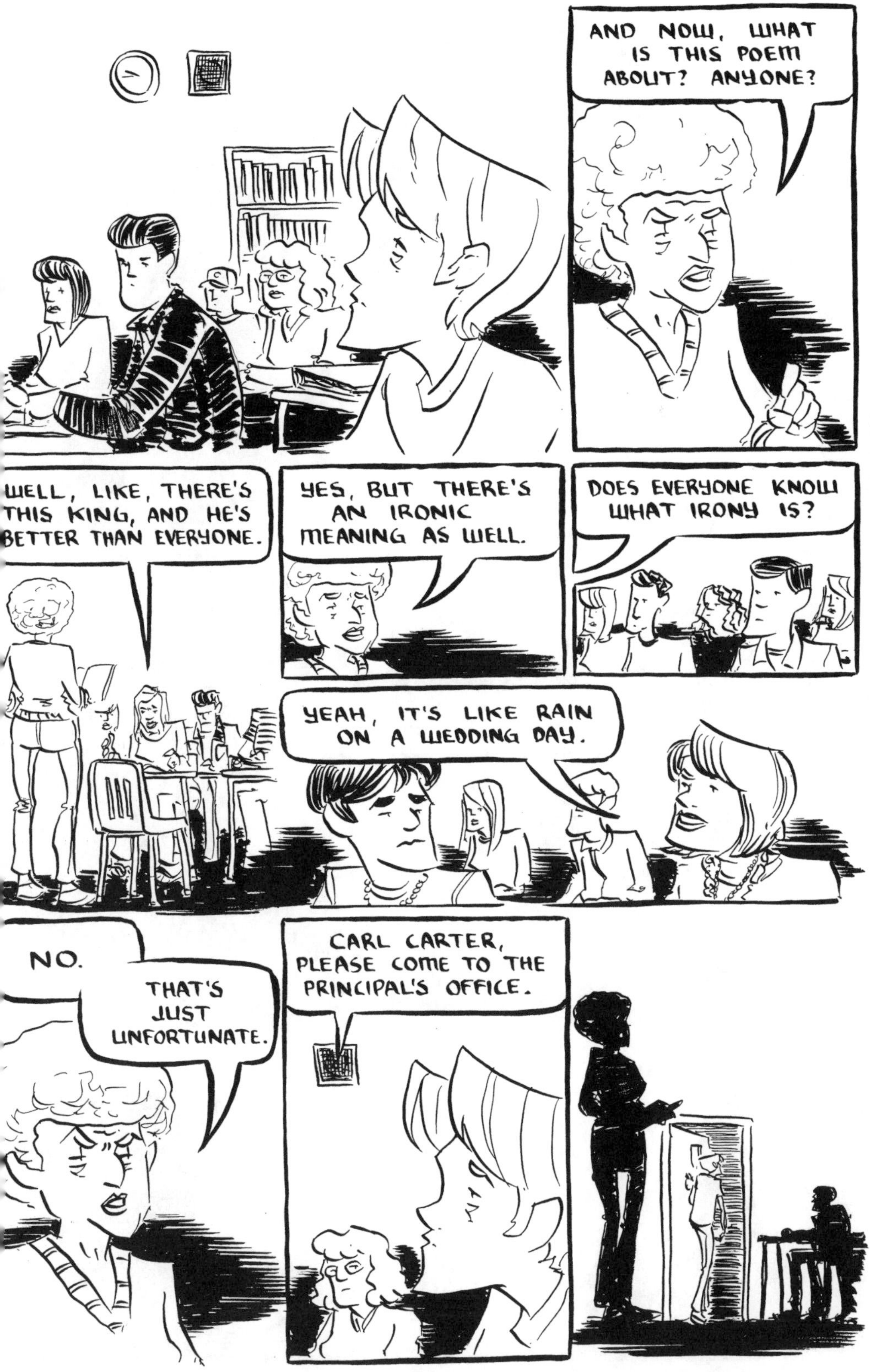
AND NOW, WHAT IS THIS POEM ABOUT? ANYONE?
WELL, LIKE, THERE'S THIS KING, AND HE'S BETTER THAN EVERYONE.
YES, BUT THERE'S AN IRONIC MEANING AS WELL.
DOES EVERYONE KNOW WHAT IRONY IS?
YEAH, IT'S LIKE RAIN ON A WEDDING DAY.
NO.
THAT'S JUST UNFORTUNATE.
CARL CARTER, PLEASE COME TO THE PRINCIPAL'S OFFICE.

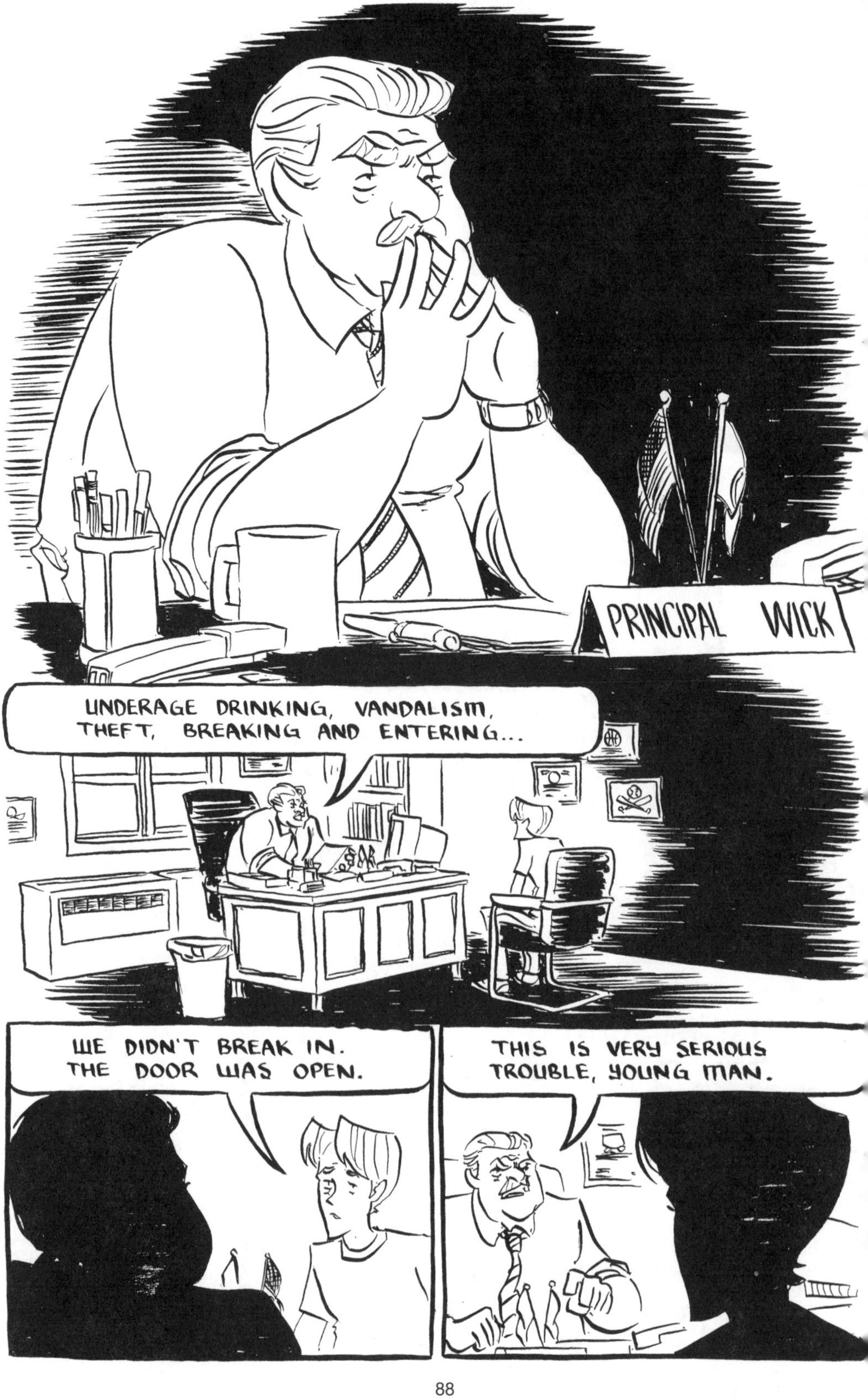
PRINCIPAL WICK
UNDERAGE DRINKING, VANDALISM, THEFT, BREAKING AND ENTERING...
WE DIDN'T BREAK IN. THE DOOR WAS OPEN.
THIS IS VERY SERIOUS TROUBLE, YOUNG MAN.

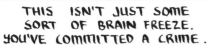

THIS ISN'T JUST SOME SORT OF BRAIN FREEZE. YOU'VE COMMITTED A CRIME.

YOU'VE GOT TO THINK ABOUT SOME OF THE DECISIONS YOU HAVE BEEN MAKING.

YOU'RE A TALENTED ATHLETE, AND YOU COULD HAVE A BRIGHT FUTURE AHEAD OF YOU.

BUT THAT DOESN'T MEAN YOU GET A GET OUT JAIL FREE CARD.

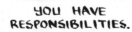
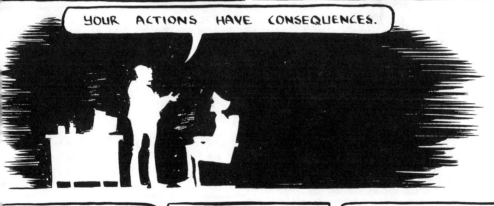
YOUR ACTIONS HAVE CONSEQUENCES.

YOU'RE NOT A CHILD ANYMORE.

YOU HAVE RESPONSIBILITIES.

NOT JUST TO YOURSELF BUT TO THIS SCHOOL AND THIS TOWN.

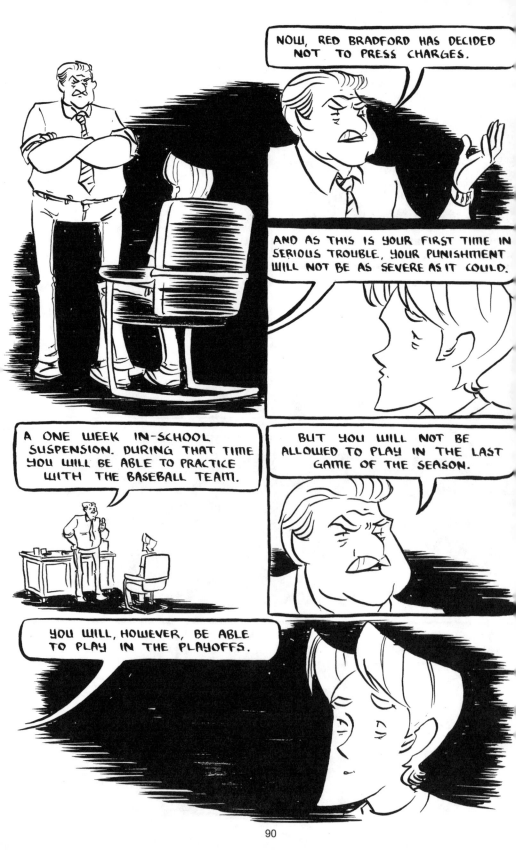

NOW, RED BRADFORD HAS DECIDED NOT TO PRESS CHARGES.

AND AS THIS IS YOUR FIRST TIME IN SERIOUS TROUBLE, YOUR PUNISHMENT WILL NOT BE AS SEVERE AS IT COULD.

A ONE WEEK IN-SCHOOL SUSPENSION. DURING THAT TIME YOU WILL BE ABLE TO PRACTICE WITH THE BASEBALL TEAM.

BUT YOU WILL NOT BE ALLOWED TO PLAY IN THE LAST GAME OF THE SEASON.

YOU WILL, HOWEVER, BE ABLE TO PLAY IN THE PLAYOFFS.

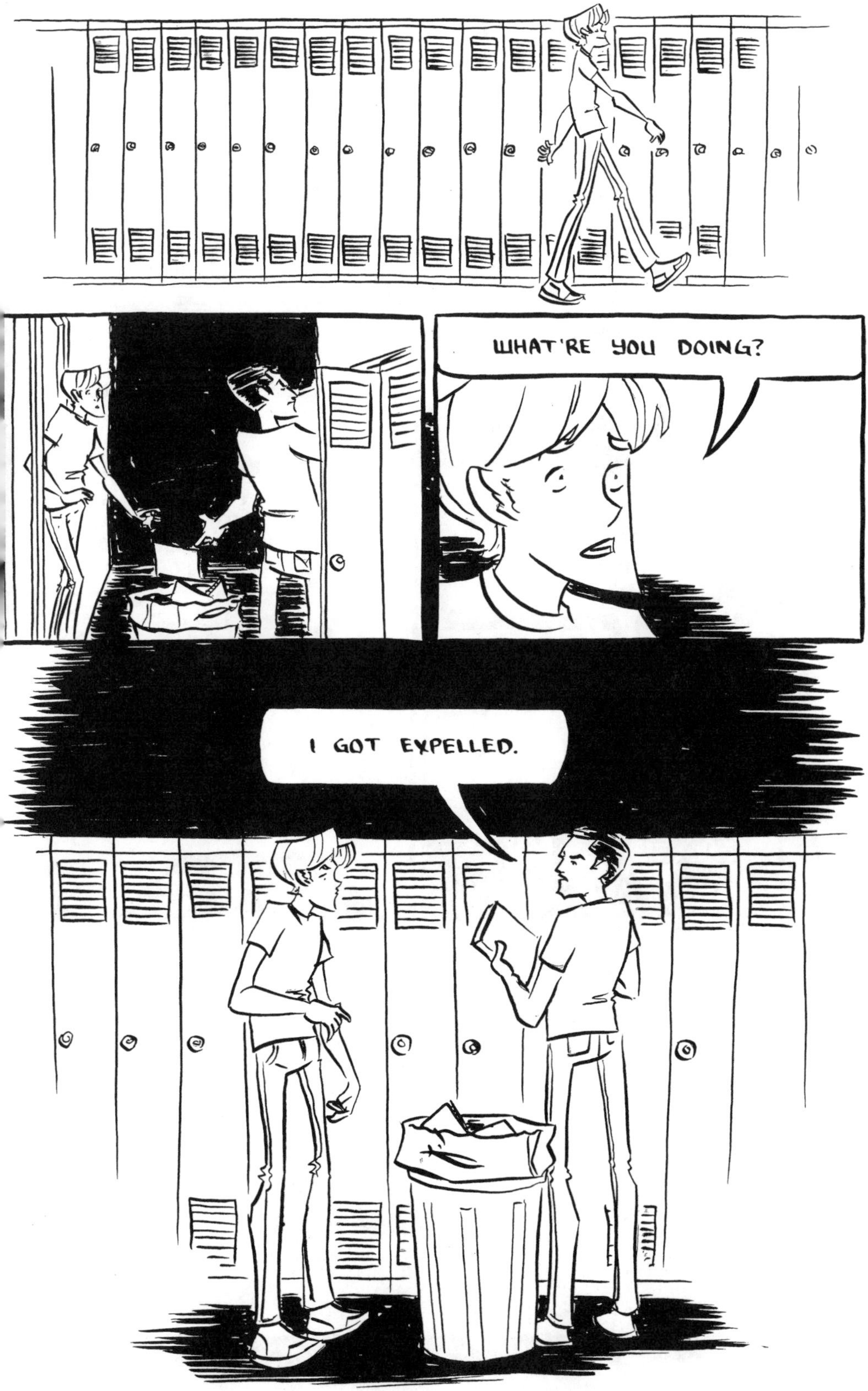
WHAT'RE YOU DOING?
I GOT EXPELLED.

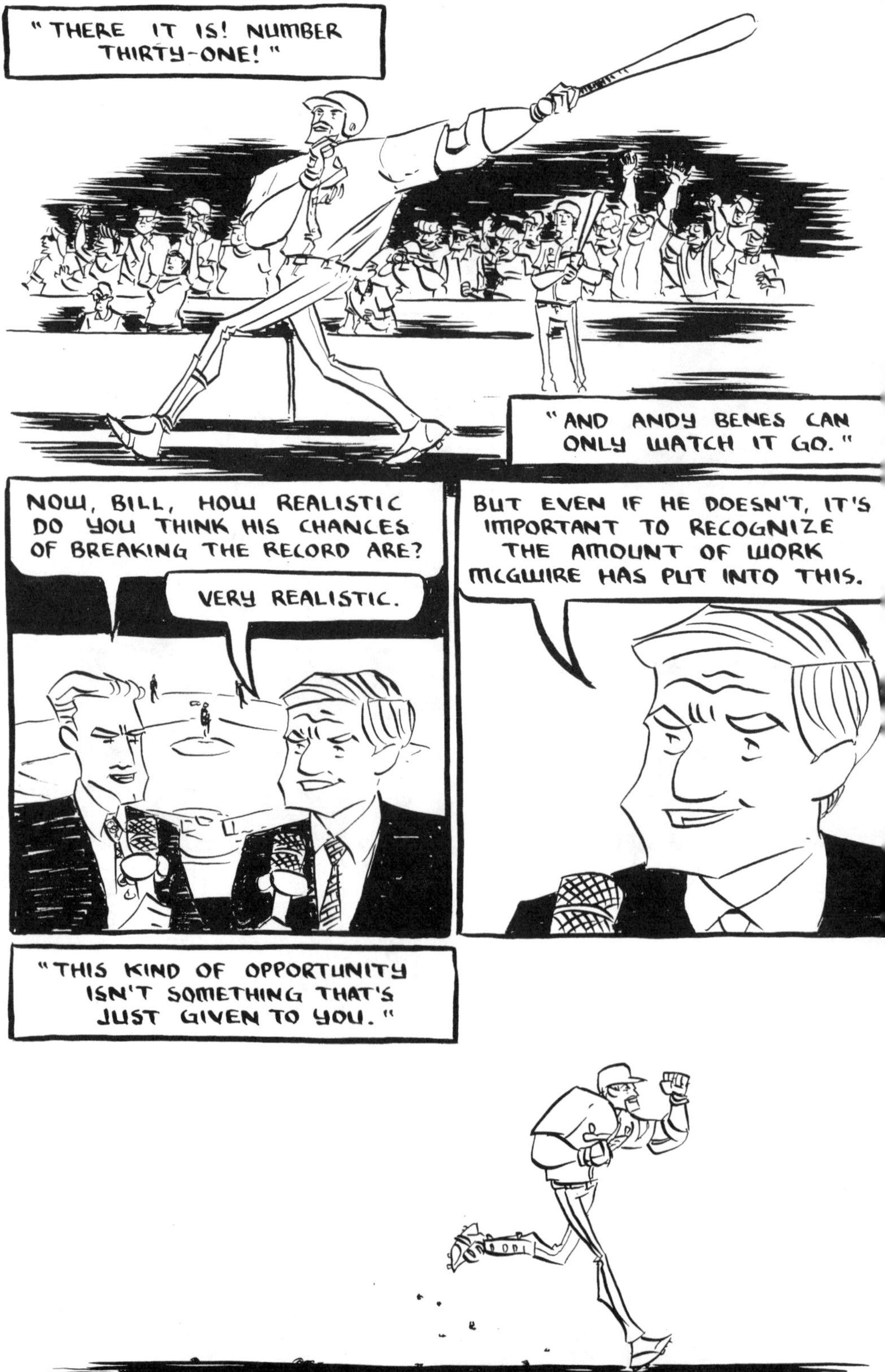
"THERE IT IS! NUMBER THIRTY-ONE!"
"AND ANDY BENES CAN ONLY WATCH IT GO."
NOW, BILL, HOW REALISTIC DO YOU THINK HIS CHANCES OF BREAKING THE RECORD ARE?
VERY REALISTIC.
BUT EVEN IF HE DOESN'T, IT'S IMPORTANT TO RECOGNIZE THE AMOUNT OF WORK MCGWIRE HAS PUT INTO THIS.
"THIS KIND OF OPPORTUNITY ISN'T SOMETHING THAT'S JUST GIVEN TO YOU."

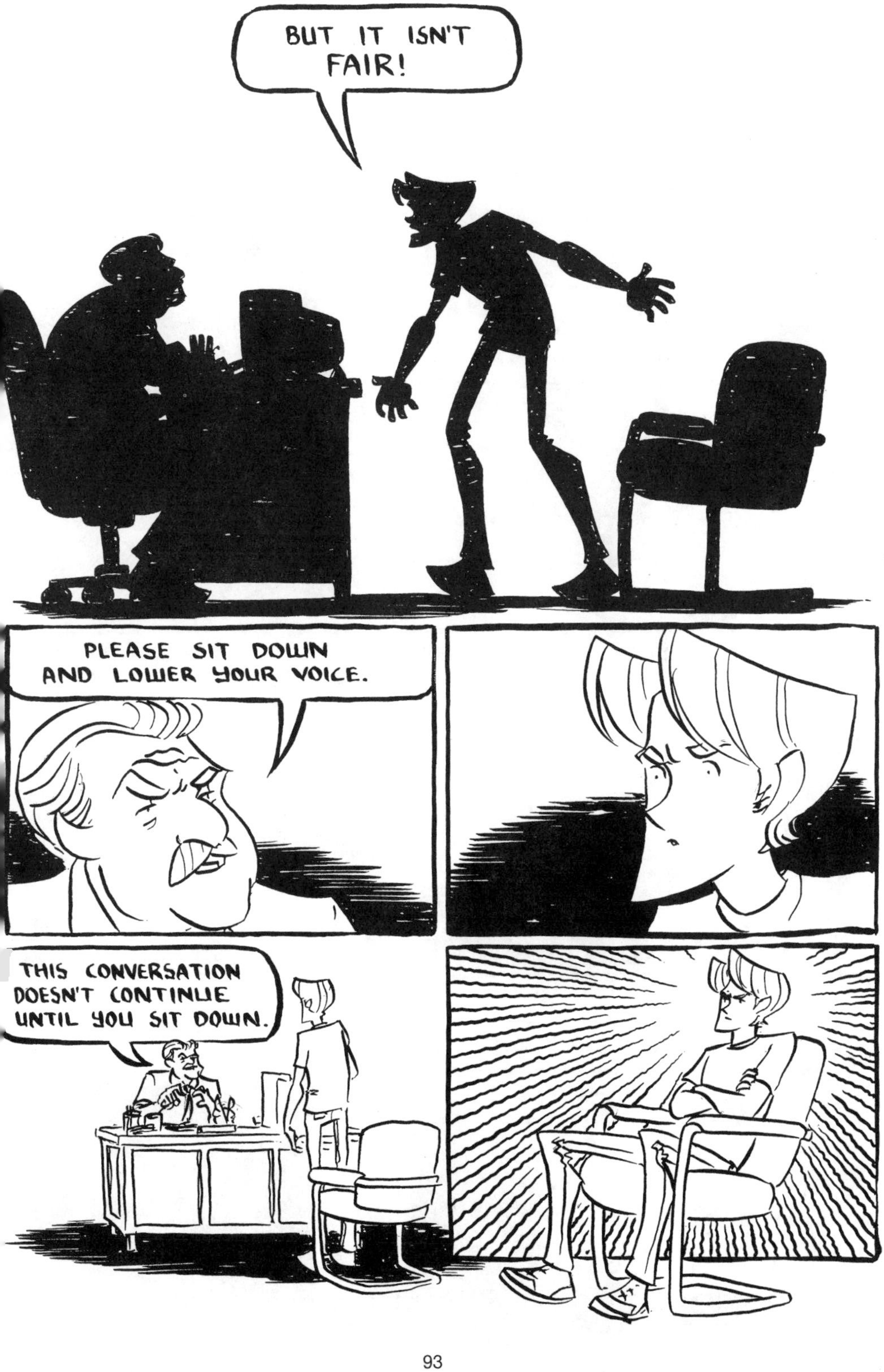
BUT IT ISN'T FAIR!
PLEASE SIT DOWN AND LOWER YOUR VOICE.
THIS CONVERSATION DOESN'T CONTINUE UNTIL YOU SIT DOWN.

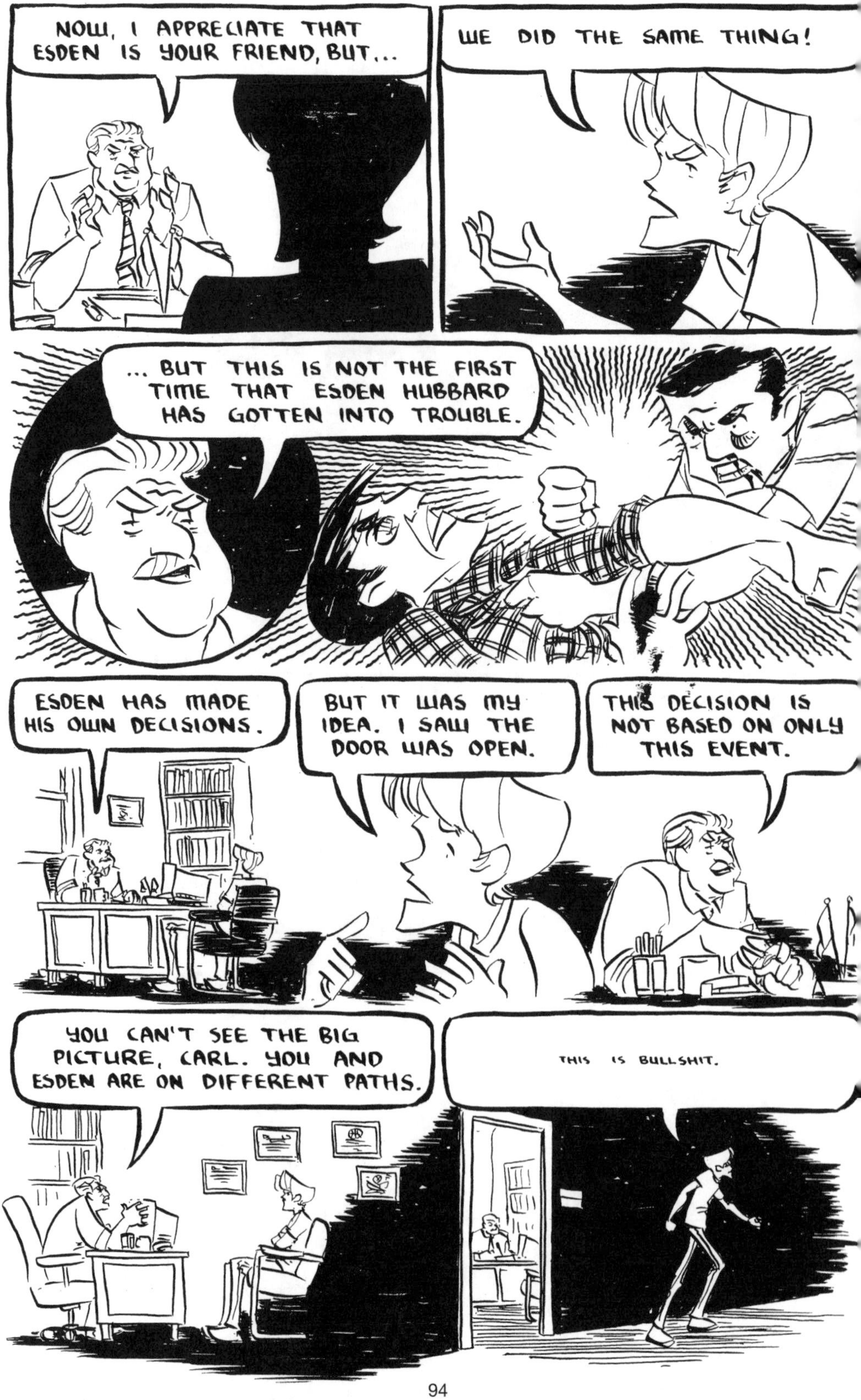
NOW, I APPRECIATE THAT ESDEN IS YOUR FRIEND, BUT...
WE DID THE SAME THING!
... BUT THIS IS NOT THE FIRST TIME THAT ESDEN HUBBARD HAS GOTTEN INTO TROUBLE.
ESDEN HAS MADE HIS OWN DECISIONS.
BUT IT WAS MY IDEA. I SAW THE DOOR WAS OPEN.
THIS DECISION IS NOT BASED ON ONLY THIS EVENT.
YOU CAN'T SEE THE BIG PICTURE, CARL. YOU AND ESDEN ARE ON DIFFERENT PATHS.
THIS IS BULLSHIT.

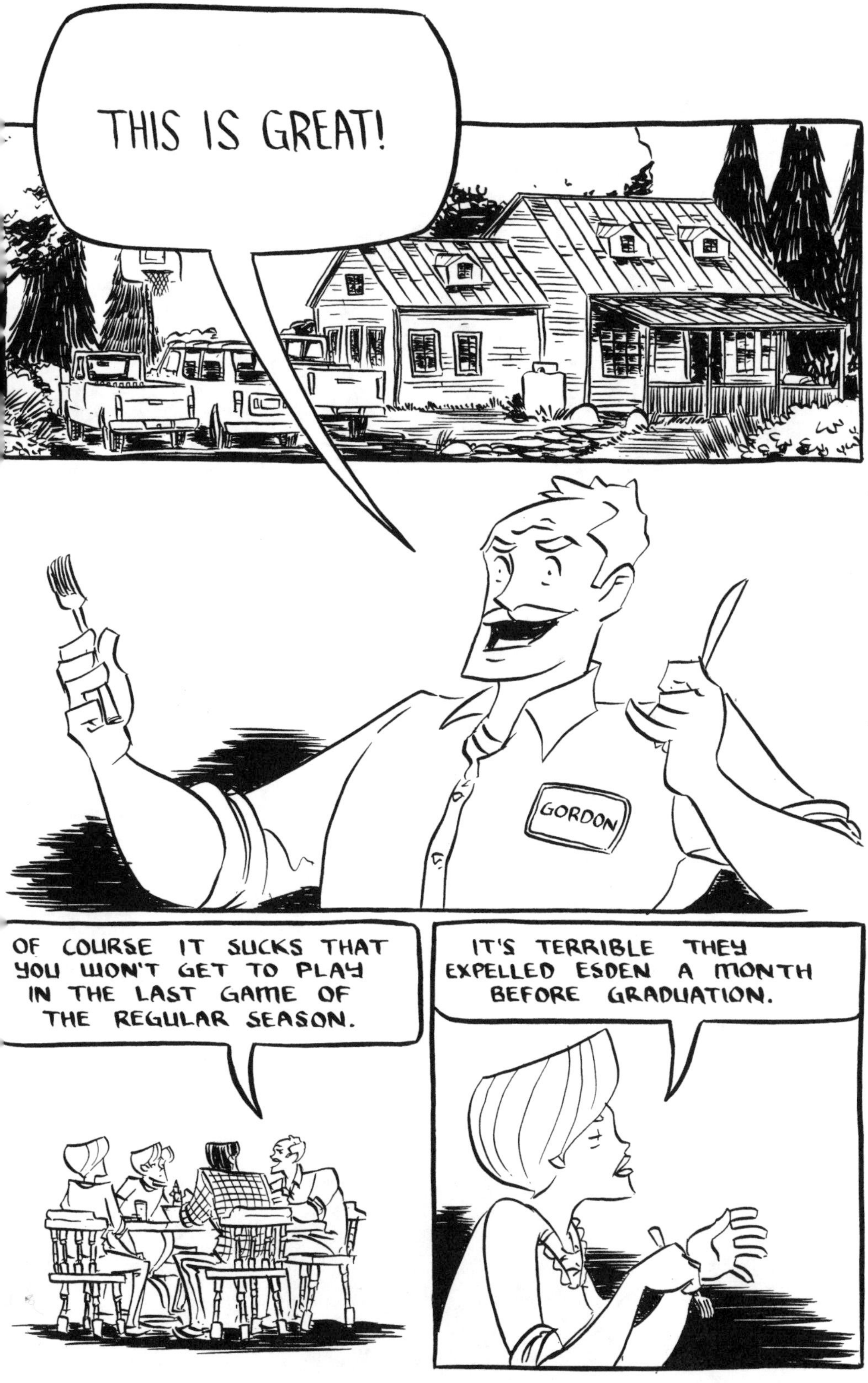
THIS IS GREAT!
GORDON
OF COURSE IT SUCKS THAT YOU WON'T GET TO PLAY IN THE LAST GAME OF THE REGULAR SEASON.
IT'S TERRIBLE THEY EXPELLED ESDEN A MONTH BEFORE GRADUATION.

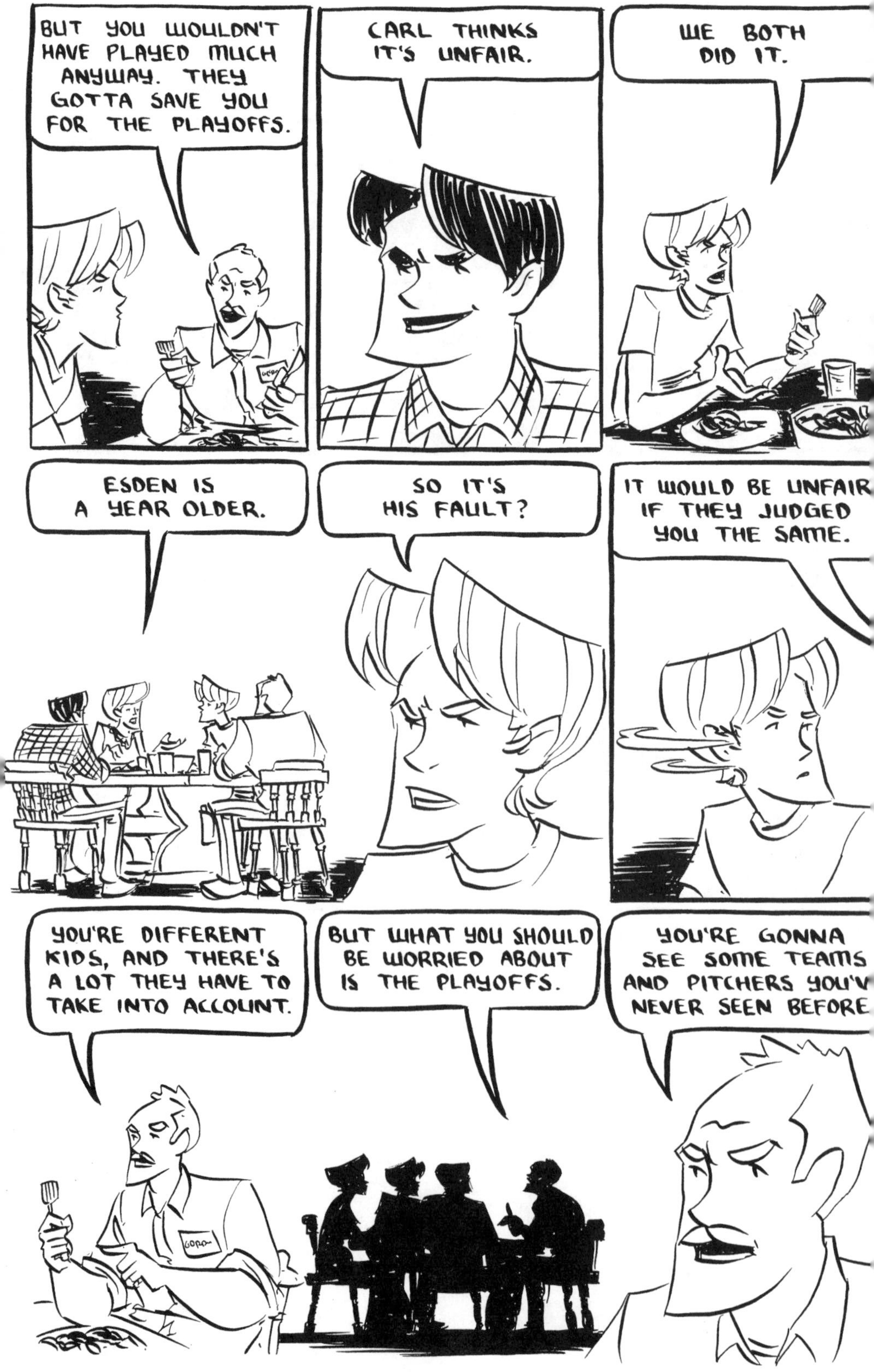
BUT YOU WOULDN'T HAVE PLAYED MUCH ANYWAY. THEY GOTTA SAVE YOU FOR THE PLAYOFFS.
CARL THINKS IT'S UNFAIR.
WE BOTH DID IT.
ESDEN IS A YEAR OLDER.
SO IT'S HIS FAULT?
IT WOULD BE UNFAIR IF THEY JUDGED YOU THE SAME.
YOU'RE DIFFERENT KIDS, AND THERE'S A LOT THEY HAVE TO TAKE INTO ACCOUNT.
BUT WHAT YOU SHOULD BE WORRIED ABOUT IS THE PLAYOFFS.
YOU'RE GONNA SEE SOME TEAMS AND PITCHERS YOU'V NEVER SEEN BEFORE

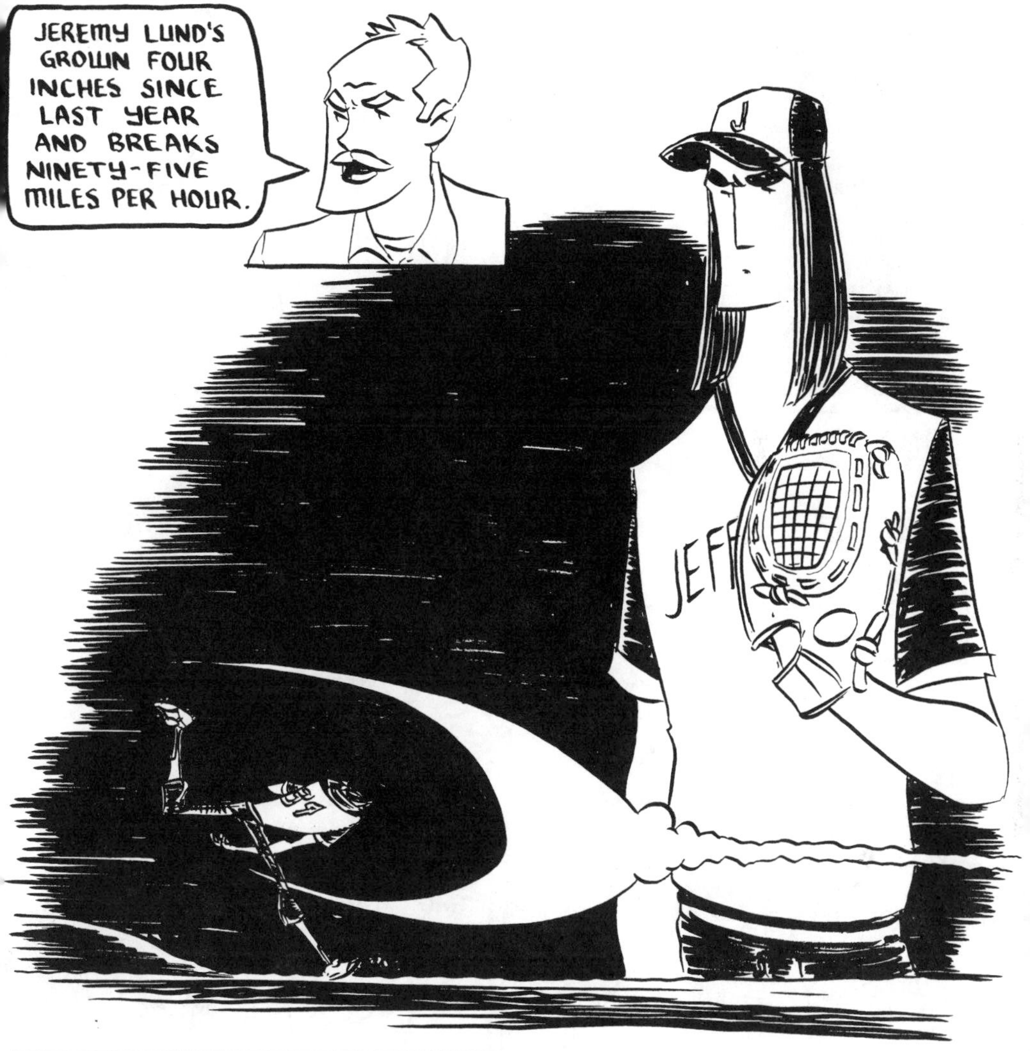
JEREMY LUND'S GROWN FOUR INCHES SINCE LAST YEAR AND BREAKS NINETY-FIVE MILES PER HOUR.
JEFF

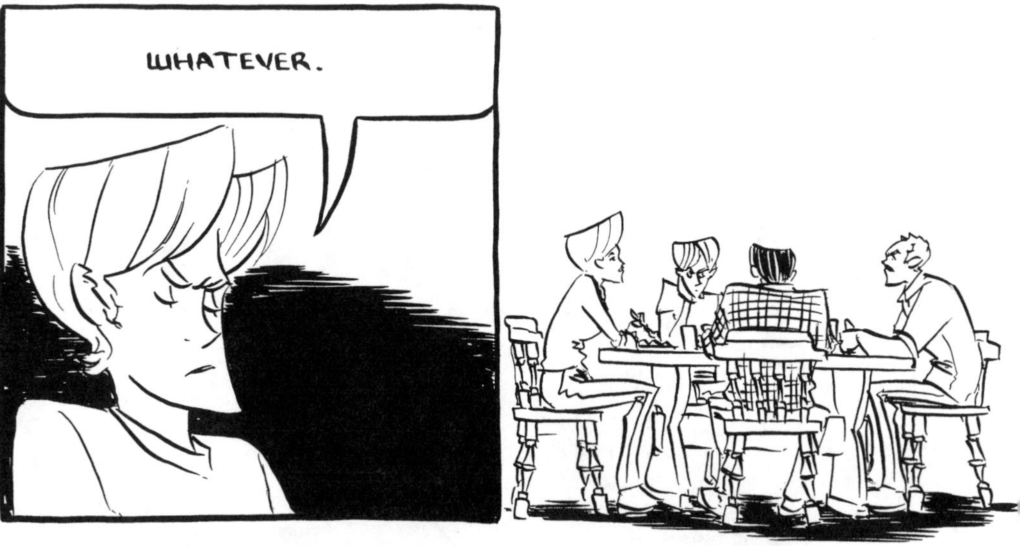
WHATEVER.

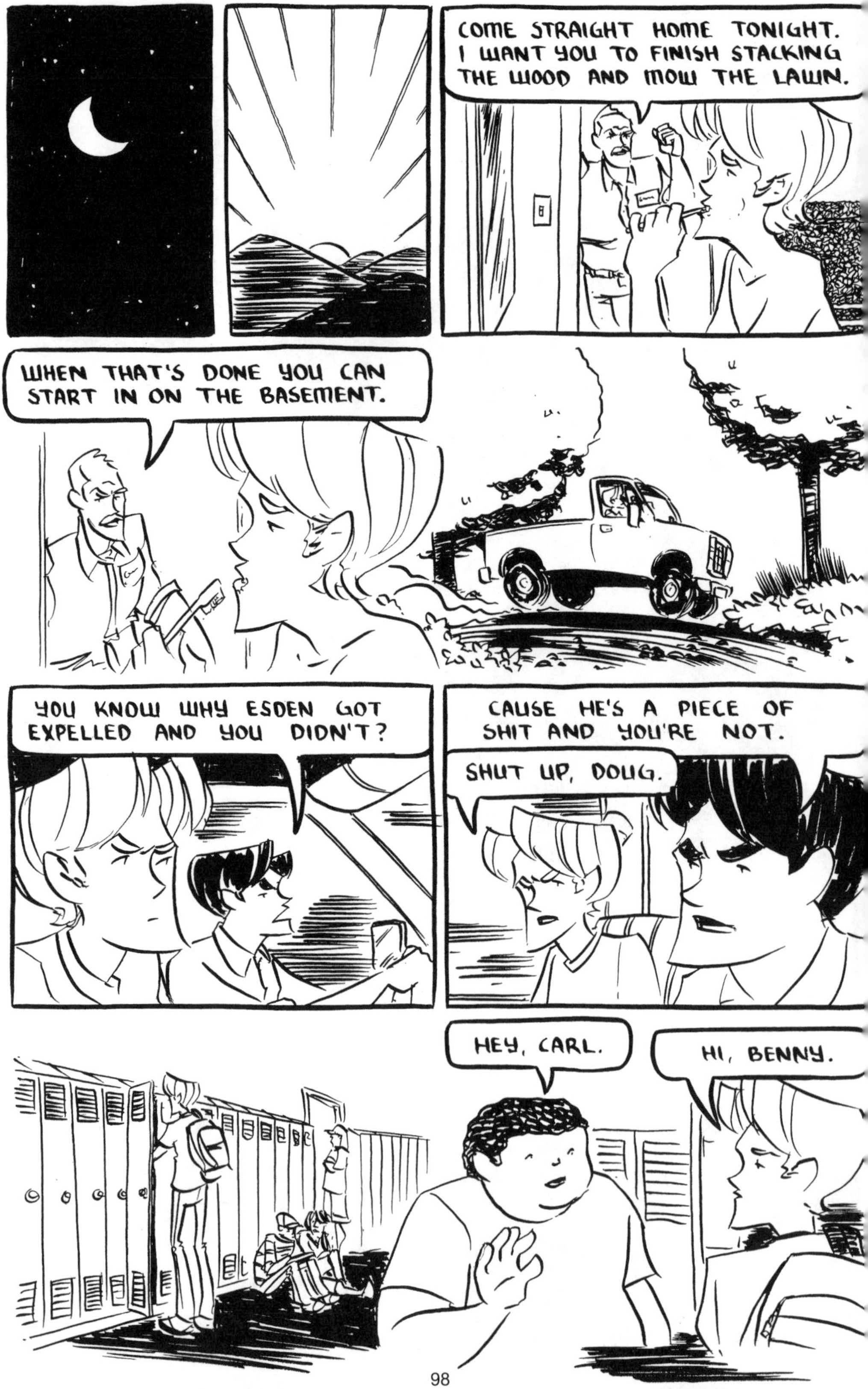
COME STRAIGHT HOME TONIGHT. I WANT YOU TO FINISH STACKING THE WOOD AND MOW THE LAWN.
WHEN THAT'S DONE YOU CAN START IN ON THE BASEMENT.
YOU KNOW WHY ESDEN GOT EXPELLED AND YOU DIDN'T?
CAUSE HE'S A PIECE OF SHIT AND YOU'RE NOT.
SHUT UP, DOUG.
HEY, CARL.
HI, BENNY.

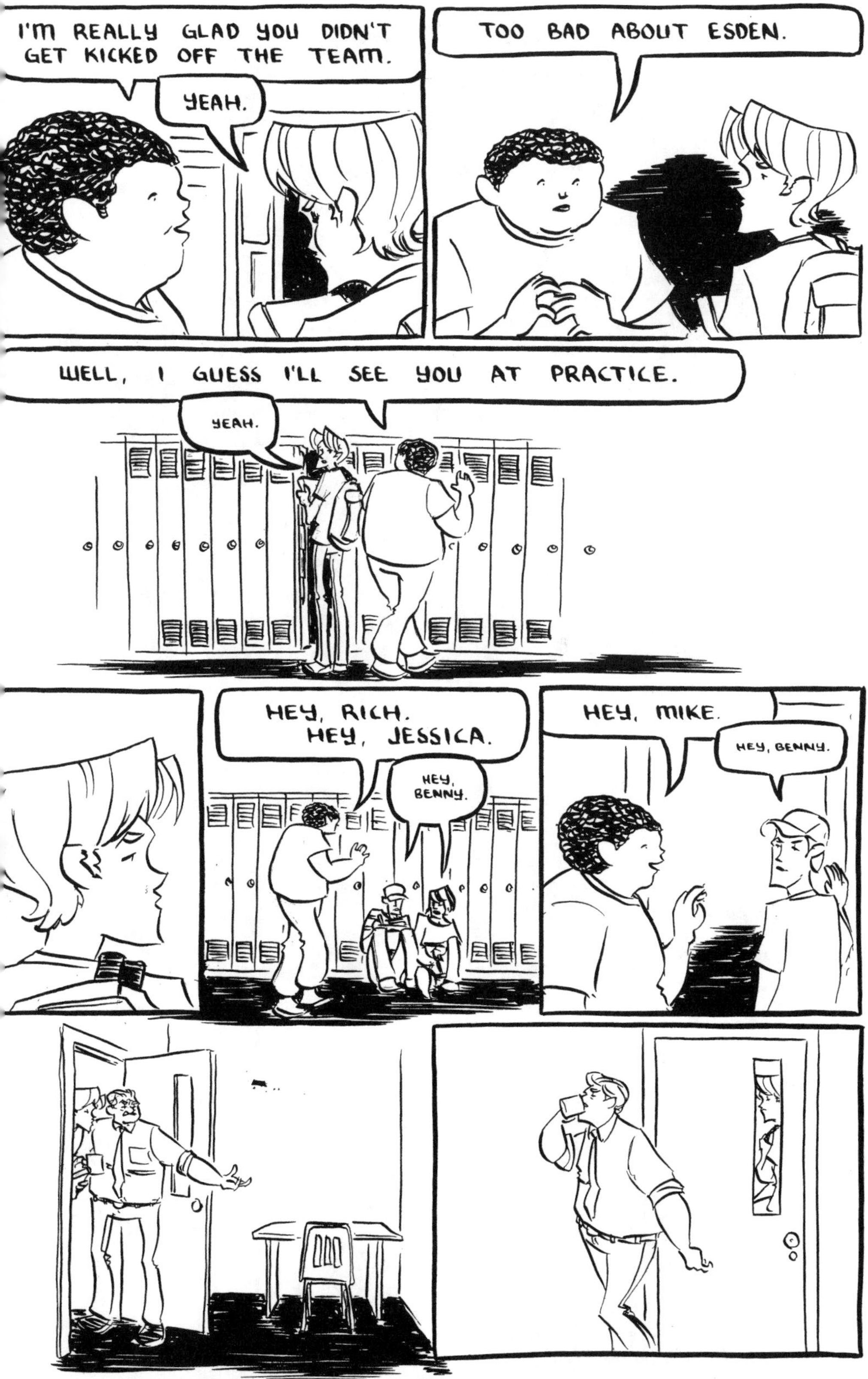
I'M REALLY GLAD YOU DIDN'T GET KICKED OFF THE TEAM.
YEAH.
TOO BAD ABOUT ESDEN.
WELL, I GUESS I'LL SEE YOU AT PRACTICE.
YEAH.
HEY, RICH. HEY, JESSICA.
HEY, BENNY.
HEY, MIKE.
HEY, BENNY.

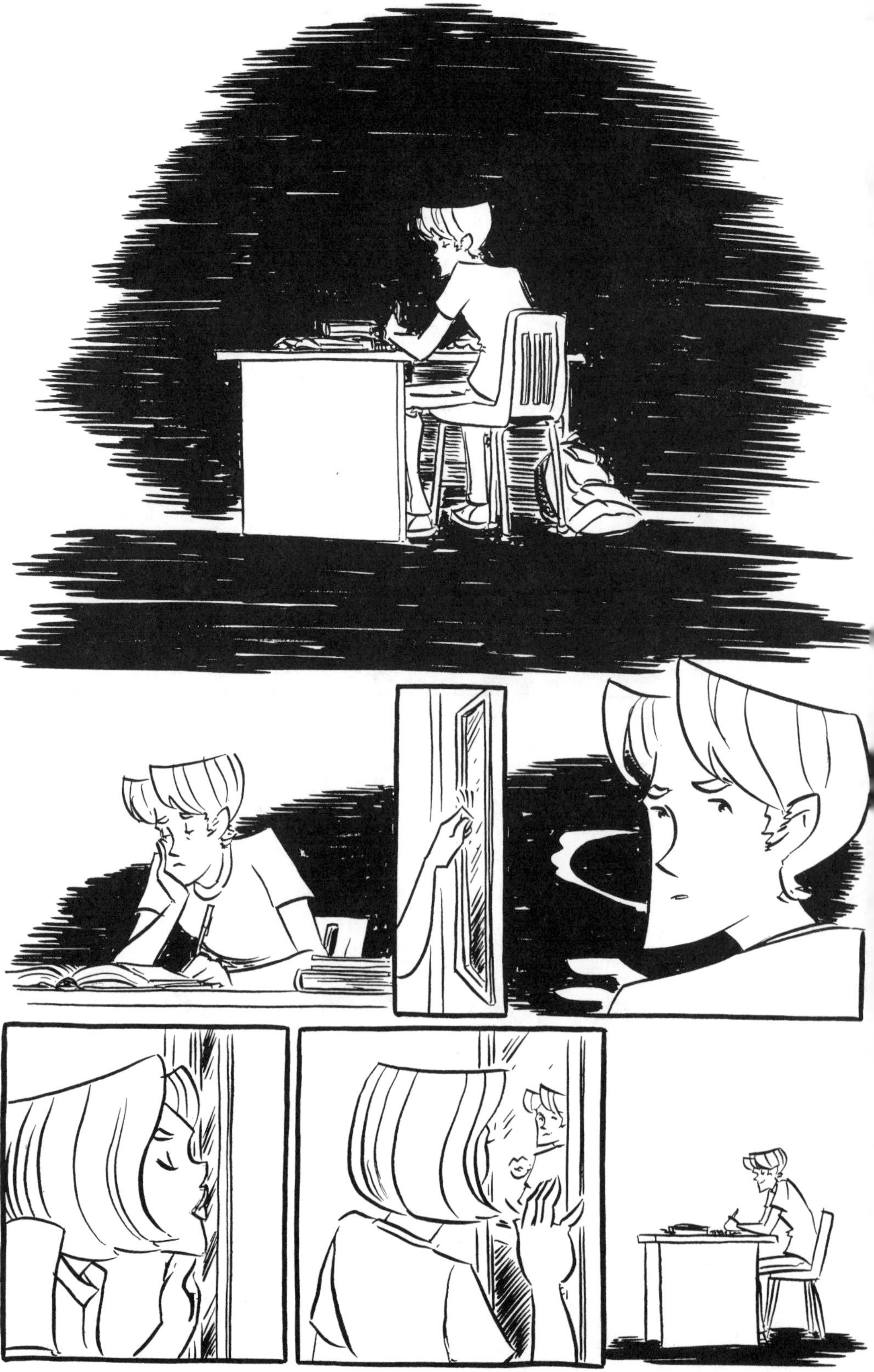

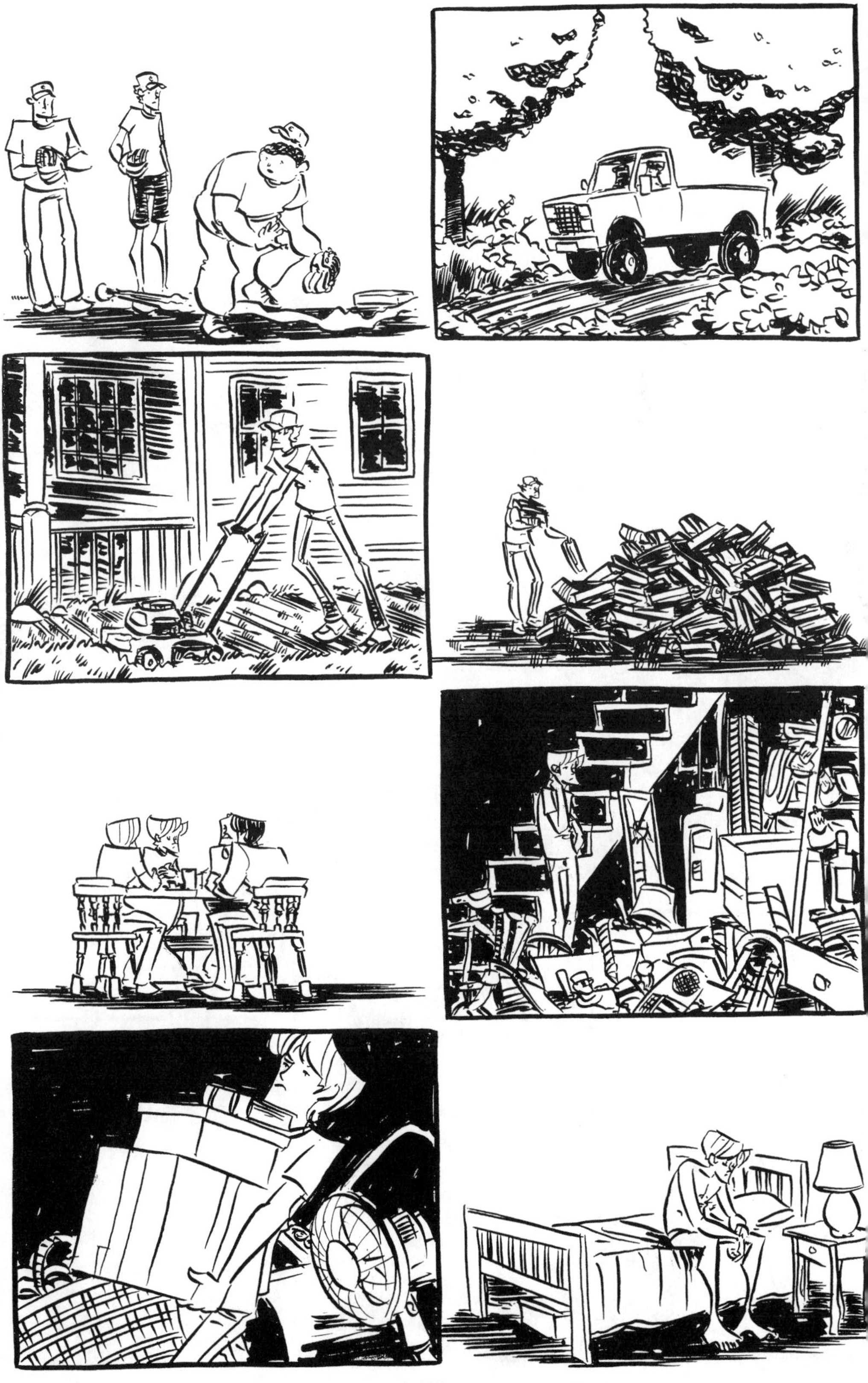

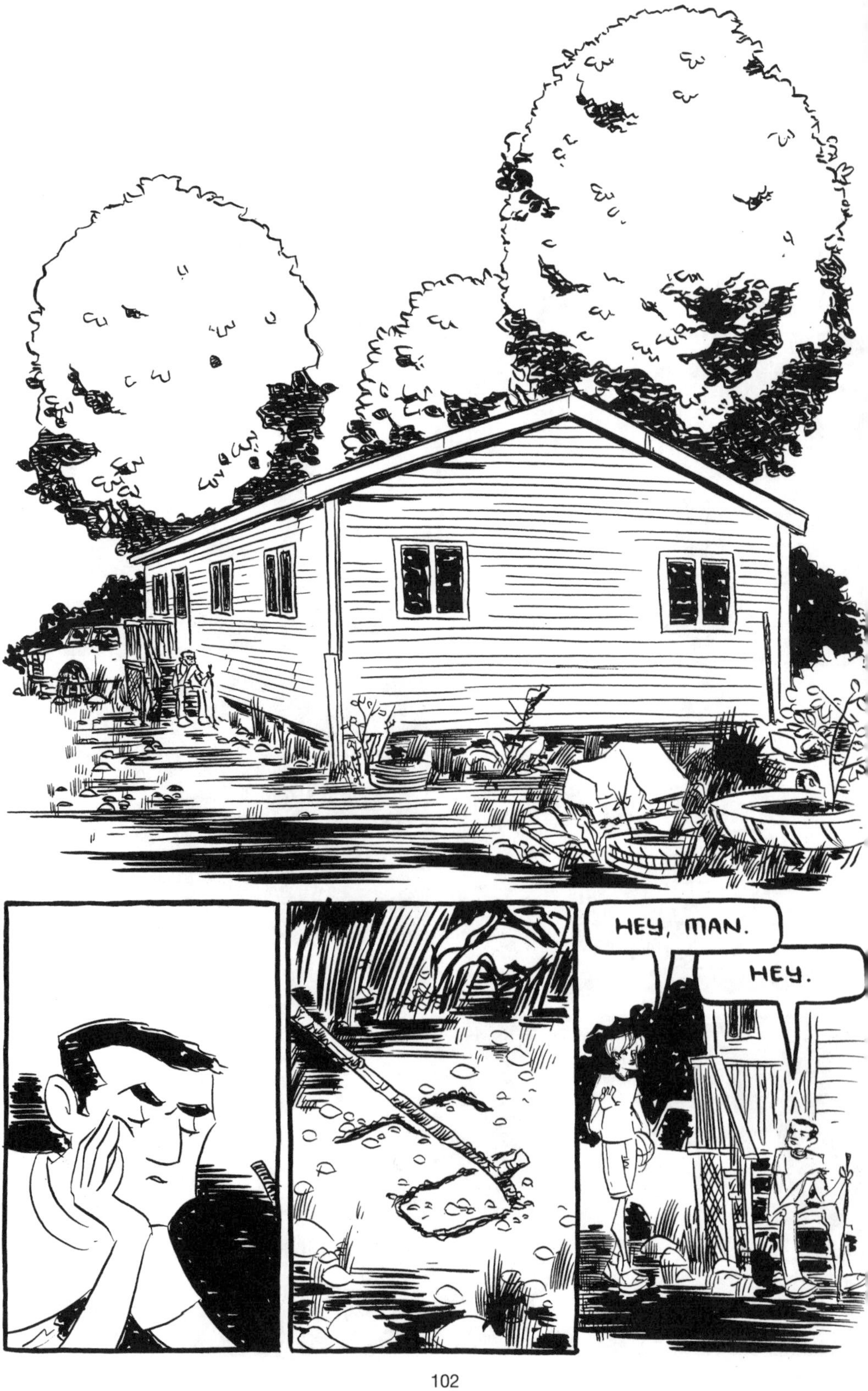
HEY, MAN.
HEY.

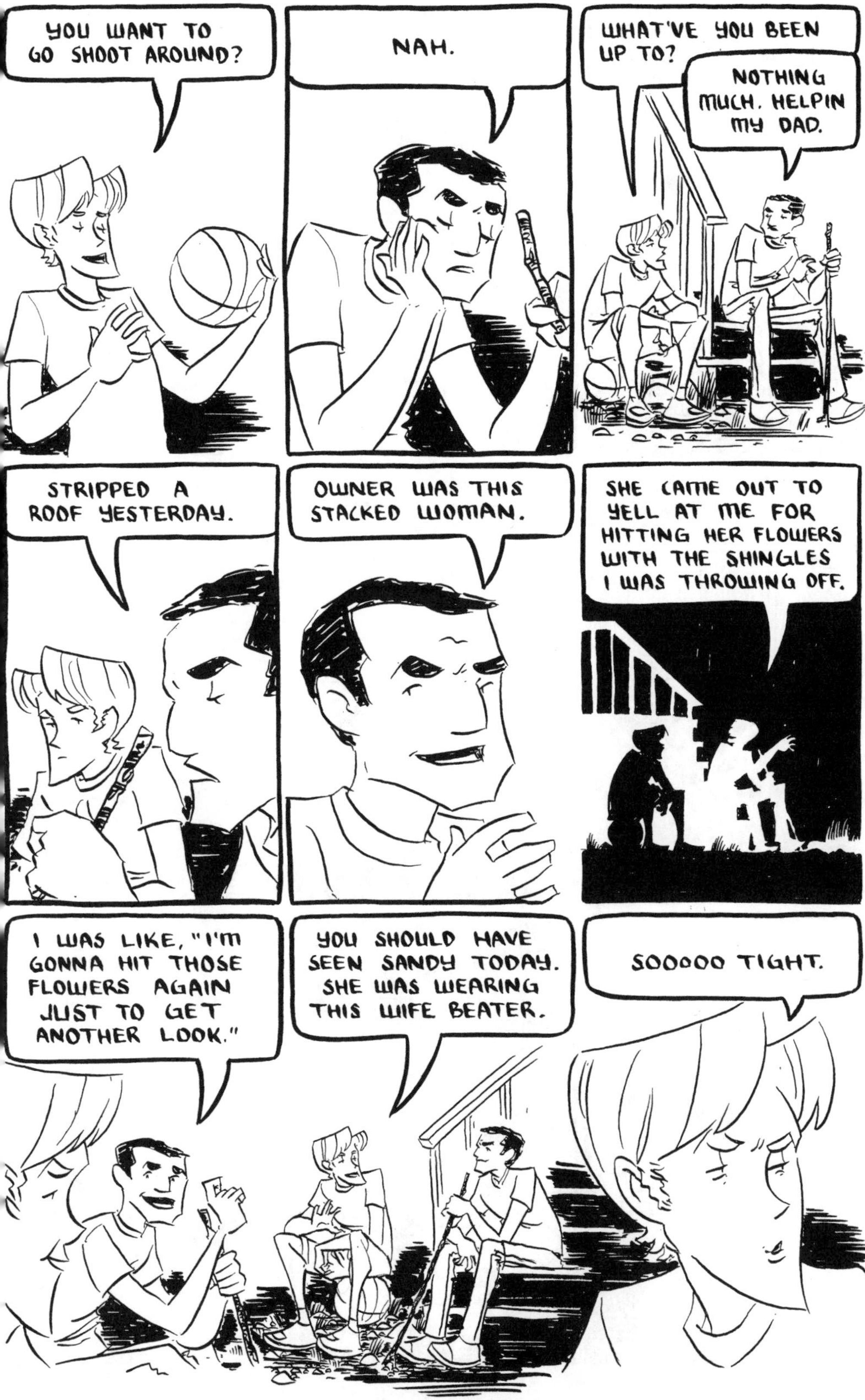
YOU WANT TO GO SHOOT AROUND?
NAH.
WHAT'VE YOU BEEN UP TO?
NOTHING MUCH. HELPIN MY DAD.
STRIPPED A ROOF YESTERDAY.
OWNER WAS THIS STACKED WOMAN.
SHE CAME OUT TO YELL AT ME FOR HITTING HER FLOWERS WITH THE SHINGLES I WAS THROWING OFF.
I WAS LIKE, "I'M GONNA HIT THOSE FLOWERS AGAIN JUST TO GET ANOTHER LOOK."
YOU SHOULD HAVE SEEN SANDY TODAY. SHE WAS WEARING THIS WIFE BEATER.
SOOOOO TIGHT.

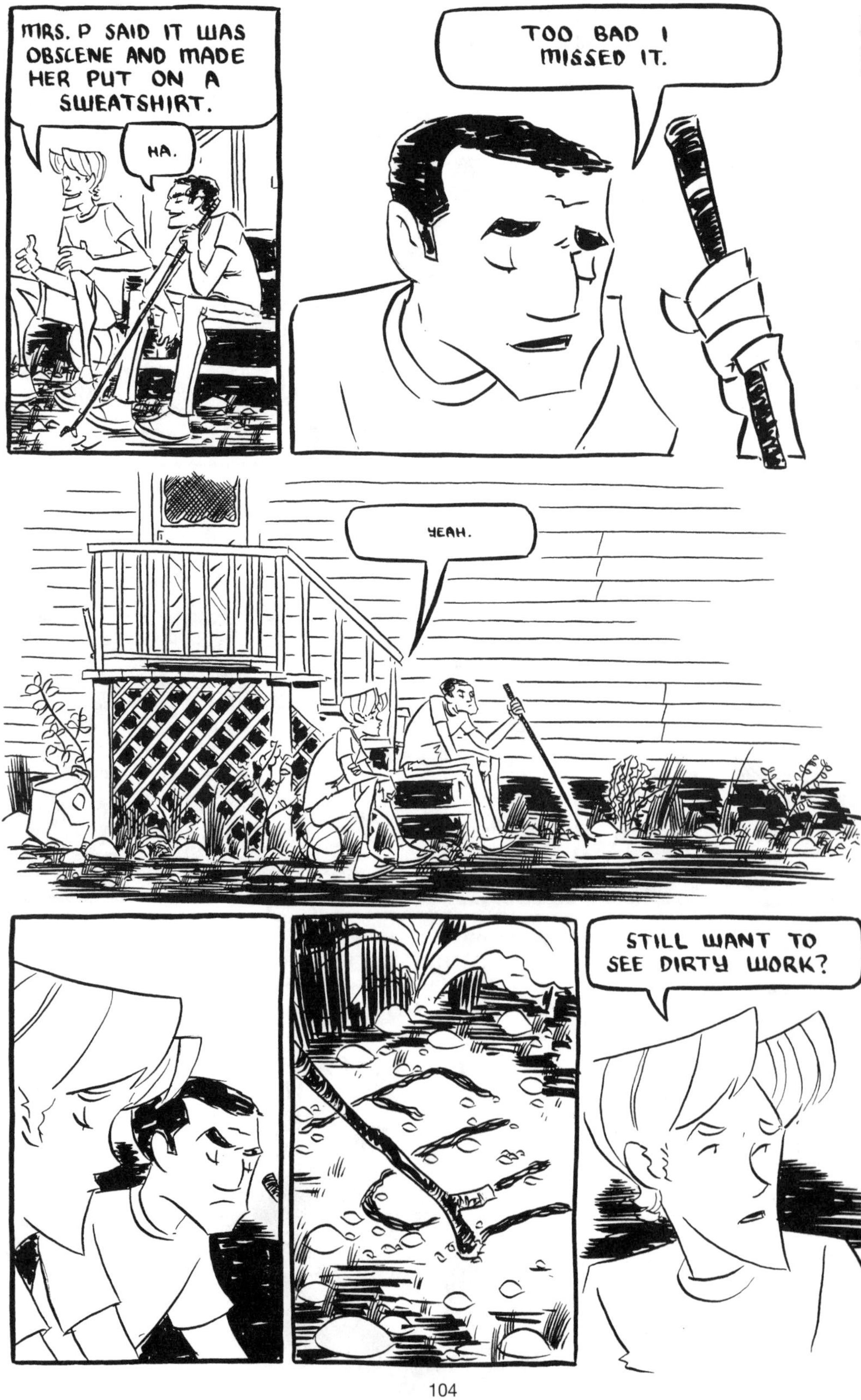
MRS. P SAID IT WAS OBSCENE AND MADE HER PUT ON A SWEATSHIRT.
HA.
TOO BAD I MISSED IT.
YEAH.
STILL WANT TO SEE DIRTY WORK?

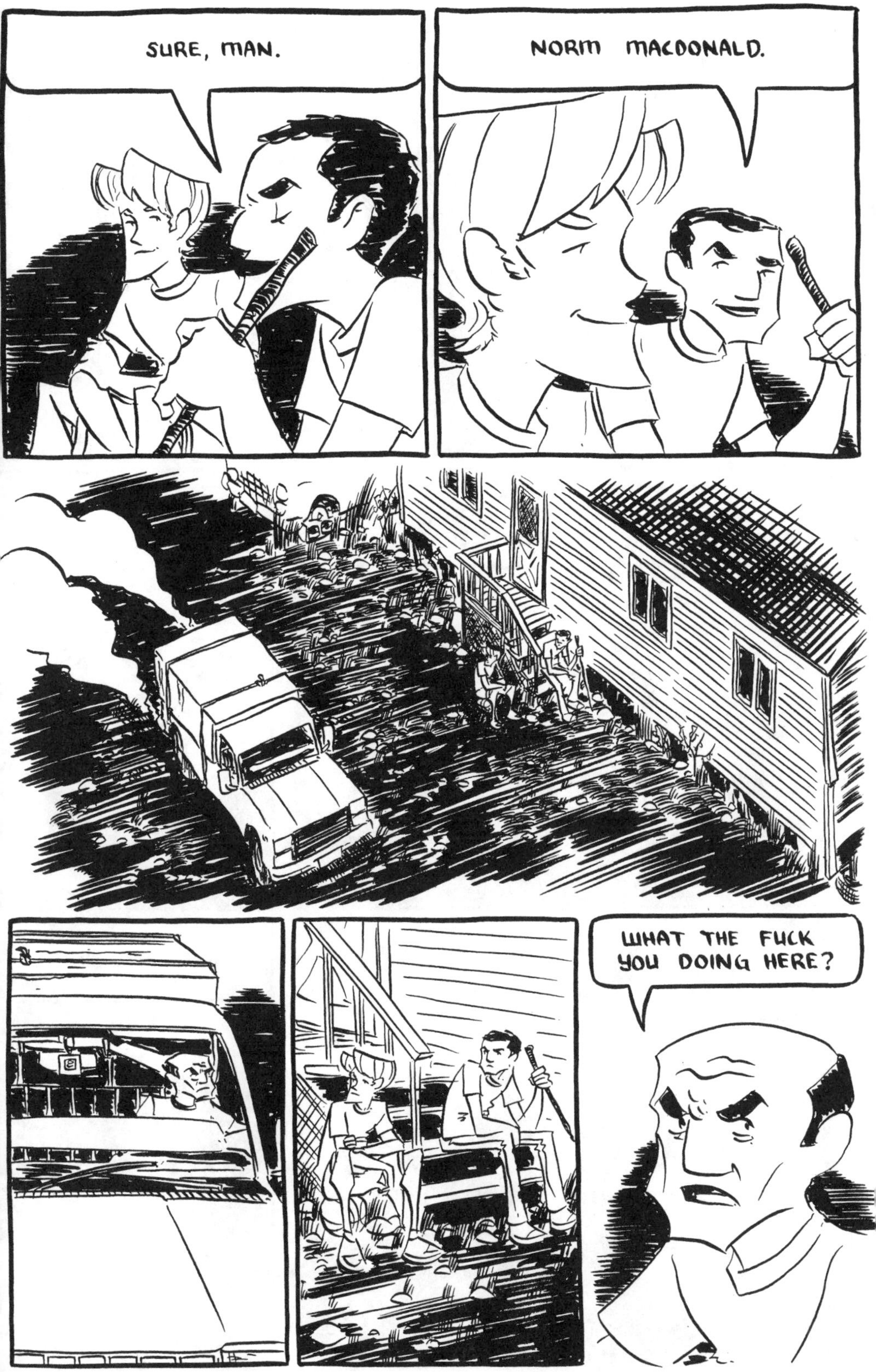
SURE, MAN.
NORM MACDONALD.
WHAT THE FUCK YOU DOING HERE?

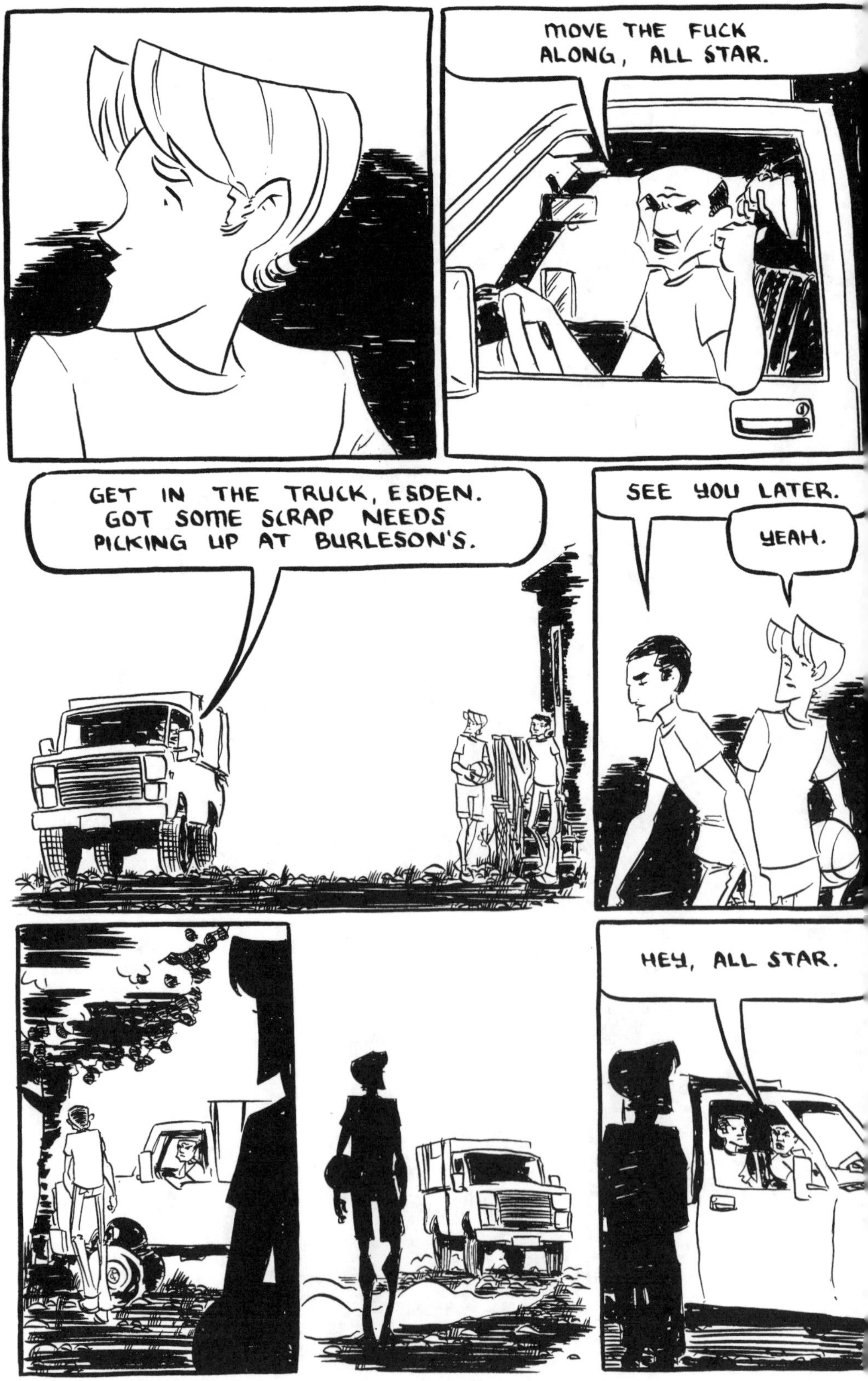
MOVE THE FUCK ALONG, ALL STAR.
GET IN THE TRUCK, ESDEN. GOT SOME SCRAP NEEDS PICKING UP AT BURLESON'S.
SEE YOU LATER.
YEAH.
HEY, ALL STAR.

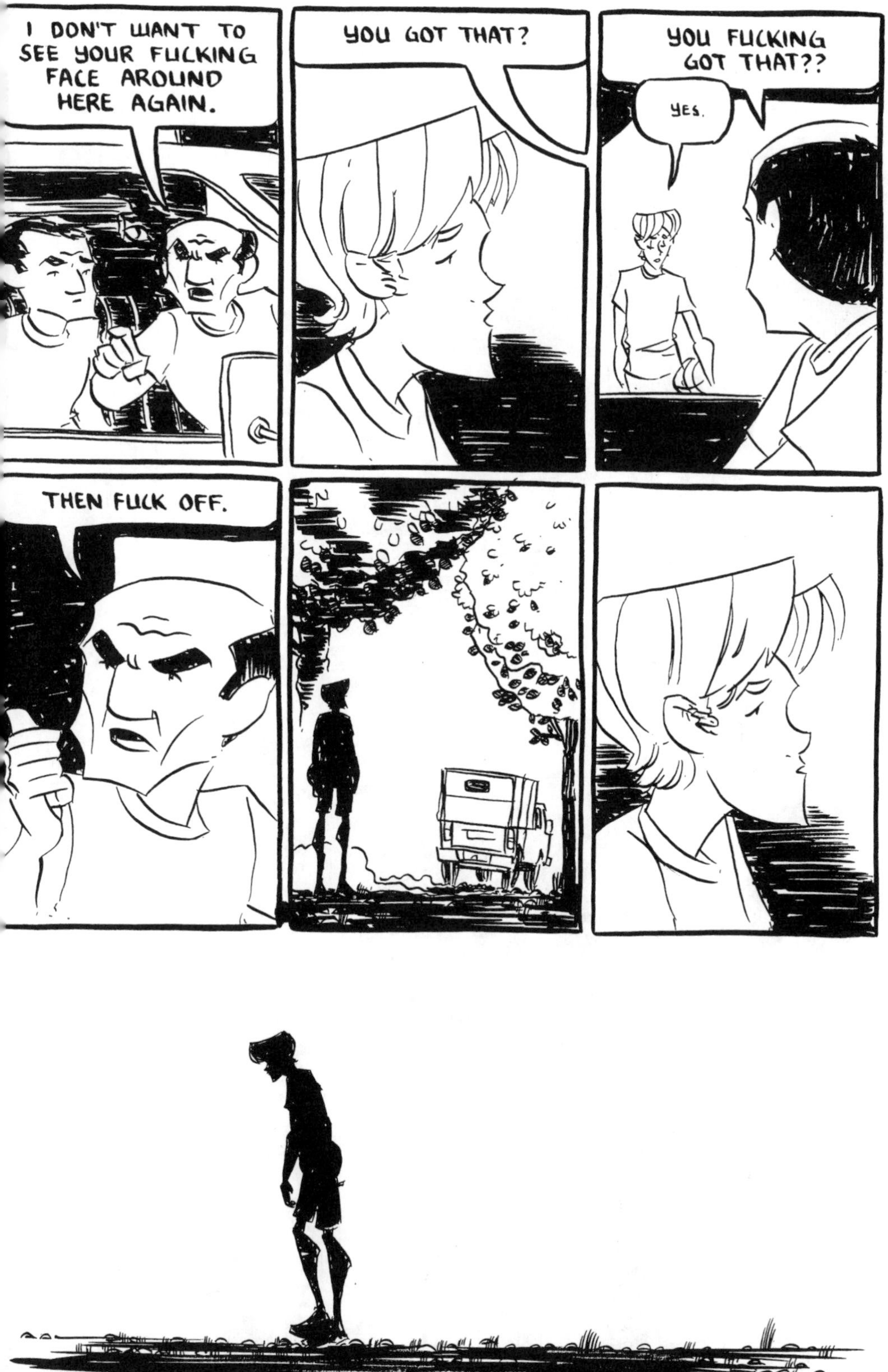
I DON'T WANT TO SEE YOUR FUCKING FACE AROUND HERE AGAIN.
YOU GOT THAT?
YOU FUCKING GOT THAT??
YES.
THEN FUCK OFF.

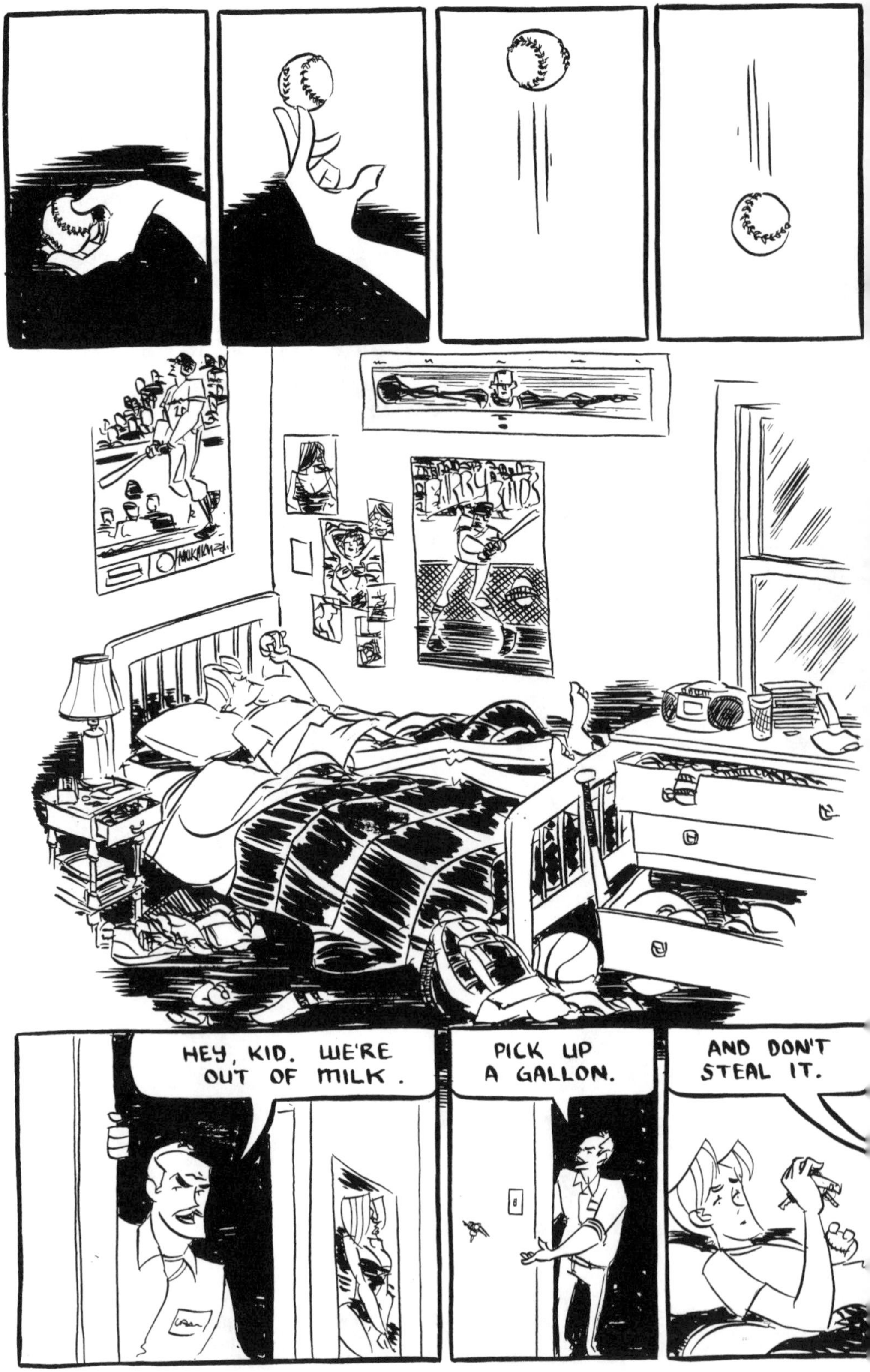
HEY, KID. WE'RE OUT OF MILK.
PICK UP A GALLON.
AND DON'T STEAL IT.

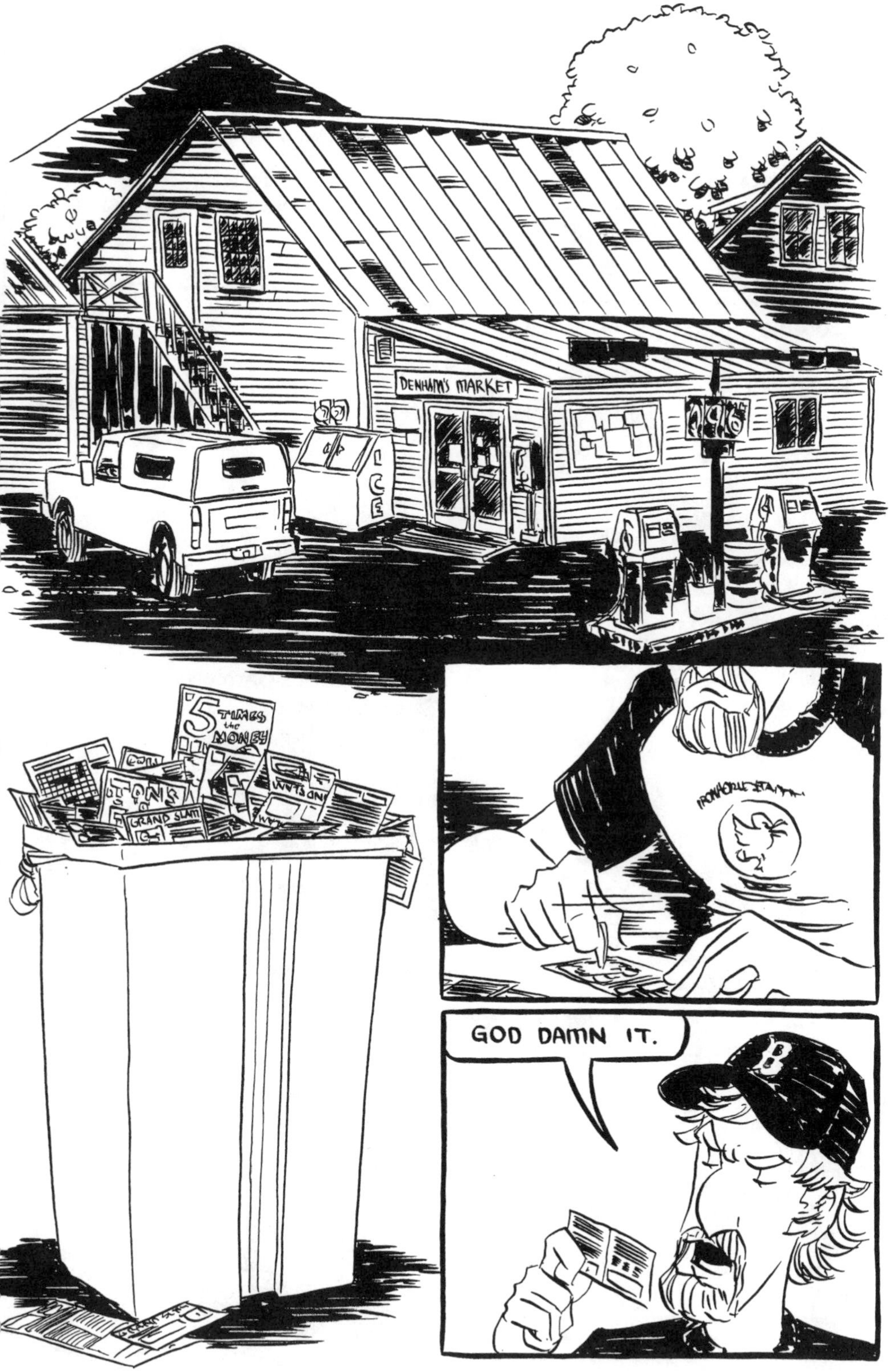

DENHAM'S MARKET
ICE
5 TIMES the MONEY
GRAND SLAM
GOD DAMN IT.

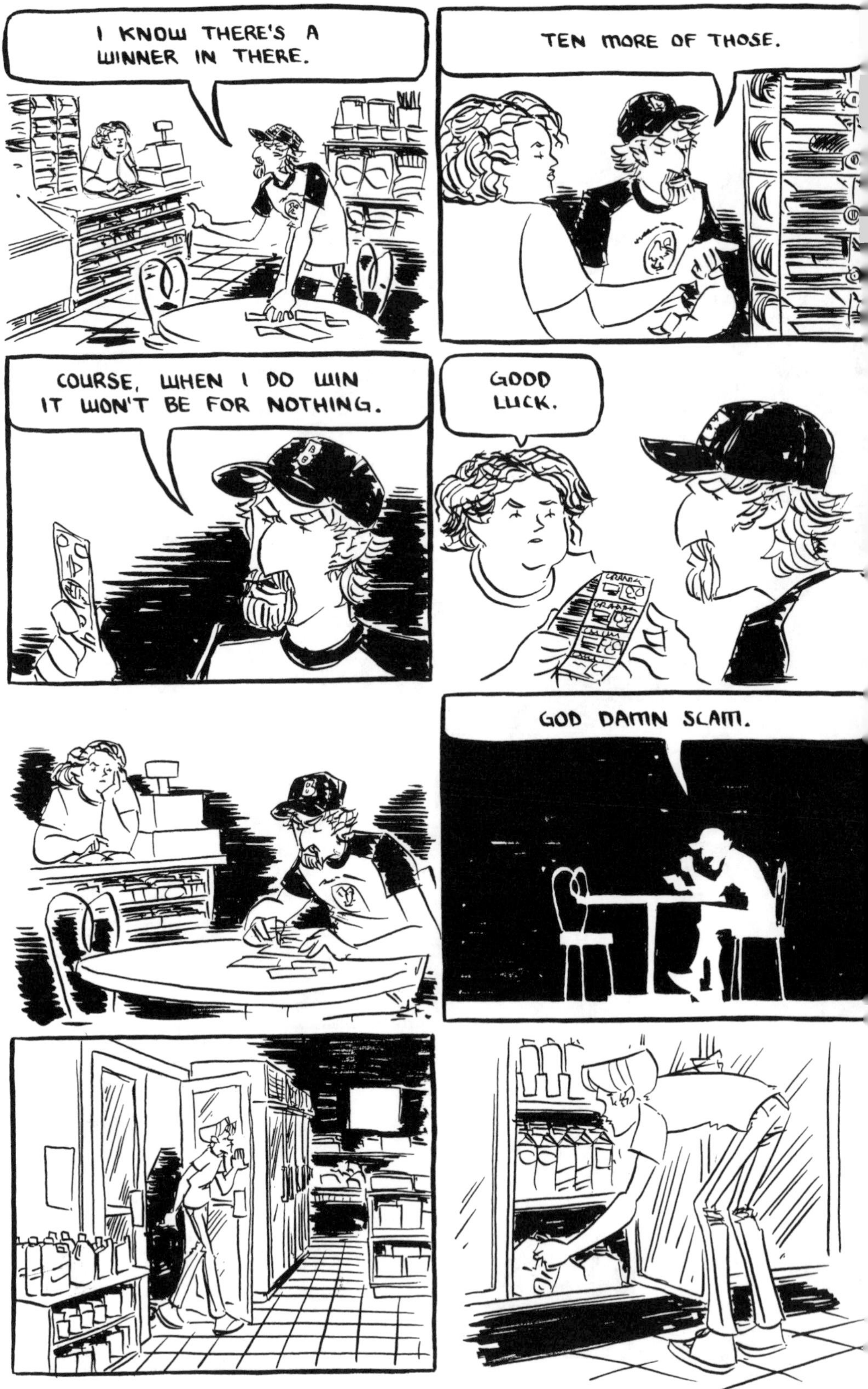
I KNOW THERE'S A WINNER IN THERE.
TEN MORE OF THOSE.
COURSE, WHEN I DO WIN IT WON'T BE FOR NOTHING.
GOOD LUCK.
GOD DAMN SCAM.

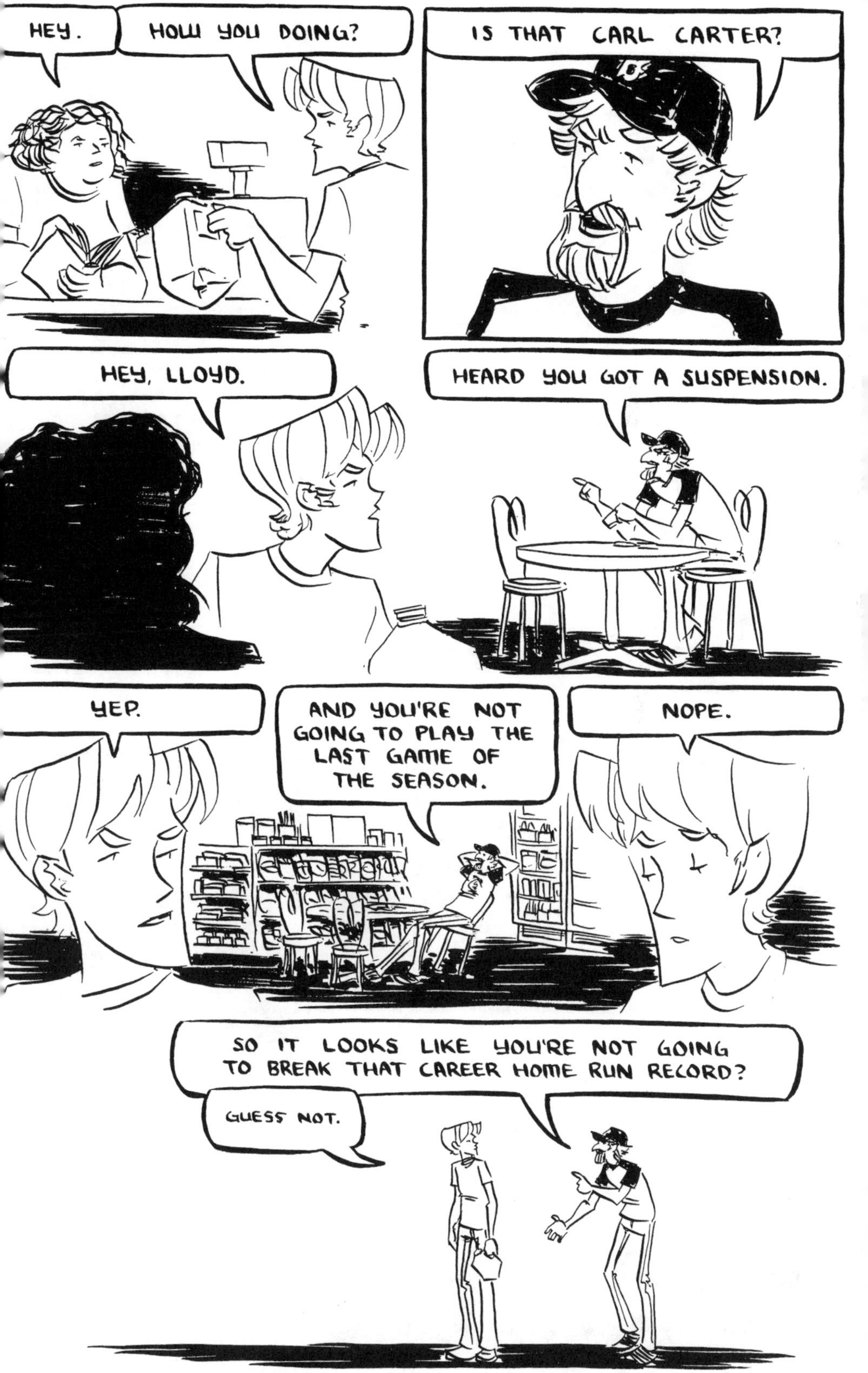
HEY.
HOW YOU DOING?
IS THAT CARL CARTER?
HEY, LLOYD.
HEARD YOU GOT A SUSPENSION.
YEP.
AND YOU'RE NOT GOING TO PLAY THE LAST GAME OF THE SEASON.
NOPE.
SO IT LOOKS LIKE YOU'RE NOT GOING TO BREAK THAT CAREER HOME RUN RECORD?
GUESS NOT.

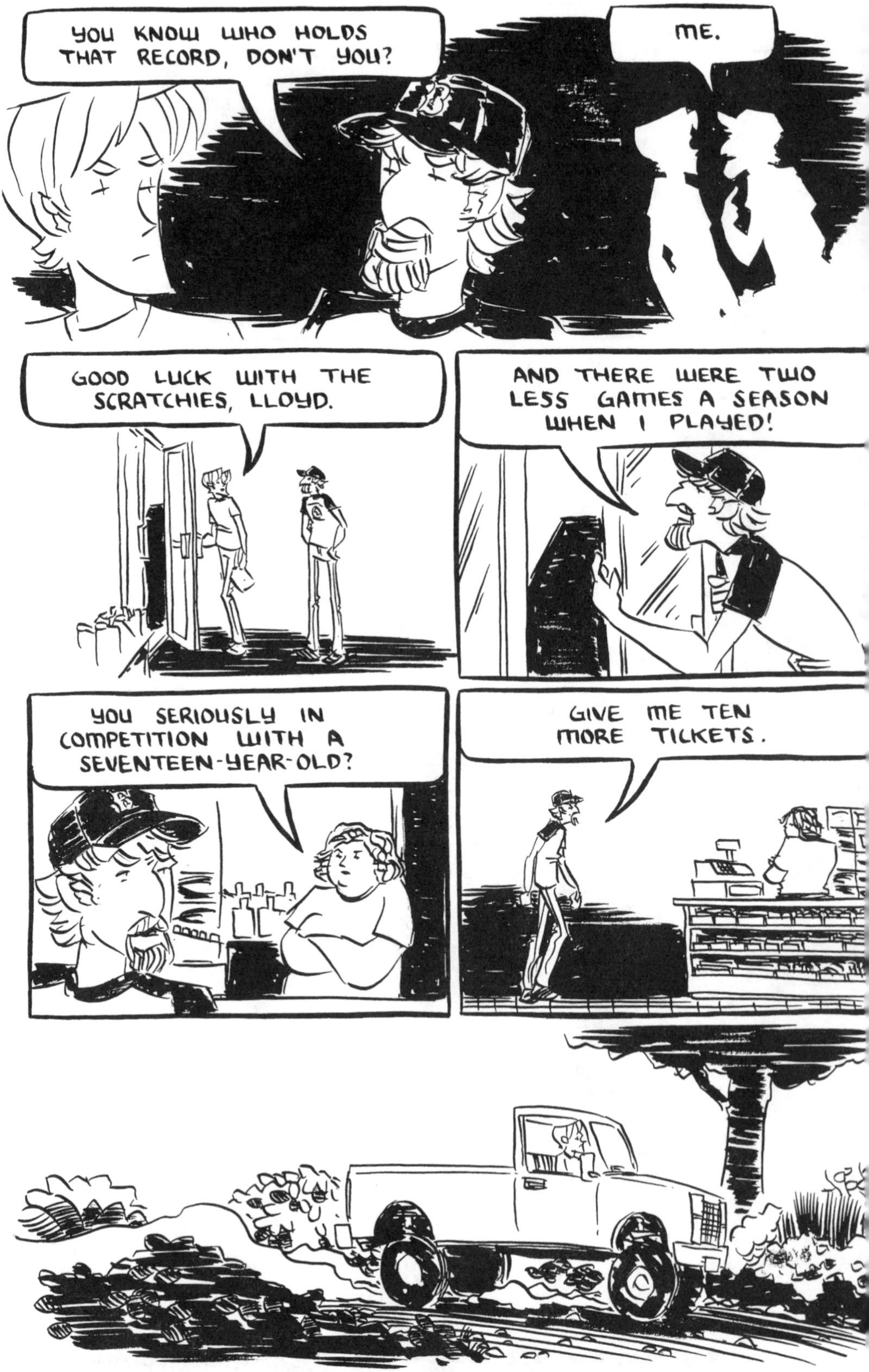
YOU KNOW WHO HOLDS THAT RECORD, DON'T YOU?
ME.
GOOD LUCK WITH THE SCRATCHIES, LLOYD.
AND THERE WERE TWO LESS GAMES A SEASON WHEN I PLAYED!
YOU SERIOUSLY IN COMPETITION WITH A SEVENTEEN-YEAR-OLD?
GIVE ME TEN MORE TICKETS.

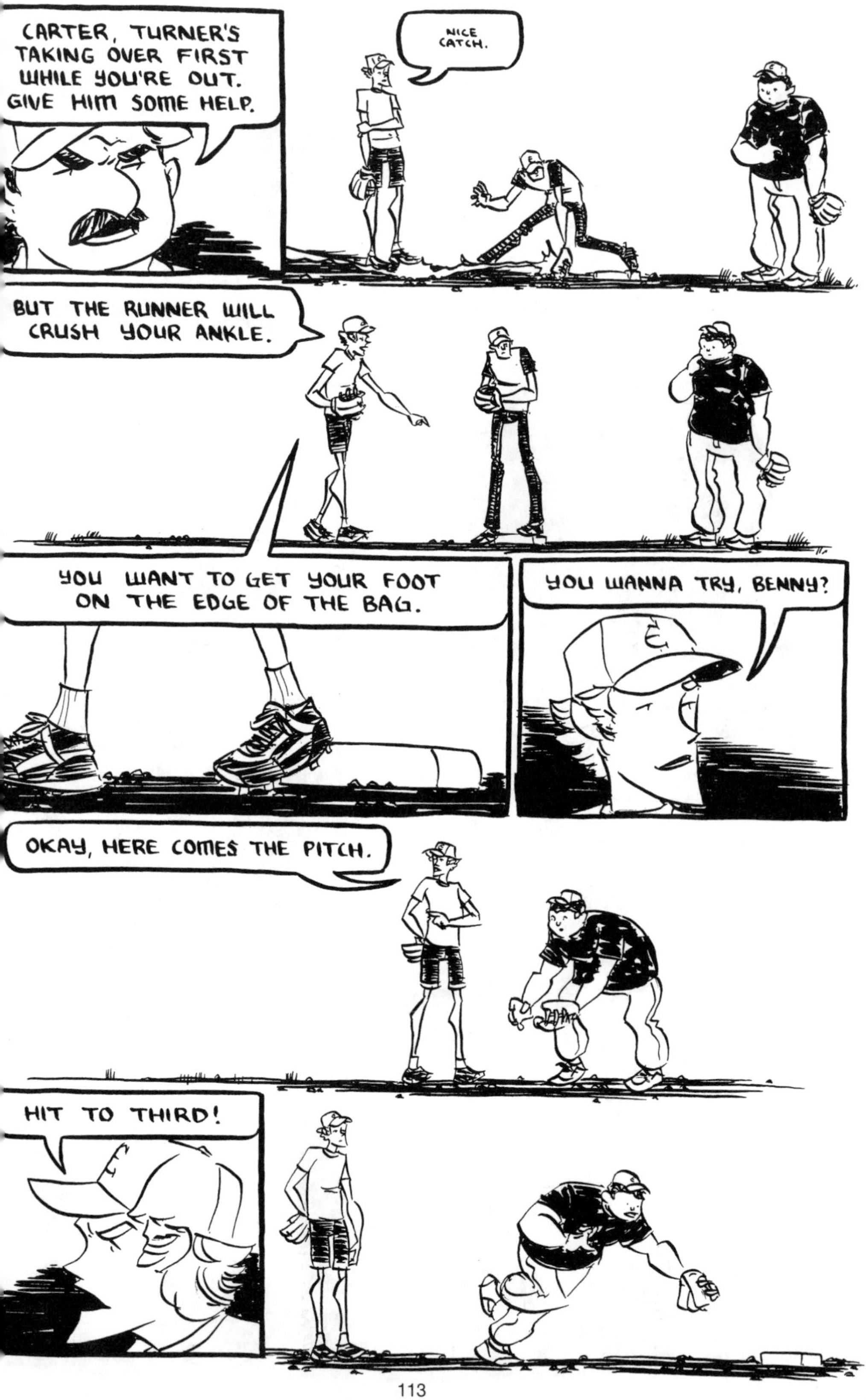
CARTER, TURNER'S TAKING OVER FIRST WHILE YOU'RE OUT. GIVE HIM SOME HELP.
NICE CATCH.
BUT THE RUNNER WILL CRUSH YOUR ANKLE.
YOU WANT TO GET YOUR FOOT ON THE EDGE OF THE BAG.
YOU WANNA TRY, BENNY?
OKAY, HERE COMES THE PITCH.
HIT TO THIRD!

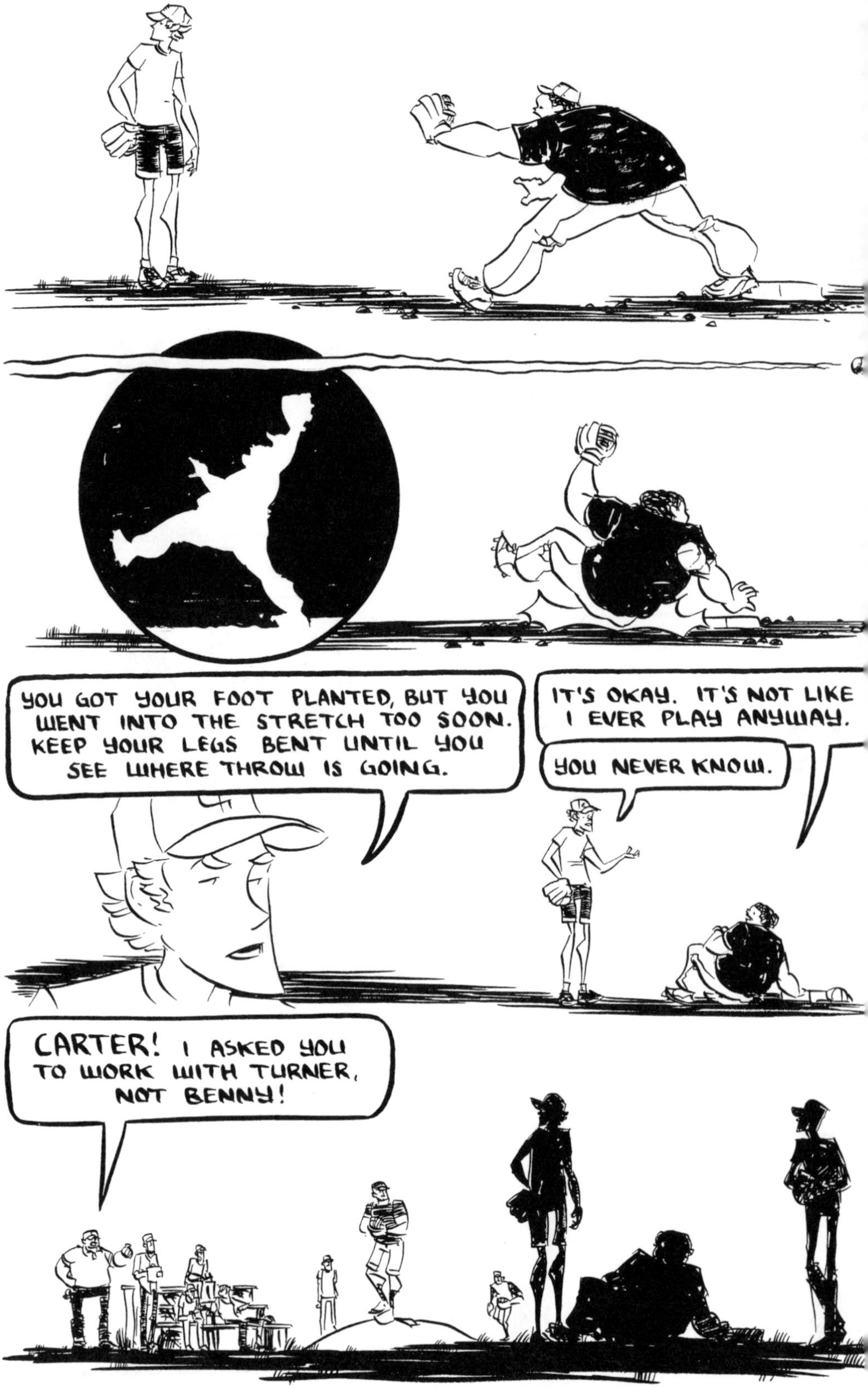
YOU GOT YOUR FOOT PLANTED, BUT YOU WENT INTO THE STRETCH TOO SOON. KEEP YOUR LEGS BENT UNTIL YOU SEE WHERE THROW IS GOING.
IT'S OKAY. IT'S NOT LIKE I EVER PLAY ANYWAY.
YOU NEVER KNOW.
CARTER! I ASKED YOU TO WORK WITH TURNER, NOT BENNY!

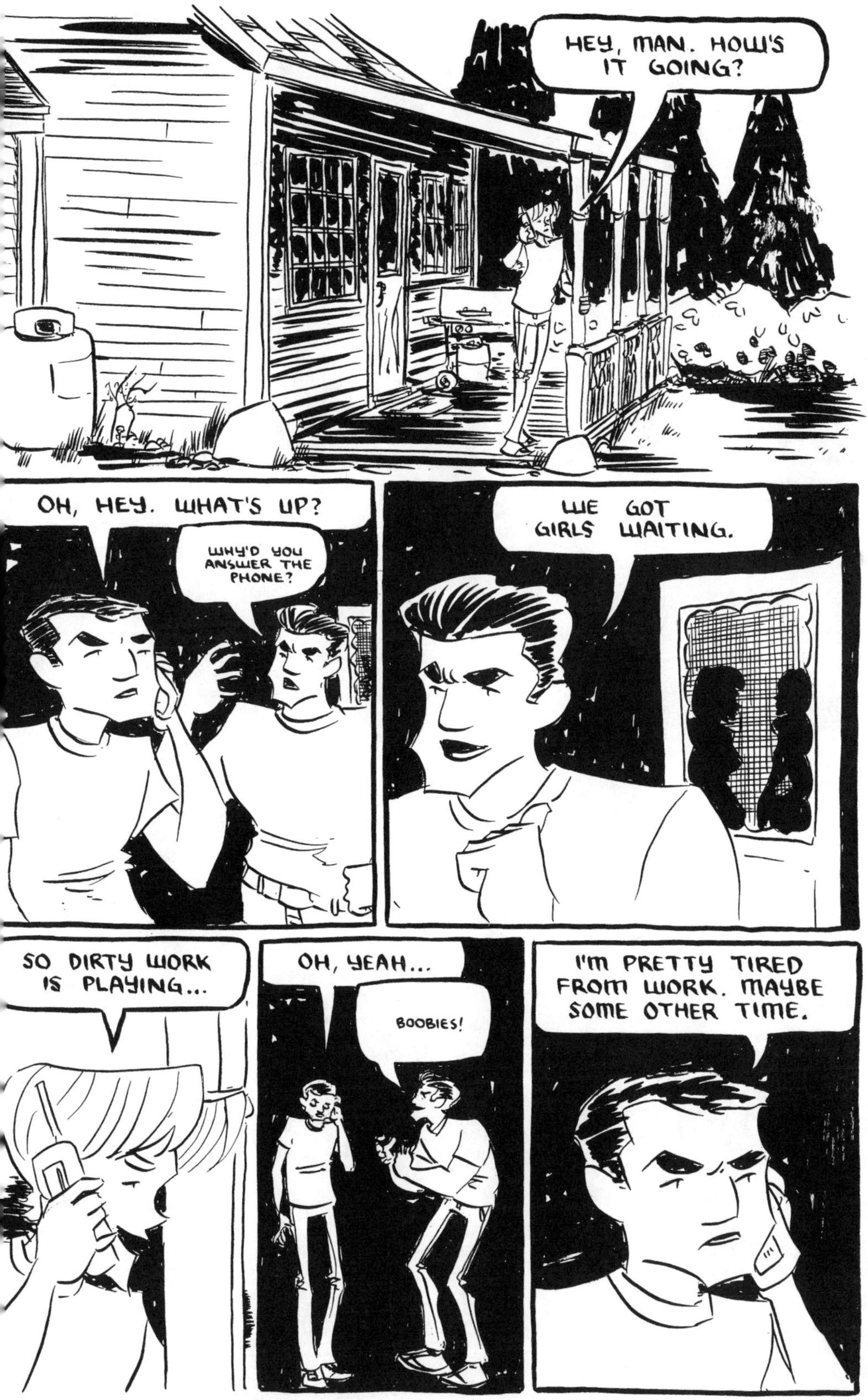
HEY, MAN. HOW'S IT GOING?
OH, HEY. WHAT'S UP?
WHY'D YOU ANSWER THE PHONE?
WE GOT GIRLS WAITING.
SO DIRTY WORK IS PLAYING...
OH, YEAH...
BOOBIES!
I'M PRETTY TIRED FROM WORK. MAYBE SOME OTHER TIME.

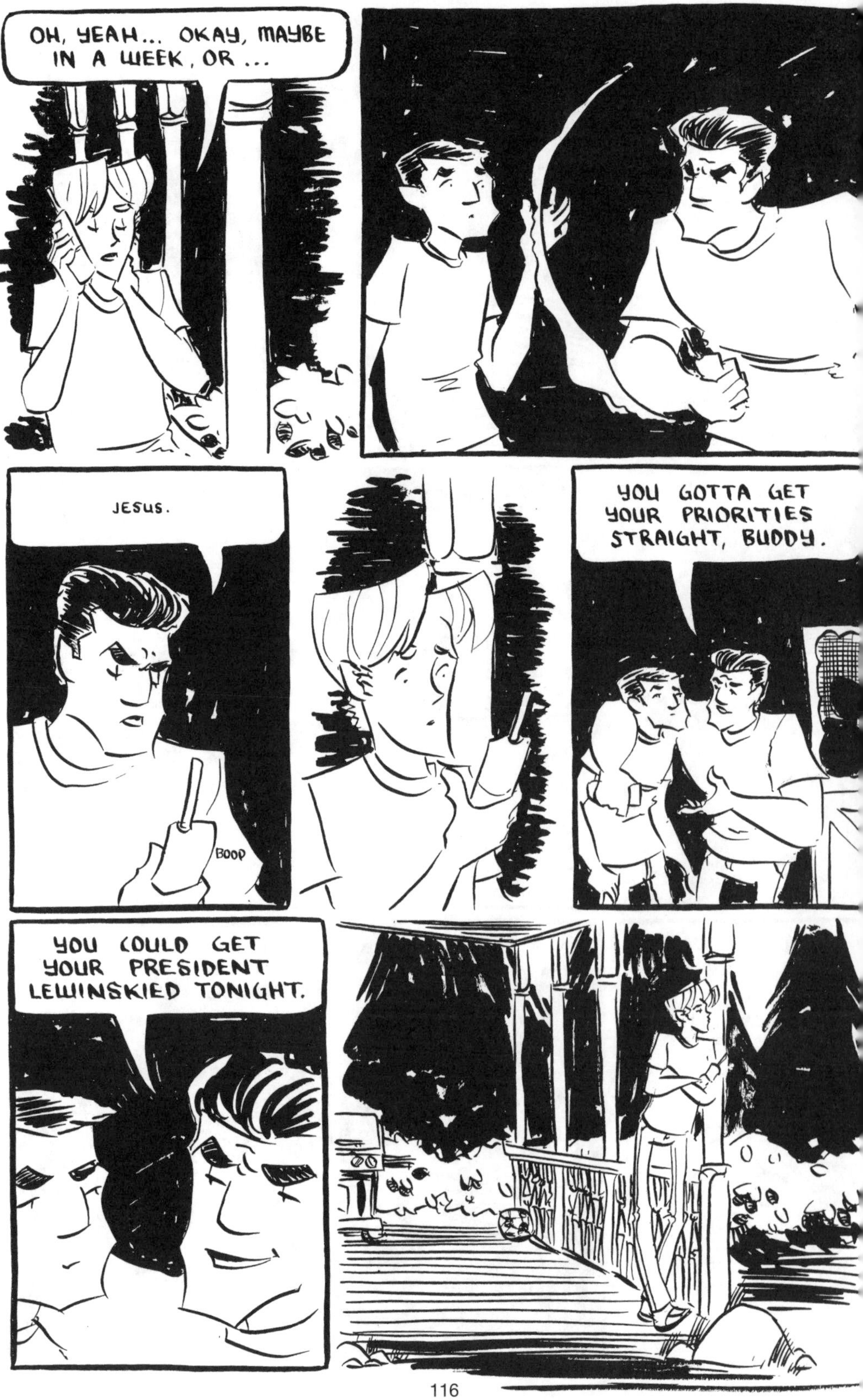
OH, YEAH... OKAY, MAYBE IN A WEEK, OR ...
JESUS.
BOOP
YOU GOTTA GET YOUR PRIORITIES STRAIGHT, BUDDY.
YOU COULD GET YOUR PRESIDENT LEWINSKIED TONIGHT.

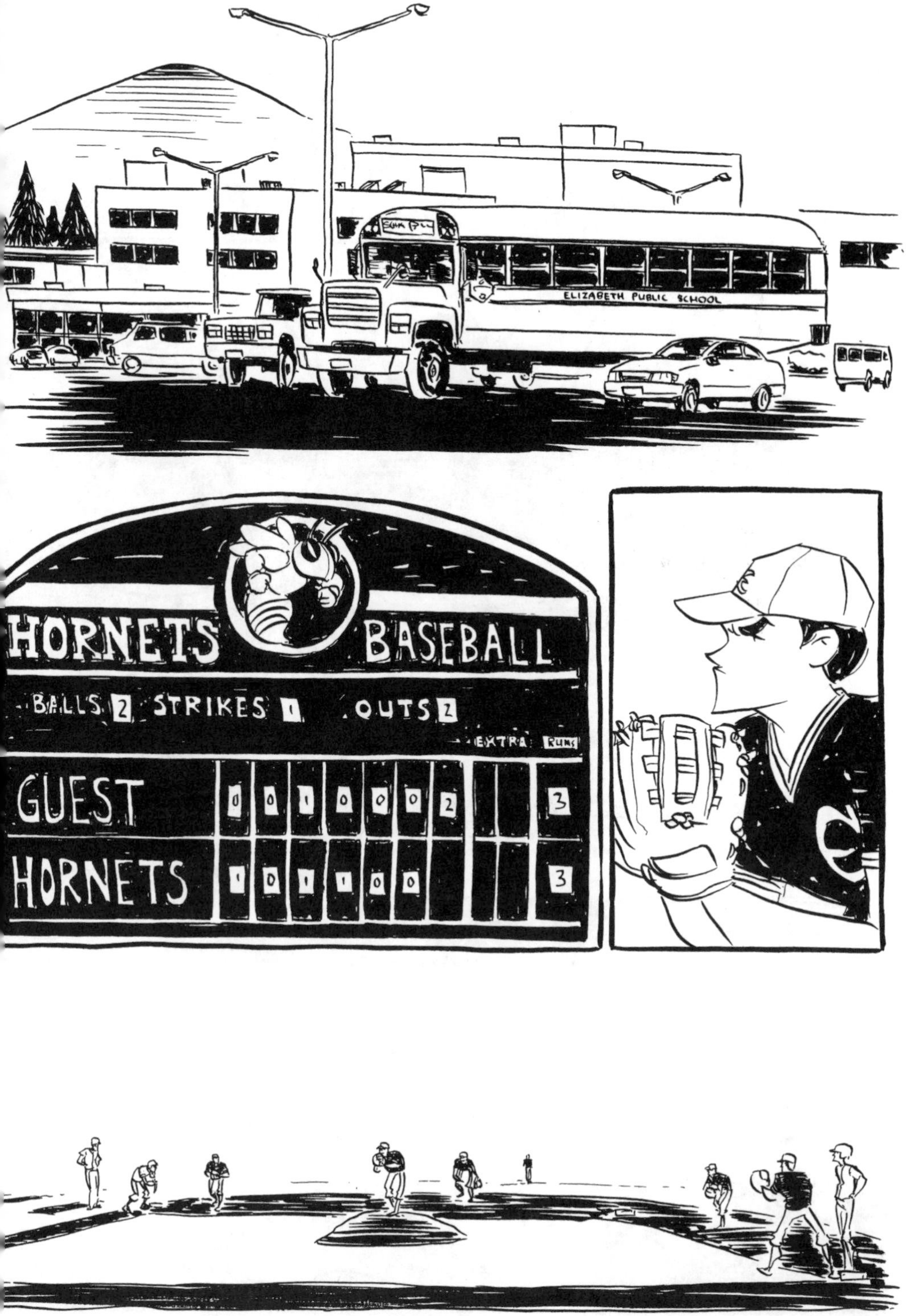
ELIZABETH PUBLIC SCHOOL
HORNETS
BASEBALL
BALLS 2 STRIKES 1 OUTS 2
EXTRA RUNS
GUEST 0 0 1 0 0 0 2 3
HORNETS 1 0 1 1 0 0 3

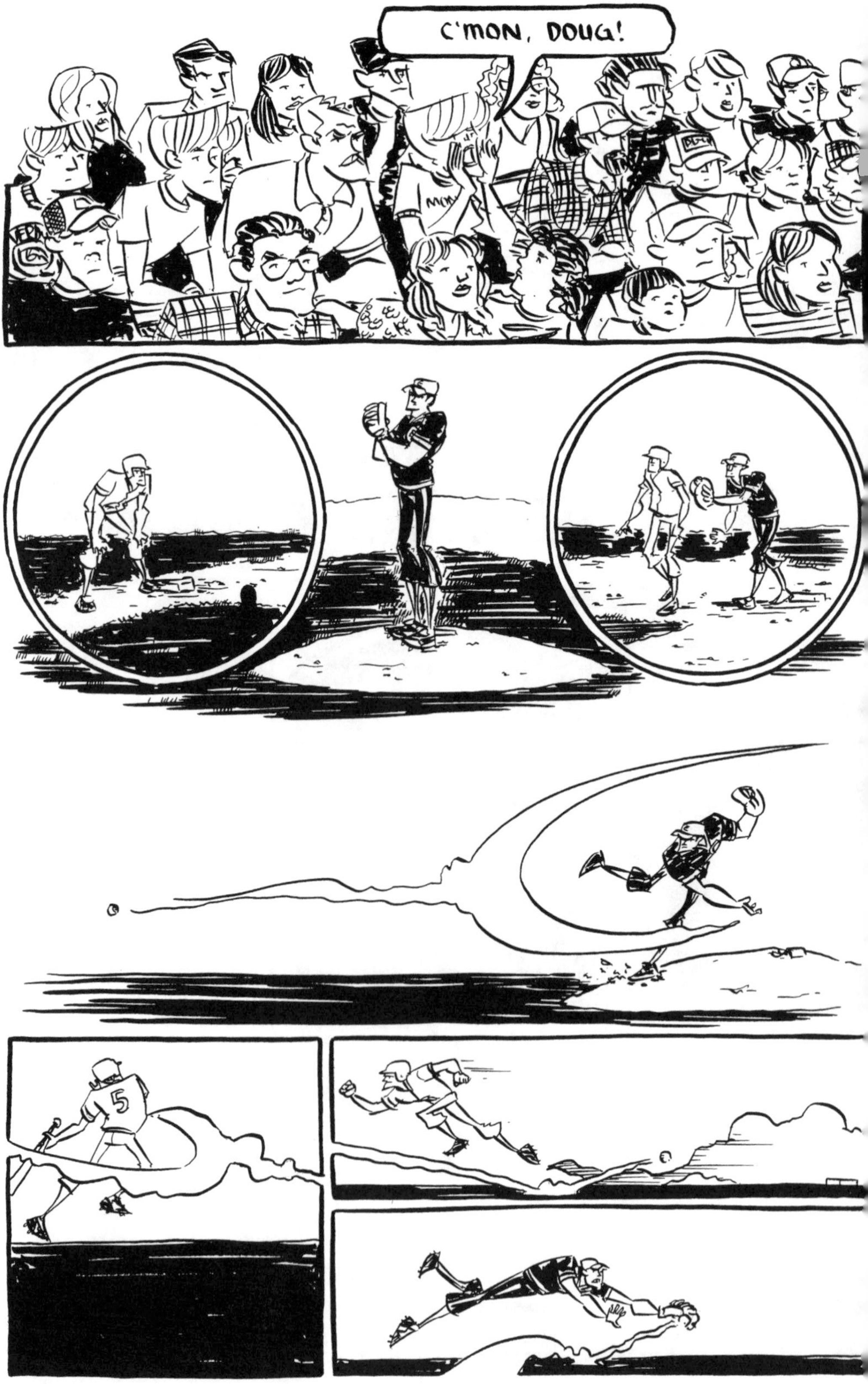
C'MON, DOUG!

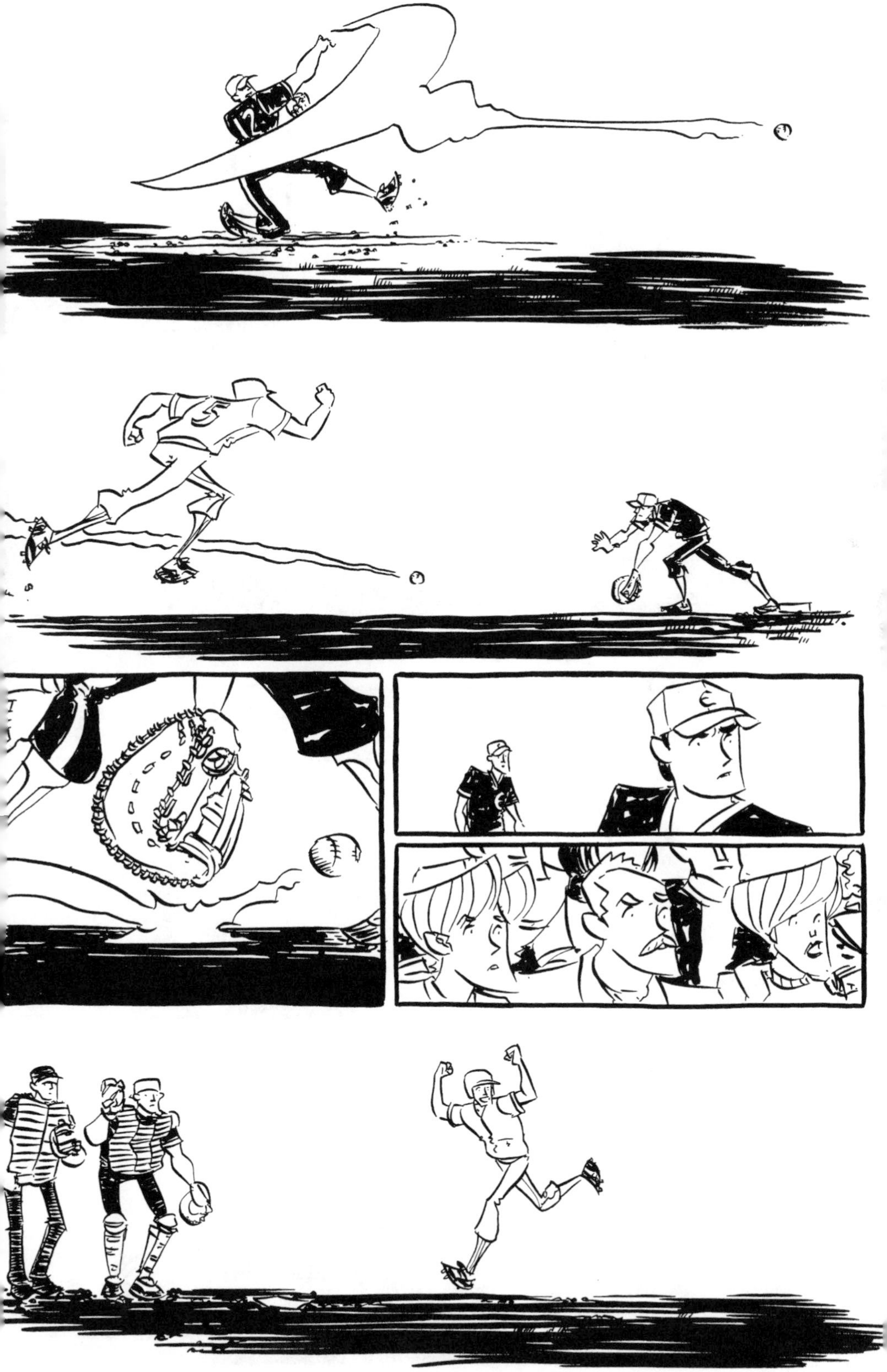

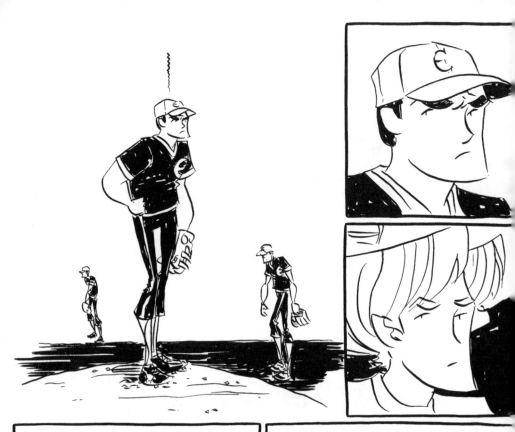

I THINK YOU WOULD HAVE CAUGHT THAT THROW.

YOU JUST BETTER BE READY FOR THE PLAYOFFS.

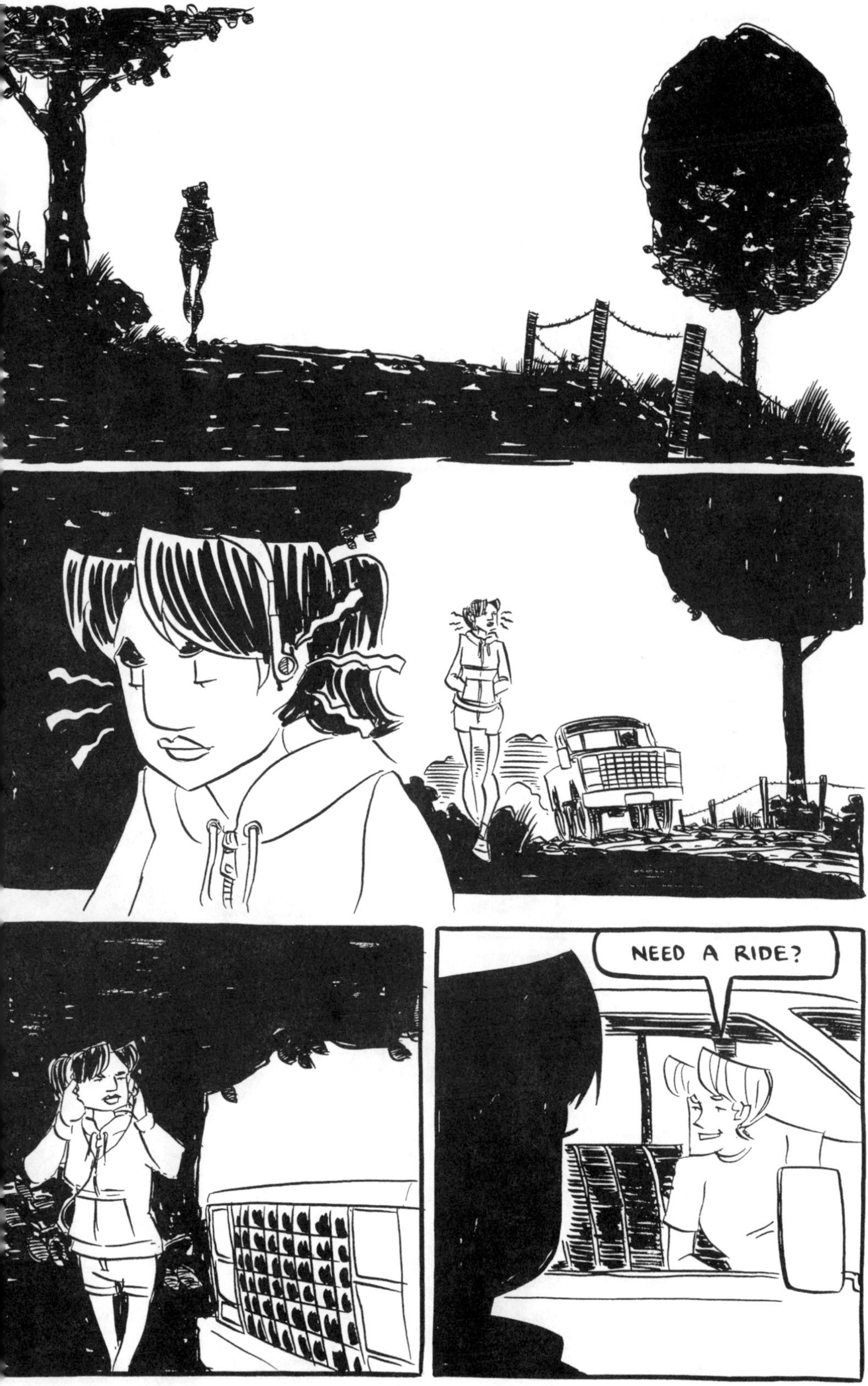
NEED A RIDE?

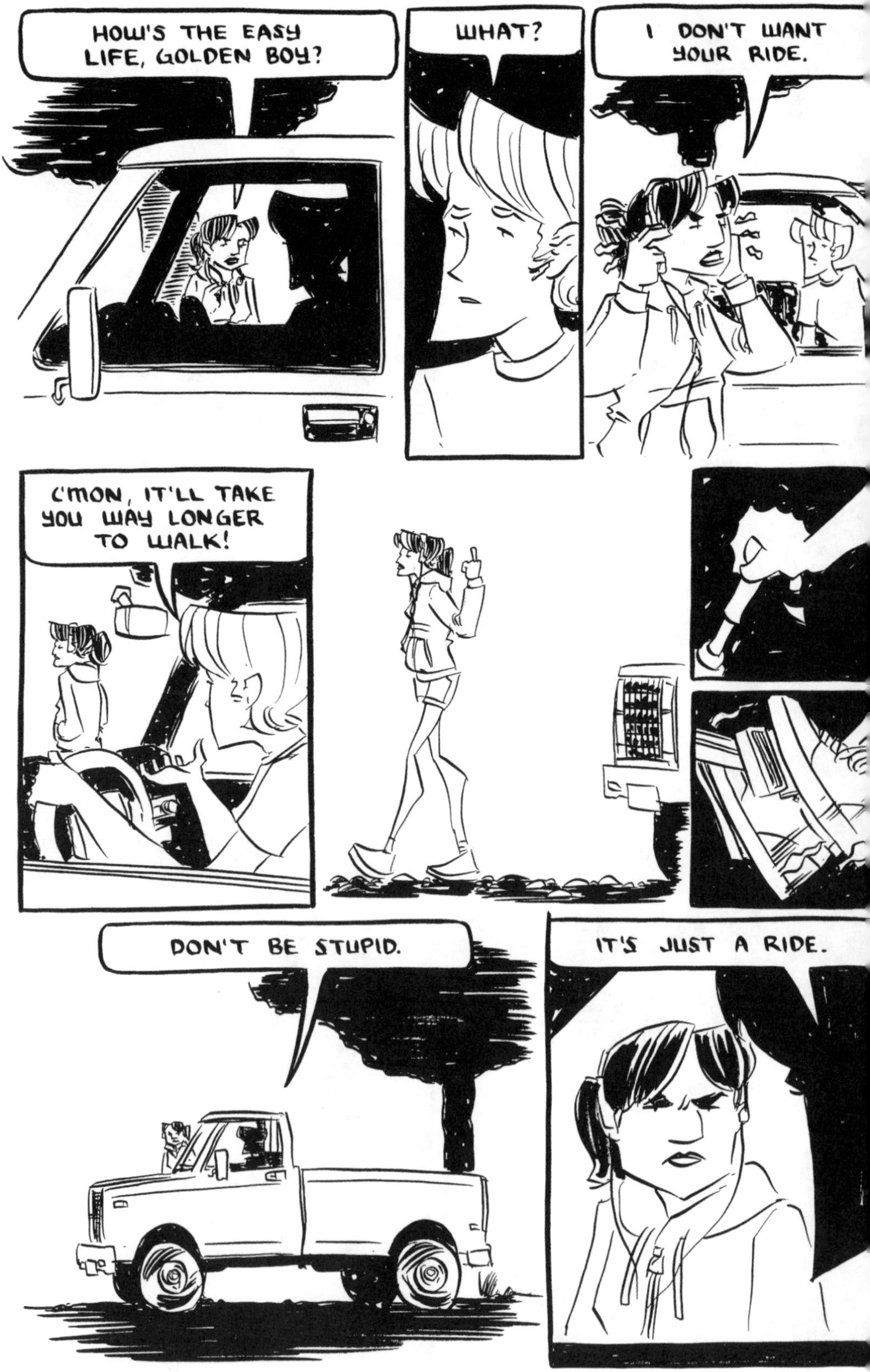
HOW'S THE EASY LIFE, GOLDEN BOY?
WHAT?
I DON'T WANT YOUR RIDE.
C'MON, IT'LL TAKE YOU WAY LONGER TO WALK!
DON'T BE STUPID.
IT'S JUST A RIDE.

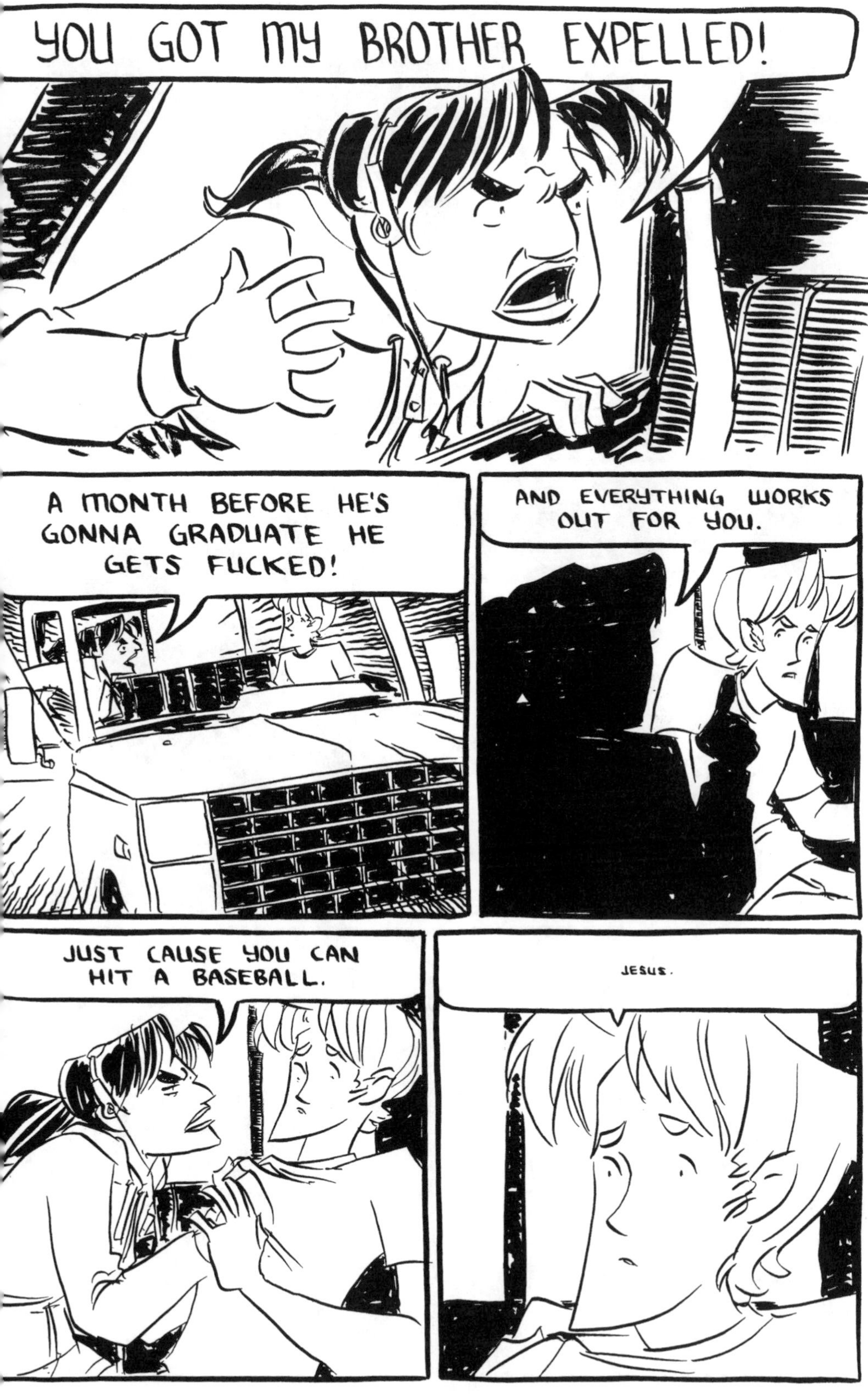
YOU GOT MY BROTHER EXPELLED!
A MONTH BEFORE HE'S GONNA GRADUATE HE GETS FUCKED!
AND EVERYTHING WORKS OUT FOR YOU.
JUST CAUSE YOU CAN HIT A BASEBALL.
JESUS.

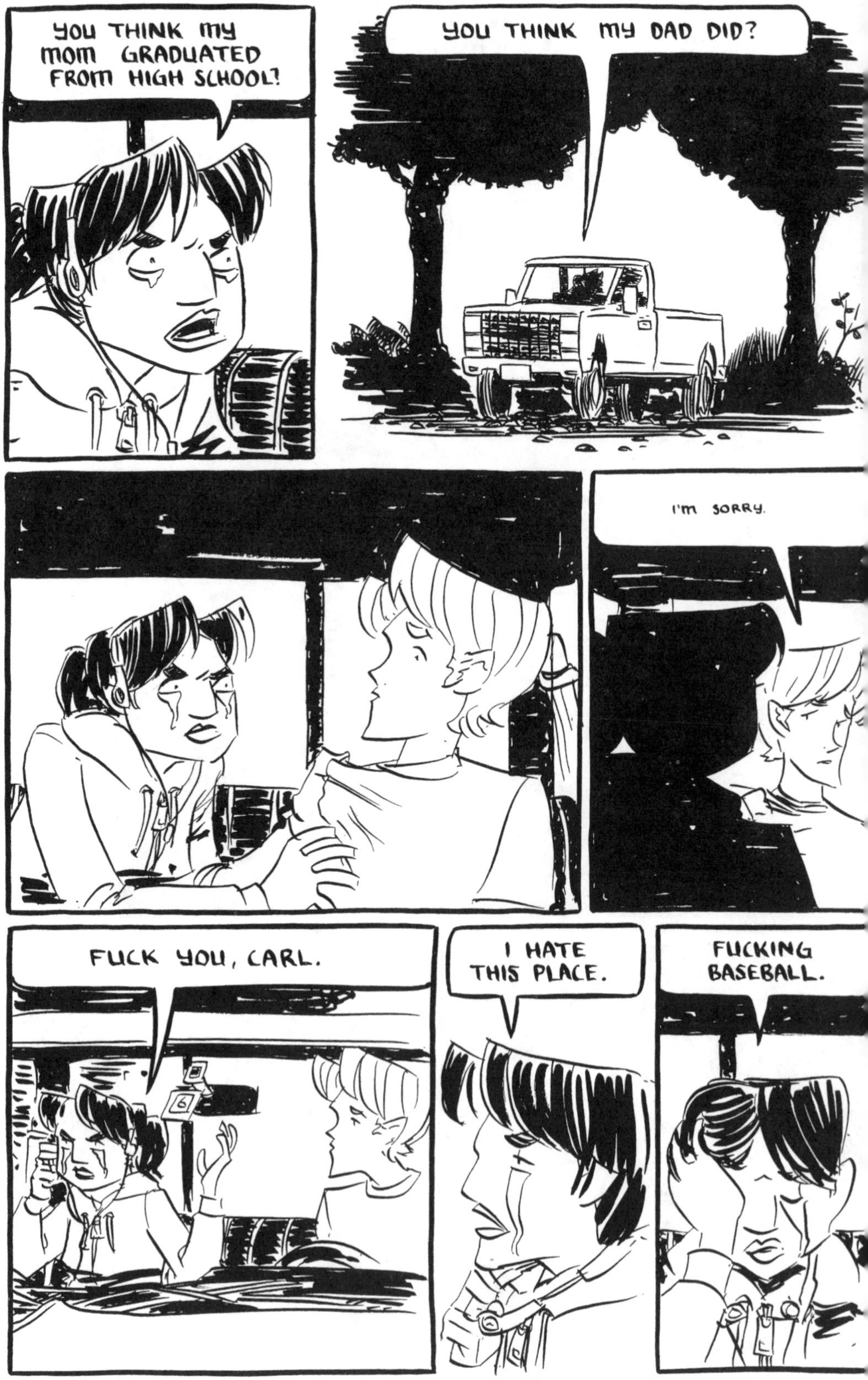
YOU THINK MY MOM GRADUATED FROM HIGH SCHOOL?
YOU THINK MY DAD DID?
I'M SORRY.
FUCK YOU, CARL.
I HATE THIS PLACE.
FUCKING BASEBALL.

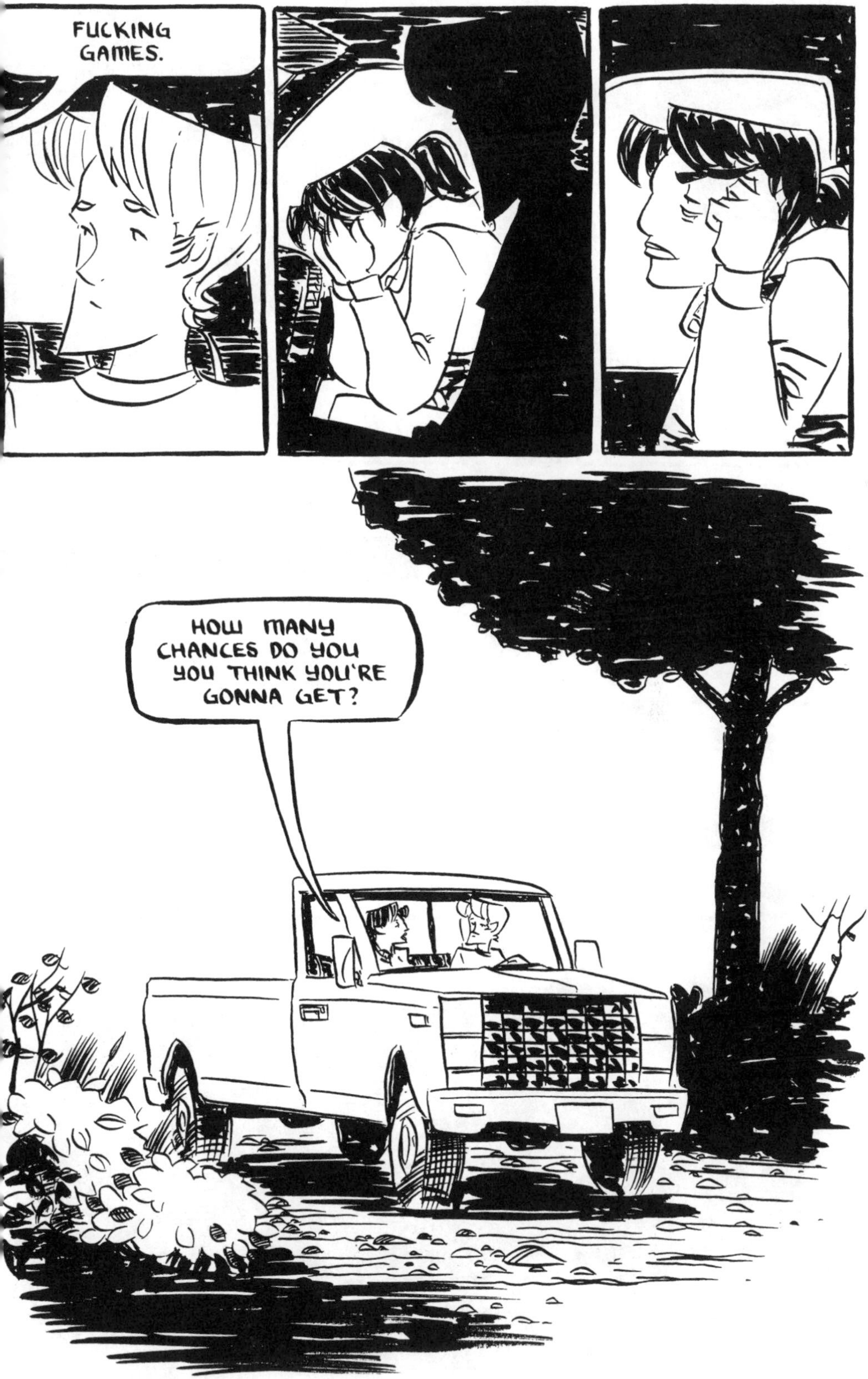
FUCKING GAMES.
HOW MANY CHANCES DO YOU YOU THINK YOU'RE GONNA GET?

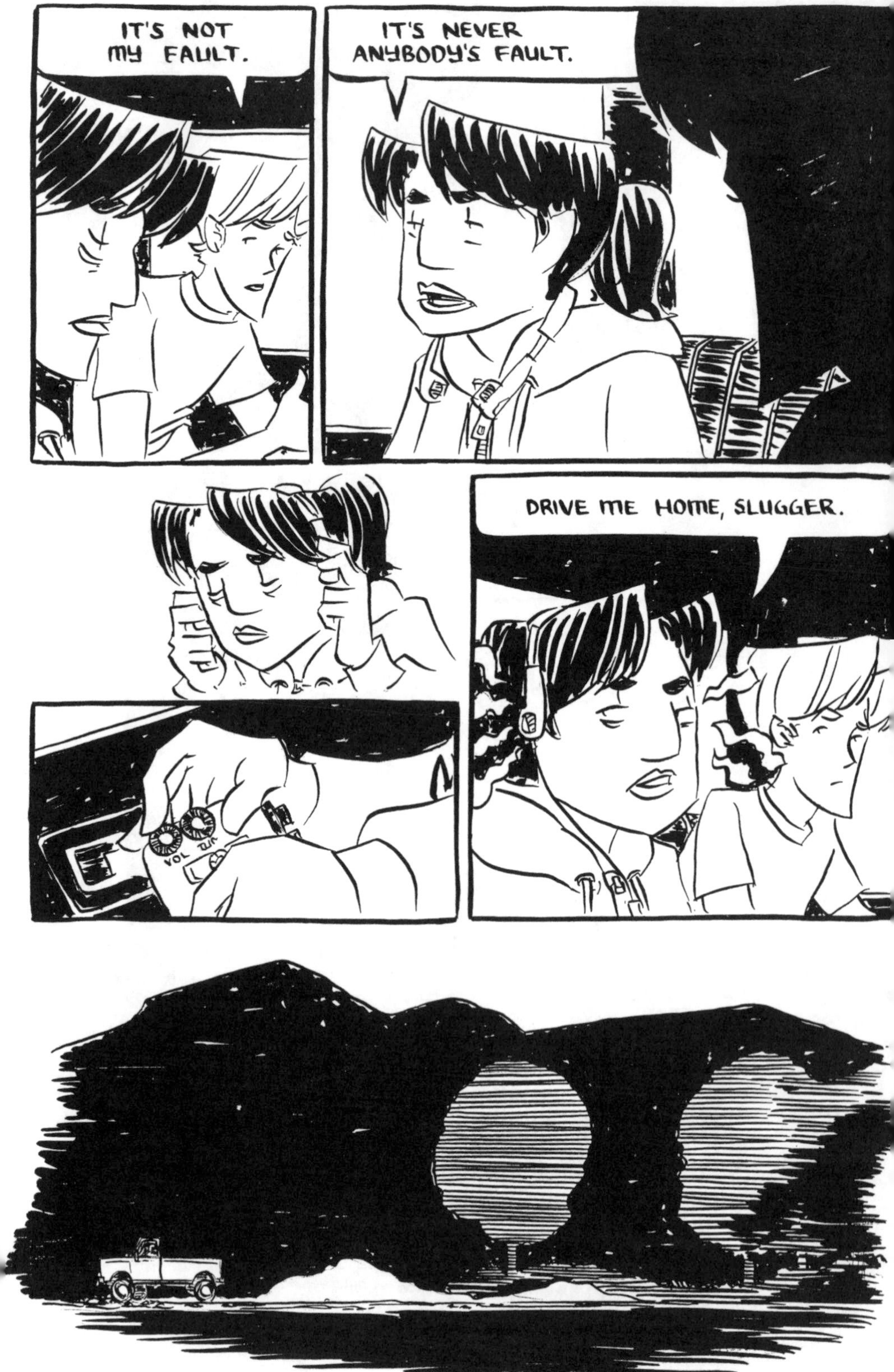
IT'S NOT MY FAULT.
IT'S NEVER ANYBODY'S FAULT.
DRIVE ME HOME, SLUGGER.
VOL

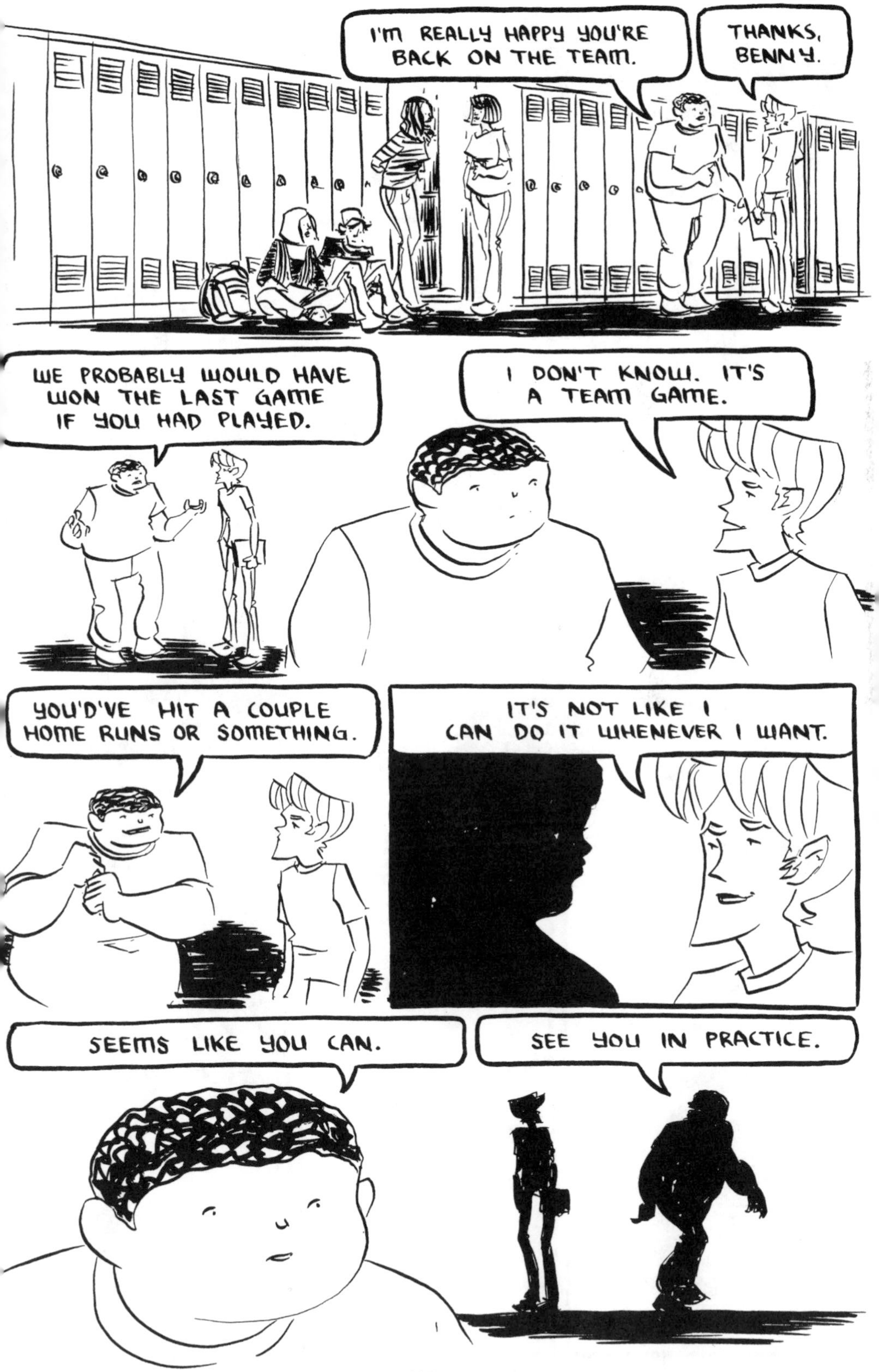
I'M REALLY HAPPY YOU'RE BACK ON THE TEAM.
THANKS, BENNY.
WE PROBABLY WOULD HAVE WON THE LAST GAME IF YOU HAD PLAYED.
I DON'T KNOW. IT'S A TEAM GAME.
YOU'D'VE HIT A COUPLE HOME RUNS OR SOMETHING.
IT'S NOT LIKE I CAN DO IT WHENEVER I WANT.
SEEMS LIKE YOU CAN.
SEE YOU IN PRACTICE.

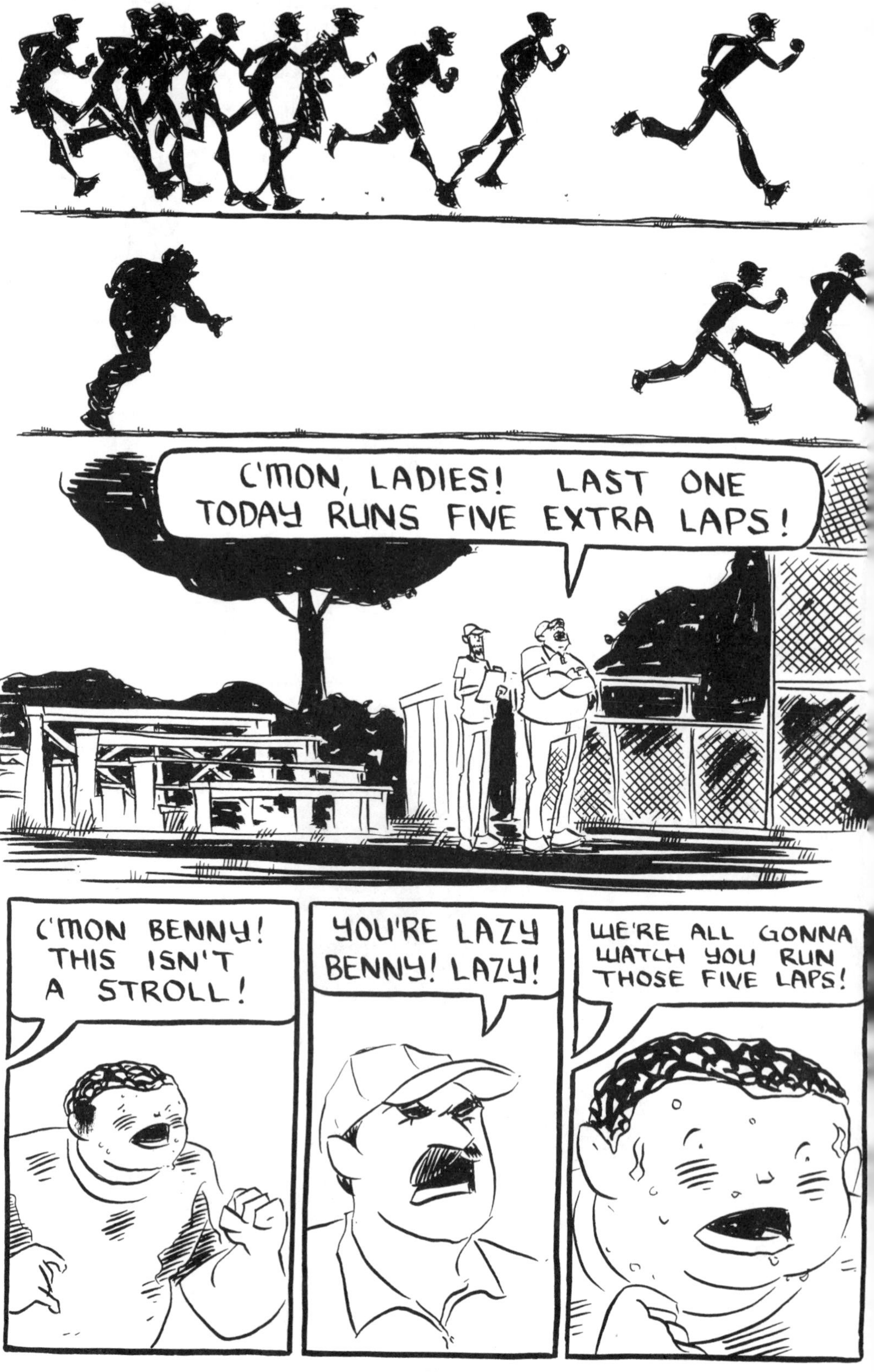
C'MON, LADIES! LAST ONE TODAY RUNS FIVE EXTRA LAPS!
C'MON BENNY! THIS ISN'T A STROLL!
YOU'RE LAZY BENNY! LAZY!
WE'RE ALL GONNA WATCH YOU RUN THOSE FIVE LAPS!

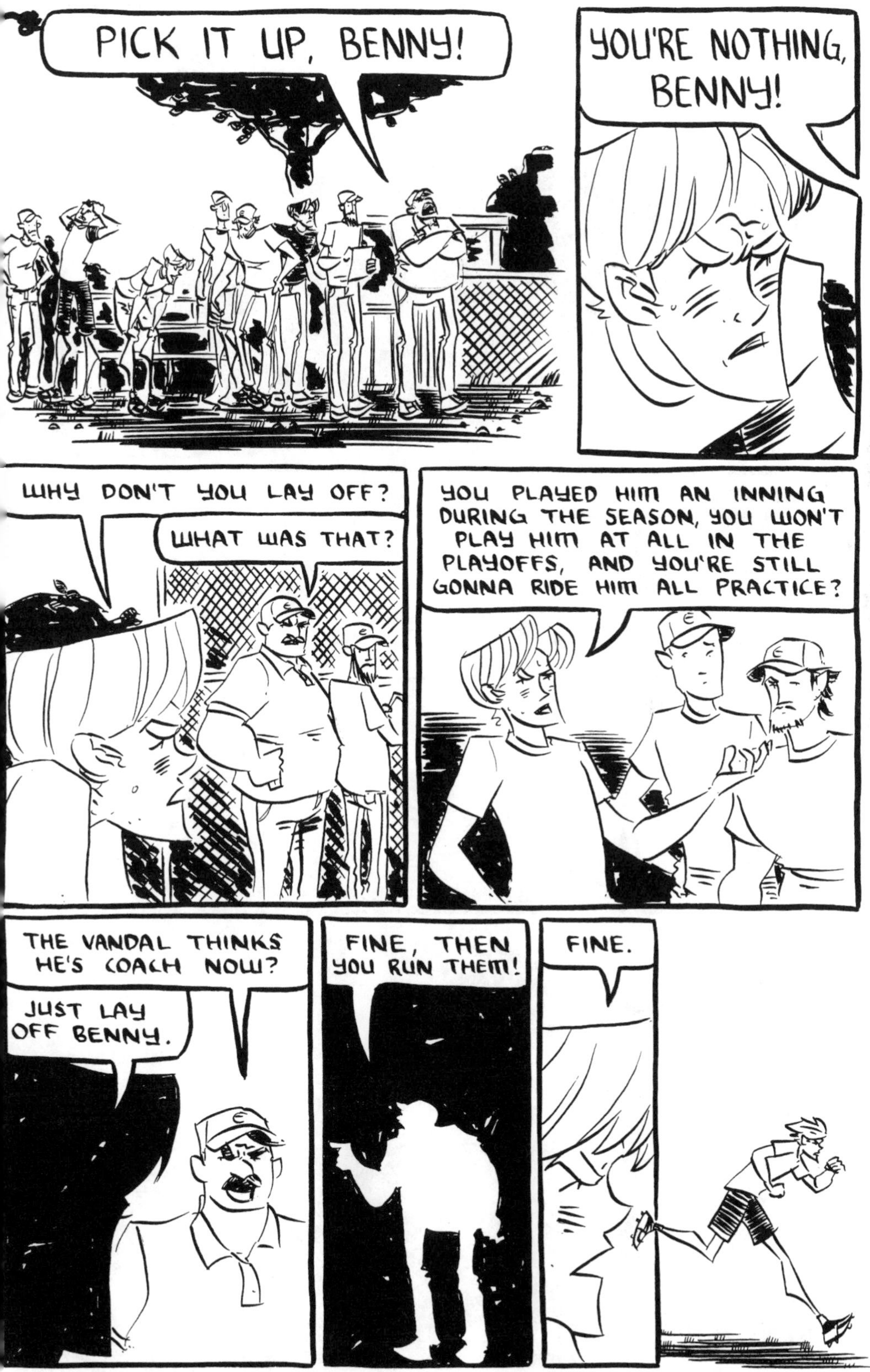
PICK IT UP, BENNY!
YOU'RE NOTHING, BENNY!
WHY DON'T YOU LAY OFF?
WHAT WAS THAT?
YOU PLAYED HIM AN INNING DURING THE SEASON, YOU WON'T PLAY HIM AT ALL IN THE PLAYOFFS, AND YOU'RE STILL GONNA RIDE HIM ALL PRACTICE?
THE VANDAL THINKS HE'S COACH NOW?
JUST LAY OFF BENNY.
FINE, THEN YOU RUN THEM!
FINE.

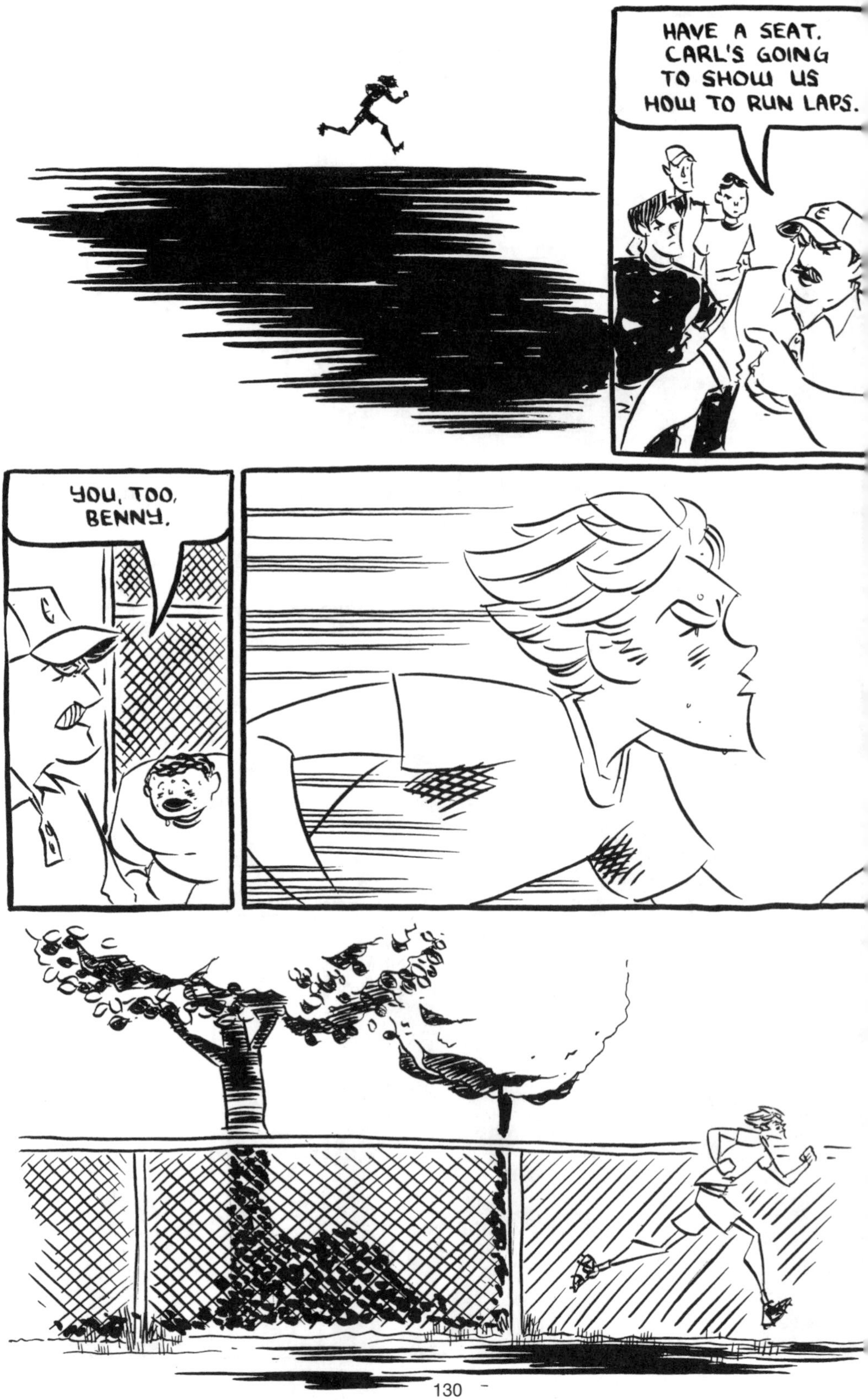
HAVE A SEAT. CARL'S GOING TO SHOW US HOW TO RUN LAPS.
YOU, TOO, BENNY.

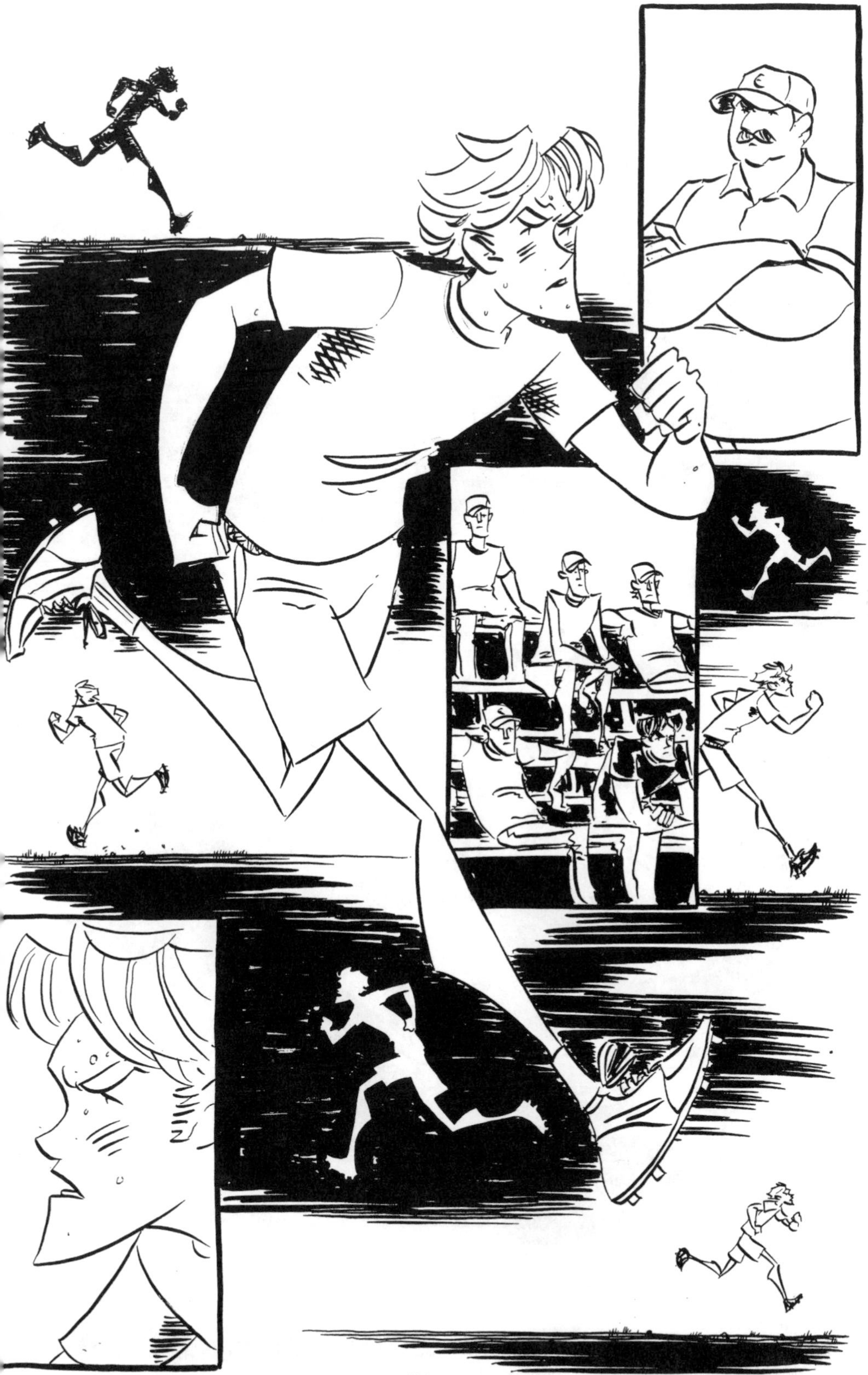

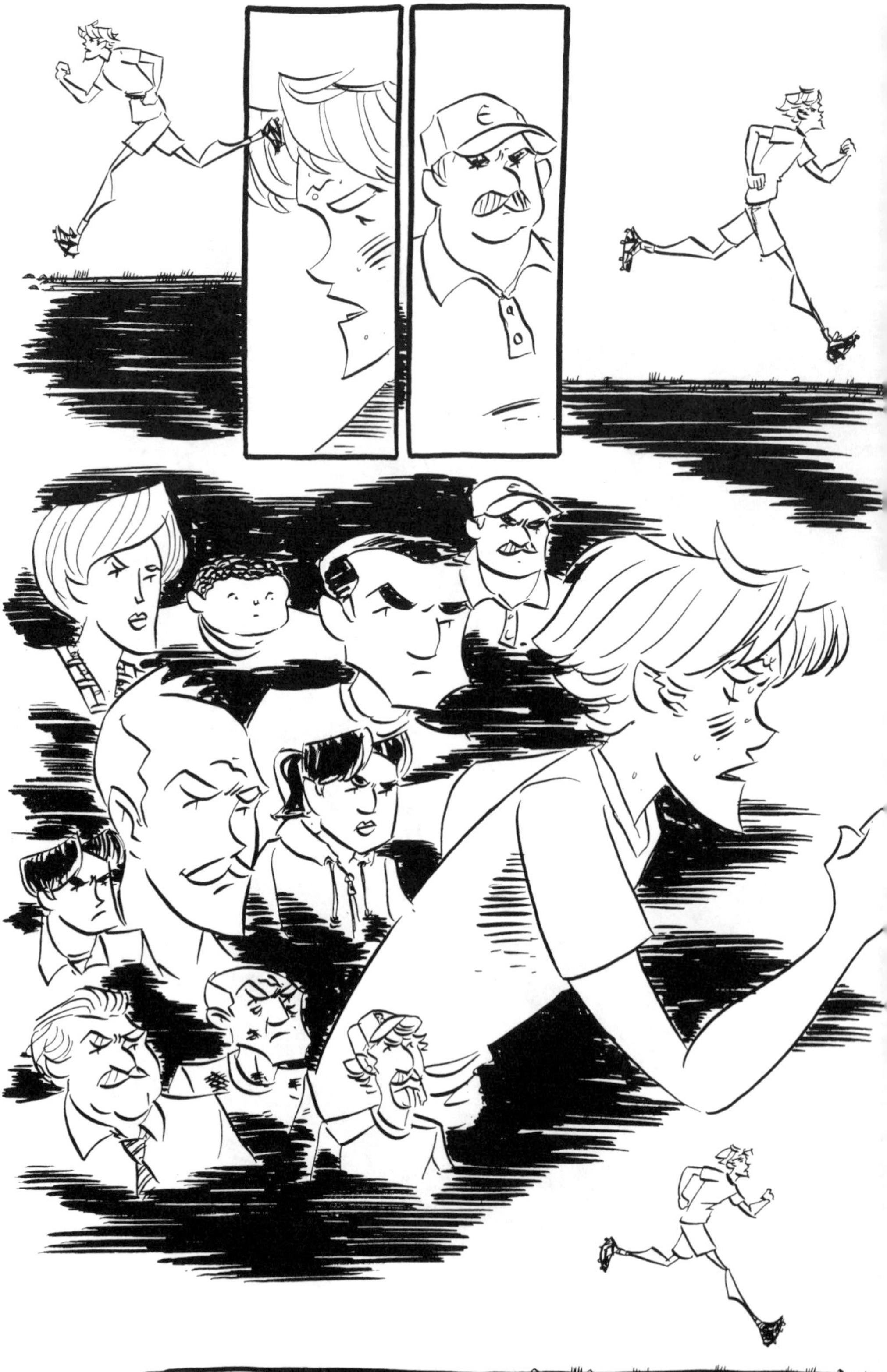

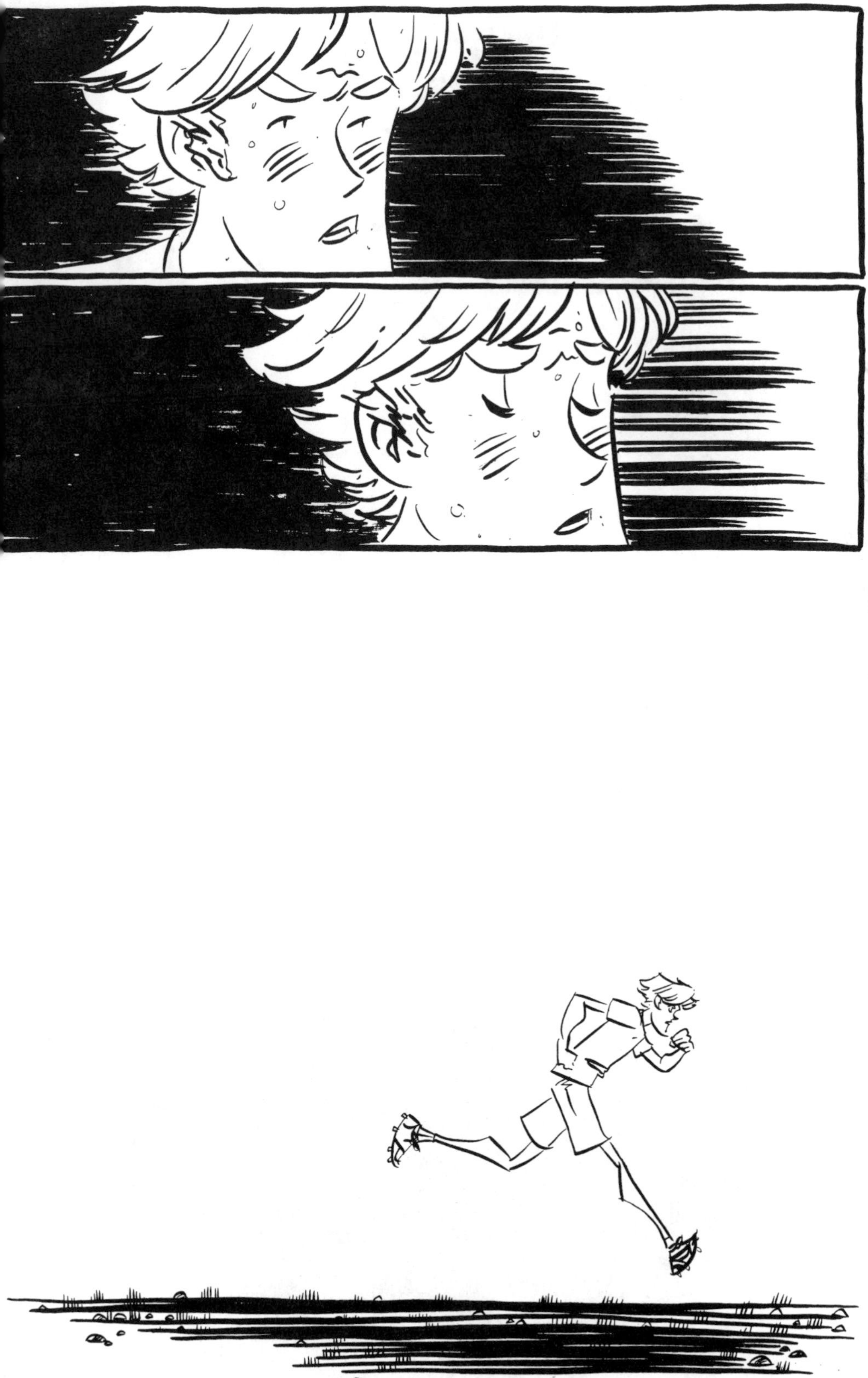

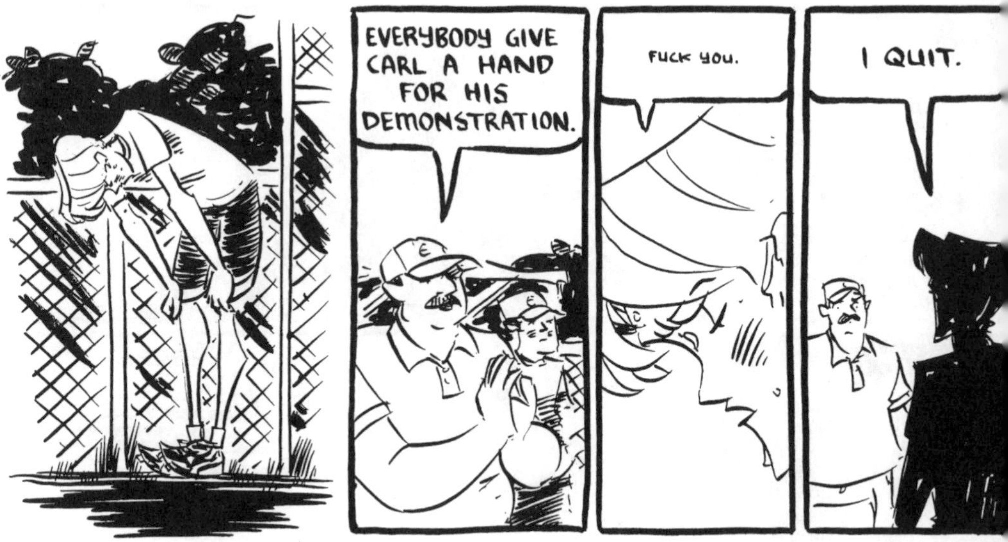
EVERYBODY GIVE CARL A HAND FOR HIS DEMONSTRATION.
FUCK YOU.
I QUIT.

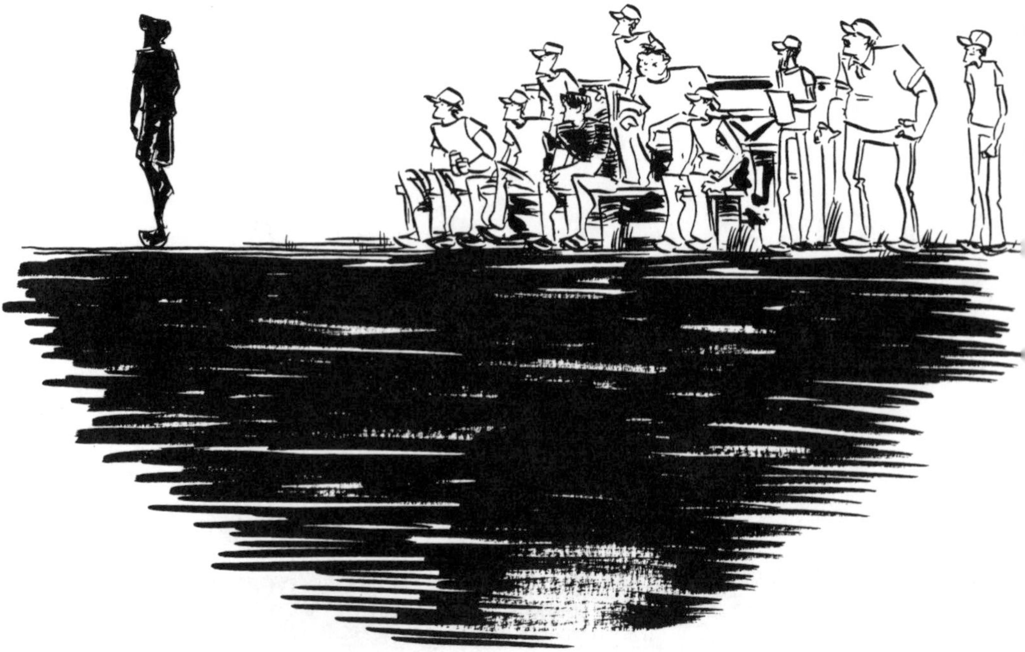

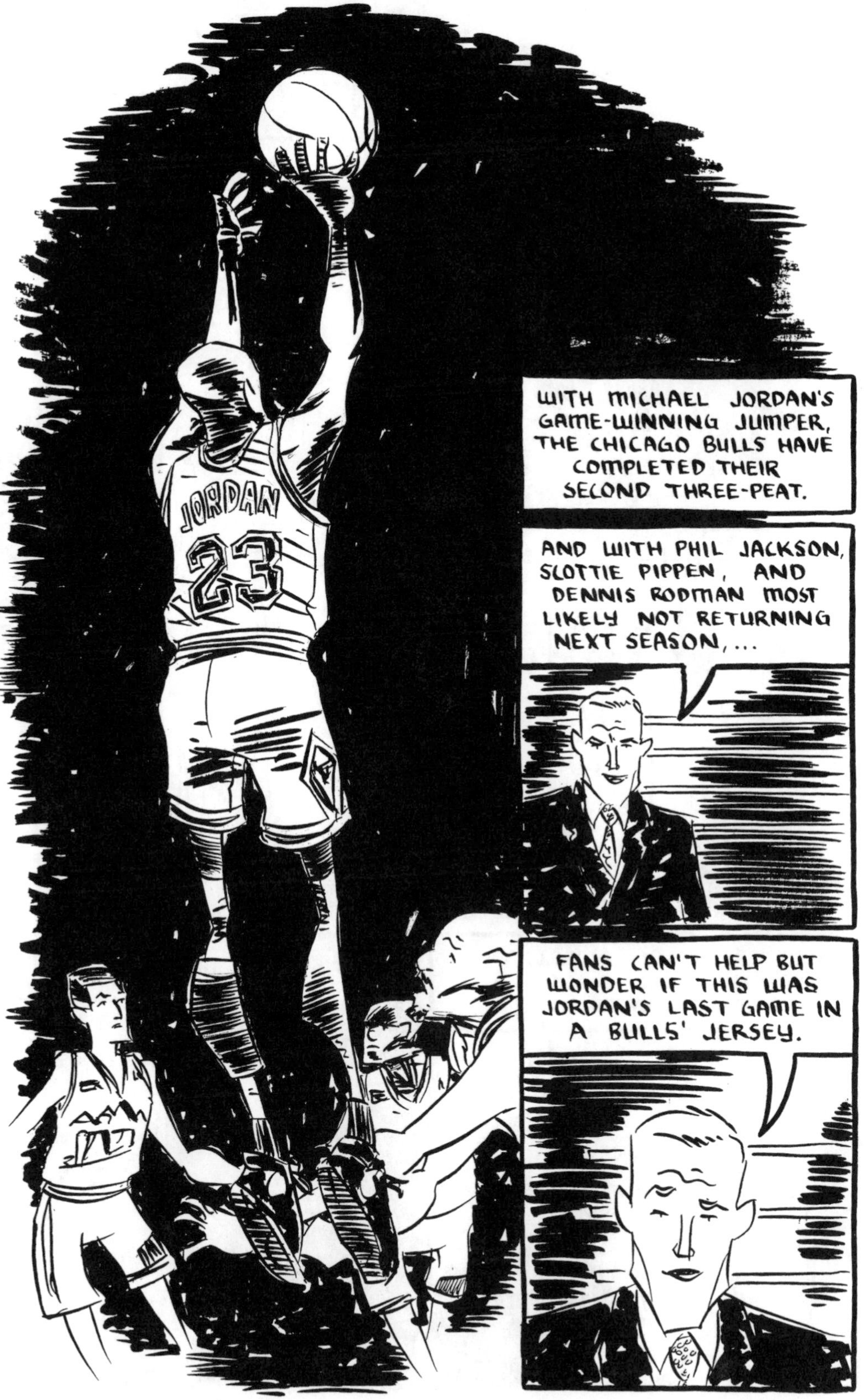
JORDAN
23
WITH MICHAEL JORDAN'S GAME-WINNING JUMPER, THE CHICAGO BULLS HAVE COMPLETED THEIR SECOND THREE-PEAT.
AND WITH PHIL JACKSON, SCOTTIE PIPPEN, AND DENNIS RODMAN MOST LIKELY NOT RETURNING NEXT SEASON, ...
FANS CAN'T HELP BUT WONDER IF THIS WAS JORDAN'S LAST GAME IN A BULLS' JERSEY.

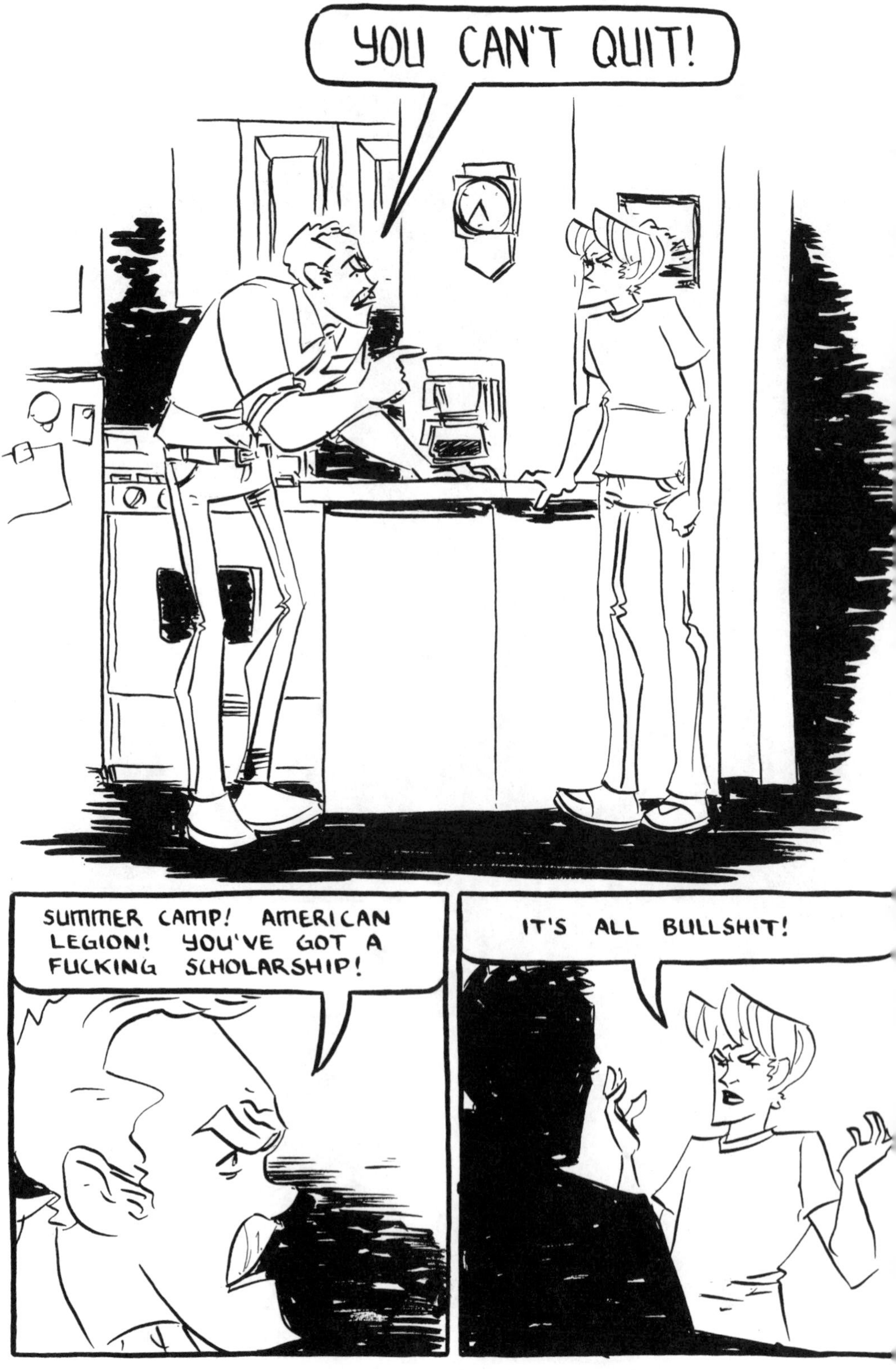
YOU CAN'T QUIT!
SUMMER CAMP! AMERICAN LEGION! YOU'VE GOT A FUCKING SCHOLARSHIP!
IT'S ALL BULLSHIT!

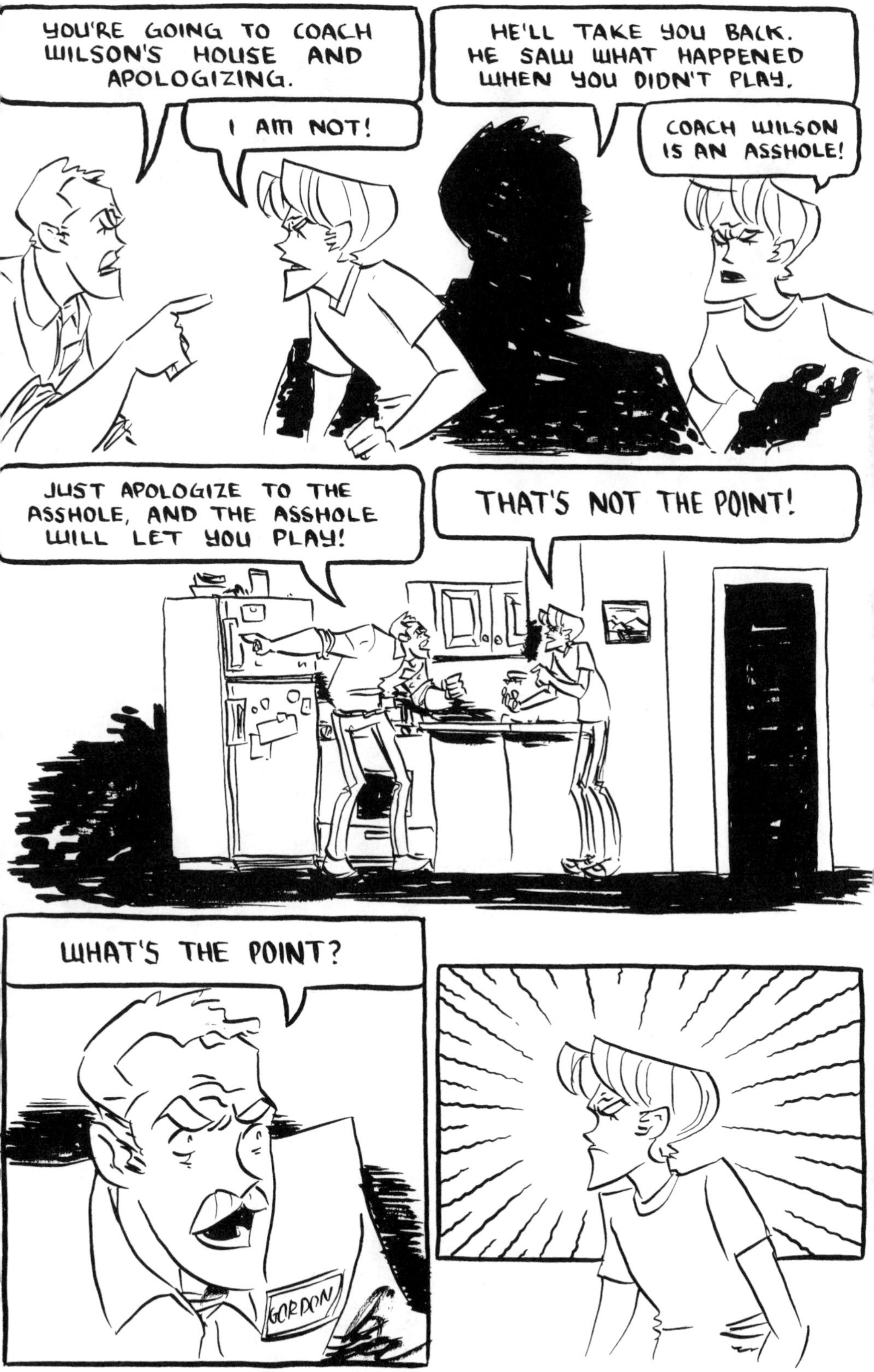
YOU'RE GOING TO COACH WILSON'S HOUSE AND APOLOGIZING.
I AM NOT!
HE'LL TAKE YOU BACK. HE SAW WHAT HAPPENED WHEN YOU DIDN'T PLAY.
COACH WILSON IS AN ASSHOLE!
JUST APOLOGIZE TO THE ASSHOLE, AND THE ASSHOLE WILL LET YOU PLAY!
THAT'S NOT THE POINT!
WHAT'S THE POINT?
GORDON

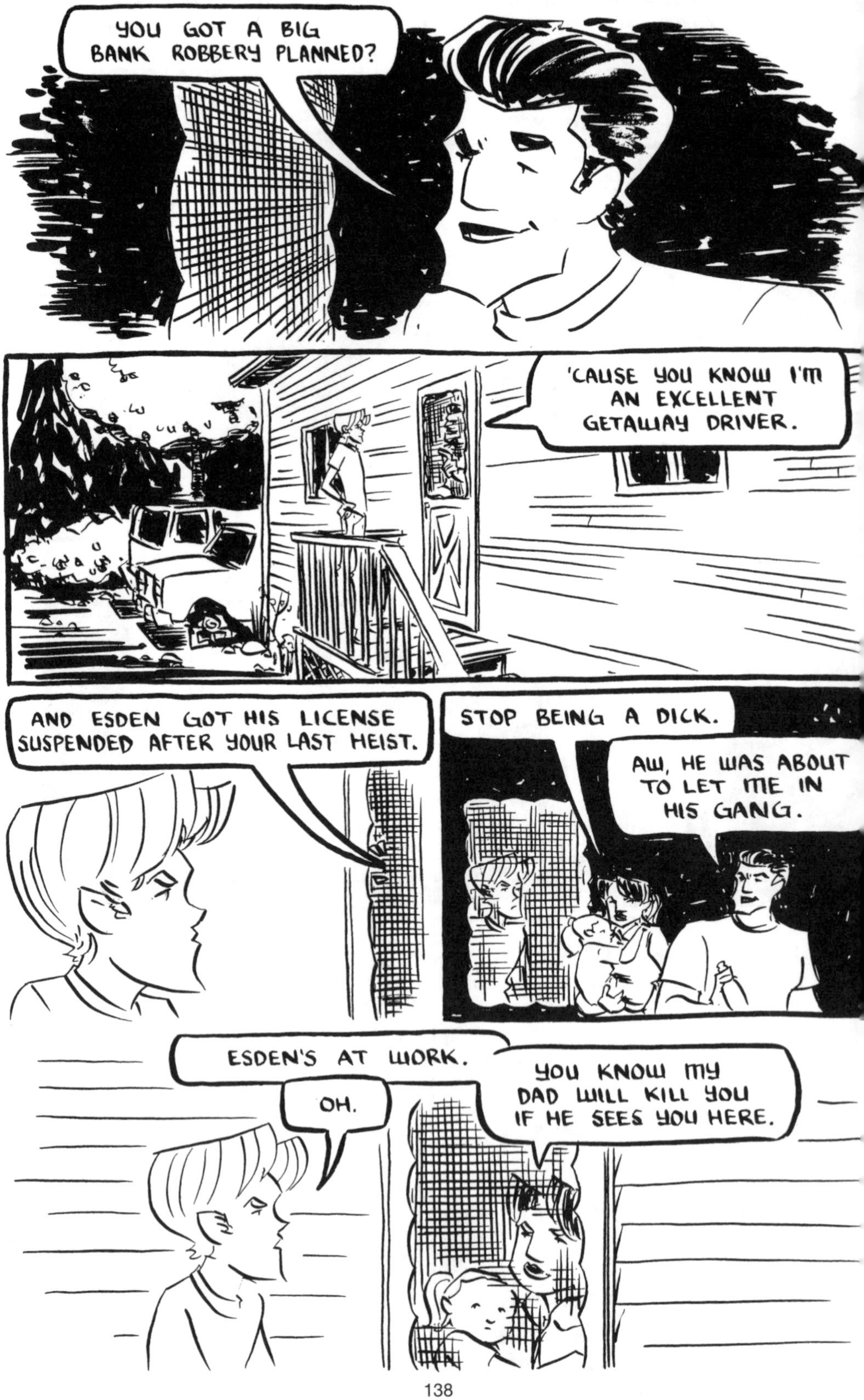
YOU GOT A BIG BANK ROBBERY PLANNED?
'CAUSE YOU KNOW I'M AN EXCELLENT GETAWAY DRIVER.
AND ESDEN GOT HIS LICENSE SUSPENDED AFTER YOUR LAST HEIST.
STOP BEING A DICK.
AW, HE WAS ABOUT TO LET ME IN HIS GANG.
ESDEN'S AT WORK.
OH.
YOU KNOW MY DAD WILL KILL YOU IF HE SEES YOU HERE.

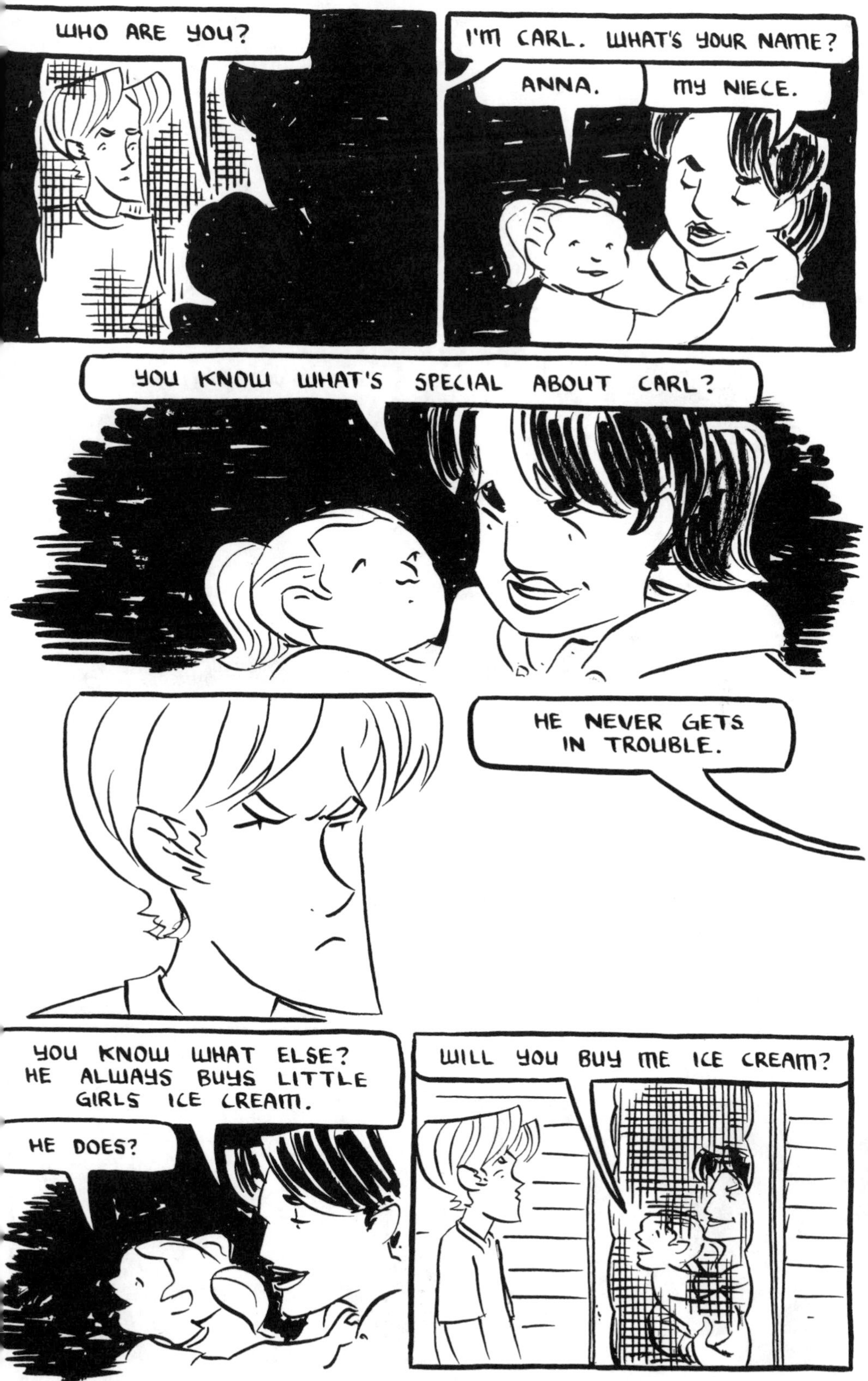
WHO ARE YOU?
I'M CARL. WHAT'S YOUR NAME?
ANNA.
MY NIECE.
YOU KNOW WHAT'S SPECIAL ABOUT CARL?
HE NEVER GETS IN TROUBLE.
YOU KNOW WHAT ELSE? HE ALWAYS BUYS LITTLE GIRLS ICE CREAM.
HE DOES?
WILL YOU BUY ME ICE CREAM?

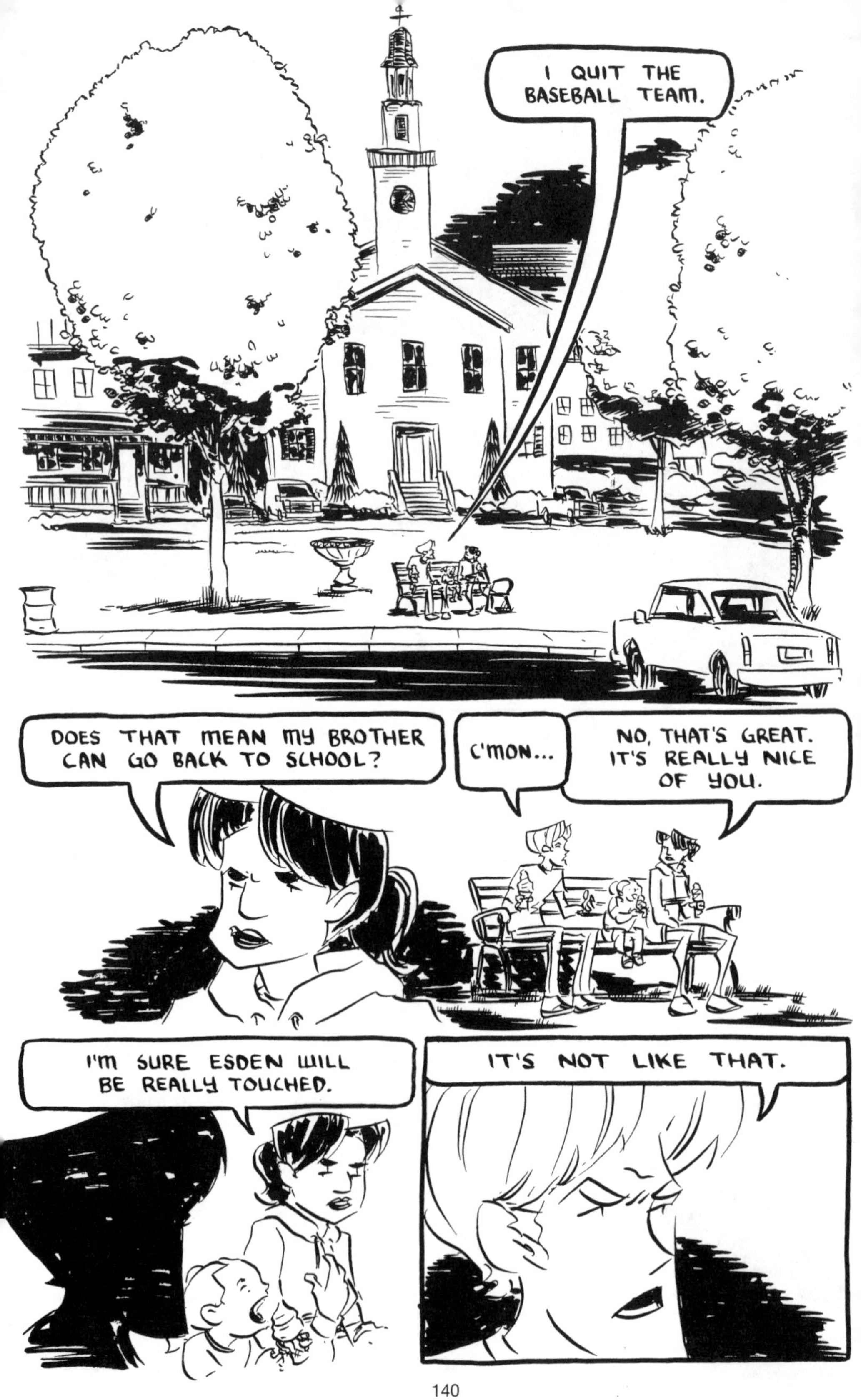
I QUIT THE BASEBALL TEAM.
DOES THAT MEAN MY BROTHER CAN GO BACK TO SCHOOL?
C'MON...
NO, THAT'S GREAT. IT'S REALLY NICE OF YOU.
I'M SURE ESDEN WILL BE REALLY TOUCHED.
IT'S NOT LIKE THAT.

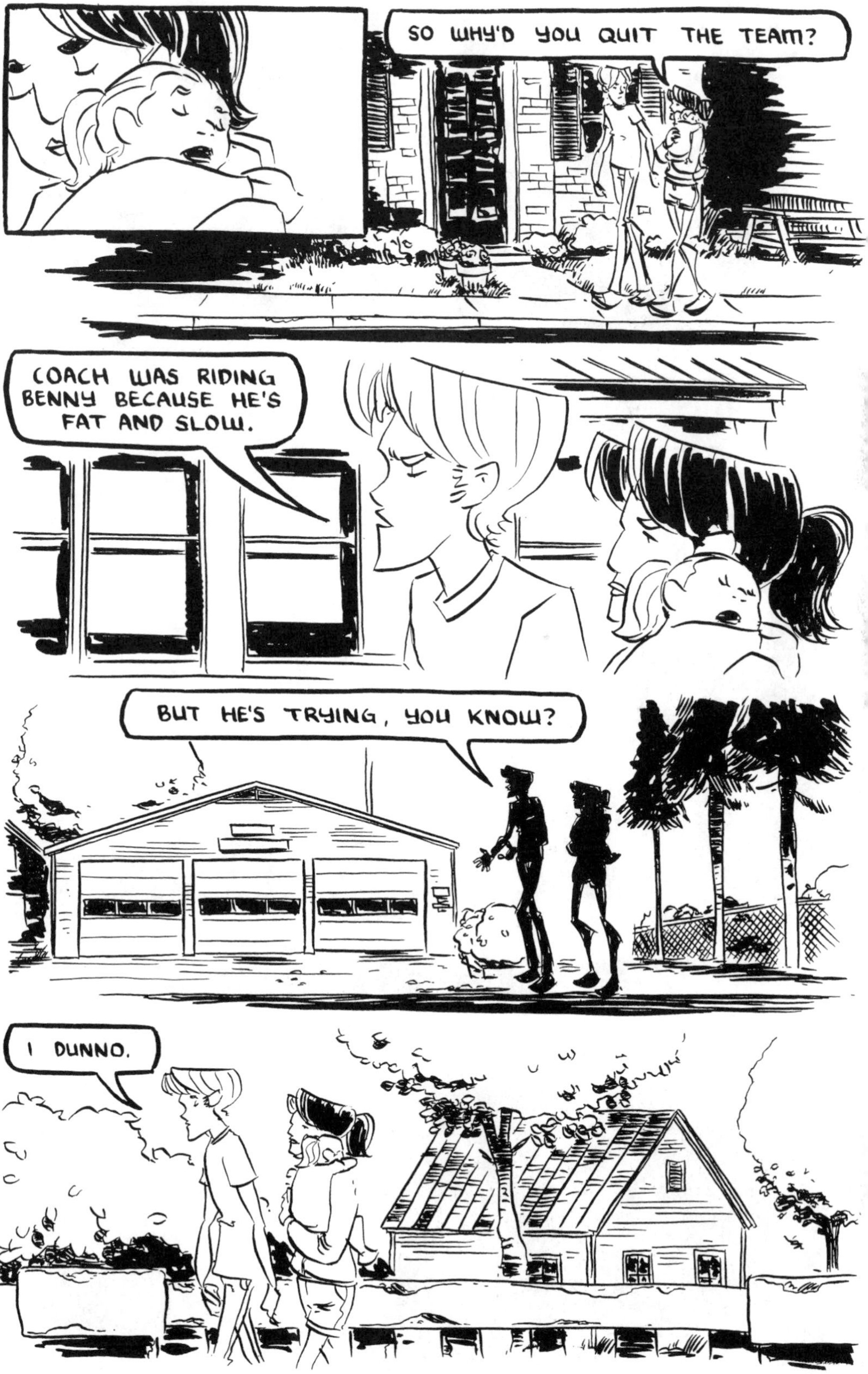

SO WHY'D YOU QUIT THE TEAM?
COACH WAS RIDING BENNY BECAUSE HE'S FAT AND SLOW.
BUT HE'S TRYING, YOU KNOW?
I DUNNO.

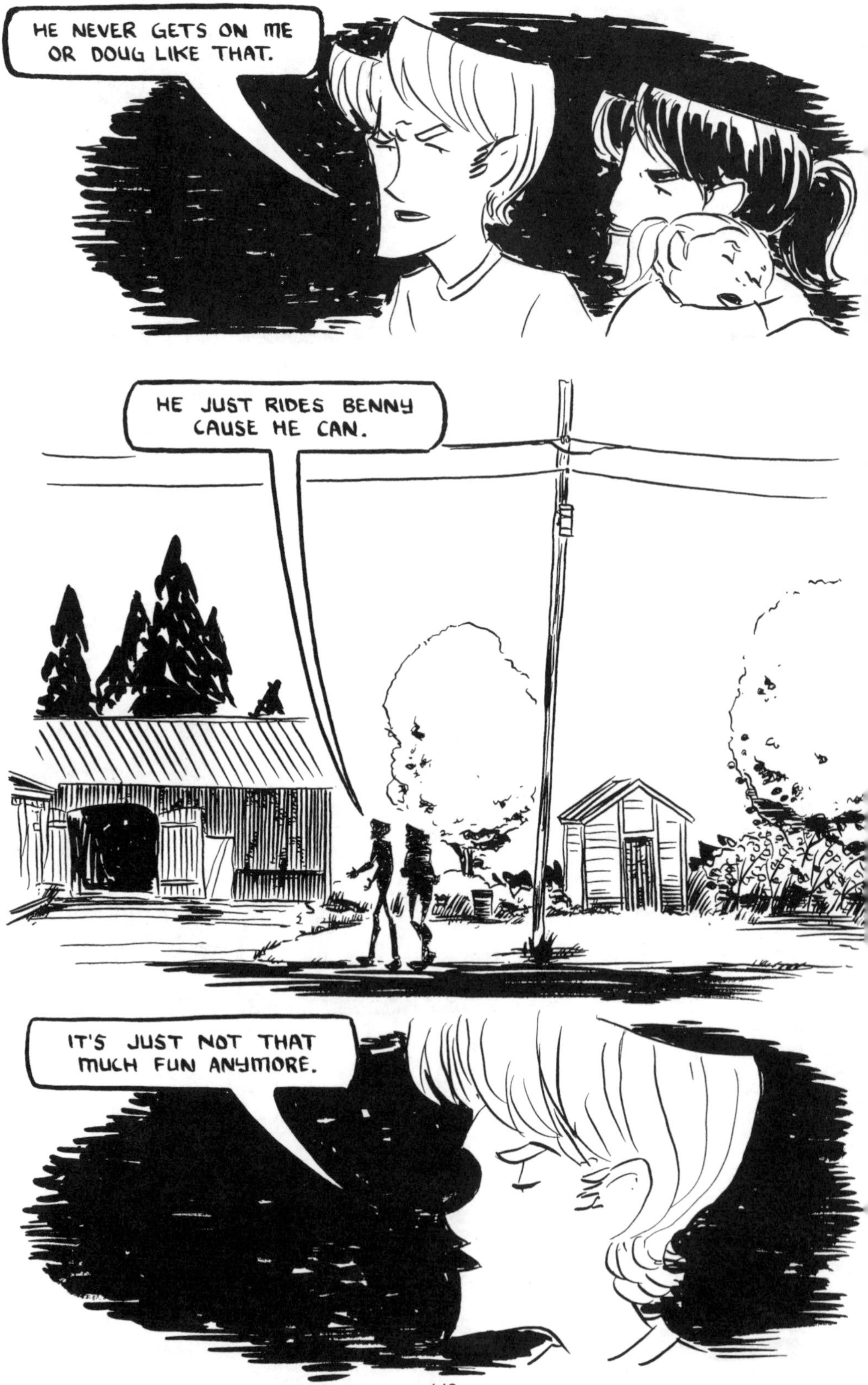
HE NEVER GETS ON ME OR DOUG LIKE THAT.
HE JUST RIDES BENNY CAUSE HE CAN.
IT'S JUST NOT THAT MUCH FUN ANYMORE.

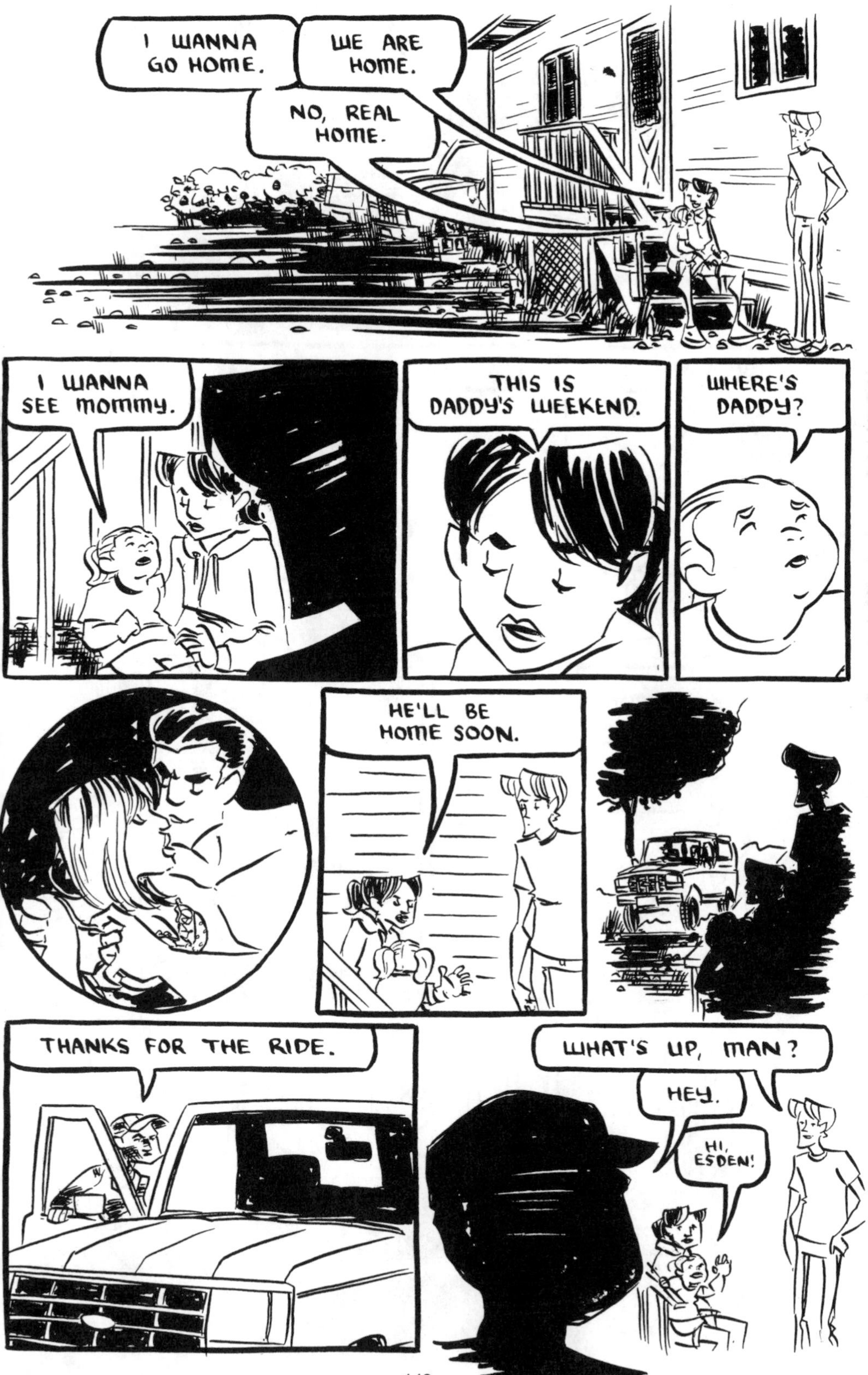
I WANNA GO HOME.
WE ARE HOME.
NO, REAL HOME.
I WANNA SEE MOMMY.
THIS IS DADDY'S WEEKEND.
WHERE'S DADDY?
HE'LL BE HOME SOON.
THANKS FOR THE RIDE.
WHAT'S UP, MAN?
HEY.
HI, ESDEN!

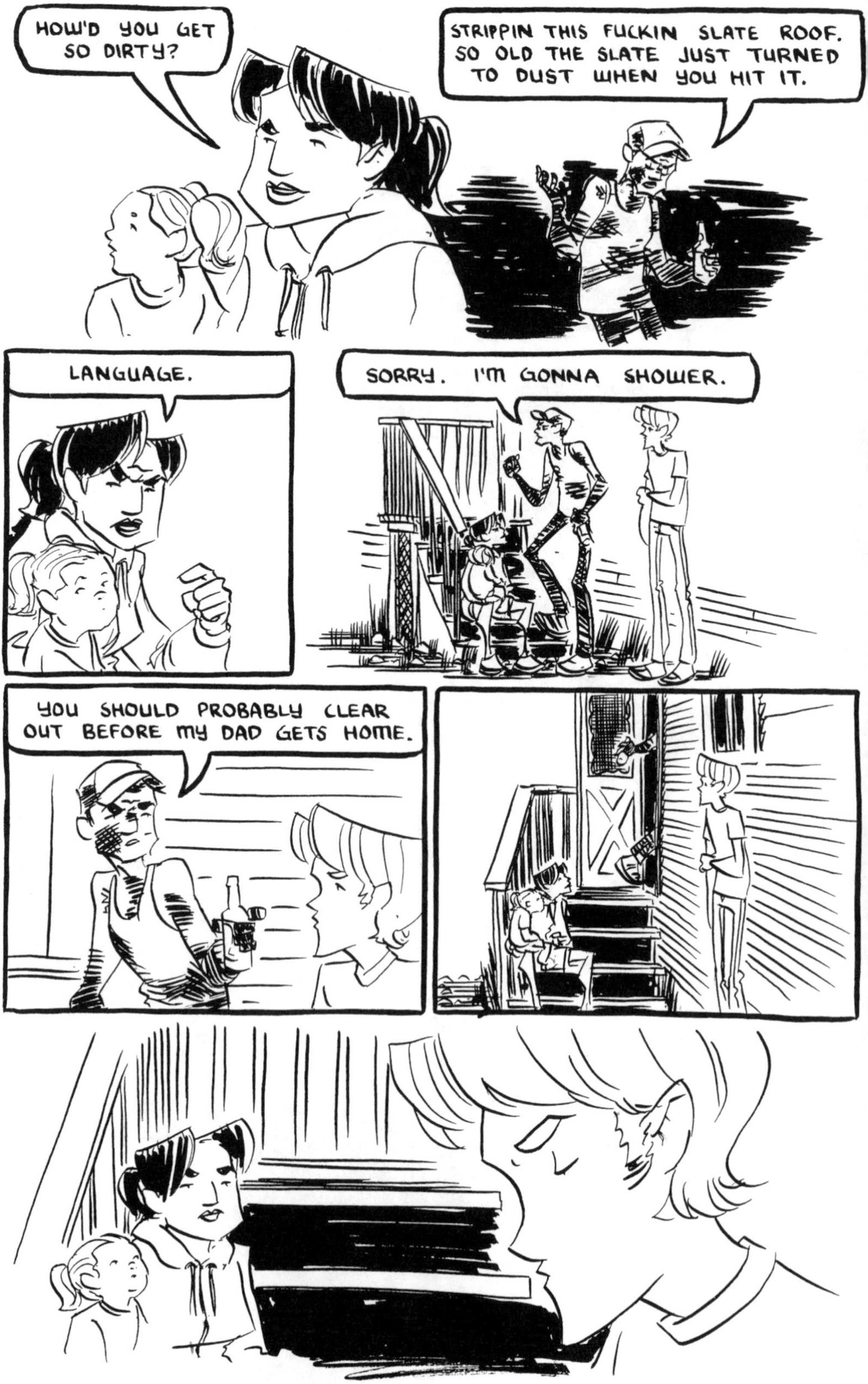
HOW'D YOU GET SO DIRTY?
STRIPPIN THIS FUCKIN SLATE ROOF. SO OLD THE SLATE JUST TURNED TO DUST WHEN YOU HIT IT.
LANGUAGE.
SORRY. I'M GONNA SHOWER.
YOU SHOULD PROBABLY CLEAR OUT BEFORE MY DAD GETS HOME.

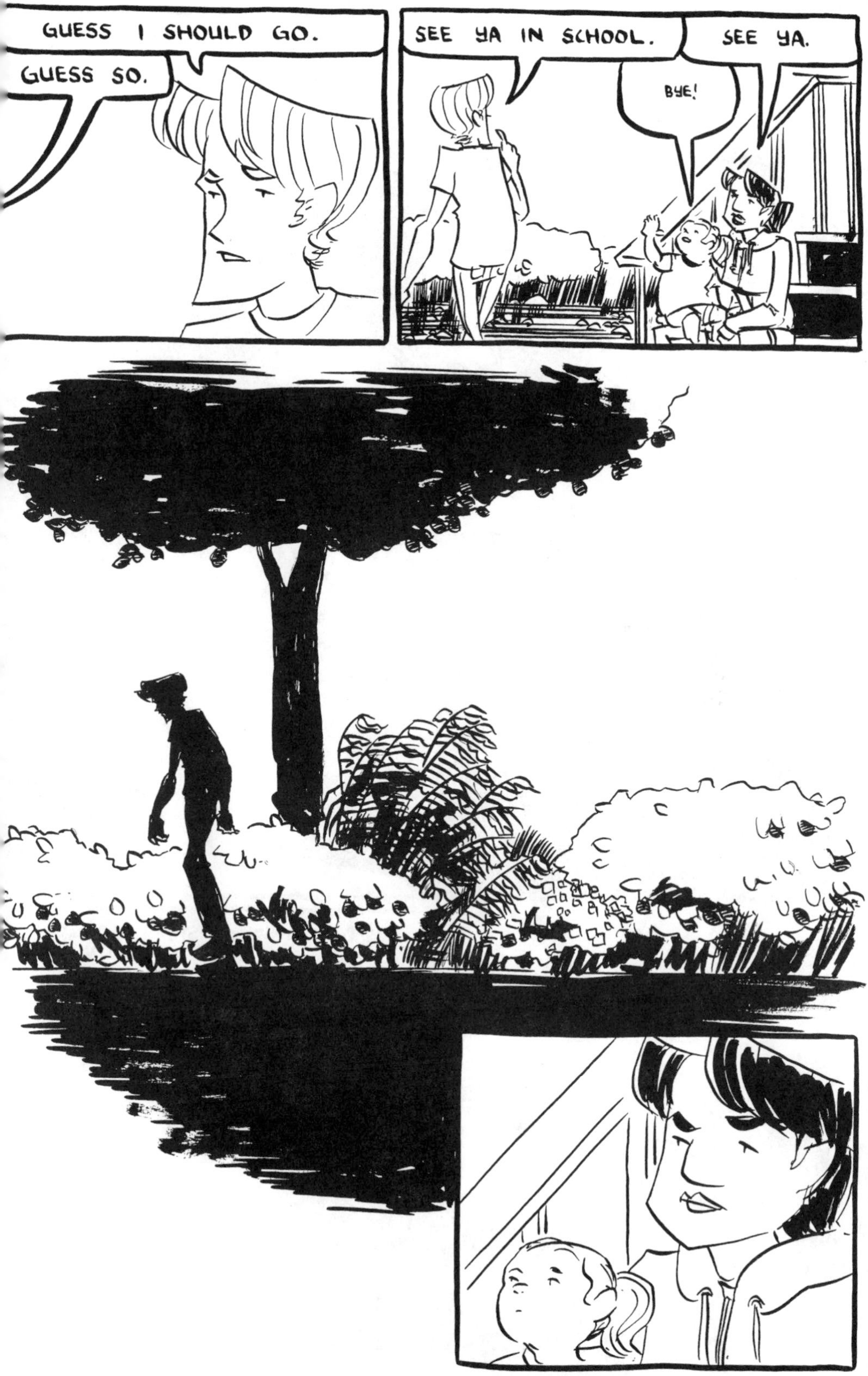
GUESS I SHOULD GO.
GUESS SO.
SEE YA IN SCHOOL.
BYE!
SEE YA.

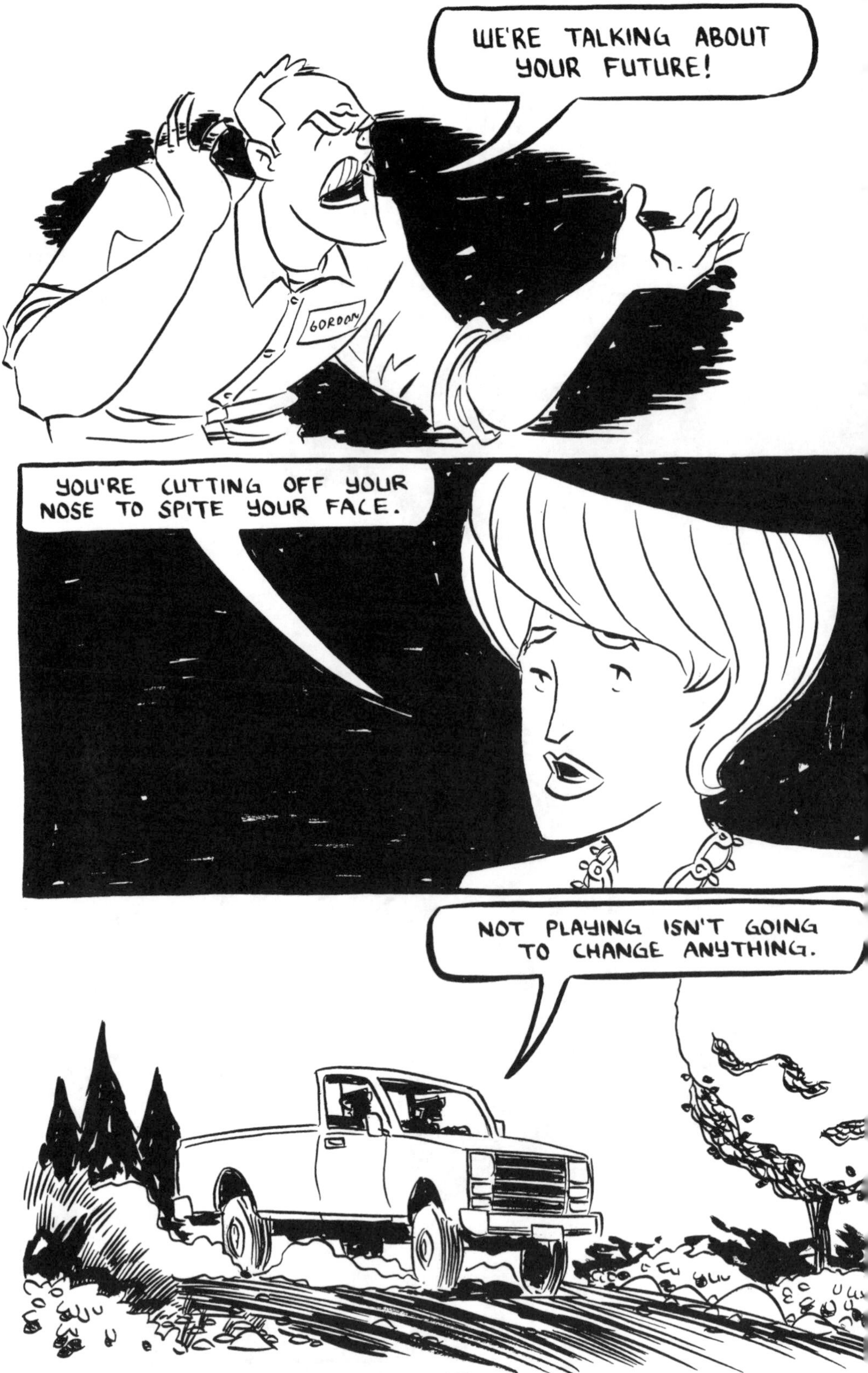
WE'RE TALKING ABOUT YOUR FUTURE!
GORDON
YOU'RE CUTTING OFF YOUR NOSE TO SPITE YOUR FACE.
NOT PLAYING ISN'T GOING TO CHANGE ANYTHING.

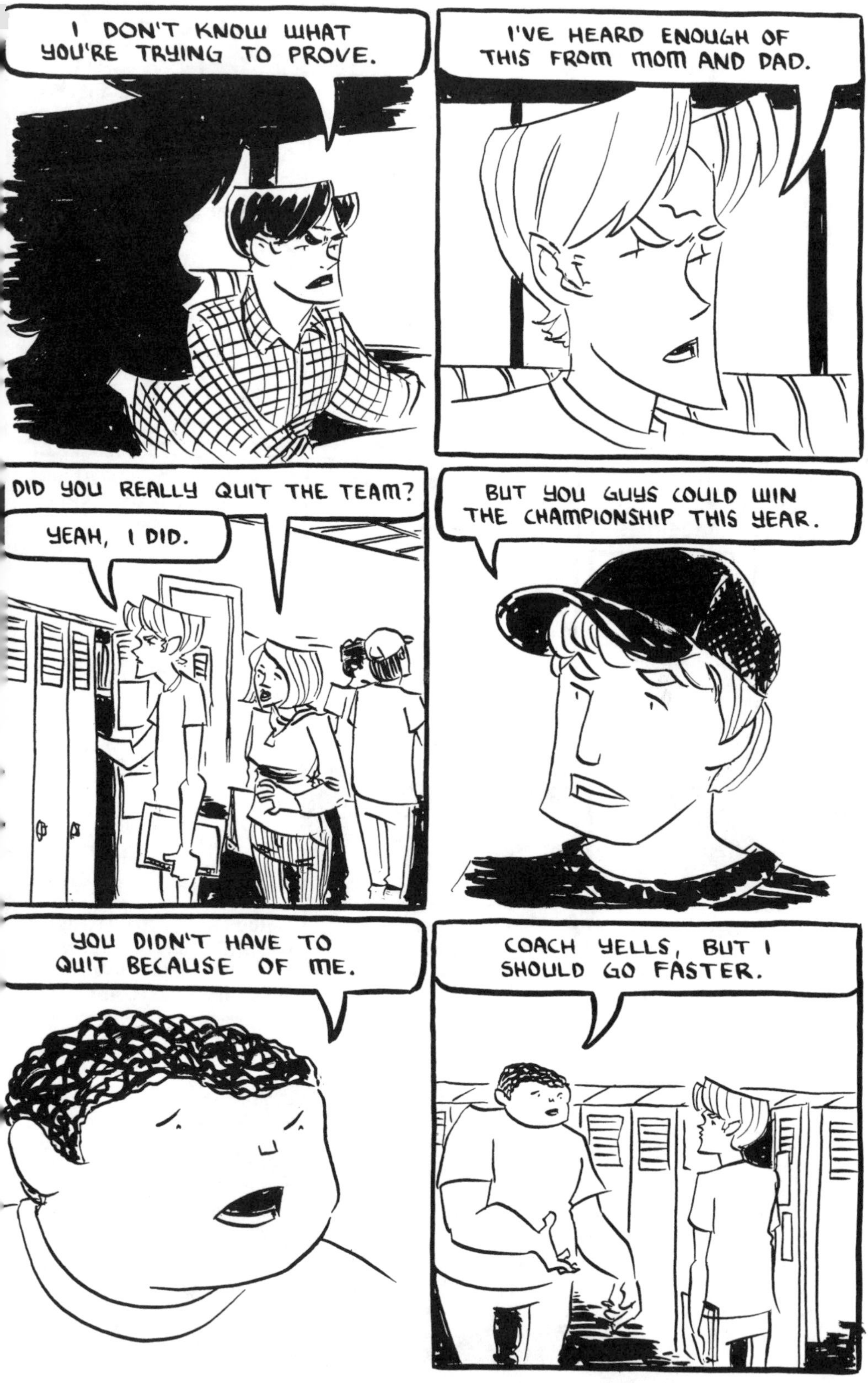
I DON'T KNOW WHAT YOU'RE TRYING TO PROVE.
I'VE HEARD ENOUGH OF THIS FROM MOM AND DAD.
DID YOU REALLY QUIT THE TEAM?
YEAH, I DID.
BUT YOU GUYS COULD WIN THE CHAMPIONSHIP THIS YEAR.
YOU DIDN'T HAVE TO QUIT BECAUSE OF ME.
COACH YELLS, BUT I SHOULD GO FASTER.

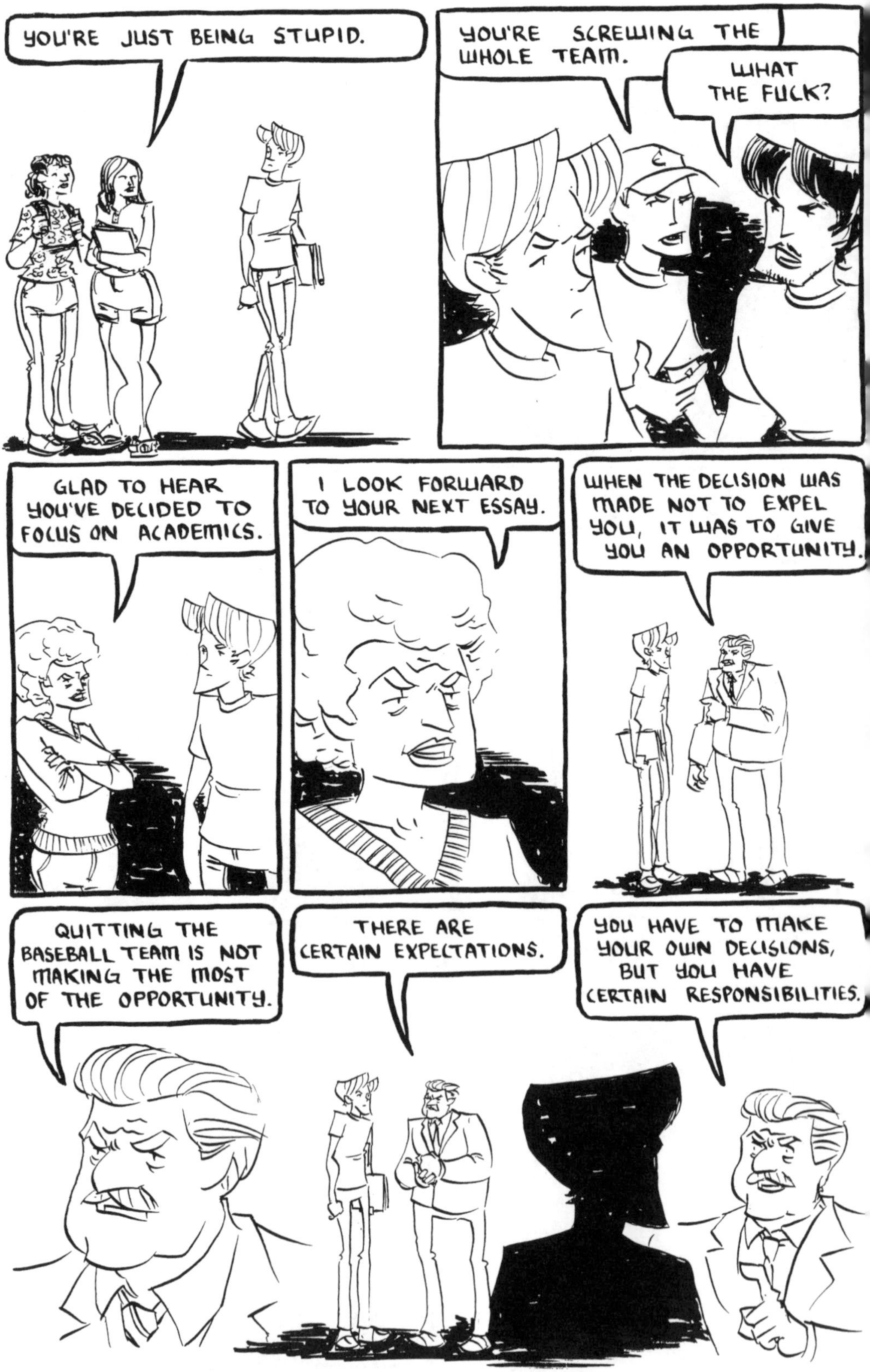
YOU'RE JUST BEING STUPID.
YOU'RE SCREWING THE WHOLE TEAM.
WHAT THE FUCK?
GLAD TO HEAR YOU'VE DECIDED TO FOCUS ON ACADEMICS.
I LOOK FORWARD TO YOUR NEXT ESSAY.
WHEN THE DECISION WAS MADE NOT TO EXPEL YOU, IT WAS TO GIVE YOU AN OPPORTUNITY.
QUITTING THE BASEBALL TEAM IS NOT MAKING THE MOST OF THE OPPORTUNITY.
THERE ARE CERTAIN EXPECTATIONS.
YOU HAVE TO MAKE YOUR OWN DECISIONS, BUT YOU HAVE CERTAIN RESPONSIBILITIES.

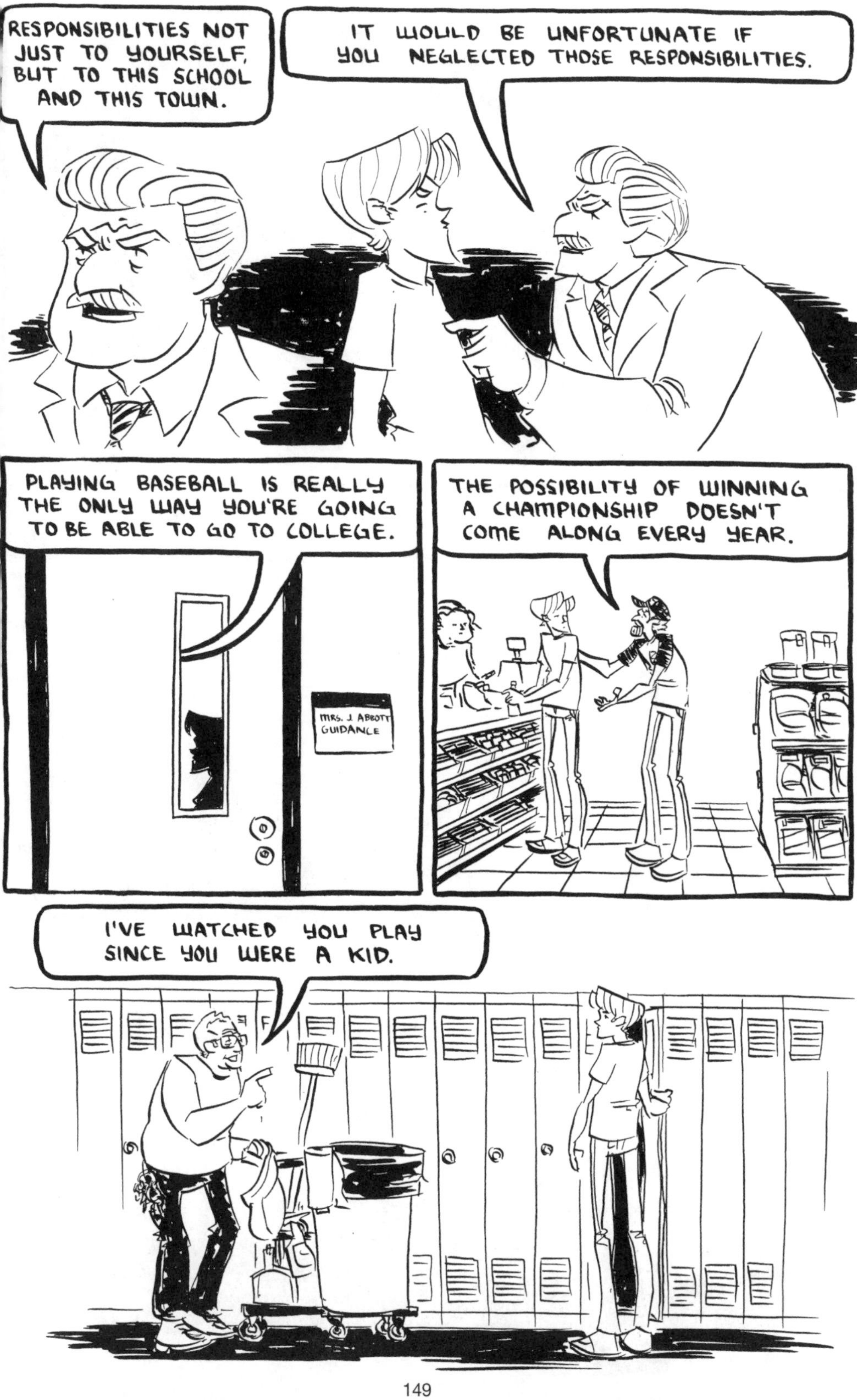
RESPONSIBILITIES NOT JUST TO YOURSELF, BUT TO THIS SCHOOL AND THIS TOWN.
IT WOULD BE UNFORTUNATE IF YOU NEGLECTED THOSE RESPONSIBILITIES.
PLAYING BASEBALL IS REALLY THE ONLY WAY YOU'RE GOING TO BE ABLE TO GO TO COLLEGE.
MRS. J. ABBOTT GUIDANCE
THE POSSIBILITY OF WINNING A CHAMPIONSHIP DOESN'T COME ALONG EVERY YEAR.
I'VE WATCHED YOU PLAY SINCE YOU WERE A KID.

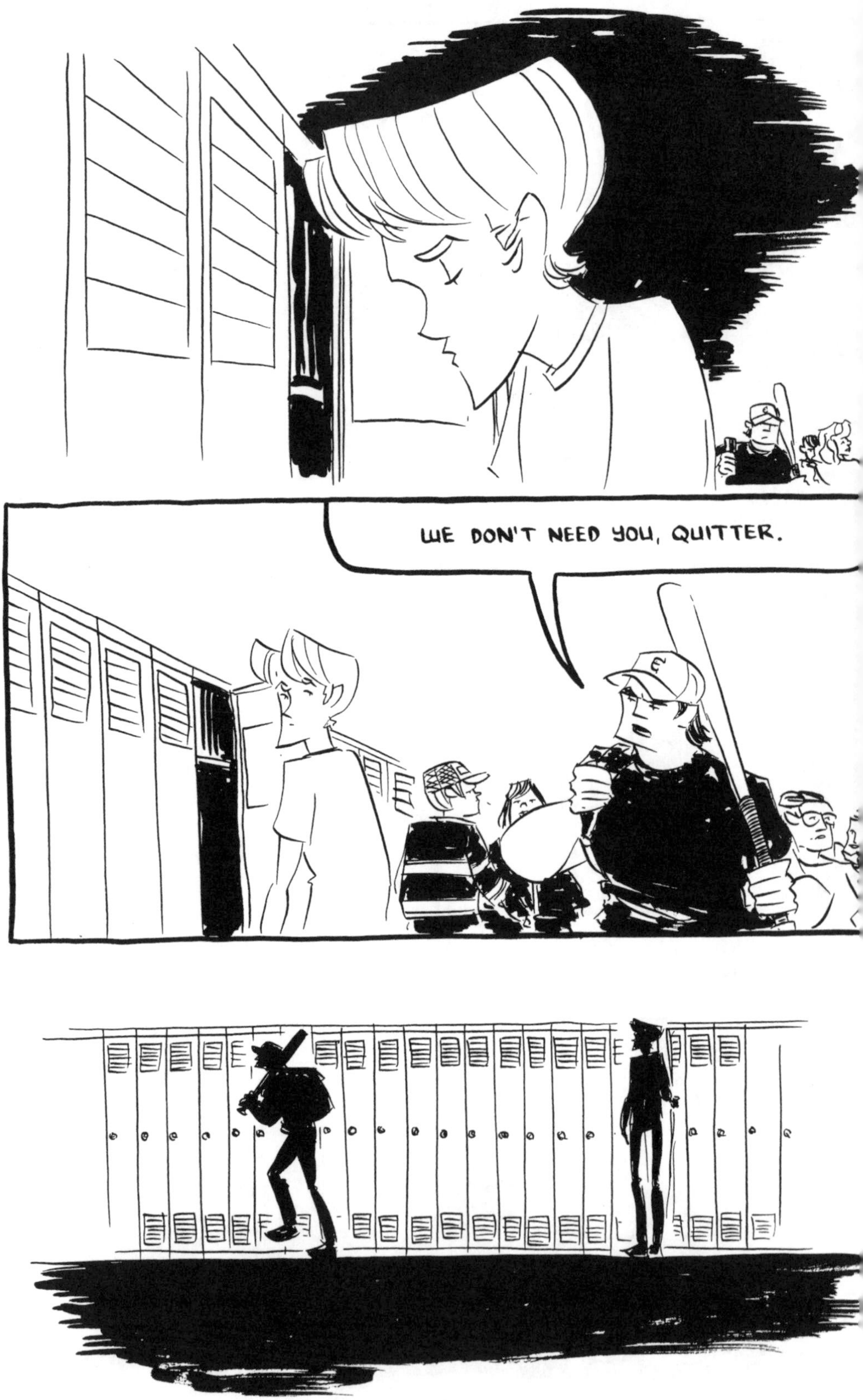
WE DON'T NEED YOU, QUITTER.

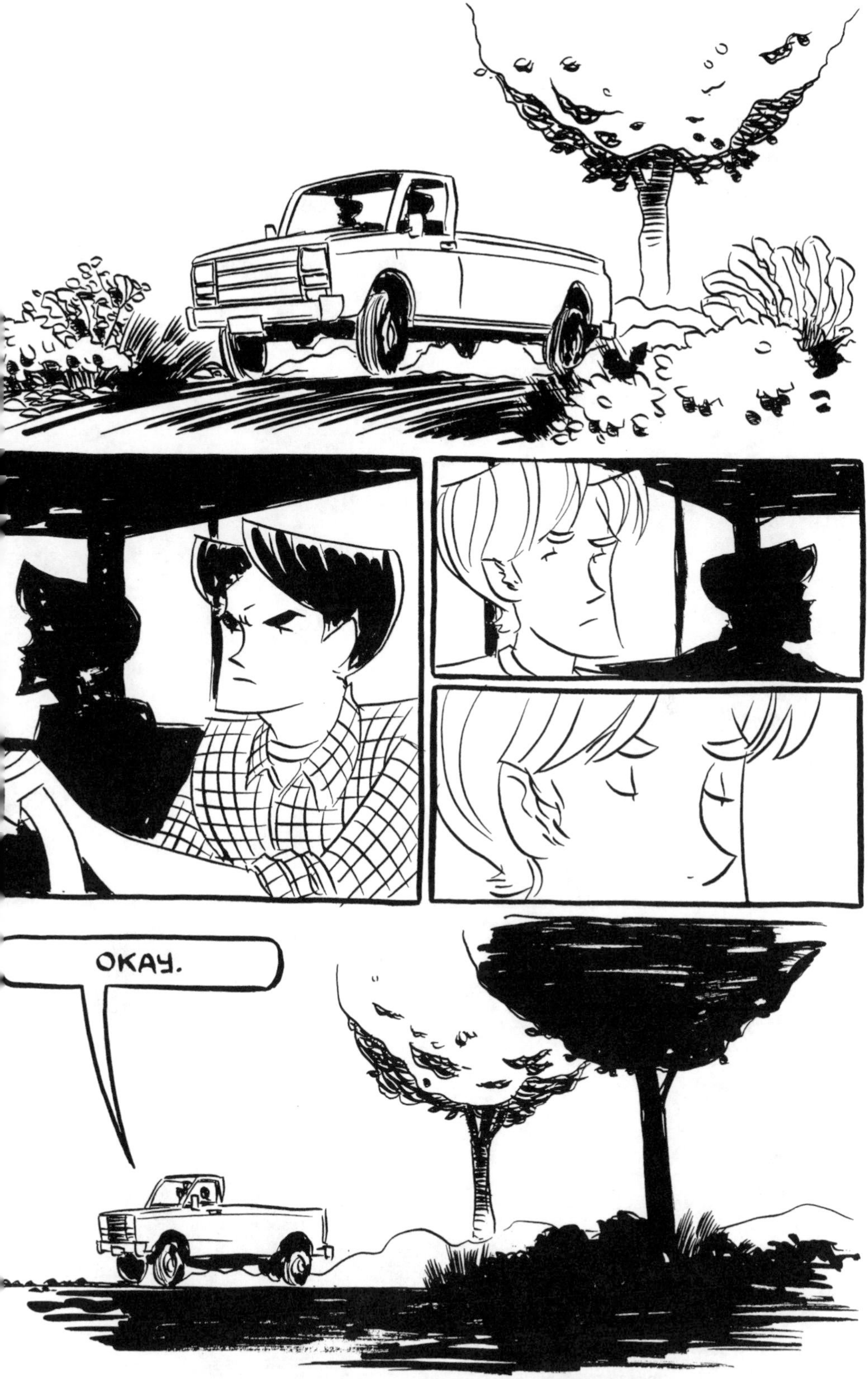
OKAY.

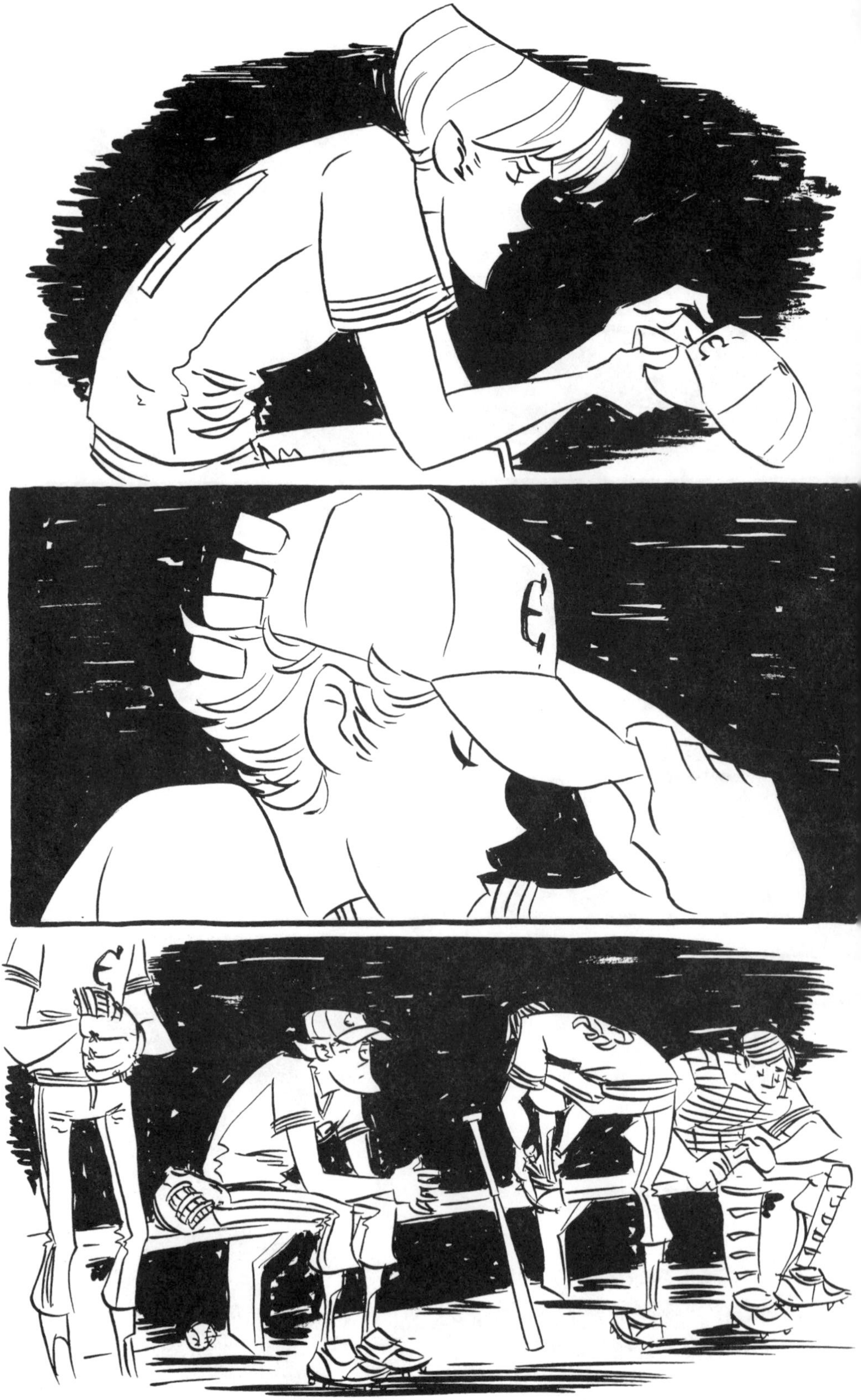

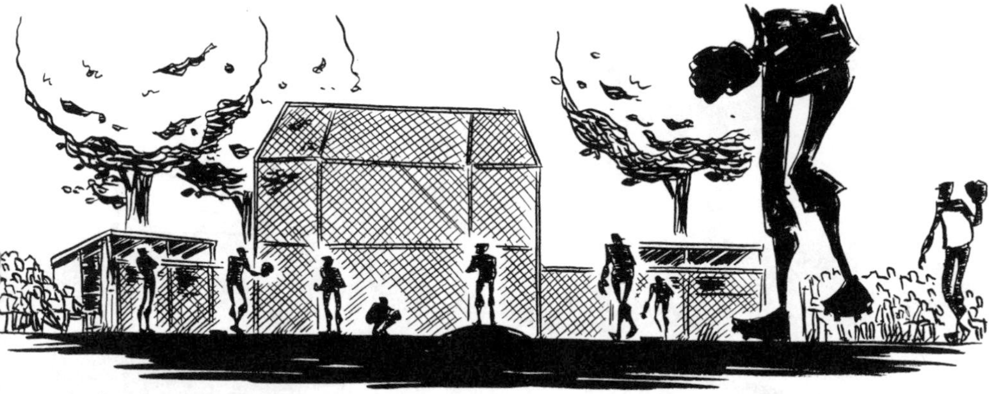

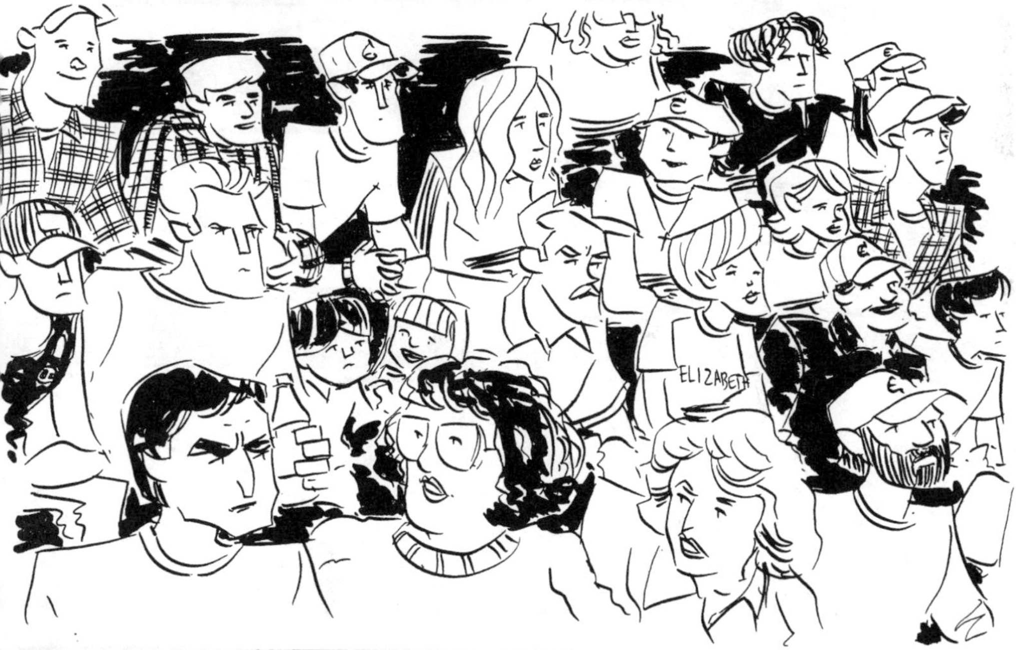
ELIZABETH

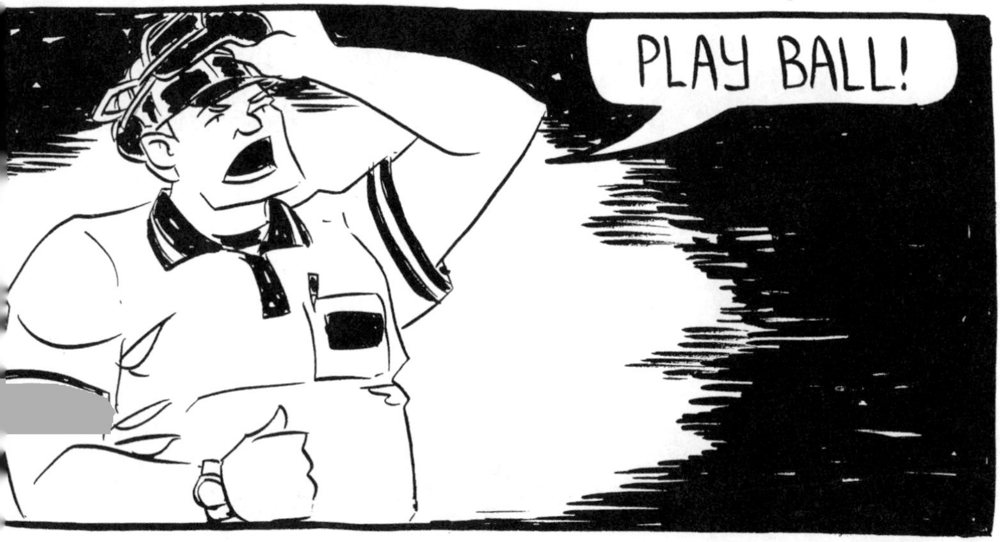
PLAY BALL!

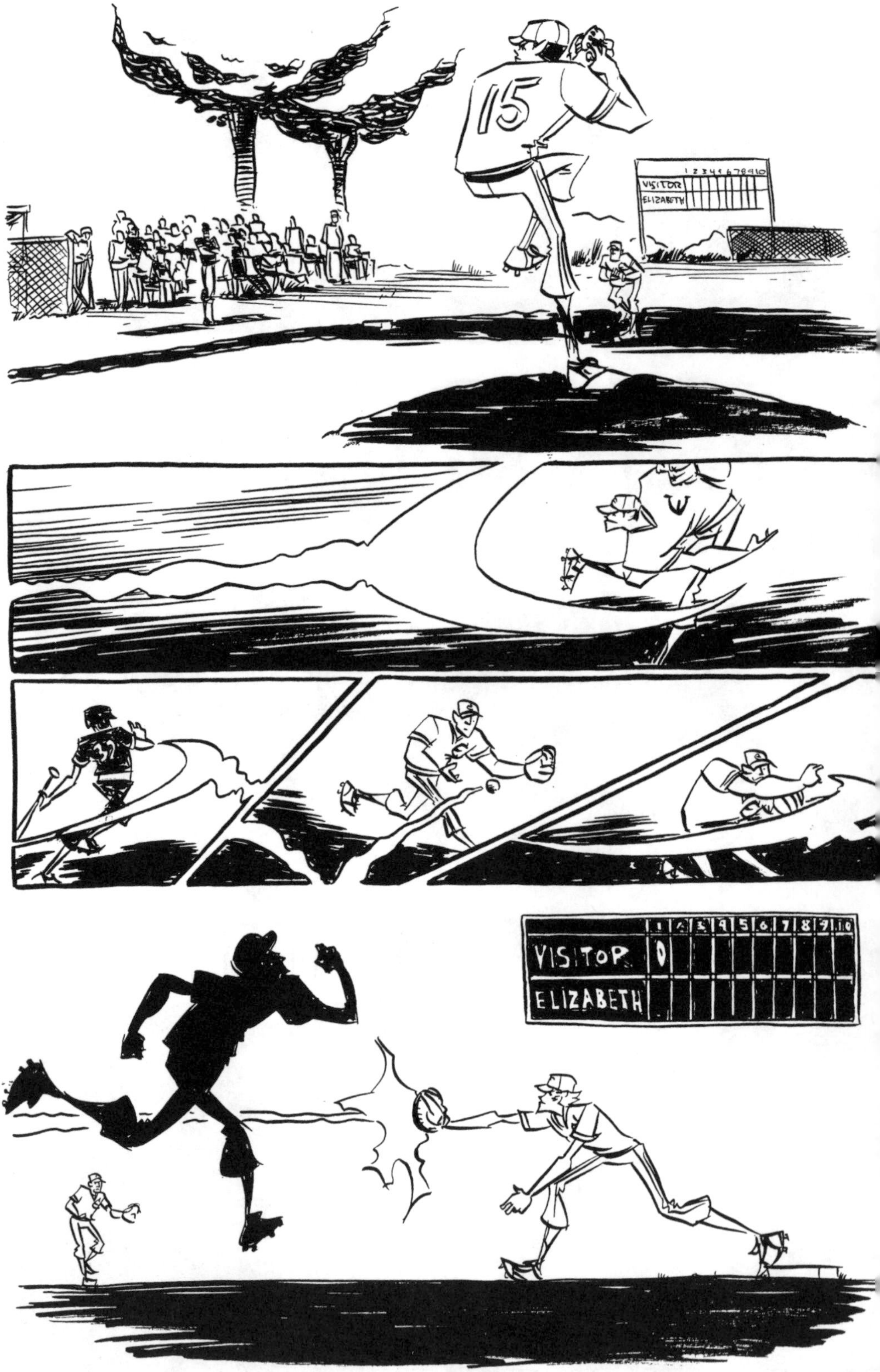
15
VISITOR
ELIZABETH
32
1 2 3 4 5 6 7 8 9 10
VISITOR 0
ELIZABETH

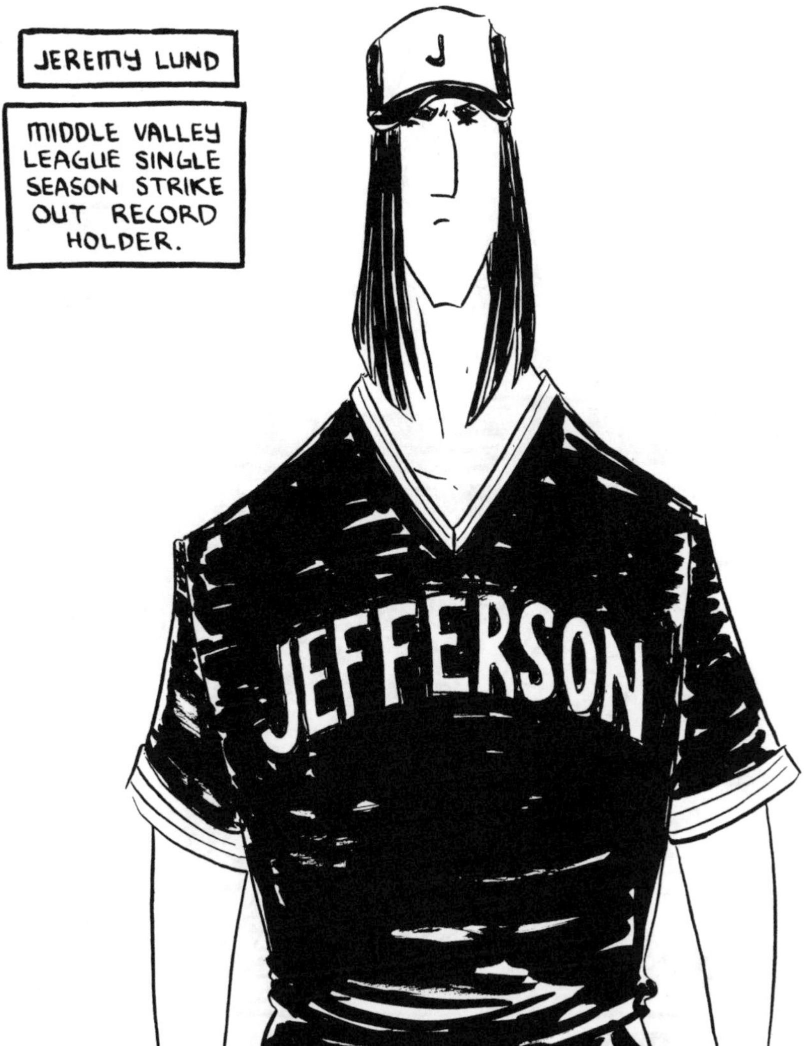
JEREMY LUND
MIDDLE VALLEY LEAGUE SINGLE SEASON STRIKE OUT RECORD HOLDER.
JEFFERSON

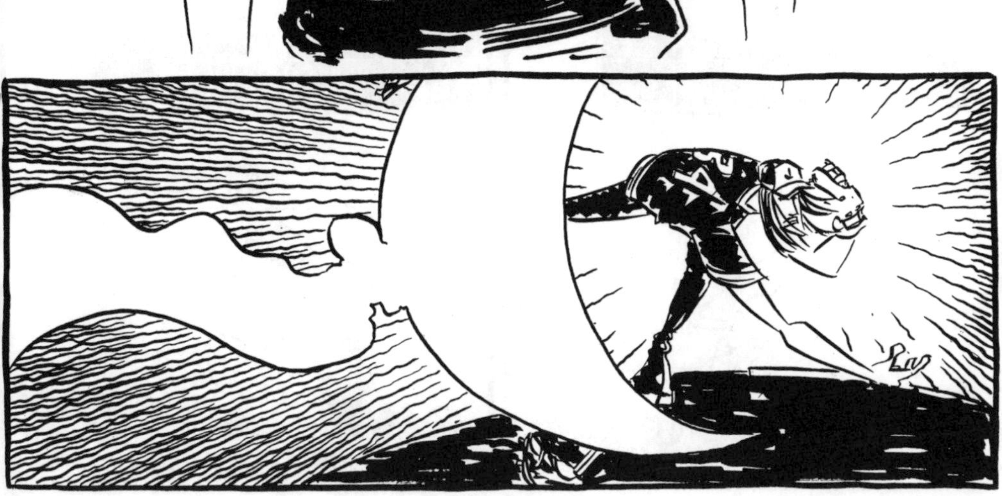

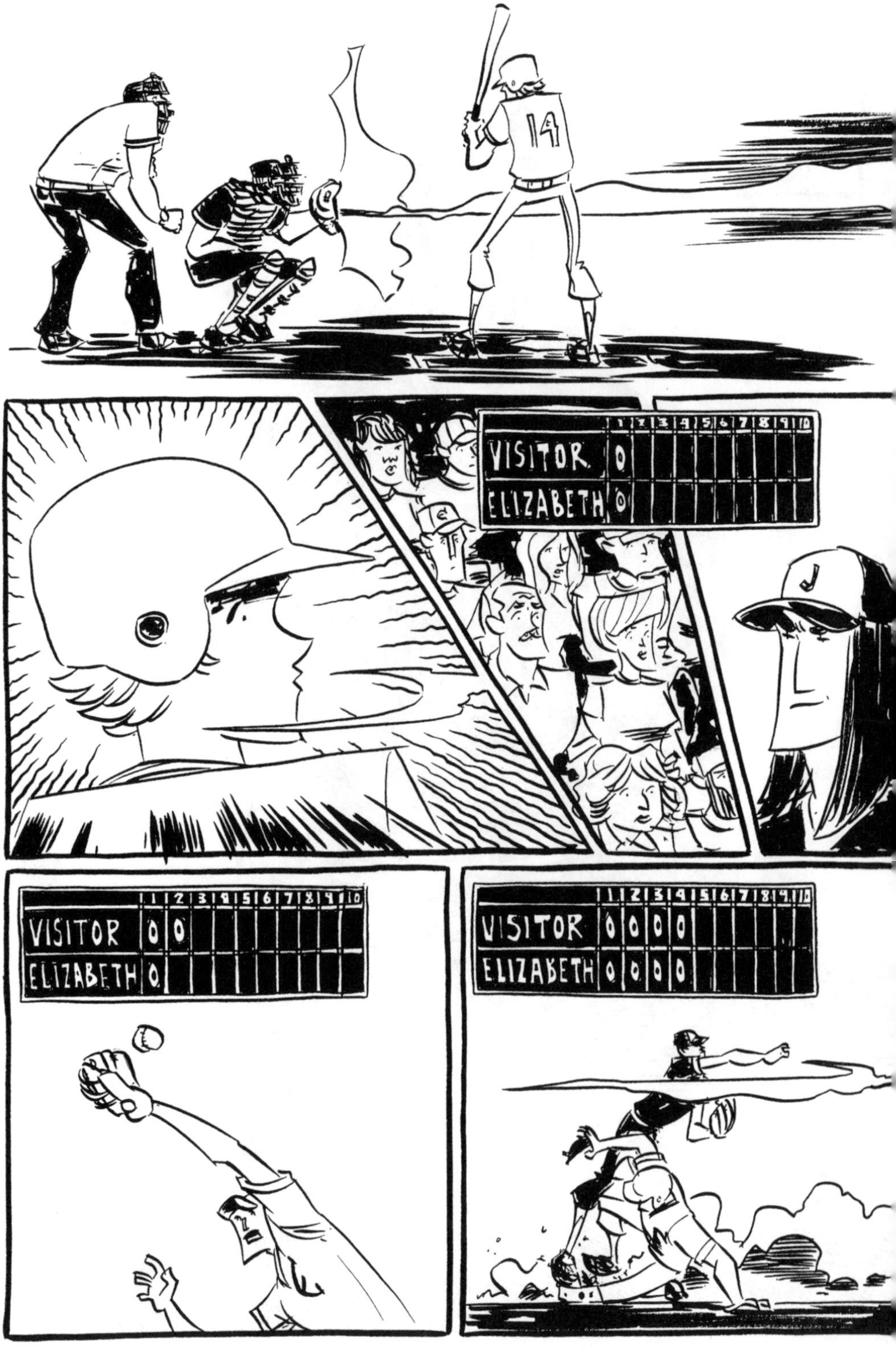
14
1 2 3 4 5 6 7 8 9 10
VISITOR 0
ELIZABETH 0
1 2 3 4 5 6 7 8 9 10
VISITOR 0 0
ELIZABETH 0
1 2 3 4 5 6 7 8 9 10
VISITOR 0 0 0 0
ELIZABETH 0 0 0 0

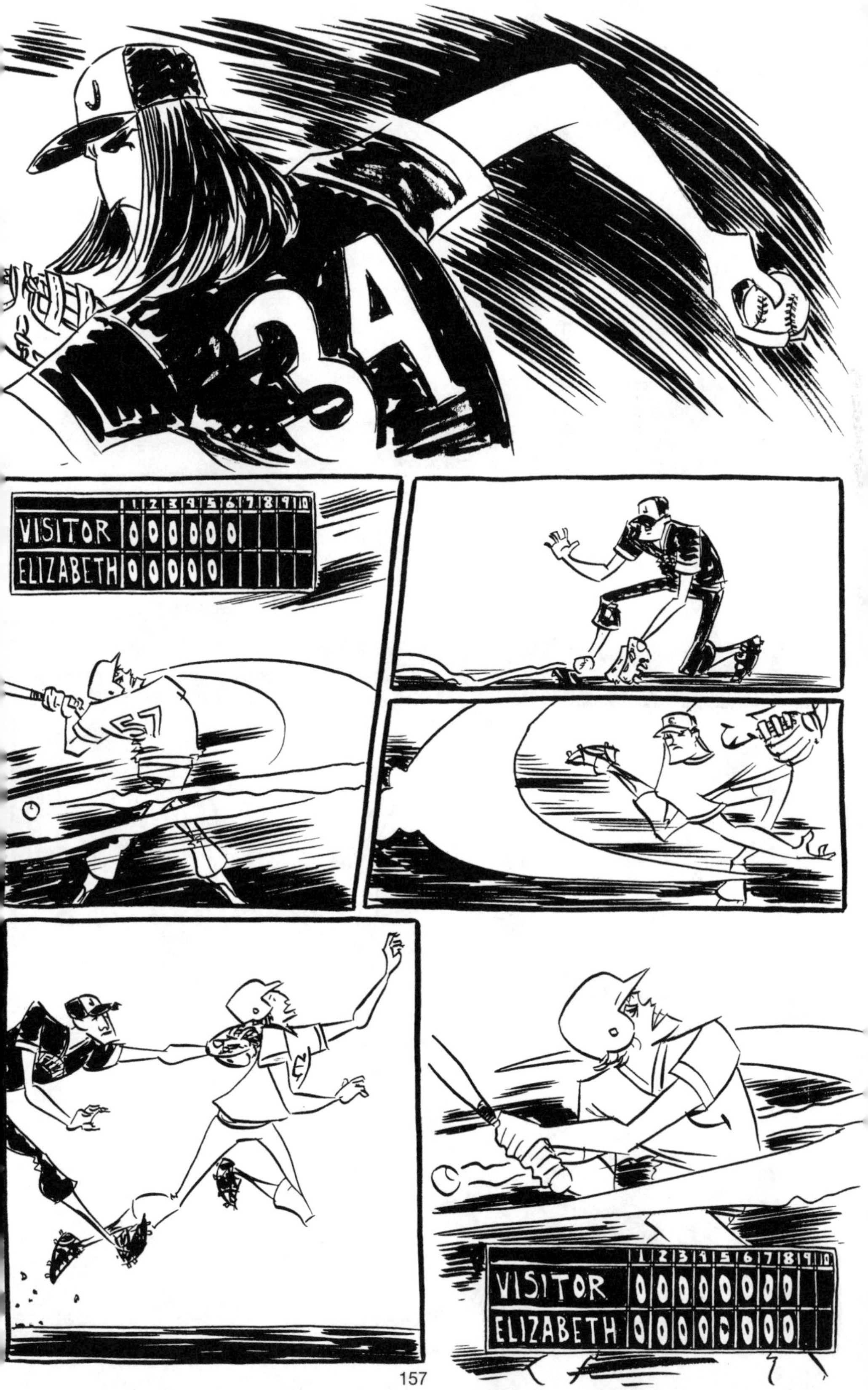

1 2 3 4 5 6 7 8 9 10
VISITOR 0 0 0 0 0 0
ELIZABETH 0 0 0 0 0
1 2 3 4 5 6 7 8 9 10
VISITOR 0 0 0 0 0 0 0 0
ELIZABETH 0 0 0 0 0 0 0 0

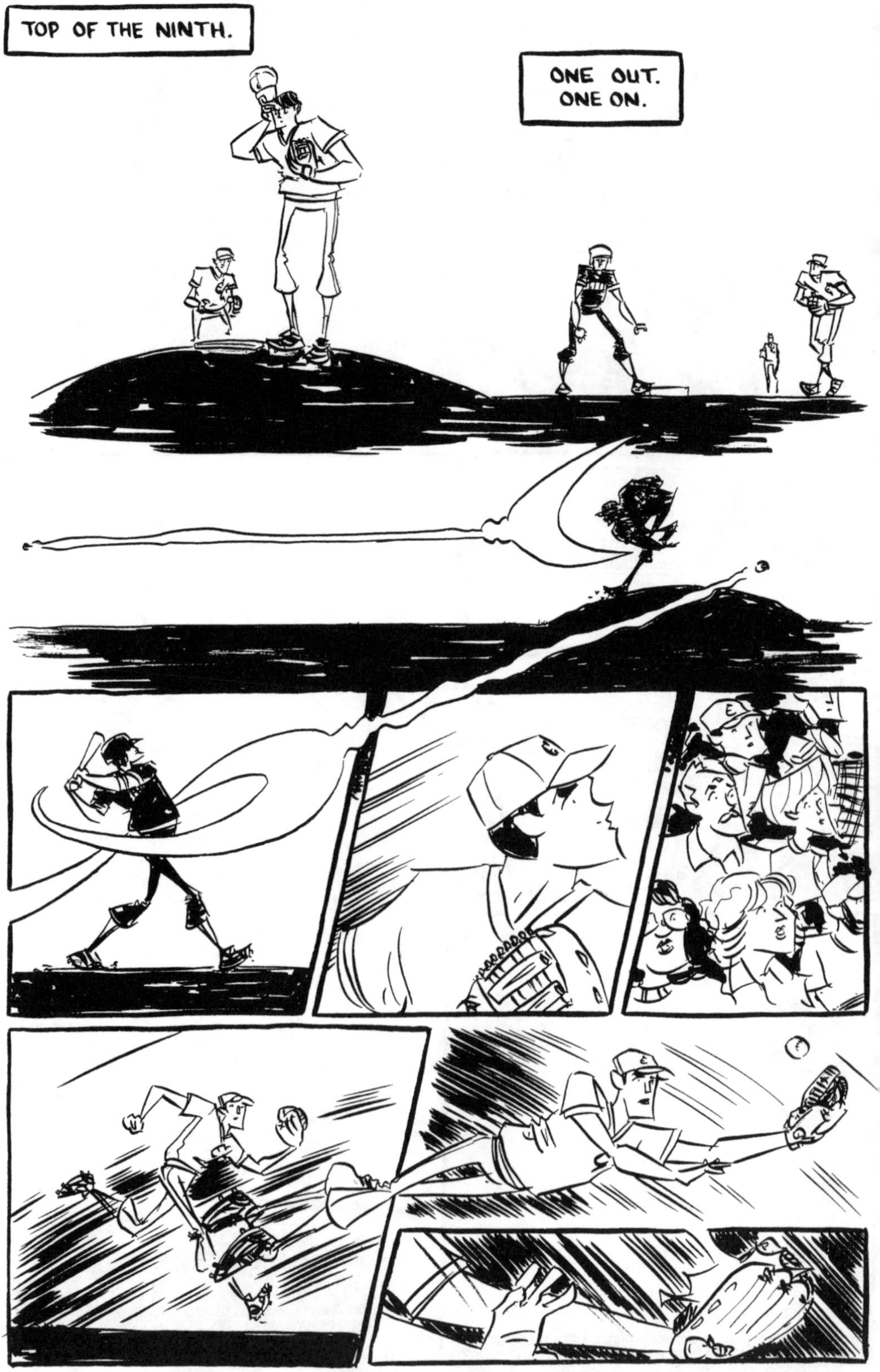
TOP OF THE NINTH.
ONE OUT.
ONE ON.

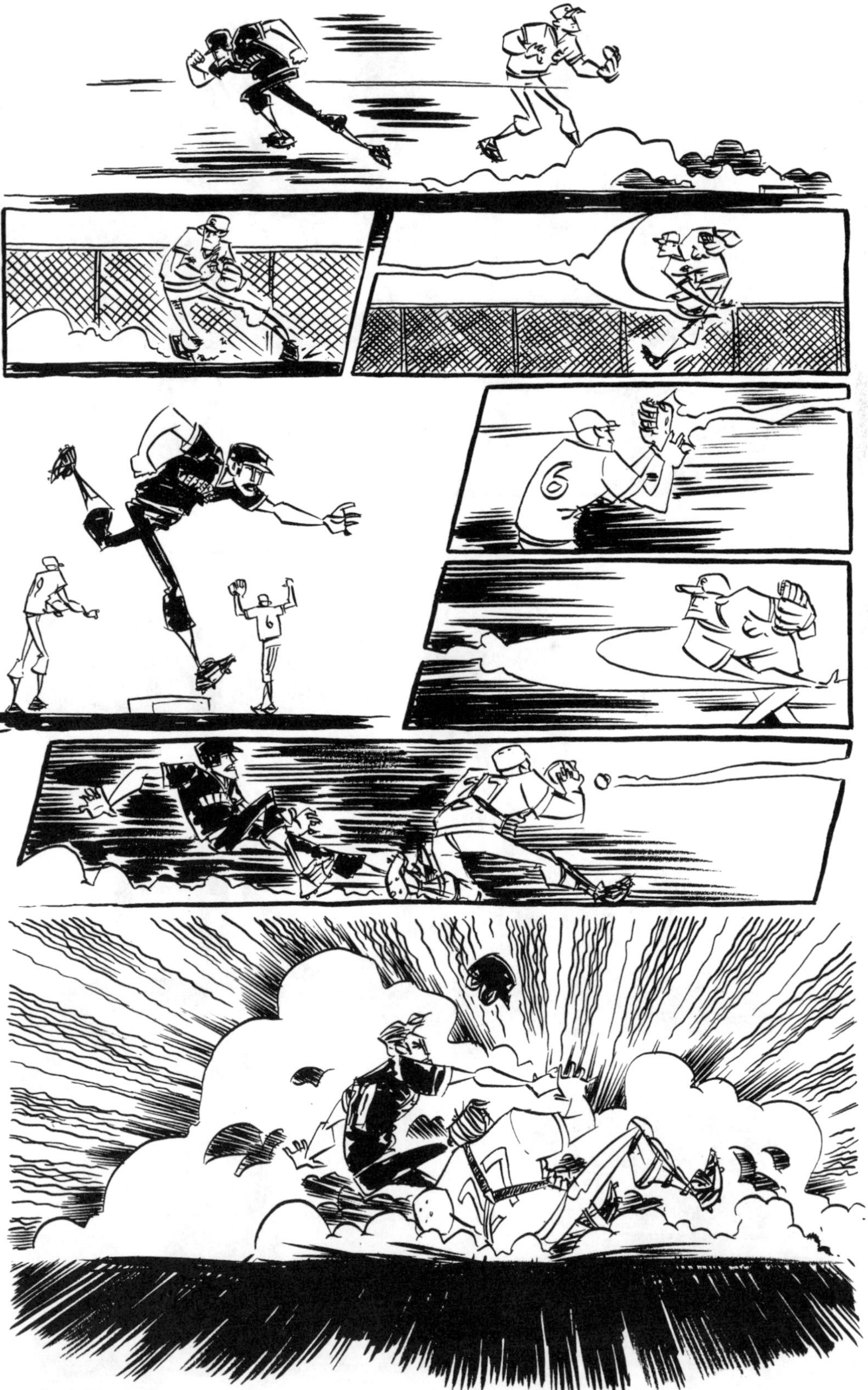

SAFE!

	1	2	3	4	5	6	7	8	9	14
VISITOR.	0	0	0	0	0	0	0	0	1	
ELIZABETH	0	0	0	0	0	0	0			

BOTTOM OF THE NINTH.

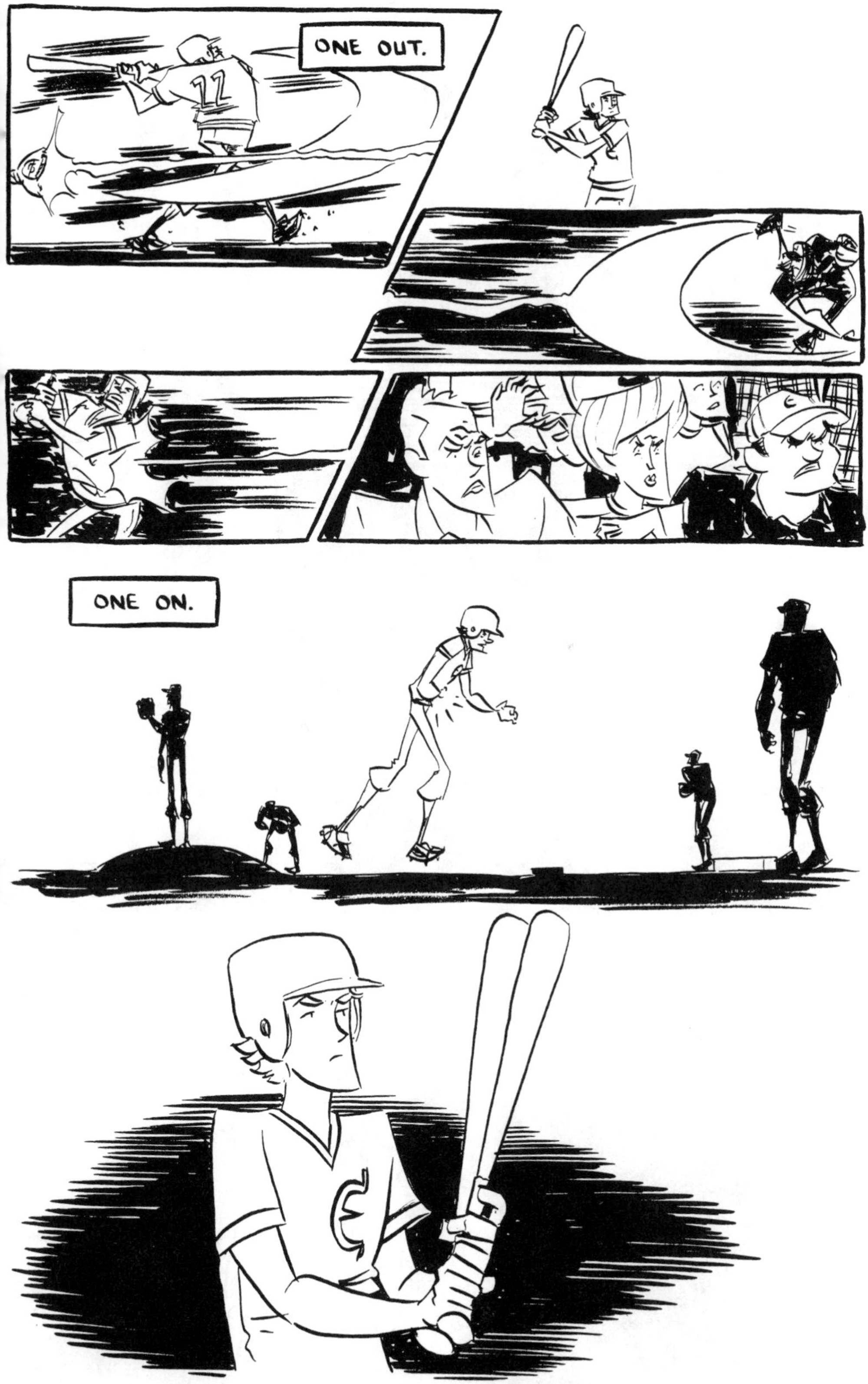
ONE OUT.
22
ONE ON.

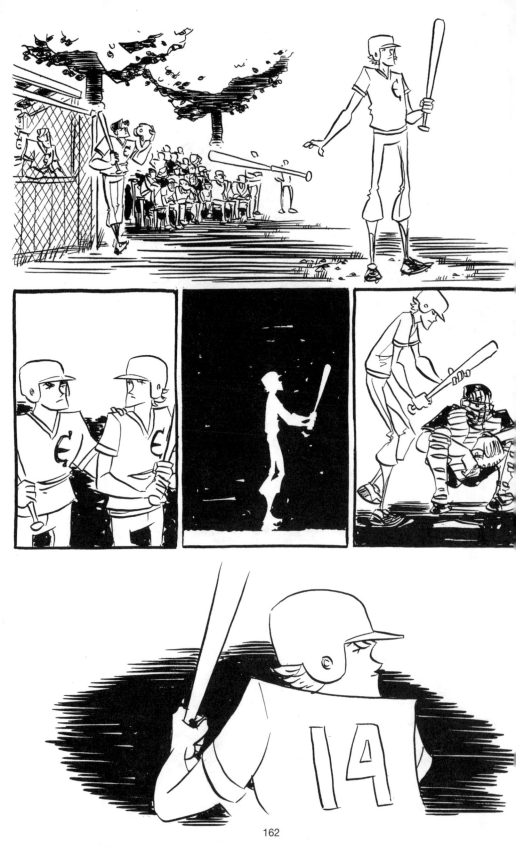

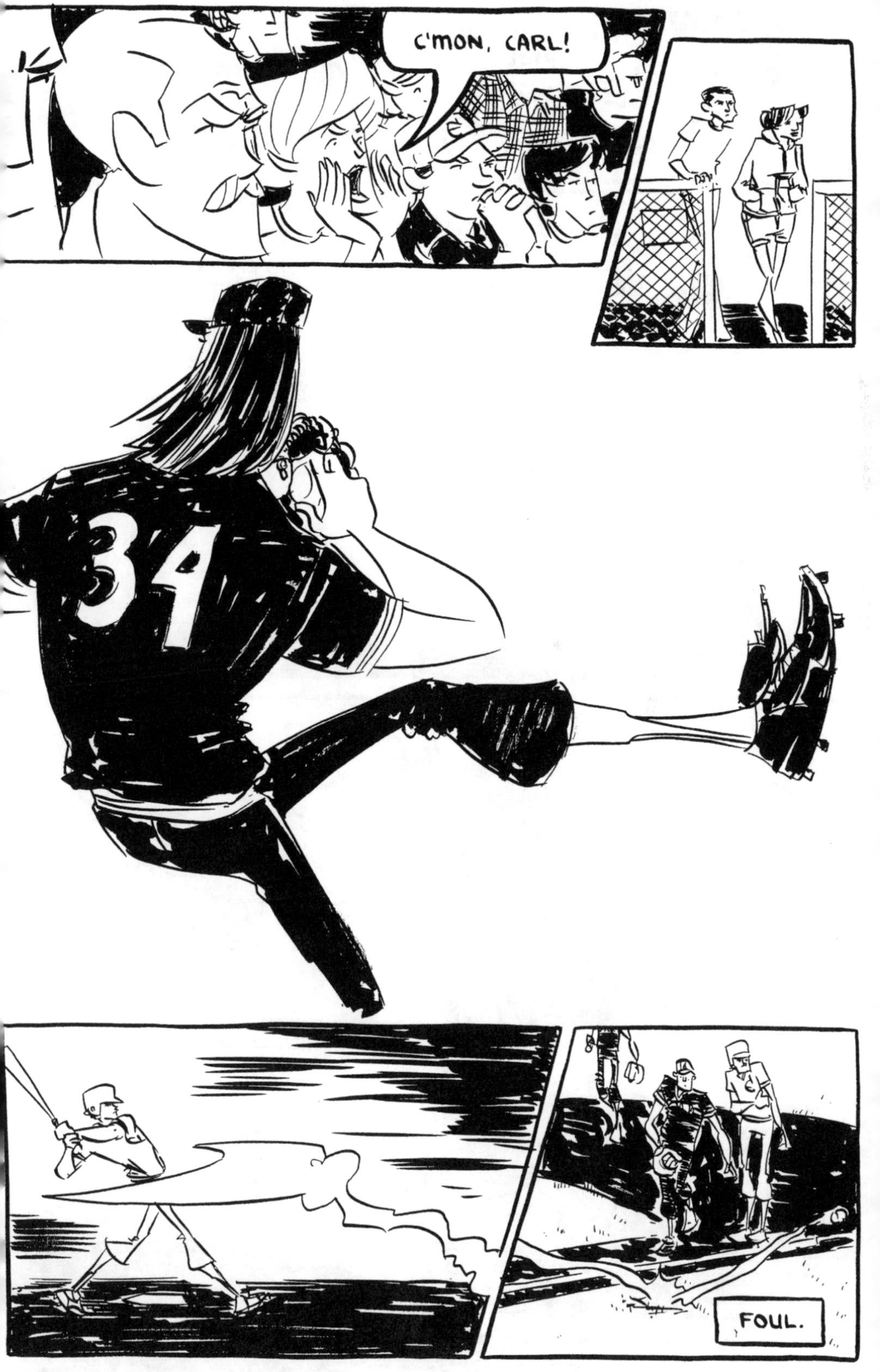
C'MON, CARL!
FOUL.

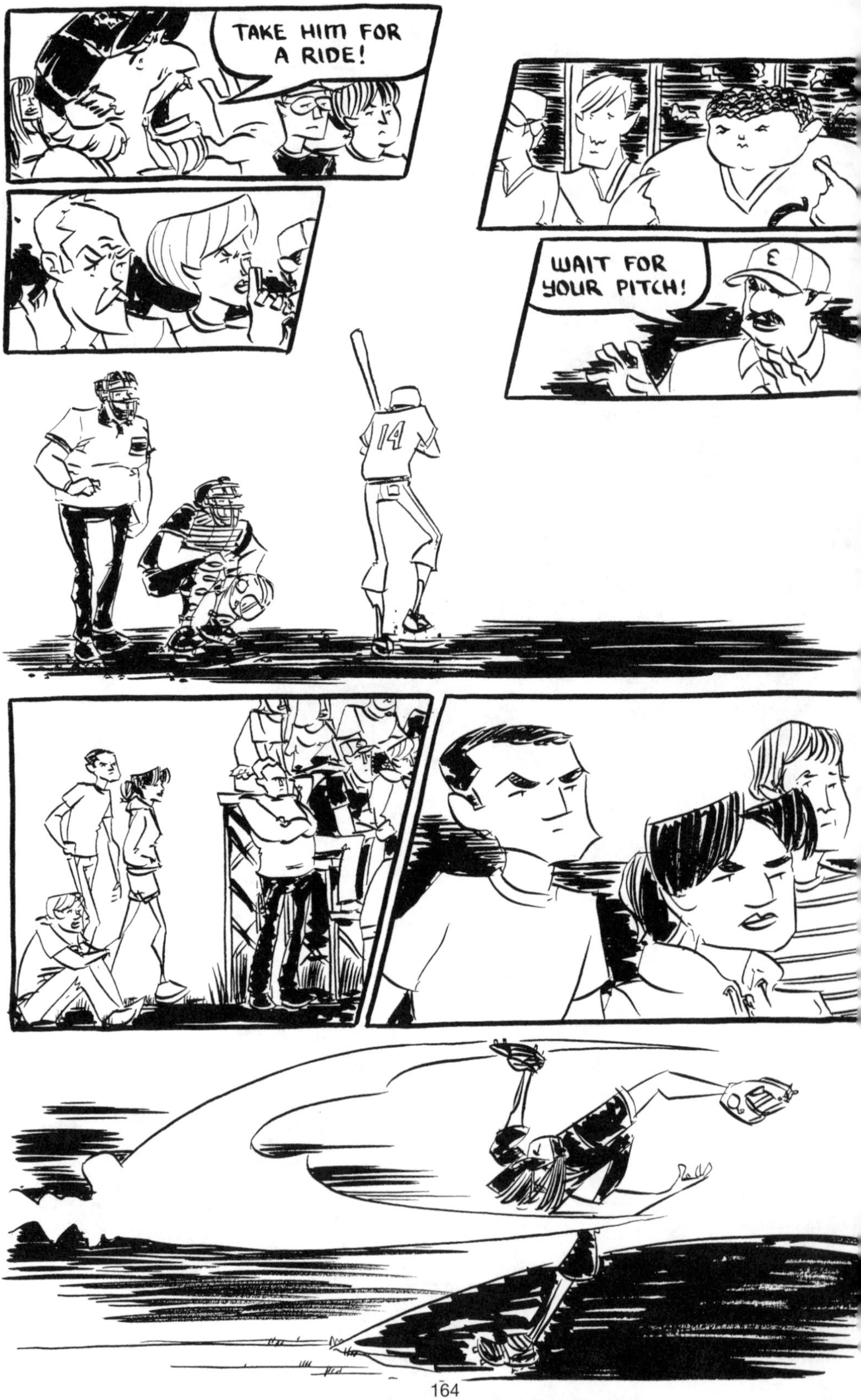
TAKE HIM FOR A RIDE!
WAIT FOR YOUR PITCH!
14

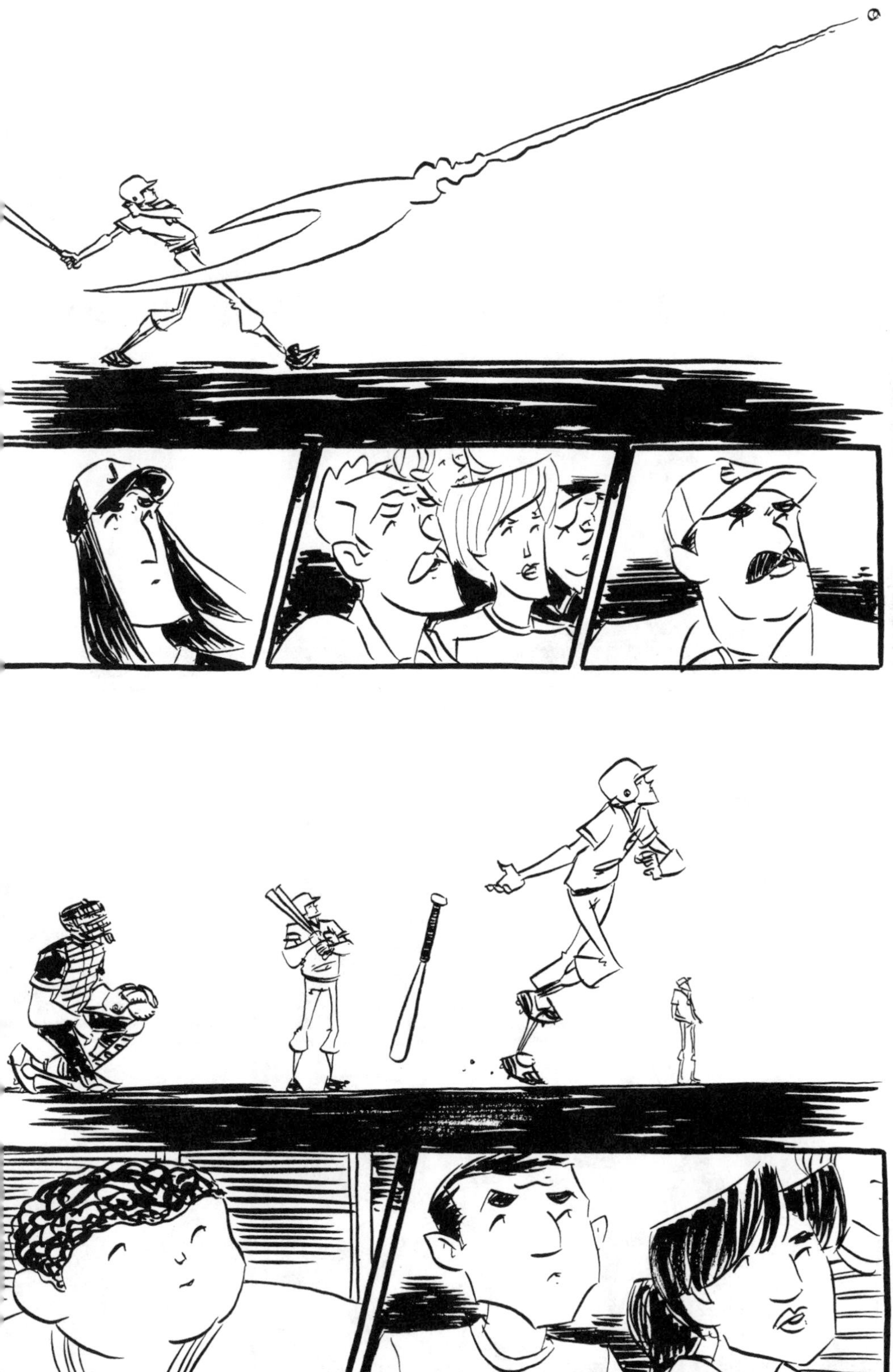

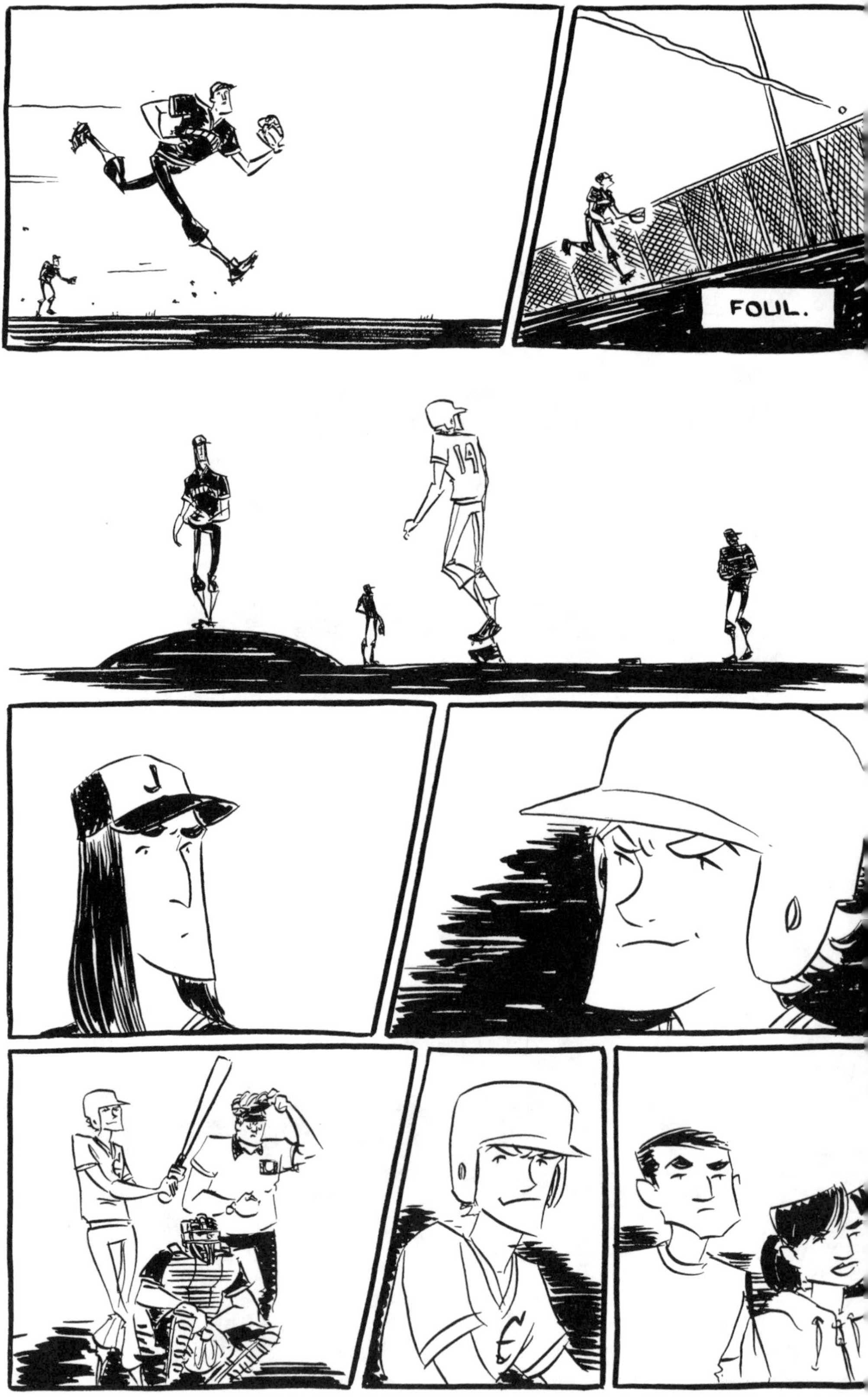
FOUL.

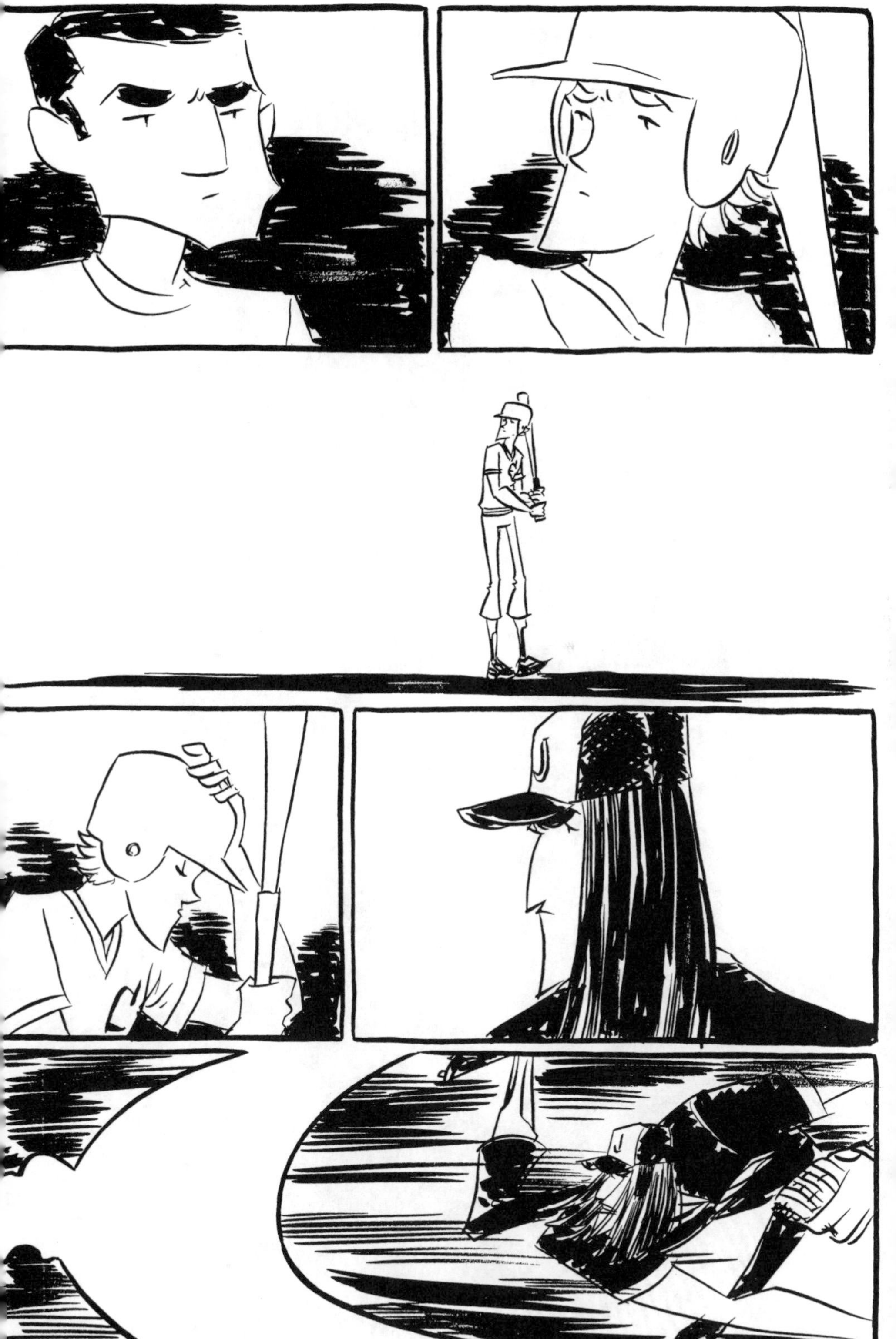

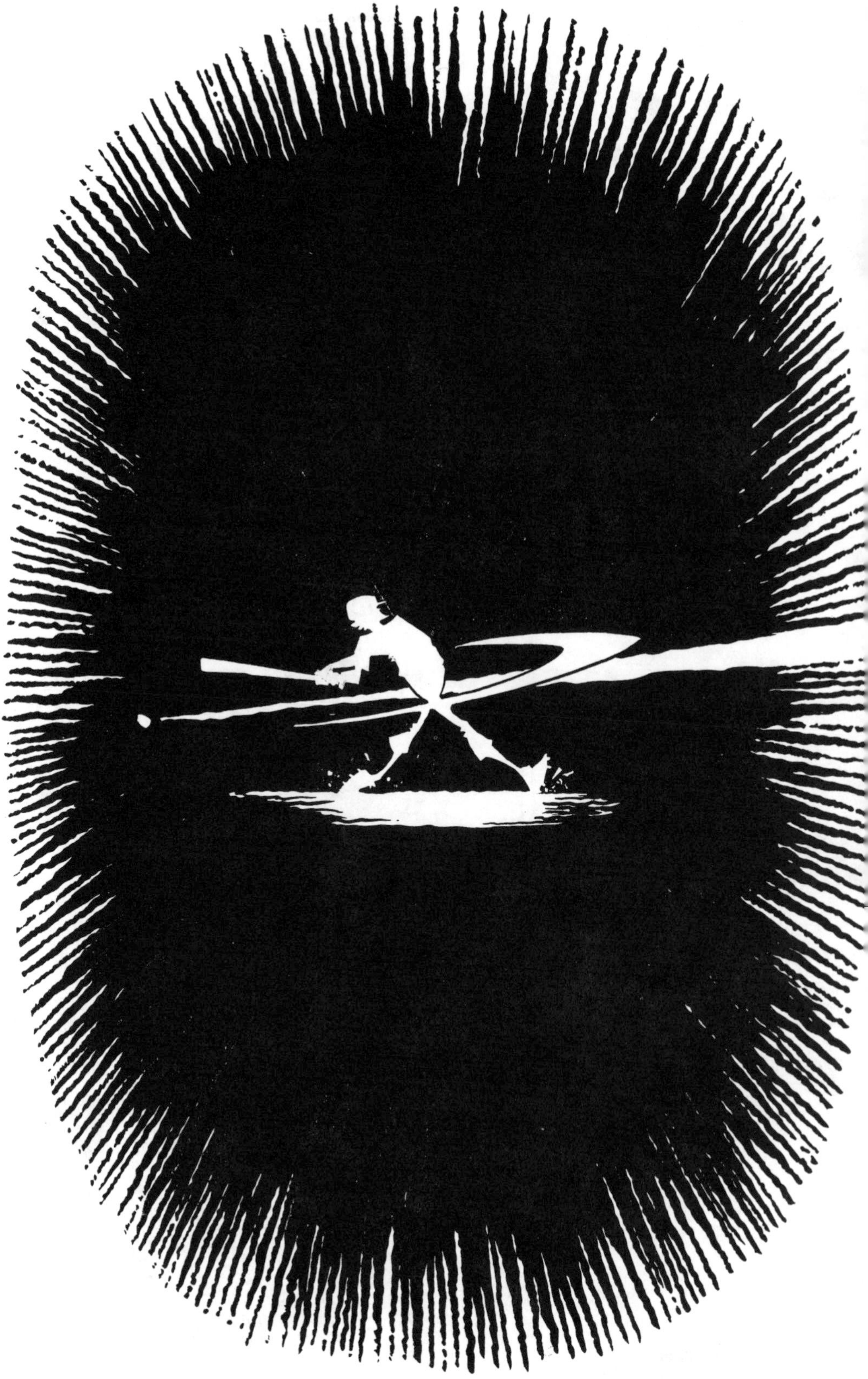

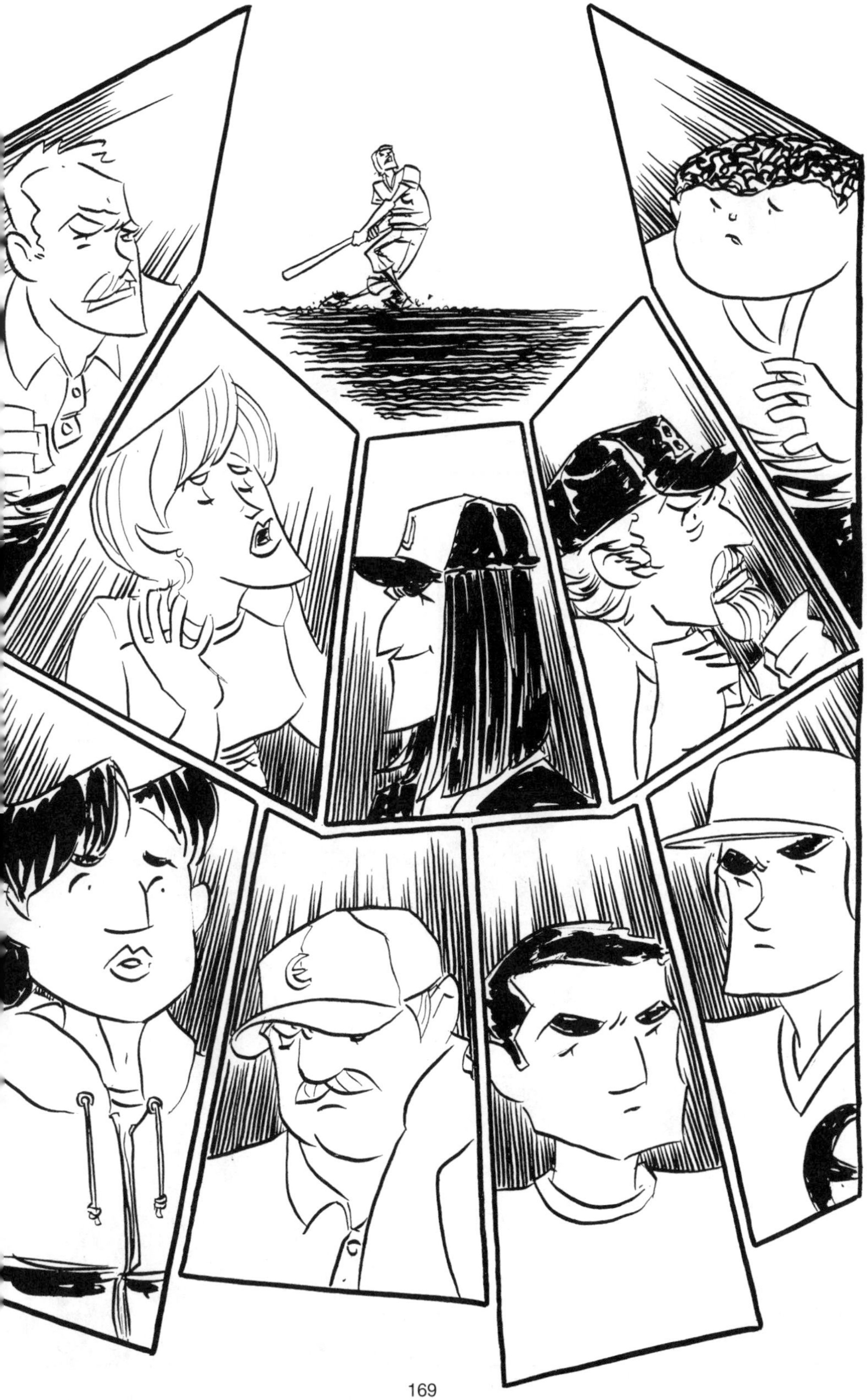

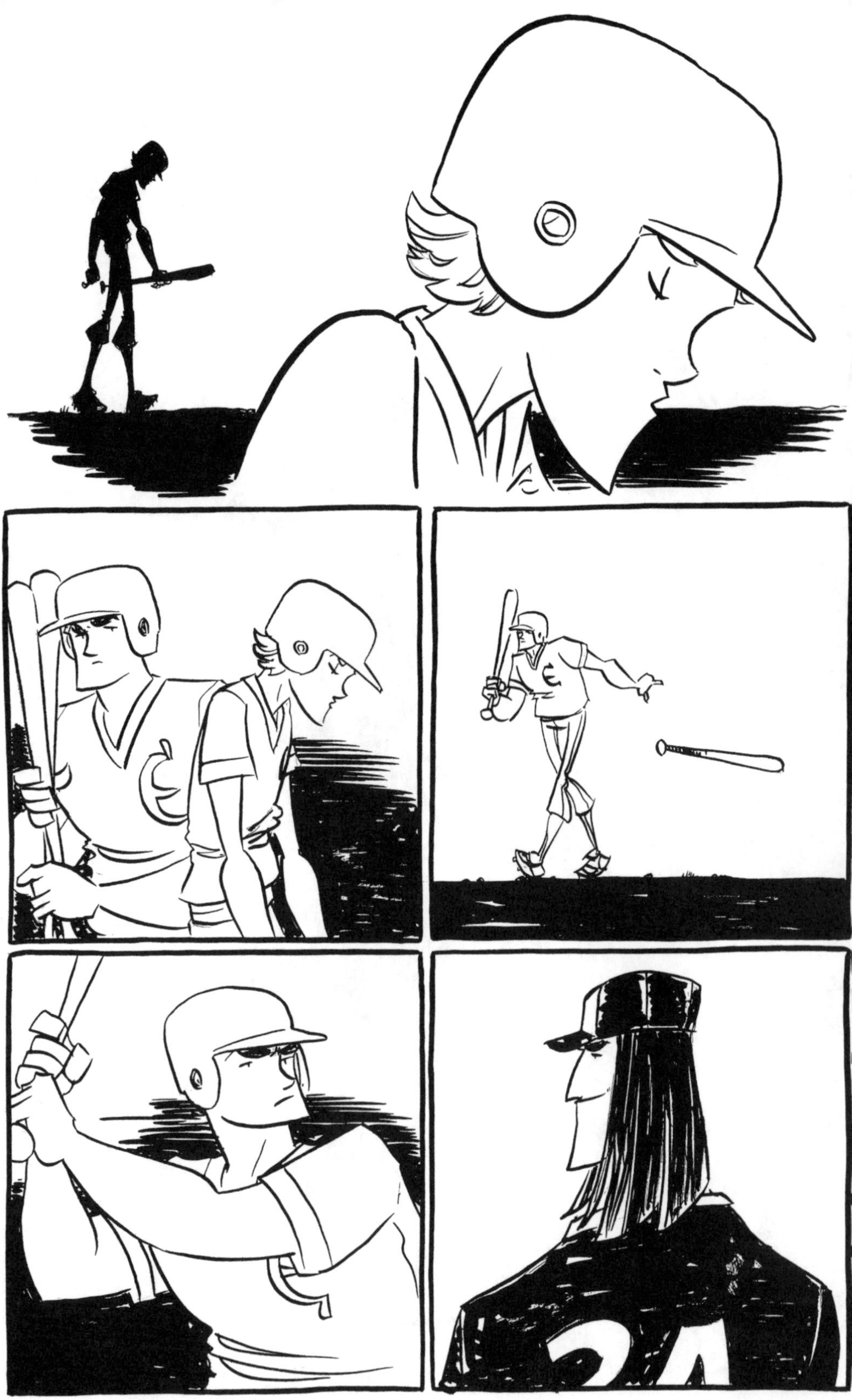

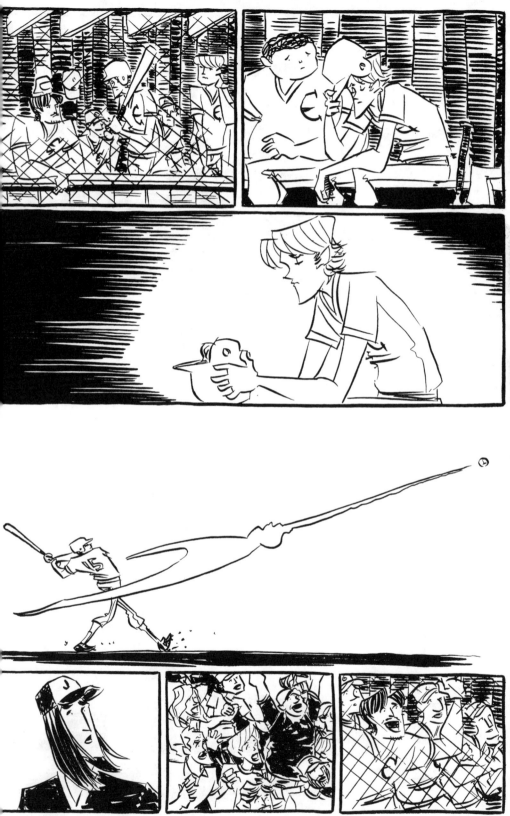

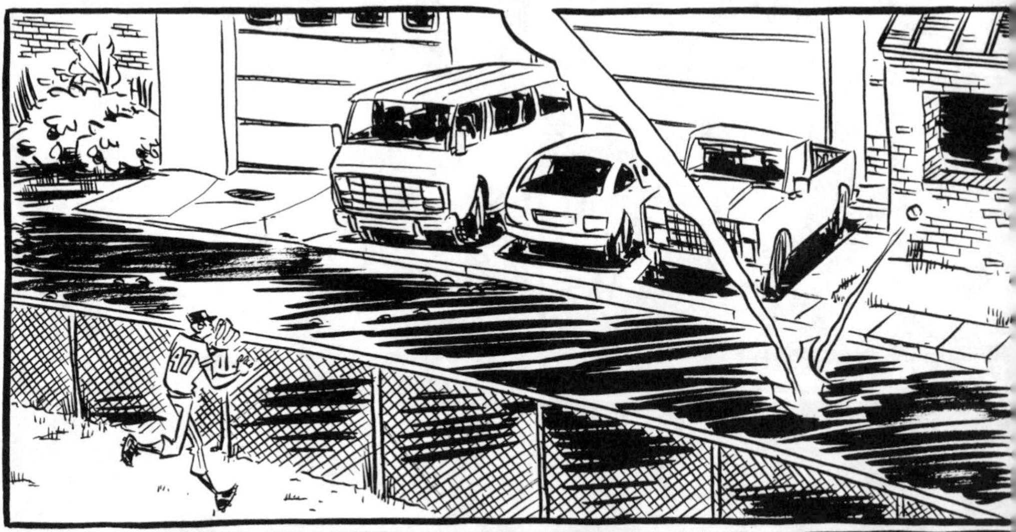

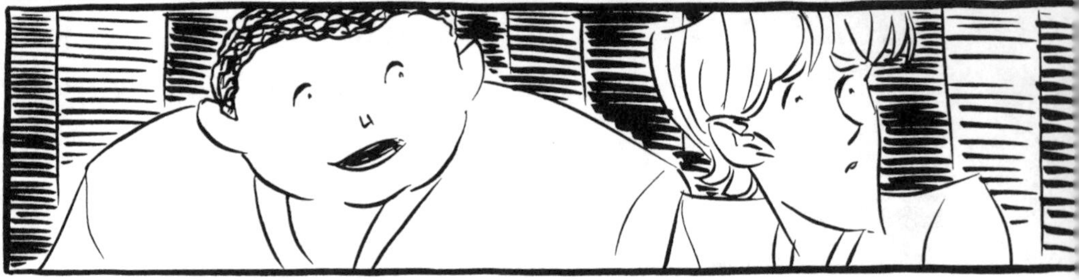

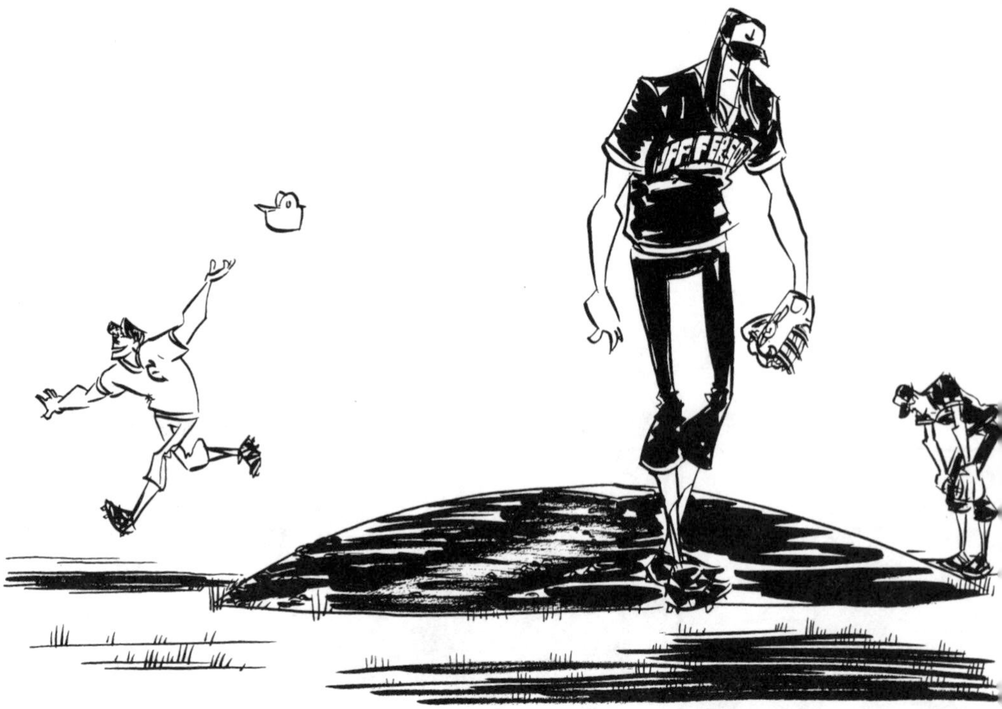

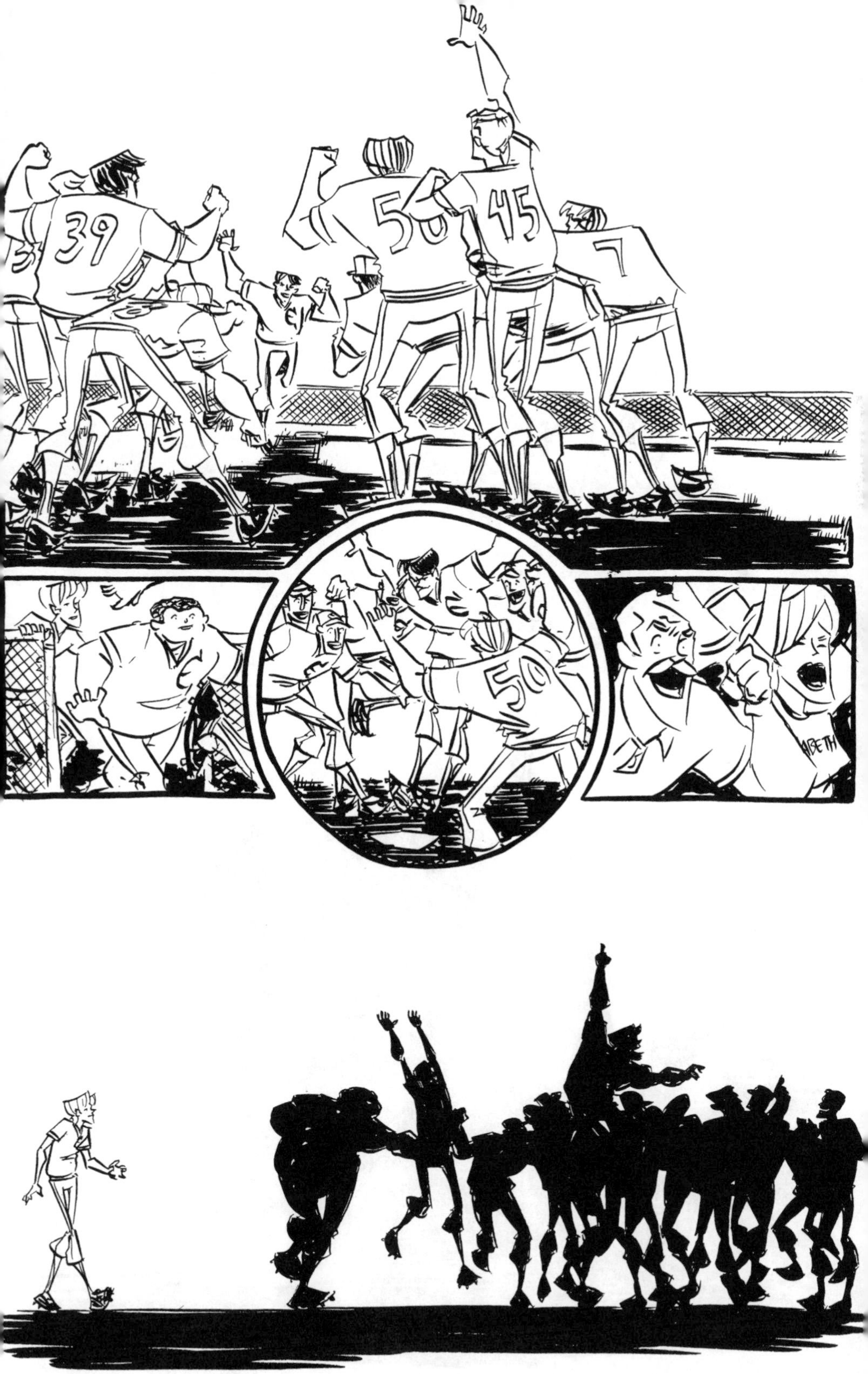
39
50
45
7
50

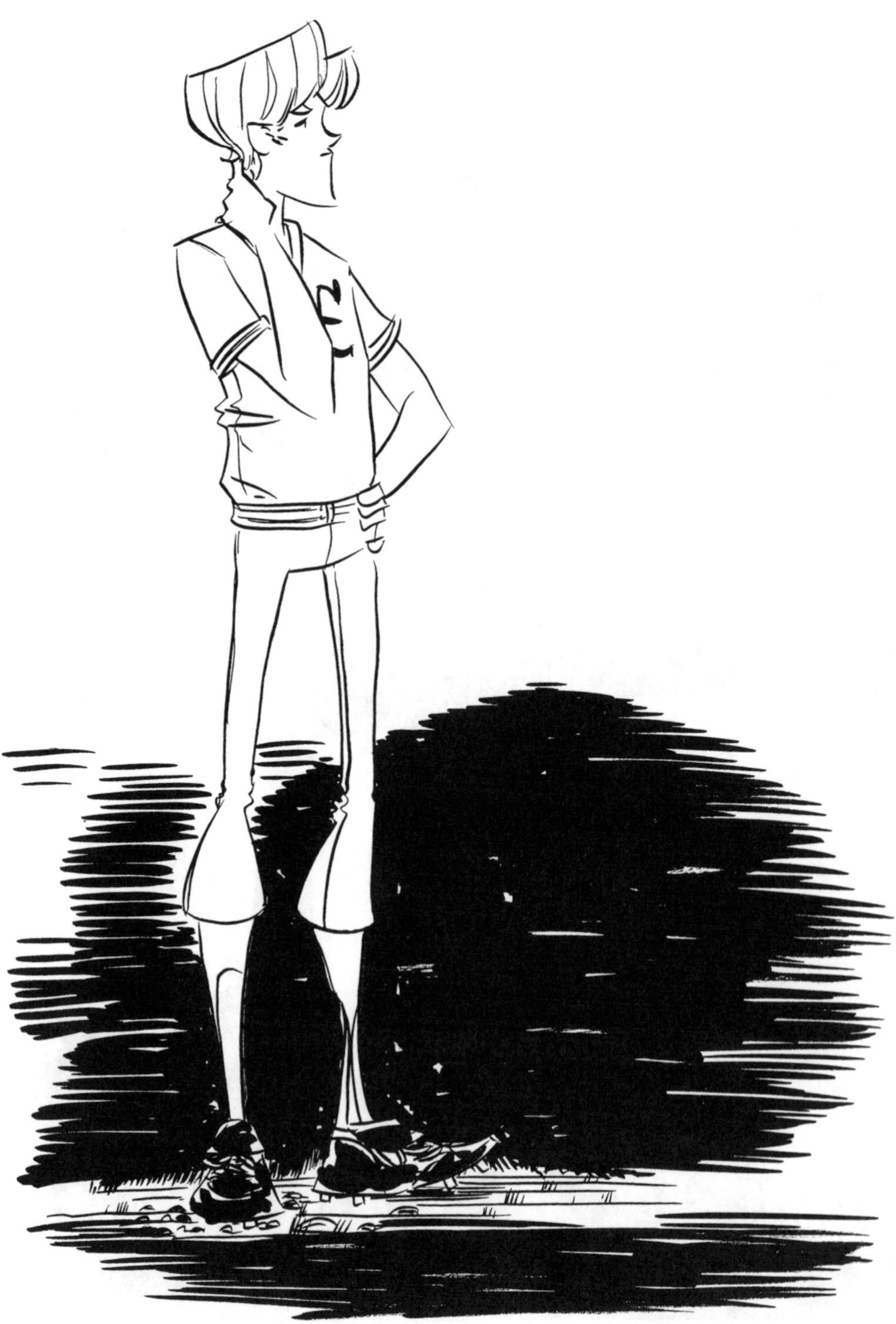

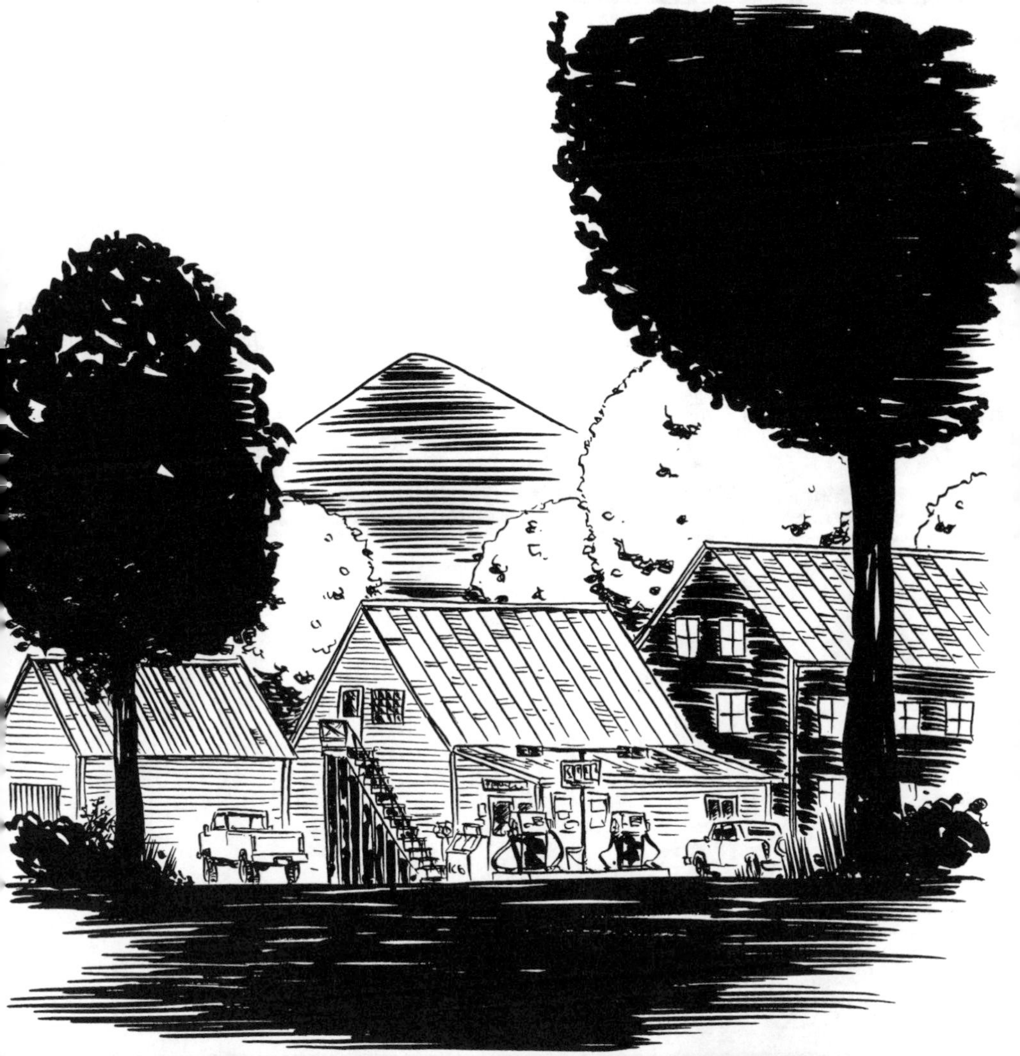

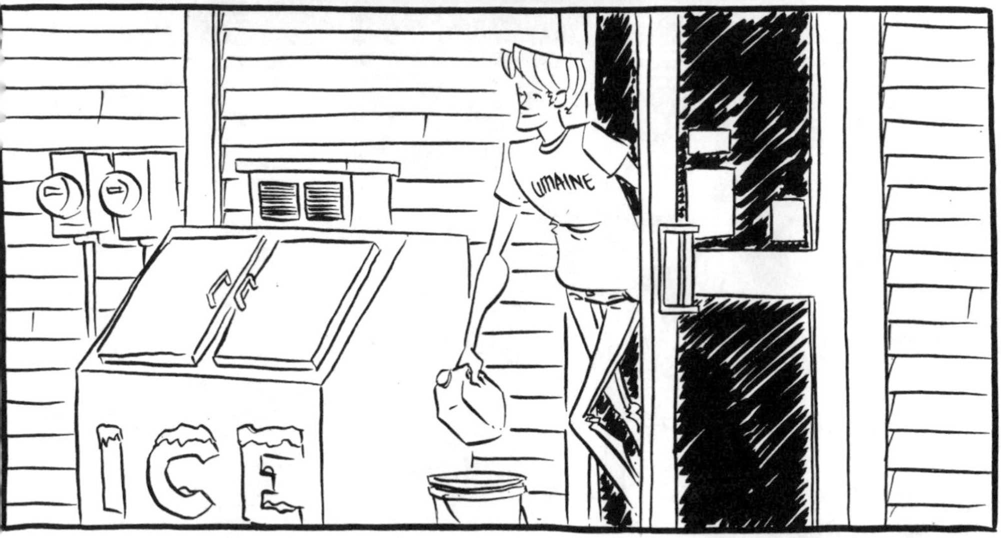
UMAINE
ICE

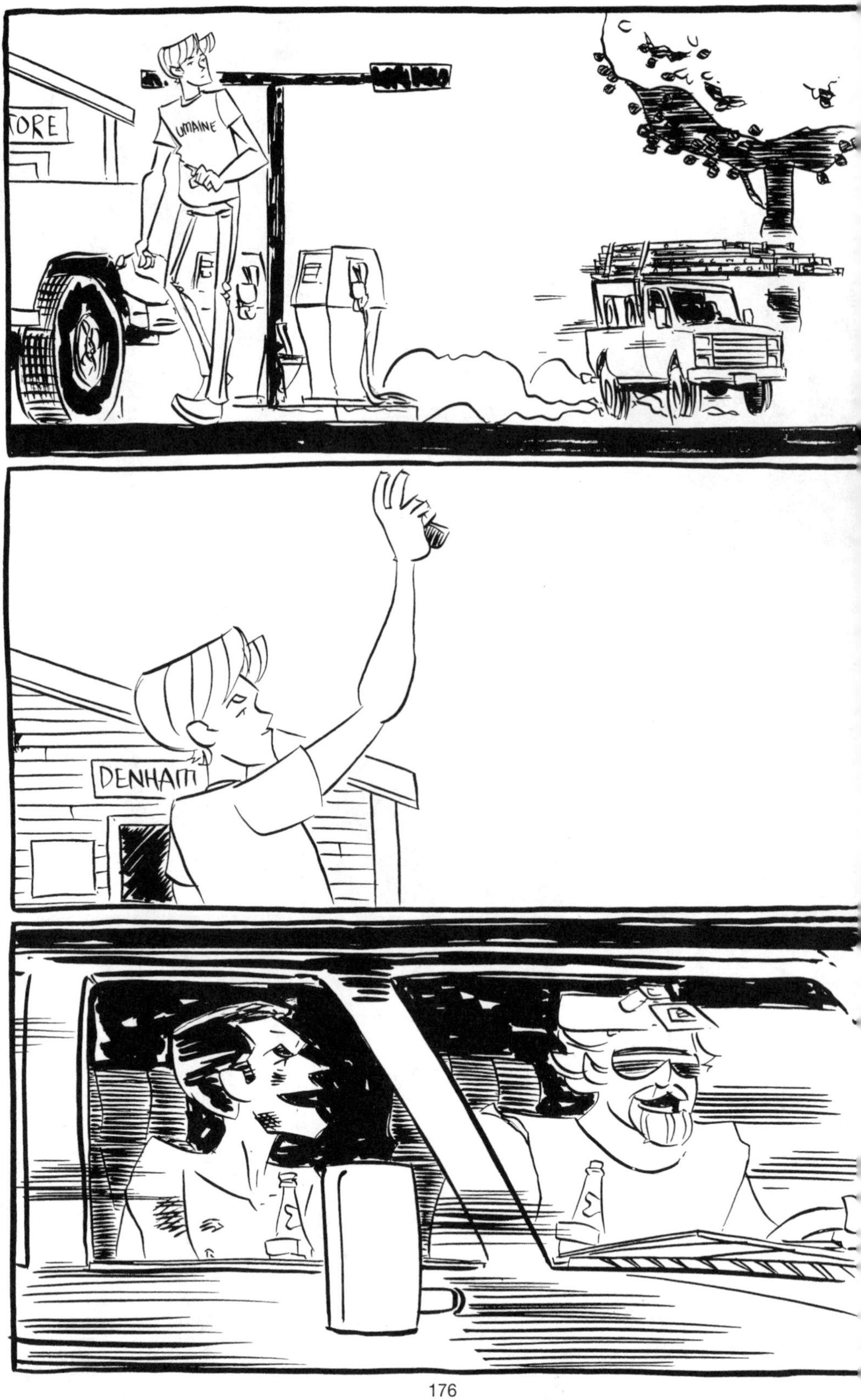

TORE
UMAINE
DENHAM

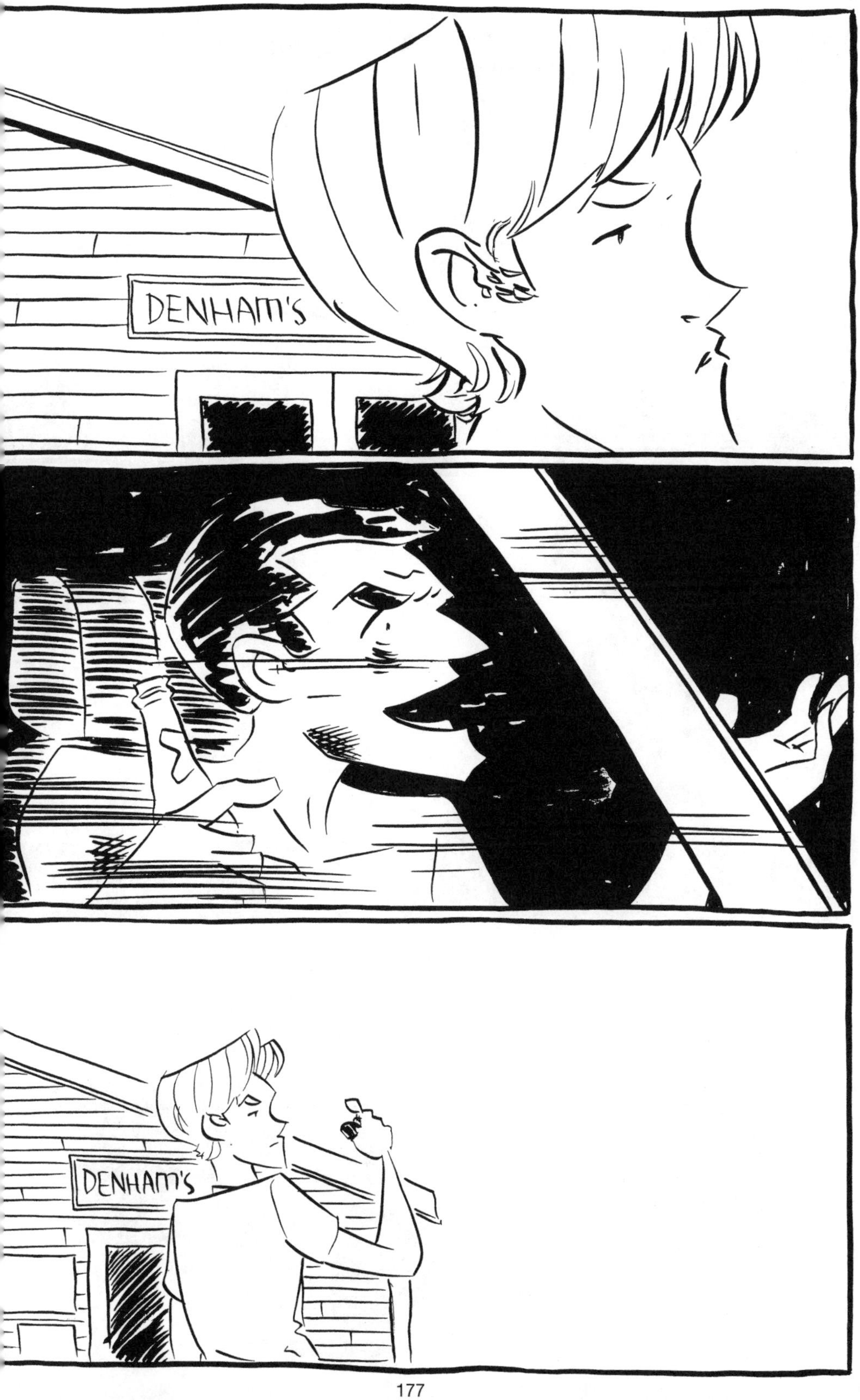
DENHAM'S
DENHAM'S

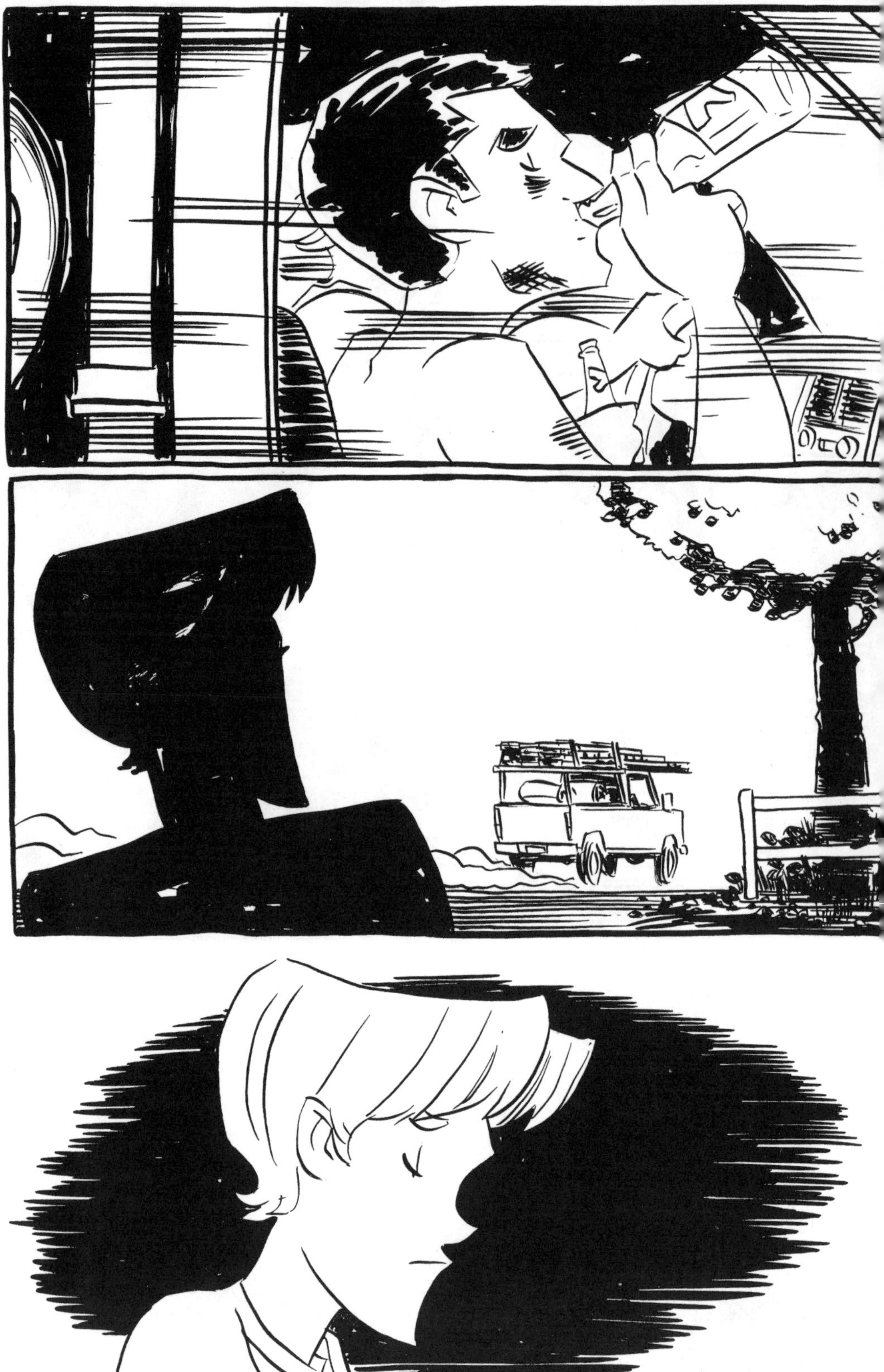

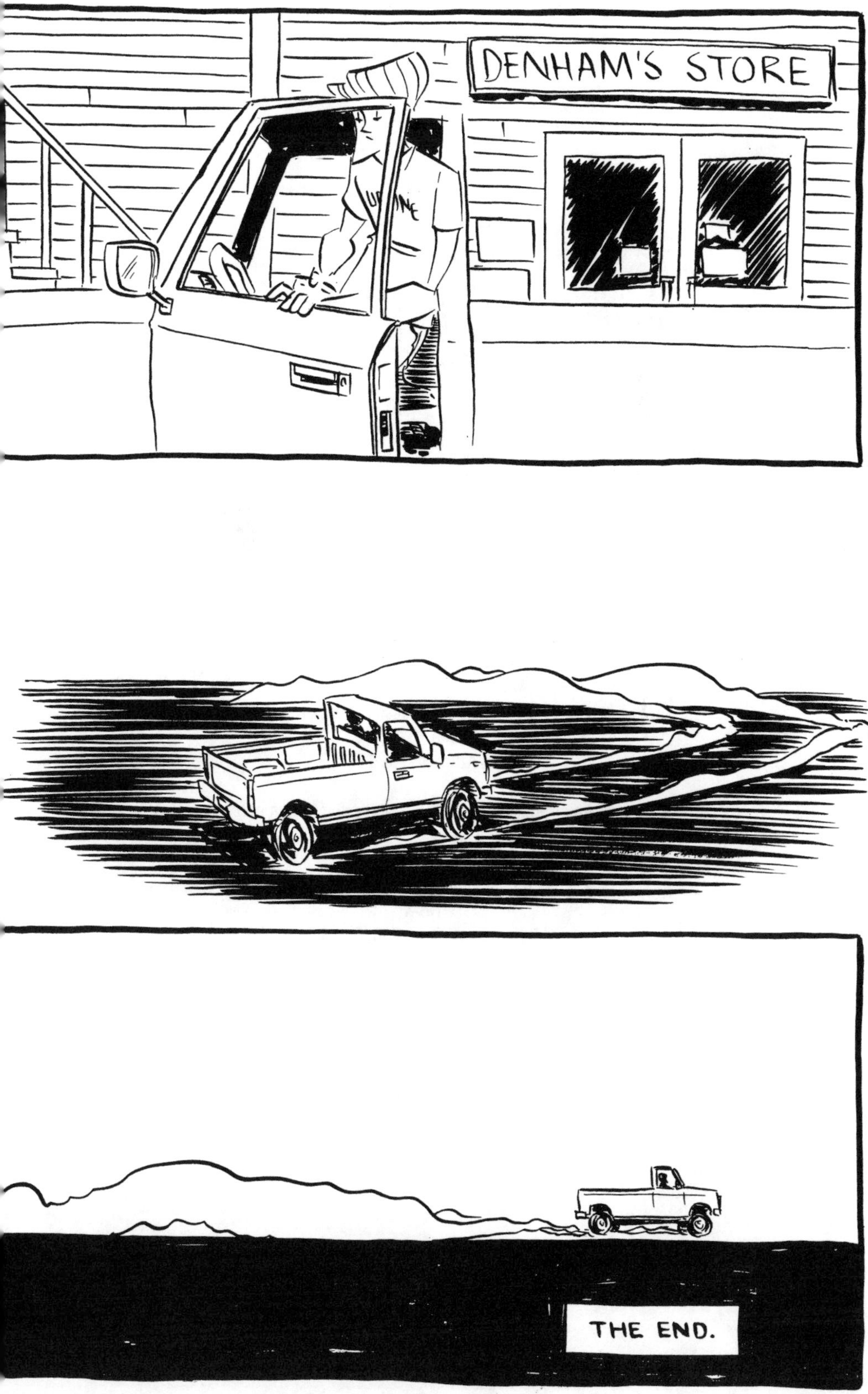
DENHAM'S STORE
THE END.

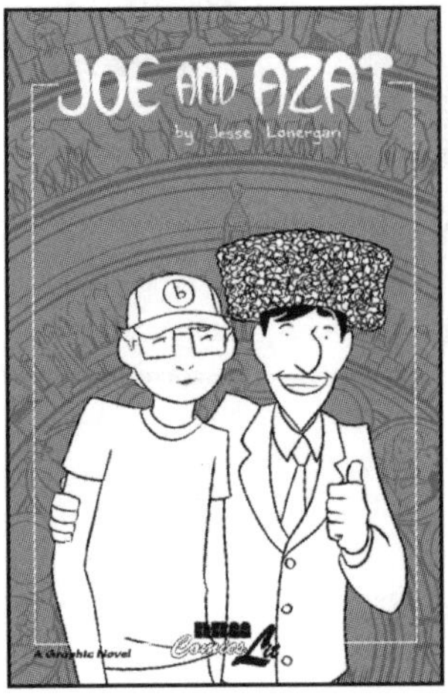
JOE AND AZAT
by Jesse Lonergan
A Graphic Novel
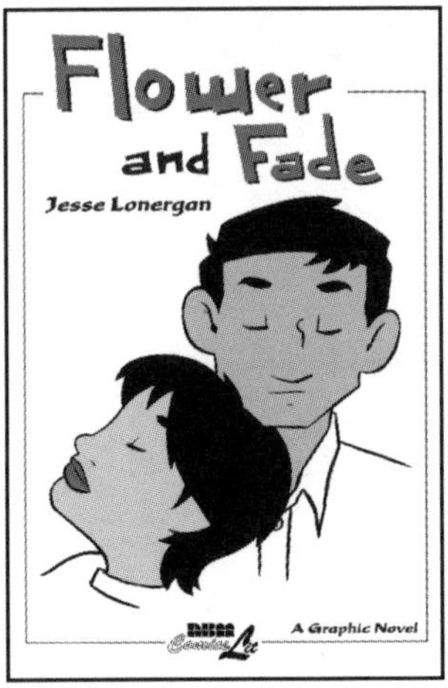
Flower and Fade
Jesse Lonergan
A Graphic Novel